Pervasive Computing: Technologies and Markets

Neil Ward-Dutton
John Davison
Robin Gear

Ovum Ltd, Cardinal Tower, 12 Farringdon Road, London EC1M 3HS UK
Telephone +44 (0) 20 7551 9000 Fax +44 (0) 20 7551 9090/1

Ovum Pty Ltd, Level 6, 388 Lonsdale Street, Melbourne VIC 3000 AUSTRALIA
Telephone +61 (0) 3 9606 0499 Fax +61 (0) 3 9606 0799

Ovum Inc. 301 Edgewater Drive, Suite 220, Wakefield, MA 01880 USA
Telephone +1 800 642 OVUM +1 781 246 3773 Fax +1 781 246 7772

Ovum Latin America, San Martín Street 674, Floor 5 (A), 1004 Capital Federal, Buenos Aires, Argentina
Telephone +54 11 4893 2902

info@ovum.com
http://www.ovum.com

ISBN 1 902566-63-7

Contents

B Pervasive computing – the new revolution?

C Market overview

D Towards pervasive applications

H Implications for suppliers

J Market development scenario and forecasts

Acknowledgements

We would like to thank the many individuals and organisations who assisted in the production of this report. With apologies to those we have omitted, we are grateful to:

Larry Roshfeld, John Czupak	Aether Software
Ed Cobb, Scott Dietzen	BEA Systems
Laurent Seraphin	Borland
John Warrants, Simon Addis	Centura
Michael Greenwood	IBM
Richard Lind, Hjalmar Winbladh, Sanjay Parthasarathy, Adam Anger	Microsoft
John Hansen, Scott Anderson	Motorola
Andrew Robinson	NetMorf
Malcolm Bird	OpenWave
Robert Brown, Ken Jacobs	Oracle
David Weilmuenster	Palm Computing
Charles Davies	Psion
Eric Chu, Curtis Sasaki	Sun Microsystems
Brendan Tutt	Tivoli Systems
John Fogelin	WindRiver

The production of this report would not have been possible without the support of a cast of thousands at Ovum, who suggested, reviewed, criticised, cajoled and, frankly, suffered to help us. Special thanks are due to Eric Woods, Phil Carnelley, Jules Hewett, Eirwen Nichols, Richard Kee, John Delaney, John Moroney, Henning Dransfeld, Shirley Brown, Katy Ring, Lee Hope, Suzanne Mucci and Katy Peek.

Neil Ward-Dutton

Robin Gear

John Davison

December 2000

A Management summary

A1 Key messages

A1.1 The new revolution

Pervasive computing is about an ideal – *any information service to any device over any network.* Pervasive computing makes digital content, applications and services available in an integrated, personalised way to users via a diverse range of devices and access networks. New services are equally accessible through wireless networks to cellular phones, vehicles, PDAs and so on; fixed narrowband connections are accessible to PCs or networked home appliances; broadband networks are accessible to digital television sets. It involves the transformation of the global data network that we call the Internet into a pervasive medium that connects users to personalised universes of dynamic content, applications and services, via any smart, connected device.

A1.2 The opportunity

Pervasive computing represents a true paradigm shift

By 2005, more than 40% of the global market for Internet services – $1.3 trillion – will be attributable to pervasive computing. Suppliers of pervasive interactive services therefore will be by far the best placed to take advantage of growing consumer and business interest in e-services. Suppliers of supporting technologies, such as infrastructure software, will have their best chances of success by supporting pervasive computing.

The adaptation of mobile handsets to the delivery of data applications (the wireless Internet) is the current preoccupation of the major industry players. However, wireless Internet is just one element of a paradigm shift that is taking place, in which PCs will play alongside not only voice handsets, but also PDAs, TVs, cars, fridges, games consoles and other devices.

No single supplier will be able to do it all

Success as a pervasive computing player requires an holistic perspective that has neither a software-centric bias nor a network-centric bias. No single supplier, or even supplier community, has access to all the skills and resources required to obtain and maintain an unassailable market position. Partnerships are the only route to success.

A1.3 Applications and services will change

The death of the application as we know it

By 2006, many computing applications will be highly granular and personalised. The lines between different types of application will become extremely blurred. The eventual transformation of the application from monolithic product to a personalised, granular set of network-based services is an inevitable consequence of the subsumption of Internet technology into application infrastructure technologies, and into different markets. E-commerce, infotainment and personal communications will be the applications areas most affected by this transformation.

Pervasive computing brings global reach and the need for localisation

There is a vital but subtle difference between today's popular Internet application (the delivery of Worldwide Web sites to PC-based browsers) and the use of the Internet as a distribution mechanism between other applications and non-PC platforms. The democratisation of digital information access will bring new applications to people whose grasp of English (or even the English alphabet or Arabic character set) is limited. The pervasive computing environment of tomorrow will be multilingual and multicultural.

Three waves of application development

Infrastructure demand will be driven by the creation of multichannel applications and services and will come in three waves, driven by application development and deployment:

- creation of new interfaces to existing uni-channel applications
- creation of completely new multichannel applications
- re-engineering of old applications in line with 'proper' design principles for multichannel applications, and tight integration between existing multichannel applications.

A1.4 Devices and access networks

Access platforms – the straw to your milkshake

Most technology constraints on the development of pervasive computing occur in access networks and devices – they are the 'straw' through which users will drink their tasty digital-content 'milkshakes'. The fast pace of innovation in devices and access networks is creating most of the current wave of interest in pervasive computing. Users are already highly sensitive to the setting of unrealistic expectations, however – so suppliers must resist the temptation to give positioning statements more weight than they deserve.

Diversity will increase – in some ways

The next five years will see increasing, not decreasing, diversity and complexity in the universe of client device form factors. However, device capabilities will become increasingly similar – and the variations in their appearance will be more a result of differences in usage contexts than differences in technology constraints (as is the case today).

Pervasive computing embraces many 'new' types of computing platform, but such platforms will not lure PC users into throwing away their investments overnight. Rather, it is likely that innovation in smart appliances will transfer to the PC community, making PCs more reliable, more secure and easier to use.

No universal platform

There will never be a single universal standard operating platform for terminals and devices. There is sufficient diversity in the range of devices that will be required and bought – and sufficient market segmentation by device usage context – to enable multiple specialist platform leaders to co-exist peacefully. The answer to the question of who will be the leading platform provider is not Microsoft or Sun Microsystems – it is Microsoft, Sun Microsystems and others.

No network nirvana

Even though third-generation technology will bring impressive improvements in the capabilities of cellular networks, parity of bandwidth across different types of access network will not be achieved in the foreseeable future. Bandwidth conservation will still be an issue in cellular networks until 2005 and beyond, unlike fixed networks.

A1.5 Infrastructure technologies

Context is king

As applications, networks and devices become more pervasive, information and communication services will play different roles in customers' lives – each of which might correspond to a different customer segment involving the use of multiple devices and networks – in other words, a different *usage context*. Usage context information, and the ability to let users manage and shape how that information controls the ways that applications are delivered to them, will become a significant value point for service providers offering applications to multiple devices over multiple networks.

Security and reliability are the big holes

The variety in access platform capabilities does not manifest itself in terms of differences in the suitability of platforms for particular applications. This is because there are two almost universal issues that are not wholly addressed by platforms themselves – issues that can therefore only be addressed through the implementation of software infrastructure:

- controlling access to applications and data through security frameworks
- ensuring reliable transmission of application data and functionality across networks.

A1.6 Industry structures

Commercial issues are as important as technology

In the long term, the development of pervasive computing will lead to demand for ever-increasing degrees of freedom of user mobility – between services, content, applications and devices. Providing users with high degrees of freedom brings many technology challenges, but the issues that suppliers must deal with concern business model flexibility as much as technology shortcomings.

Customer ownership must be shared

In order to provide seamless, high-quality services to subscribers in a pervasive computing environment, service providers will have to share all sorts of information about users as they navigate around their personalised universes of content, applications and services. Suppliers' ability and willingness to share such information, and the creation of information-sharing agreements, will therefore be a 'make or break' point for the wide market development of pervasive computing. Without information-sharing agreements, only the largest suppliers and service providers will be able to provide users with the service options that they will demand – everyone else will be locked out of the market.

Regulators need to get moving

It is on questions regarding information sharing and co-operation that industries normally turn to regulators for answers – but much of the existing data privacy regulation is not able to accommodate the market's requirements in the world of pervasive computing. Furthermore, there is currently no regulatory body that has the remit to impose its authority on such a sprawling 'industry' – and there is little evidence that the regulatory bodies that have influence over its constituent parts are working with each other to seek out potential areas for concern.

A1.7 Technology suppliers

Ignore positioning statements

All potential suppliers of pervasive computing devices, access networks, applications, content and services must focus their efforts on delivering achievable goals – and must make clear distinctions between these practical delivery strategies and their positioning statements. Accidental or deliberate confusion of the two will only cause trouble. As for today's grand positioning statements – such as 'Bluetooth everywhere', 2Mbit/s mobile network bandwidth and universally available content, applications and services within the next few months – the future will be much more prosaic and slower to arrive, but no less important to the computing, telecommunications and broadcast media industries.

The big infrastructure suppliers are investing heavily in pervasive computing

Many of the world's largest software and network infrastructure suppliers are starting to build bridges between the key supply chains. These companies realise that interworking across these supply chains will be the key to enabling pervasive computing, and are busy expanding their spheres of influence accordingly. Companies such as Cisco Systems, Ericsson, IBM, Microsoft, Nokia, Sun and Oracle are investing heavily in building out capabilities in markets outside their traditional territories.

Only the biggest suppliers will be able to provide the platforms

The development of pervasive computing depends on the availability of access platforms – and applications – that are secure, reliable and perform well. However, pervasive computing application infrastructure must also support cost-effective deployment of applications to multiple access platforms. Much of the software infrastructure that optimises the quality of service of application delivery also has to be specialised for particular access platforms.

The huge complexity associated with addressing these challenges means that there can only be a few serious players in this area. Only companies with significant multichannel experience, international operations and product development budgets can afford to attempt to build such a platform and support it properly. Other players will have opportunities, but they must work around the major infrastructure providers, rather than compete with them, to succeed.

A1.8 Standards

IP still has some way to go

The evolution of IP into a globally accepted networking protocol, as a key enabler of the Internet and the Worldwide Web, has played an important part in driving developments in pervasive computing. However, its transformation into a universally available piece of pervasive computing fabric is not a foregone conclusion. Three significant challenges need to be overcome by suppliers in order to make IP suitable as a core piece of pervasive computing technology:

- device addressability
- quality of service assurance
- IP mobility.

Bluetooth has an important role to play in the long term

Bluetooth has huge possibilities as an enabler for device innovation, but it is already suffering from over-hype and there is significant potential for a backlash before products even hit the market in volume. Other technologies can play part of Bluetooth's role (IEEE 802.11 in the office, HomeRF in the home) but Bluetooth's strength lies in its potential for ubiquity. Until any personal area network technology becomes truly useful, however, a critical mass of devices must be enabled to take advantage of it. Take-up is currently hampered by the high cost of the technology.

XML is a fundamental pervasive computing enabler

XML has a wide role to play in the provision of pervasive computing infrastructure. It is already being used to enhance prospects for multichannel delivery of applications and content, and the advertisement by mobile devices of their capabilities to remote, server-based application platforms. It is also a key component of most business-to-business application integration suites, which are likely to form the operational backbones of tomorrow's service provider information-sharing initiatives.

A2 Pervasive computing – ubiquitous e-services

A2.1 The pervasive computing ideal

The rapid adoption of thin-client, Internet-based business computing, together with the speed with which the Internet is penetrating business and consumers' lives, is driving every technology-dependent company to look for ways of maximising its potential as a vehicle for transformation. Pervasive computing is the new vision that promises to do this, as well as satisfying the need for a suitable infrastructure for e-business.

Pervasive computing is about an ideal – *any information service to any device over any network.* Pervasive computing makes digital content, applications and services available in an integrated, personalised way to users via a diverse range of devices and access networks – new services are equally accessible through wireless networks to cellular phones, vehicles, PDAs and so on; fixed narrowband connections are accessible to PCs or networked home appliances; broadband networks are accessible to digital television sets. It involves the transformation of the global data network that we call the Internet into a pervasive medium that connects users to personalised universes of dynamic content, applications and services, via any smart, connected device.

Big industry players are looking to play significant roles – and it is not pre-ordained that Microsoft will win, which is, of course, why Sun Microsystems, IBM, Oracle and others are so keen to enter the contest.

A2.2 Ovum's definition of pervasive computing

Ovum defines pervasive computing as follows:

> *Pervasive computing is a vision of the future of digital information and computation, in which digital content, applications and services are made available in an integrated, personalised way to users, and accessed by users, via a diverse range of devices and access networks.*

The Internet is not strictly a part of our definition of pervasive computing, but Internet technology forms the information conduit around which media convergence is occurring, and around which delivery of multiple types of application, content and services is starting to be facilitated. The adoption of packed-switched networks and the IP protocol throughout increasing numbers and varieties of network is what is really priming the broadcast media, IT and telecommunications industries for the pervasive computing revolution.

Figure A2.1 shows the pervasive computing ideal of personalised service universes.

Figure A2.1 **Personalised service universes**

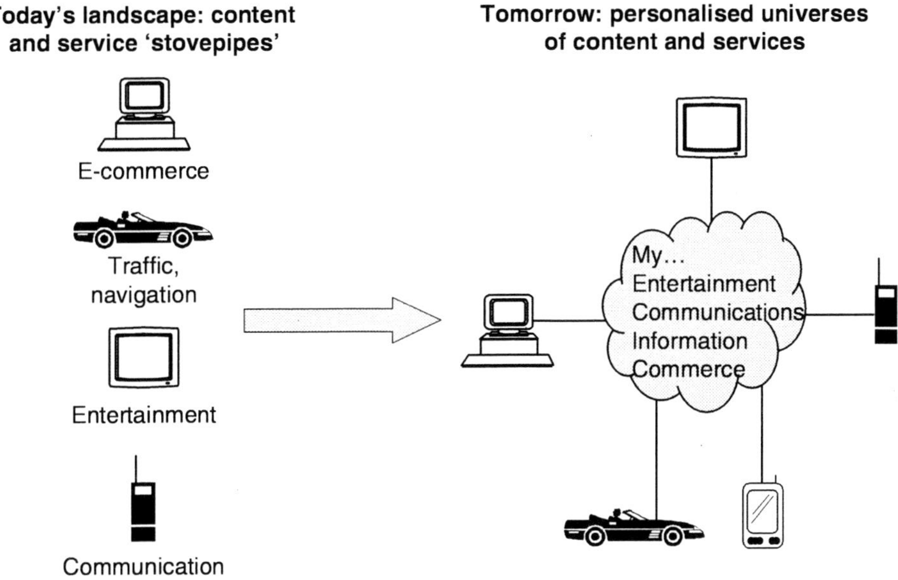

Source: Ovum (Pervasive Computing: Technologies and Markets/Chapter A)

Pervasive computing, in Ovum's definition, does not just mean 'computers everywhere' – it represents 'computers, networks, applications and services everywhere'. However, it is important to realise that the pervasive computing ideal of 'any service to any device over any network' is a statement of enablement; it does not mean that *every* service will be made available to *every* type of device over *every* type of network.

A2.3 Why now?

Market drivers for suppliers

Why now? The short answer is to gain a share of a global market that will be worth nearly $1.3 trillion by 2005 – a huge figure that represents more than 40% of the global market for Internet-based services.

There are three main drivers:

- the threats of commoditisation and increased competition from globalisation and deregulation
- the opportunity to sell existing assets (or incremental enhancements to these) to new markets
- the opportunity for competitive differentiation through the provision of high-value services.

Market drivers for consumers and corporate users

Consumers want mobility

Consumer interest in access to applications, services and content through new smart, connected devices is driven by three factors:

- increased mobility of workforces and consumers in general – not just geographically, but in terms of mobility between roles. As technology improves people's geographic mobility, their home and work lives will also merge
- the increasing expectation in many developed countries (largely driven by past technology innovations) of 24-hour service availability – whether the service in question is a corner shop, a television programme or a website
- general interest in the Internet (largely driven by ISP and merchant advertising), combined with an antipathy (by some) to PCs.

Corporate users want operational efficiency

Corporate users of pervasive computing technology are interested in making their corporate IT systems and applications pervasive. Corporate pervasive computing technology users have more obvious reasons for wanting the technology than consumers. In many respects they are the same reasons as those that have driven historical vertical industry innovation in device hardware – the desire to reduce operational costs and increase company productivity. Examples of opportunities include:

- an automobile manufacturer looking to deploy the same set of features in all its models, implementing them as microprocessor-controlled services rather than as hard-wired features. Buyers pay for certain services to be enabled; if the car is sold to someone else who can afford to pay for extra services (such as electric seats or advanced security features, for example) the manufacturer 'switches on' those services – remotely, via a wireless network – for a fee
- a retailer using its brand to offer free PDAs and network connections (and thus acting like a mobile data service provider) to allow its customers to carry out e-shopping at both the retailer's site, and the sites of its partners. Once the retailer's customers are provided with the devices and the connections, they can use these channels and conduits for all kinds of value-added services that increase the level of customer lock-in.

A2.4 What will pervasive computing affect?

The emerging pervasive computing movement will prove as disruptive to the IT software and hardware industries as the client-server movement of the early 1990s. However, unlike client-server technology, it will affect the broadcast media and telecommunication industries equally.

Pervasive computing is about much more than mere wireless connectivity (a common misperception). Wireless connectivity is currently hot, but it is just one element of the overall pervasive computing picture. Pervasive computing represents the final step in the transformation of computing technology from a scarce resource that could only be used by priest-like operatives, working behind closed doors, to a technology for which access is truly democratised.

The changes brought about by the pervasive computing revolution will be profound:

- applications as we think of them today will no longer be built. Pervasive computing applications will be collections of co-operating e-services that deliver personalised groups of functions to support users' favourite activities, the way they like them
- devices will be disaggregated. New, modularised personal computing platforms, enabled by Bluetooth, will be composed and re-composed dynamically by users as they move between different locations and roles.

A3 Infrastructure is key to market evolution

A3.1 Infrastructure – the hammer and glue

A key aspect of the trend towards pervasive computing is the evolution of the infrastructure 'glue' that will bind today's (and tomorrow's) applications to users, regardless of the access platform that they use, and which will break the walls of today's information delivery 'stovepipes' and enable the vision of universal access associated with pervasive computing.

Pervasive computing infrastructure encompasses a myriad of software, hardware and communications functions. Together, these functions have one fundamental aim:

> *to help break the bonds that currently tie users to devices, devices to networks and applications to both of these, and thereby enable more direct relationships between users and applications, regardless of the device and network being used.*

Figure A3.1 illustrates this aim.

Figure A3.1 **Pervasive computing infrastructure – breaking the bonds**

Without pervasive computing technology...

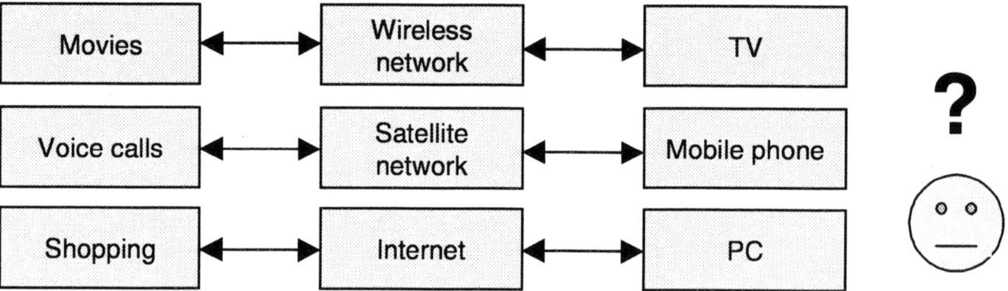

With pervasive computing technology...

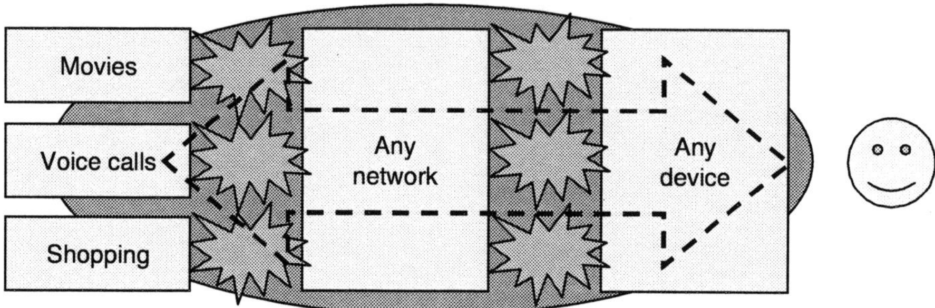

Source: Ovum (Pervasive Computing: Technologies and Markets/Chapter A)

This is a grand statement of ambition for the role of infrastructure. But what does it mean? Breaking the bonds involves addressing three main challenges:

- the majority of applications in use today are not deployed as network-based services, nor are they designed to be suitable for delivery to multiple types of access platform
- outside the realm of the PC and the corporate LAN, today's digital information access platforms vary widely in their capabilities – and therefore their suitability for delivering certain types of application to users
- industries have been created and have matured around the delivery of particular types of digital information to particular types of device over particular types of network. These 'stovepipes' make the level of industry interworking that will be required to deliver truly pervasive computing applications, very difficult.

A3.2 The need for end-to-end solutions

In order to enable pervasive computing, infrastructure technology must deliver end-to-end solutions. It must play a central role in supporting:

- the creation of content, applications and services that can be delivered to multiple access platforms
- the creation and optimisation of access platforms for particular applications
- the delivery of content, applications and services to access platforms.

However, given the diversity of technologies required and the scale and scope of even one of these supporting roles, it is apparent that no single infrastructure supplier will be able to supply everything that the market needs. Without standards that can enable interworking between different 'islands' of infrastructure, market development could be severely constrained.

A3.3 Which technologies will play a part?

The pervasive computing vision requires a huge amount of infrastructure – enabling technology products – in order to develop fully. The foundation of pervasive computing infrastructure is hardware and access network infrastructure; software infrastructure is layered on the 'bare bones' provided by these to build complete 'living environments' for pervasive computing activity. Development and operational management services are complementary to these run-time infrastructure elements.

Figure A3.2 shows the main technologies that form the elements of hardware and network infrastructure, software infrastructure, and development and operational management services. These technologies are the building blocks for device-, network- and application-independent infrastructure solutions – they are not specific to any single type of device or access network, nor are they tailored for the delivery of particular applications.

Figure A3.2 **The building blocks of pervasive computing infrastructure**

	Main technologies
Hardware and network infrastructure	Client devices; server hardware; access network infrastructure; core network infrastructure
Software infrastructure	Client operating systems; service invocation and brokerage; user interfaces; storage management; security and subscriber ID; data synchronisation; device management; quality of service optimisation and integrity assurance
Development and operational management services	Content/application authoring tools; content/application integration tools; content adaptation tools; personalisation tools and engines; context management frameworks; billing systems; subscriber management systems; service monitoring tools; usage analysis tools; service integration platforms

Source: Ovum (Pervasive Computing: Technologies and Markets/Chapter A)

A4 The future of applications and content

A4.1 How and when will applications become multichannel?

Application providers, software infrastructure providers and service providers will engage in three distinct types of multichannel application development activity, which will come to market in three distinct waves:

- construction of new platform-specific extensions to existing applications
- construction of new applications that are designed to be multichannel from the outset
- re-engineering of older applications and integration of these with new applications that are designed to be multichannel.

The first wave has already begun. It is the result of a short-term strategy to get multichannel capabilities to market quickly, involving a 'top-down' approach to multichannel application architecture. The need for a strategy that enables quick time-to-market will be stimulated by steady advances in the transformation of application products into network-based services, which are already occurring and will continue over the next three years.

The second wave is starting now, and is largely the preserve of new-entrant service providers, working in partnership with innovative software infrastructure providers and systems integrators to deliver multichannel applications that are designed that way from the 'ground up'.

The third wave will start in earnest in around 2002, as cost and profitability pressures on established players, brought about by competition from new entrants, force them to analyse their ongoing investment in infrastructure and platforms and find new ways of deploying services that are more cost-effective.

By 2006, new pervasive computing applications will not be recognisable as such. Many applications will be highly granular and personalised, and the lines between different kinds of application will be extremely blurred. The eventual transformation of the application from monolithic product to personalised, granular set of network-based services is an inevitable consequence of the subsumption of Internet technology into application infrastructure technologies, and into different markets. E-commerce, infotainment and personal communications will be the applications most affected by this transformation.

A4.2 Critical success factors for multichannel applications

There are three critical success factors that must be addressed in order for a service provider to deliver a multichannel application:

- service-based delivery of the application
- implementation of a high-quality, multichannel application architecture that allows cost-effective deployment of the application to new access platforms
- implementation of infrastructure that enhances the overall quality of service of application delivery, which is implemented throughout the delivery environment (not just on the access platform).

Quality of service assurance is a theme running through these factors. It requires the co-ordinated enlistment of the service provider's operational management services, the infrastructure underpinning the network-based application and the access platform itself.

Today, such an undertaking is difficult – the infrastructure platforms that confer high quality of service to applications do not promote the types of design principle that underpin the cost-effective delivery of multichannel applications; if you try to design a multichannel application, you will get little support from 'off-the-shelf' infrastructure products.

The co-ordination of end-to-end assured delivery quality requires service providers wanting to offer multichannel applications to form technology and implementation partnerships with infrastructure providers, application and content providers, network operators and device manufacturers.

A4.3 Application transformation – pressurising supply chains and platforms

Application convergence will pressurise players in today's channel-specific supply chains to interwork much more effectively. The 'stovepipes' will eventually be broken down for two reasons:

- the delivery of multichannel applications requires service providers to partner with multiple network operators and device suppliers working in multiple channel-specific markets
- application convergence means that, increasingly, no single service provider will be able to provide all the services that every user will want to access. Service providers will therefore have to partner with their peers working in other channel-specific and application-specific markets.

The personalisation, granularity and convergence of application types will not happen smoothly – and will not happen at all without significant evolution in access platforms and software infrastructure.

Devices are evolving from application-specialised objects into general computing platforms. However, in the short term they will not be sufficiently capable to support converged application environments. Broadcast access networks are today used to deliver infotainment and, increasingly, e-commerce applications, but as these applications become more granular and personalised, broadcast will become an inefficient application delivery model. Broadcast delivery in this environment can only work if personalisation and aggregation functions are provided by access platforms, rather than by central application-serving platforms. This distributed computing arrangement brings its own set of infrastructure challenges.

Another factor that will inhibit application convergence is that the software infrastructure used today, in supporting the quality of service of application delivery, either does not support multichannel applications or is highly proprietary and therefore less easy to promote across multiple supply chains.

A5 The future of devices and access networks

A5.1 Access platforms: different, but becoming more similar

There is considerable variation today in the capabilities of device and network components of major pervasive computing access platforms. The main factors that limit the capabilities of individual access platforms are:

- the capability of cellular networks to support data services
- the fundamental limitations of broadcast networks
- the slow evolution of battery technology (relative to the pace of mobile device innovation).

Device differentiation: from technology limitations to usage contexts

The wide variation in access platform capabilities will continue, even when current technology constraints are removed. Today, it is hard constraints such as battery technology that limit the capability of particular devices; tomorrow it will be soft constraints – primarily, the usage contexts in which people like to use devices – that will lead to variation in device capabilities and form factors. In particular, device manufacturers are keen to increase the level of commonality between different device types, in order to improve accessibility to digital information over networks. Many see this capability as being a key short- to medium-term differentiator in markets that are highly competitive.

There is no such thing as the specialised device

Many manufacturers talk of their pervasive computing devices as specialised appliances, but application convergence means that such an approach has fundamental limitations in the long term. Slowly but surely, devices are evolving from application-specialised objects into more open computing platforms. As infotainment, e-commerce and personal communications applications in particular converge, device manufacturers will have to look to the overall requirements of the converged application space to determine the capabilities of next-generation devices.

The challenges are significant. The fact that broadcast networks work best when every subscriber wants the same information, means that devices that are used in conjunction with broadcast networks in particular must be designed to take on increasing amounts of the overall application processing burden. When everyone gets everything, delivery of specialised, aggregated sets of converged application components requires the bulk of that work to be carried out post-transmission rather than pre-transmission.

A5.2 The road to network convergence

Carriers are set to gradually replace today's 'spaghetti' mass of core network infrastructure with unified, IP-friendly, multiple class-of-service fibre backbones. That much is well-understood. However, a similar, but less dramatic shift is also coming to pass in access networks. This shift makes converged applications easier to deliver to users.

The increasing penetration of digital services over broadband access networks is allowing existing cable and copper infrastructure to be used much more efficiently. Operators are increasingly installing infrastructure that allows them to deliver voice, data and video over the same wires (or through the same area of spectrum). Furthermore, applications are converging in their use of transmission schemes. For example:

- rich media Internet applications are slowly moving from unicast to multicast protocols
- sophisticated interactive TV services are bringing requirements for certain data to be unicast to particular subscribers, in tandem with other common elements that are broadcast.

The convergence of voice, video and data through digital network transmission is not the same thing as the emergence of uniform availability of broadband transfer speeds, however. Increasing numbers of mobile operators are starting to move the development of broadband mobile services down their agendas. They fear that the high prices that they have paid for operating licences might preclude the requisite infrastructure spend.

A5.3 Partnerships are vital for building the right access platforms

The variety in access platform capabilities does not manifest itself in differences in the suitability of platforms for particular applications. This is because there are two almost universal issues that are not wholly addressed by platforms themselves – issues that can therefore only be addressed through the implementation of software infrastructure:

- controlling access to applications and data through security frameworks
- ensuring reliable transmission of application data and functionality across networks.

Differences in access platform capabilities do, however, affect the ways in which gaps between platform capabilities and applications' technology requirements can be addressed. The more restricted the access network, the more information bandwidth must be optimised, but the more restricted the device, the less dynamic optimisation can be performed. The suitability of software infrastructure solutions for enhancing quality of service is therefore highly dependent on the details of the access platform. For example, reliability and security issues are being dealt with by implementations of the relatively lightweight WAP set of protocols (WTP, WSP and WTLS) in mobile wireless access platforms, but reliability is being addressed in a more proprietary but heavyweight fashion by IBM (with its MQSeries Everyplace messaging middleware) on PDA platforms.

Success requires access platform suppliers to ignore the temptation to develop proprietary infrastructure solutions, and to work with best-of-breed third-party technologies. This in turn means manufacturers must ensure that their products are open enough to stimulate partnerships, and partner with the biggest and best. If standards are involved then so much the better.

A6 The future of digital information supply chains

A6.1 Today's digital information stovepipes

There are three main industries involved in the delivery of particular types of digital information, which have historically been implemented as closed 'stovepipes':

- the telecommunications industry – in which most activity has historically focused on facilitating voice communication across fixed and mobile telecommunications networks
- the IT industry – in which most activity has historically focused on delivering applications to PCs
- the broadcast media industry – in which most activity currently focuses on delivering infotainment content to TVs.

However, the huge growth in use of the Internet and its protocol (IP) in both business and consumer contexts, is fast dissolving the binds that have historically tied particular digital information delivery industries to particular applications, networks and devices. The proliferation of IP services is driving convergence between these industries, networks and applications, as shown in *Figure A6.1*.

Figure A6.1 **IP adoption is driving convergence**

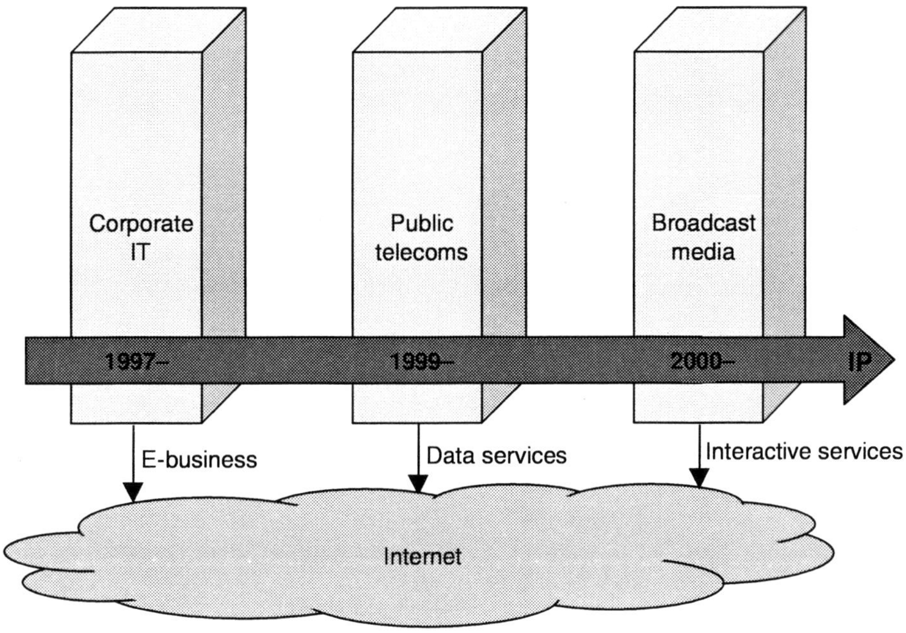

Source: Ovum (Pervasive Computing: Technologies and Markets/Chapter A)

Pervasive computing presents opportunities for companies to break out of these rigid supply chains and enter either the other stovepipes, or new supply chains being constructed around the delivery of content, applications and services to new types of smart, connected device. Of course, migration of suppliers from their 'home' stovepipe brings them into contact with suppliers that they have not had to partner or compete with before. For example, automobile and home appliance manufacturers are now working with software companies, network operators and content providers to enable the delivery of applications and services to vehicles and domestic appliances respectively.

A6.2 Major supplier migrations

Convergence of the major digital information delivery industries is in many ways the engine behind the development of pervasive computing – because suppliers migrating across the major digital information supply chains will be the pioneers of multichannel service provision. Over the next five years, content and applications, networks and devices currently tied together within today's computing, telecommunications and broadcast media stovepipes will become increasingly interwoven to create an environment where applications are delivered over multiple networks, to multiple types of device. The major migrations of suppliers that will facilitate this weaving will occur around four events:

- the maturation of the wireless Internet, through 2001 and 2002
- the popularisation of digital interactive TV services, through 2001 and 2002
- the widespread availability of broadband point-to-point access services to the home, through 2003 and 2004
- the widespread availability of broadband access speeds in mobile networks, through 2005 and 2006.

As these events occur, we will also see a degree of access platform substitution and the growth in importance of new types of smart, connected device – the connected PDA, car and home appliance.

A6.3 Breaking the stovepipes – market, technology and geographic issues

Market issues

'If you play in my park, you play by my rules'

Suppliers moving from a position of strength in one supply chain will not be able to rely on that strength translating to their target market. Successful ventures will be built from partnerships between what may seem at first to be unlikely allies, for in many cases partners will compete in some areas.

The value of information is changing – but not as you might expect

In order to provide seamless, high-quality services to subscribers in a pervasive computing environment, service providers will have to share all sorts of information as users navigate around their personalised universes of content, applications and services. Without such information exchanges, the pervasive computing vision is a flawed one for suppliers: there will be no simple subscriber billing, no interactive advertising and no open access to the Internet, for example. Consequently, the value of information increases the more it is shared between suppliers. This change in the nature of the value of information will bring major changes in the relationships that service providers must form with their customers, and with the information that they hold about those customers, in order to succeed as a pervasive computing player.

Information-sharing models have the potential to overcome two of the most difficult questions that face pervasive computing service providers:

- how can they afford to provide open access to other providers' applications and services if this means that revenues will stop flowing to them and start flowing to the other providers?
- how can they support a user (and avoid blame) if a problem occurs somewhere in a third party's delivery of a service?

Technology issues

Dealing with specialised quality of service infrastructure

The development of pervasive computing depends on the availability of access platforms – and applications – that are secure, reliable and perform well. However, pervasive computing application infrastructure must also support cost-effective deployment of applications to multiple access platforms. Furthermore, software infrastructure ('middleware') that optimises the quality of service of application delivery, has to be specialised for particular access platforms. This presents a major challenge for the software providers that are trying to build next-generation infrastructure products hosting multichannel applications – as well as providing platforms that need to help providers build multichannel assets, and potentially scale to millions of users, significant chunks of the software must be specialised and rigorously tested for each access platform supported.

The scale and complexity of this challenge means that there can be few serious players in this area. Since many variations in access platforms are peculiar to particular regions, only companies with significant multichannel experience, international operations and product development budgets can afford to attempt to build such a platform and support it properly.

Facilitating information sharing

Information sharing is at the heart of enabling interconnection between service providers – just as it is a key part of the regulations that allow interconnection between telecommunications carriers. There are three broad areas that need to be considered:

- **usage information**: in order for providers to be able to support open access to other providers' applications, services and delivery channels, revenue needs to be able to flow between them. However, the amount of revenue that flows in some way has to be related to patterns of user activity
- **operational management information**: users see their 'primary' service providers (the parties that bill them) as the parties responsible for problems in delivering paid-for services. This will be their view even if the problem actually occurs within another service provider's domain. Service assurance is therefore a difficult issue – primary service providers become responsible for the quality of services and infrastructure that they do not own or control. Primary service providers will therefore need to have confidence that the third-party operated applications, services and

infrastructure that they allow their subscribers to access, is being managed to a high standard

- **context information**: session context information identifies user sessions and what and whom those sessions involve, so it makes sense that session context information should be the foundation of the information processing that individual providers have to carry out. However, the promotion of session context information to being something that is shared not only between components of an application or service, but also between providers, brings a number of further technology challenges.

Geographic issues

Some people say that we live in an age where national boundaries no longer matter. The truth, unfortunately, is nothing like that. Quite apart from differences in penetration of particular types of application and access platform, matters of geography create widely differing environments that affect the ability of suppliers from particular markets to migrate to other positions in other markets. The considerable variation that exists across national boundaries brings yet another set of complexities for suppliers to consider when they migrate from one position to another:

- application and content issues – for example, requirements for content localisation and variations in cultural attitudes to advertising
- service provision issues – for example, variations in regulation that restricts ownership of media channels
- device issues – for example, variations in the cultural acceptance of 'traditional' computers.

A7 Key messages for suppliers

A7.1 All suppliers must consider both sides

Successful development of pervasive computing requires all supplier communities to avoid hype and implement open products and services using standards wherever possible. However, the major issue that supplier communities must deal with is realising that what they do not know is as important as what they do know:

- software-centric players understand issues surrounding delivering specialised products and services to highly segmented markets, and differentiating those products and services based on features and functions
- network-centric players understand issues surrounding the very high-quality delivery of mass-market services that are differentiated based on price and performance.

Both perspectives are vital, yet – with very few exceptions – neither community recognises the importance of the other perspective.

A7.2 Device manufacturers

- For the vast majority of device suppliers, success in pervasive computing will require more than just delivering the 'sexiest' device.
- You will have to complement your device offering with digital content, applications and services – but bring these to market by partnering with established service providers; do not attempt to build a service provider business from scratch.
- Keep services and portals relevant to your core device offerings, ensure they add value and do not price them too highly or take-up will be stifled.
- Use standards to bring the widest universes of content, applications and services to your user base – but do not rely on them to solve all your problems. Partner with experienced software infrastructure providers to ensure that your platform is good enough to deliver the right mix of services.
- Be aware that implementing an open platform will decrease your hold over the supply chain – but that not having control over it is a precursor to your success. You must compete based on the quality of your partnerships, not through a market stranglehold.

A7.3 Network operators

- You can play a powerful role in the pervasive computing revolution by offering network services – but only if you understand your target market and work with other established players to build the right offerings.
- You have lots of specialised strengths – these go way beyond mere ownership of the 'bit pipes'. The user information that you have the potential to mine is valuable – use it.

- You will not succeed if you try to do everything yourself. Success requires a hybrid IT/telecoms view and a shift in focus away from delivery of mass-market network services offered on the basis of price/performance, towards delivery of specialised services for highly segmented audiences, differentiated on features and functions.
- Don't just see users in terms of ARPUs – they will be turned off by information and advertising overload. Start by thinking about what content, applications and services *people* want, rather than thinking about how much money you need to gain from each *subscriber* in order to recoup investments. Partner with others to explore this question.

A7.4 Content and application providers

- In order to re-use your content or application assets across multiple delivery channels you will have to do a lot of work in the short term – but it is vital that you carry this out, in order to reap rewards in the long term.
- Digital rights management infrastructure is critical to your ability to make money from your assets, but implementing it requires wide-ranging partnerships with software infrastructure, network and device suppliers.
- Choose your software infrastructure partners carefully – their ability to help you deliver your assets across multiple channels with minimum effort is critical to your long-term success. Their level of commitment to standards is key – lip-service is not enough. The more open the infrastructure through which your assets are deployed, the wider your potential audience.
- Make sure your pricing and business models are consistent across multiple channels. Users will exploit weaknesses and/or inconsistencies to their advantage – and your disadvantage.

A7.5 Service providers

- You have the opportunity to play many key roles in the pervasive computing revolution, because your ability to deliver content and/or applications as services is a vital precondition of their delivery within a pervasive computing environment.
- Success depends on more than just interposing yourself between one or more content and application providers, and users. Without an established brand behind you, it may be best to provide wholesale technology e-services rather than consumer-focused services.
- Customer 'ownership' is a dangerous pursuit, as it may shut you out from lucrative collaborative partnerships with other providers. Exchange of information with other providers is likely to be vital to your success in the long term.
- Partner with software infrastructure as well as network infrastructure players – you will not succeed without their expertise.

- Your ability to store, manage and use usage context information does not just enable you to allow customers to obtain seamless multichannel experiences. It can help you add further value by allowing users to personalise their own online universes, and avoid information overload.

A7.6 Infrastructure vendors

- You are key to the development of pervasive computing – but unless you work with each other, particularly across the network/software divide, you will not reap the rewards.
- Only the biggest providers will be able to build end-to-end solutions for customers. If you are not one of them, it makes more sense for you to work with a major supplier, rather than try to usurp them. You will have to work with them anyway.
- Do not try to make everything perfect. Time-to-market is critical – particularly in the short term.
- In the medium-to-long term, most of the value-add you provide to your customers will be in helping them deal with the complexity inherent in the specialisation of content, applications and services, rather than their homogenisation.
- Internet services or corporate application infrastructure specialists must work with partners – including specialist technology providers, service providers, network operators and device manufacturers – to provide the right offerings to customers of wireless Internet and interactive TV services.

A8 The pervasive computing technology opportunity

A8.1 A major revenue opportunity

By 2005, Internet service revenues attributable to pervasive computing access – revenues obtained by service providers offering multichannel access – will be nearly $1.3 trillion. This will account for more than 40% of the global market for Internet services in 2005 – a significant increase on 2001, when multichannel access revenues will account for less than 5% of overall global Internet service revenues. The total will comprise a mixture of commerce, access and advertising revenues.

In order to enable the pervasive computing revolution, application and content providers, network operators, service providers, device manufacturers, corporate users and consumers worldwide will spend over $21 billion in 2005 on software infrastructure to enable multichannel content, applications and services.

A8.2 Regional variations

The pervasive computing service opportunity – and, correspondingly, the infrastructure opportunity – is heavily skewed toward North America and Western Europe. By contrast, the long-term opportunity in Asia-Pacific is significantly lower than that in North America – despite that region's current advanced state in the provision of mobile data services, when compared to the rest of the world.

It is the balanced provision of multichannel access that creates the environment for pervasive computing to flourish, and the dominance of the mobile access channels in Asia-Pacific means that the opportunity for pervasive computing is limited compared with North America and Western Europe. This does not mean that the absolute level of Internet adoption will necessarily be lower, just less involved with pervasive, multichannel access.

Figure A8.1 shows that North America will account for two-thirds of total revenues from multichannel Internet services by 2005 – a decline from its early market domination in 2001 of just less than 80%. *Figure A8.2* shows that this dominance is mirrored by infrastructure spend – in 2005 North America will account for 51% of the global total.

Figure A8.1 **Internet service revenues from pervasive computing, $ billion**

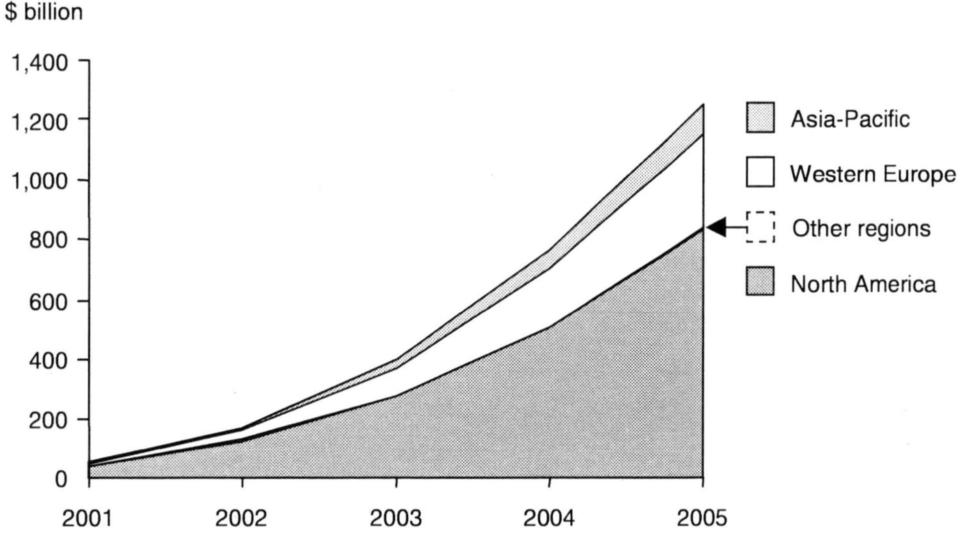

Source: Ovum (Pervasive Computing: Technologies and Markets/Chapter A)

Figure A8.2 **Software infrastructure spend, $ billion**

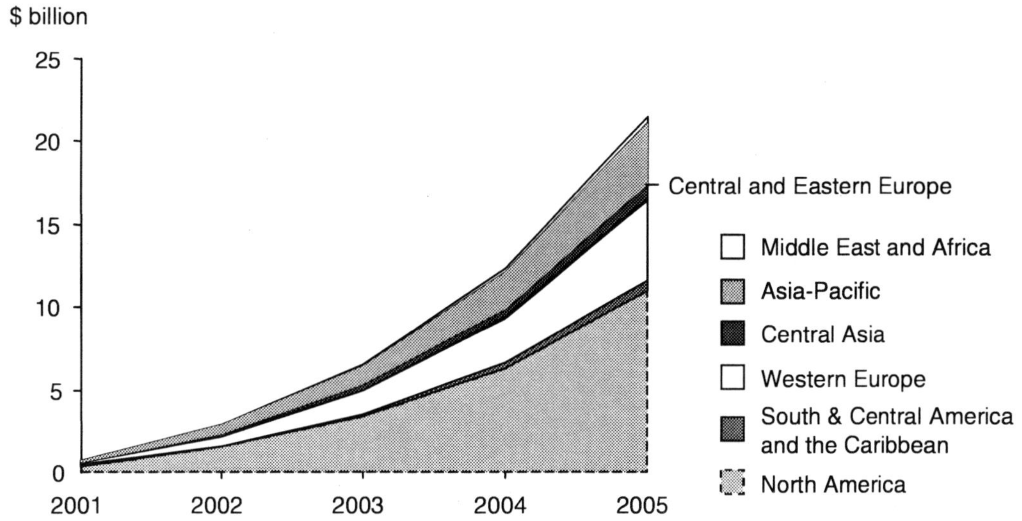

Source: Ovum (Pervasive Computing: Technologies and Markets/Chapter A)

A8.3 Waves of application development

As outlined in *Section A4.1*, pervasive computing applications and services will come to market via three waves of development. The different waves of adoption bring new multichannel assets to market, but improve business for supplier communities in different ways.

Infrastructure technologies associated with the first wave of multichannel application development and deployment – channel-specialised content adaptation technology, for example – are designed to get multichannel assets to market quickly, and thus generate new revenues for providers. However, infrastructure technologies associated with the second and third waves of deployment are primarily designed to reduce operating costs and make operations more efficient, rather than open up new markets.

Figure A8.3 shows how the overall market for software infrastructure associated with pervasive computing will be affected by the development of these three deployment waves over time. In 2001, the vast majority of users' software infrastructure spend will be on first-wave infrastructure technologies (a total of just over \$4.25 billion worldwide). However, by 2003 the influence of the first wave of technologies will have waned so that it accounts for around 44% of overall spend (a total of just over \$11.8 billion worldwide). By 2003, the first-wave software infrastructure opportunity will be eclipsed by other infrastructure technologies.

Figure A8.3 **Infrastructure spend by adoption wave, \$ billion**

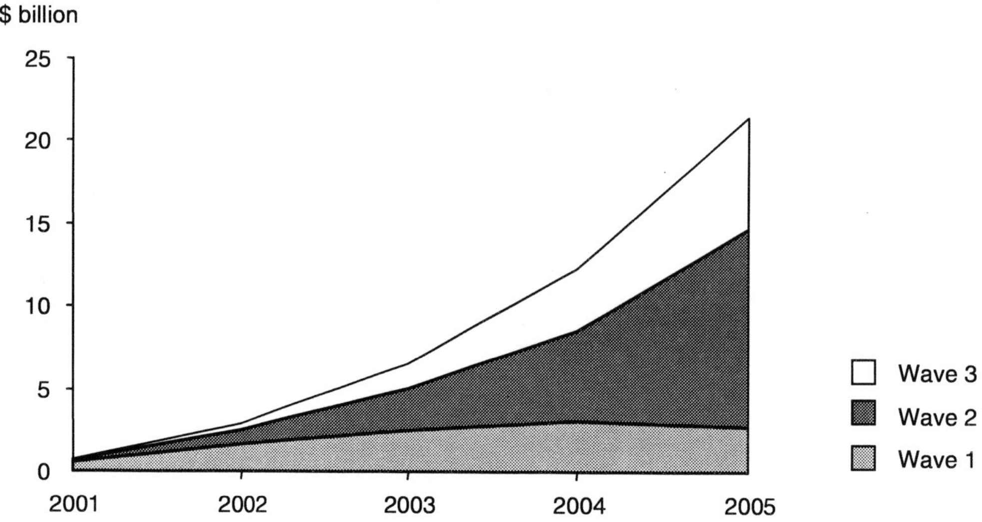

Source: (Pervasive Computing: Technologies and Markets/Chapter A)

B Pervasive computing – the new revolution?

B1 Looking for the new revolution

B1.1 Client-server redux?

In the early 1990s, the IT industry – users and suppliers – closed its collective eyes and wished for something better. They wished for a new technology that would empower employees, free large companies from the shackles of their proprietary mainframe computer systems and bring affordable computing power to smaller companies.

Client-server technology was the answer it came up with. One reason for its widespread uptake was that it made vast fortunes for software and hardware companies, including Microsoft, Sun Microsystems and Oracle. Vendor push is as important to a new market as user pull.

But it was not the full answer. Client-server brought its own problems – high management costs being one of the biggest. The speedy adoption of thin-client, Internet-based business computing is a testament to this fact. This adoption, together with the speed at which the Internet is penetrating business and consumers' lives, is driving every technology-dependent company to look for ways of maximising the Internet's potential as a vehicle for transformation.

The new vision that promises to do what client-server computing failed to do, satisfying the new needs of consumers and providing a suitable infrastructure for e-business, is pervasive computing.

B1.2 The new vision

Pervasive computing is about an ideal: *any information service to any device over any network*. It is about making digital content, applications and services available in an integrated, personalised way to users through multiple devices and access networks, so that new services are equally accessible through wireless networks to mobile phones, through corporate LANs to PCs, or by broadcast to digital television.

All the major players in the IT industry are investing significant amounts of time and money on transforming the global data network that we call the Internet, into a pervasive medium that connects users to personalised universes of dynamic content, applications and services, via any smart, connected device. The consequent changes will be profound:

- applications as we think of them today will no longer be built. Pervasive computing applications will be collections of co-operating e-services that deliver personalised groups of functions to support users' own favourite activities – the way they like them
- devices will be disaggregated. New modularised personal computing platforms, enabled by Bluetooth, will be composed and re-composed dynamically by users as they move between different locations and roles.

This vision of the 'next-generation Internet' is a long way from what the Internet is today – a medium for transporting messages and relatively static web content between traditional PC computing platforms. It is truly a paradigm shift. To play a role in the development of pervasive computing need not be the goal for every supplier: but suppliers that do not understand the potential effect of the pervasive computing revolution and adjust their strategies accordingly, will find themselves marginalised.

B1.3 Pervasive computing is as disruptive as the client-server movement

The transformation of today's Internet into tomorrow's pervasive computing fabric, together with associated evolutions in application architectures, hosting platforms and devices, will create a market for infrastructure technologies worth more than $20 billion worldwide by 2006.

The emerging pervasive computing movement will prove as disruptive to the IT software and hardware industries as the client-server movement of the early 1990s. Moreover, it will affect the broadcast media and telecommunication industries equally significantly – something which the client-server movement never did.

Pervasive computing is about much more than mere wireless connectivity (a common misperception). Wireless connectivity is 'hot', but it is just one element of the overall pervasive computing picture. Pervasive computing represents the final step in the transformation of computing technology from a scarce resource that could only be used by priest-like operatives, working behind closed doors, to a technology with access that is truly democratised.

Figure B1.1 shows how the extent of access to digital information and processing power has changed over time, with the introduction of new computing paradigms worldwide – and how pervasive computing is taking access to digital information, and processing power, to billions of users.

Figure B1.1 **The effect of pervasive computing**

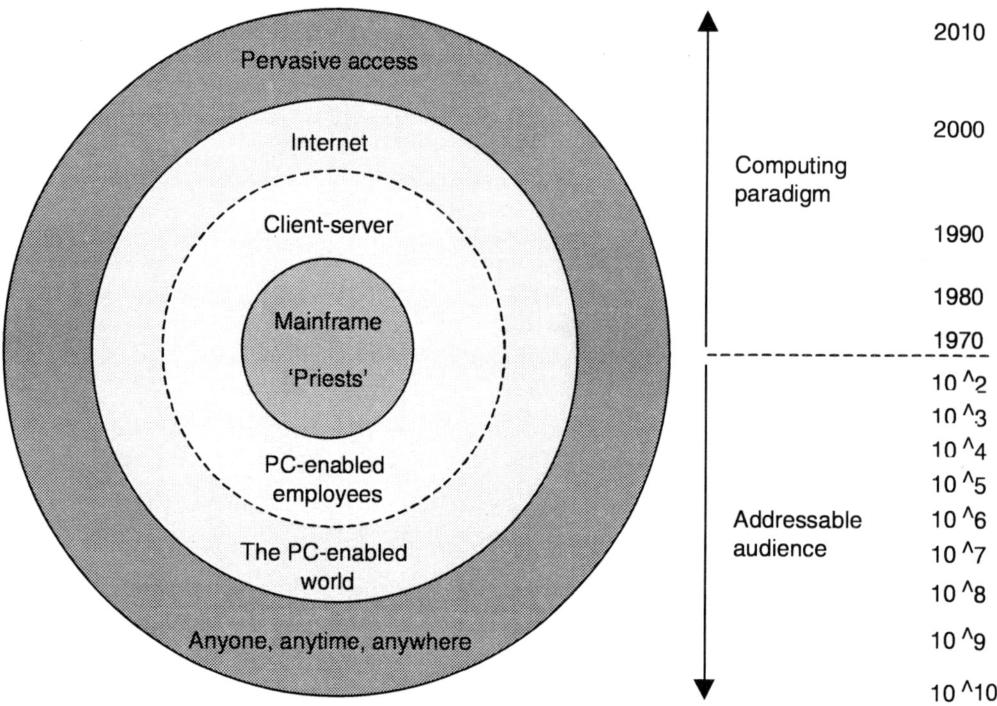

Source: Ovum (Pervasive Computing: Technologies and Markets/Chapter B)

The changes induced by pervasive computing will not follow the same path as client-server computing, however. Web-based computing has swept through industries so quickly because client-server introduced problems of manageability and heterogeneity: even the rise of a *de facto* standard (the Microsoft client platform) could not prevent a steady shift towards the web paradigm.

There is no doubt that pervasive computing will bring its own heterogeneity and management problems. But this time, the heterogeneity will not be circumvented – it is user-driven. The pervasive computing ethos almost mandates heterogeneity. Consequently, pervasive computing is no 'milk run'. It represents a paradigm shift, and there are rich rewards to be gained, but the journey will be long and arduous.

Vendor push

Just as with client-server, big IT industry players (especially those that made fortunes from client-server) are looking to satisfy the demand. Successful players must apply hybrid IT/communications perspectives to find solutions that really work for users. It is not pre-ordained that Microsoft will win this fight: which is, of course, why Sun Microsystems, IBM, Oracle and others are so keen to enter the ring.

And this time, the telecommunications, broadcast media, automotive, home appliances and retail industries want to be part of the game.

> *'This idea that we need a new platform, a platform that takes as its centre the Internet and the user, and then takes the devices and services, rather than having the devices at the centre; that idea has been emerging for a long time. And the question is what can be done to get enough of those pieces together to really get that to critical mass.'*
>
> Extract from a keynote speech by Bill Gates on Microsoft's .NET strategy

B2 Why are we moving towards pervasive computing?

Different communities want different things from the future of information technology. Not all suppliers will want to play in the pervasive computing market (although, right now, it seems that every technology company wanting to grab some mindshare is keen to carve out a chunk of the opportunity for itself). For a multichannel service delivery environment to be viable, all the players that want something from pervasive computing (IT, telecommunications and media providers, and service users) must have something to gain. 'High-end' suppliers of every type will need to take a position.

The current situation does not provide a long-term viable market infrastructure, not least because content and applications today have to be authored for specific devices and networks. Some content or service providers can afford to do this, but it is expensive and a long-term headache. Many service and content providers will not be able to do this. If this situation continues, the move towards pervasive computing will be stifled because:

- users (as a community) will only be able to access content, applications and services that have been explicitly designed and authored for the device and network they are using
- the majority of content owners and service providers will only be able to reach parts of the user community that use particular devices to access information.

B2.1 What do suppliers want?

The short answer is a share of a products and services market that will be worth a colossal $1.3 trillion by 2006.

The long answer is that there are three main drivers:

- the threats of commoditisation and increased competition from globalisation and deregulation
- the opportunity to sell existing assets (or incremental enhancements to those) to new markets
- the opportunity for competitive differentiation through provision of high-value services.

Accessing new markets

Application, content and service providers are keen to take their assets to new audiences. As they look to advertising or subscription revenue as core components of their business models, the number of 'eyeballs' they can reach becomes more and more important. Pervasive computing promises to bring new audiences to these players. Companies such as AOL, Time Warner, Yahoo!, Vivendi and the BBC are all looking to re-use their assets across multiple delivery channels. As owners or brokers of the scarcest resource in any digital information delivery market – content – they are finding no shortage of service providers willing to help them.

Infrastructure providers are also looking to move beyond the corporate IT and telecommunications worlds, which have been their home for so long. Pervasive computing opens up relatively untapped markets to companies such as BEA, Ericsson, IBM, Microsoft, Motorola, Nokia, Oracle and Sun Microsystems – all of whom have initiatives in place. Telecommunications network operators such as BellSouth, BT, Cable & Wireless, NTT DoCoMo and Vodafone are looking at ways of delivering value-added services; pervasive computing will not only bring the network operators these opportunities, but will also drive more voice and data traffic through their networks, as a side-effect.

Perhaps most importantly, the investment community is keenly looking beyond 'wired web' dot.coms to new investment opportunities and the next revolution. The current focus is infrastructure companies enabling wireless Internet services, and the money is flooding in. It will not be long before the community turns its gaze to interactive services infrastructure providers, telematics infrastructure providers and so on.

Competitive differentiation through new service offerings

Service providers and network operators have the potential to build roles for themselves as brokers between content and application suppliers and users – for multiple information delivery channels. Service providers and network operators will improve their competitive positions if they can take advantage of the new service provision opportunities that will arise from the evolution of pervasive computing:

- content and application suppliers will be more likely to forge relationships with service providers and network operators if those companies can demonstrate the ability to grow content and application suppliers' subscriber bases and usage
- users are more likely to subscribe to a single service provider that can offer them the services they want, through all the delivery channels that they use, rather than subscribe to multiple service providers that each offer content and applications through single channels.

B2.2 What do users want?

Consumers

Consumers are interested in access to applications, services and content through 'new' channels, for three reasons:

- increased mobility of workforces and consumers in general – not just geographically, but in terms of mobility between roles. As technology improves people's geographic mobility, their home and work lives merge too
- the increasing expectation in many developed countries (largely driven by past technology innovations) of 24×7 service availability – whether the service in question is a local shop, a television programme or a website
- general interest in the Internet (largely driven by ISP and merchant advertising), combined with an antipathy (by some) to personal computers.

The majority of consumers are not technology-savvy, and so technology barriers to multichannel service delivery mean nothing to them. A consumer told that they can access a personal banking service through their mobile phone, for example, will be nonplussed if the service is not the same (within reasonable limits) as that provided through their TV.

Corporate users

Corporate users of pervasive computing technology are interested in making their own corporate IT systems and applications pervasive. Corporate pervasive computing technology users have much more easily-identified reasons for wanting the technology than do consumers. In many respects they are the same reasons as those that have driven historical vertical-industry innovation in device hardware.

Reducing costs

As microprocessors and networking equipment become cheaper, suppliers in many industries are interested in using pervasive computing technologies – typically, utilising wireless networking of some kind – to either turn their products into services, or to lower the cost of delivering their services. Examples include a soft drinks machine supplier examining the business case for embedding inventory management and wireless networking technology into each deployed machine – to allow it to only visit machines needing servicing or re-filling, rather than having to make regular visits to all its deployed machines.

Adding value

Retailers, banks and utilities in particular have the opportunity, through pervasive computing technology, to not only reduce operational costs (through more efficient management of their assets and networks) but also to add value to their products or services – by improving the quality, or enriching the features, of their products or services. Examples include:

- an automobile manufacturer looking to deploy the same set of features in all its models, implementing them as microprocessor-controlled services rather than as 'hard-wired' features. Buyers of the cars then pay for certain services to be enabled. If the car is then sold to someone who can afford extra services (such as electric seats or advanced security features), the manufacturer can then 'switch on' those services remotely, via a wireless network – for a fee

- a retailer using its brand to offer free PDAs and network connections (and thus acting like a mobile data service provider), which allow customers to carry out e-shopping at both the retailer's own site, and the sites of its partners. Once the retailers' customers are provided with the devices and connections, they can use these channels and conduits for all kinds of value-added services that increase the level of customer lock-in.

B3 Defining pervasive computing

B3.1 The network is the computer...

When Sun Microsystems invented its strapline 'the network is the computer' in the mid-to-late 1990s, many people were confused. For several years it appeared that the company was using its network-centric ethos merely to promote its server technology and to outflank Microsoft. But whether by accident or by design, the concept of 'the network is the computer' has come of age. It captures a lot of the spirit of the pervasive computing vision.

Bill Gates' opinion on the same issue is interesting for its parallels to Sun's stated position. When describing Microsoft's .NET strategy, Gates talks about 'a platform that takes as its centre the Internet and the user, and then takes the devices and services – rather than having the devices at the centre' – something remarkably similar in spirit to Sun's concept.

Many of the major infrastructure suppliers' strategies – not just Sun's and Microsoft's – share the same core: focusing on enablement of network-based applications, services and content; and their delivery to multiple types of computing device, via multiple types of network.

B3.2 Ovum's definition of pervasive computing

The pervasive computing ideal is simply stated – 'any information service to any device over any network' – but to really tie down what is occurring, particularly for forecasting purposes, we need a tighter definition:

> Pervasive computing is a vision of the future of digital information and computation in which digital content, applications and services are made available in an integrated, personalised way to users, and accessed by users, via a diverse range of devices and access networks.

Figure B3.1 shows the pervasive computing ideal of 'personalised service universes'.

Figure B3.1 **Personalised service universes**

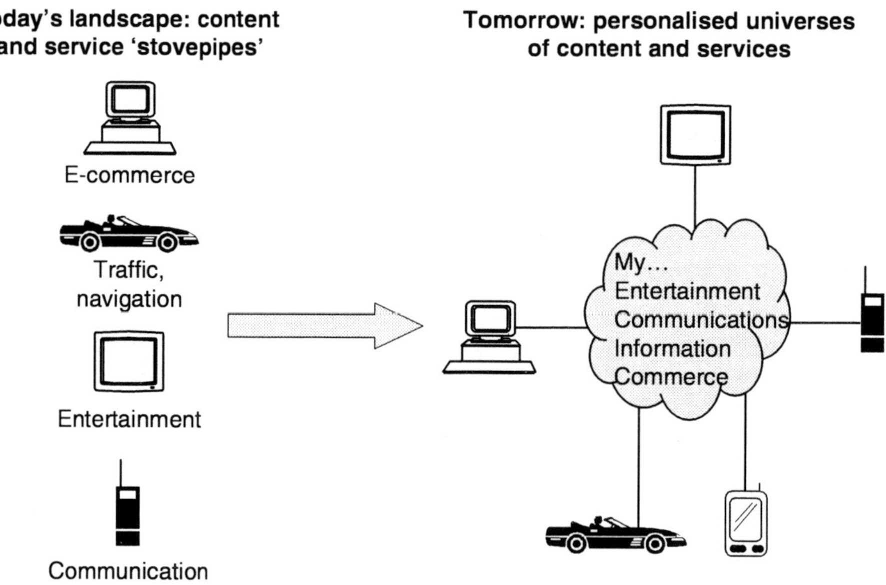

Source: Ovum (Pervasive Computing: Technologies and Markets/Chapter B)

Pervasive computing, in Ovum's definition, does not just represent 'computers everywhere': it represents 'computers, networks, applications and services everywhere'. However, it is important to realise that the pervasive computing ideal of 'any service to any device over any network' is a statement of enablement; it does not mean that *every* service will be made available to *every* type of device over *every* type of network.

There are five important elements to our pervasive computing definition.

A range of content, applications and services to a range of devices

Pervasive computing takes advantage of the increasing coverage and capability of data networks to broaden the services that can be delivered to particular devices. For voice handhelds this is about delivering combinations of voice and data services; for digital TVs it is about enriching programming with interactive elements, and using those as a launch point for wider streams of interactive services.

Digital delivery

Content, applications and services have been delivered to various types of computing device for many years – via physical media such as tape, floppy disks and CD-ROMs. Pervasive computing is predicated on delivery of content and services digitally over networks, rather than via physical media. Digital network delivery of information has only really become both straightforward and widely-performed since the invention of the Worldwide Web.

It may sound obvious, but it is important to note, then, that pervasive computing places e-services providers in a pivotal role in the supply chain of content, applications and services to devices. As the central aggregator of relationships, the role of the service provider is the target for much of the change and opportunity that pervasive computing will bring.

Personalisation

Variations in the capabilities of devices, and the contexts in which they are used, mean that personalisation of content, applications and services will be key to the success of pervasive computing. Without both imposed and voluntary personalisation, providers will find it hard to offer high-value services to their customers; and users will find it hard to digest and navigate around information.

Integration

An integrated approach to delivery of content, applications and services across multiple channels is a pre-requisite of truly pervasive computing. Without integrated approaches, service providers will find it very difficult to offer continuity of experience to users of their services. Unless implementations of an application are integrated across all the delivery channels to which it is made available, service providers will find it difficult to offer personalised features without requiring them to specify their preferences multiple times, for example.

The Internet

The Internet is not strictly a part of our definition of pervasive computing, but Internet technology forms the information conduit around which media convergence is occurring, and around which the delivery of multiple types of application, content and services is starting to be enabled. The adoption of packet-switched networks and IP protocol throughout increasing numbers and varieties of network is what is really priming the broadcast media, IT and telecommunications industries for the pervasive computing revolution.

B4 Technology evolution: making it all possible

Ovum's definition of pervasive computing is predicated on the availability of smart, connected devices. Without any kind of connectivity to the outside world, people can use smart devices to carry out tasks; but those tasks will be limited and highly static. This is because most of the new computing devices that are catching people's attention are not designed to be programmed directly through their own user interfaces (as is the case with personal computers). Without a network, such devices cannot take on new functions or have their capabilities altered. And it is not worth connecting a device with no 'brain' to a network – another device or computer at the other end of a network connection to such a device would not be able to ask it to do anything.

B4.1 The evolution of smart connected devices

The genesis of pervasive computing can be traced back approximately 25 years, when (at the same time as the birth of the microcomputer) very simple micro-controllers were first embedded in high-end consumer products such as washing-machines; and when simple microprocessors started to power electronic cash registers, digital watches and pocket calculators. All this embedded computing activity started to fuel ideas about computers becoming pervasive, moving beyond the realm of science-fiction paperback books, and into news programmes on slow news days.

However this increasingly rich computing medium has not been enough, historically, to enable true pervasive computing. *Figure B4.1* shows why devices alone are not enough.

We can think of increasingly smart devices as being the seeds of pervasive computing. Without a fertile soil, the seeds will not germinate; it is networks that provide that fertile soil. Only over the past five years, when data-capable networks have started to become more pervasive, have the world's developed economies really begun to accelerate towards much closer interconnectivity between the physical world and the electronic world. Pervasive computing will only really start to flourish, however, when compelling applications rain down on those devices and networks.

Figure B4.1 **Smart devices are only the seeds of pervasive computing**

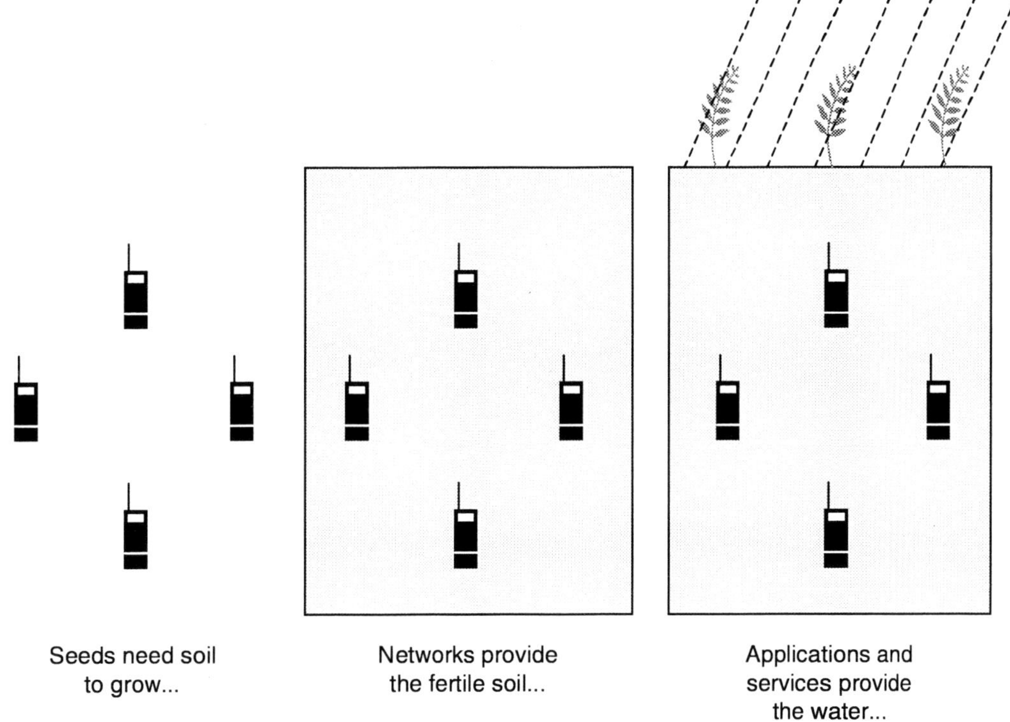
Seeds need soil
to grow...
Networks provide
the fertile soil...
Applications and
services provide
the water...

Source: Ovum (Pervasive Computing: Technologies and Markets/Chapter B)

Chips with everything

Device smartness is, in a sense, a measure of a device's capability to carry out computing tasks. The smarter the device, the wider range of tasks it can carry out. Smartness depends on two things:

- hardware capabilities – a combination of raw processing power and primary & secondary data storage capacity
- software capabilities – a combination of the degree to which the hardware can be controlled by software instructions, and the flexibility with which those software instructions can be changed.

Thus, a device with a sophisticated operating system that resides in memory and that can run any suitable program residing in memory is smarter than a device that has a simple operating system, and can only run a small number of programs burnt onto a ROM chip.

The hardware and software innovation necessary to bring all sorts of devices into the pervasive computing fabric has come from a variety of industries, including defence, retail and consumer electronics – as shown in *Figure B4.2*.

Figure B4.2 **Cradles of hardware and software innovation**

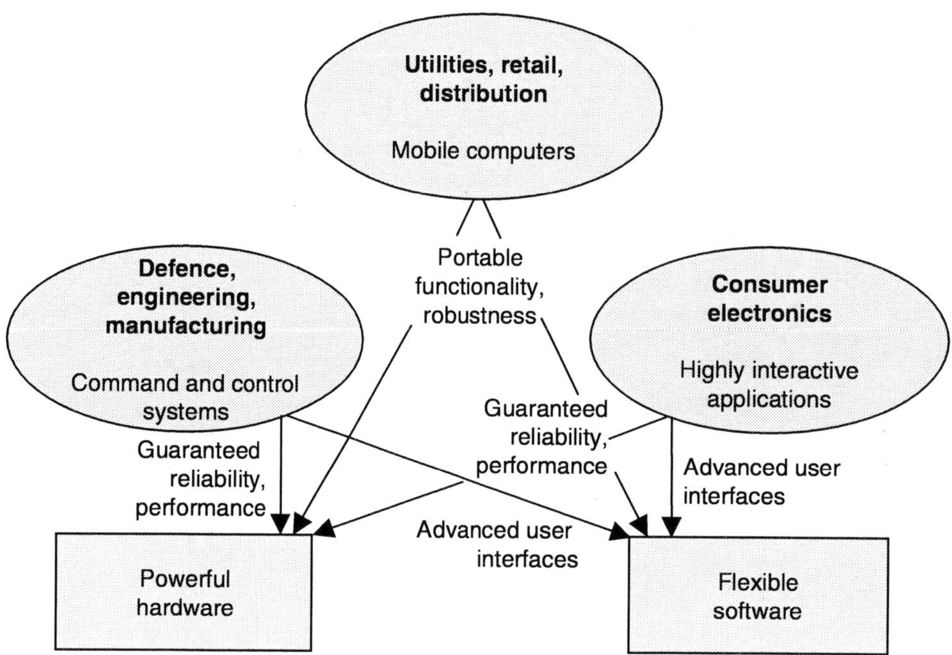

Source: Ovum (Pervasive Computing: Technologies and Markets/Chapter B)

Drivers for hardware and software innovation

The principal drivers behind innovation in hardware and software systems, and their suitability for implementation outside PCs, have been the same as the age-old business drivers – cost reduction and service improvement.

The defence, engineering and manufacturing industries have spent large sums of money embedding systems into their assets (whether missiles or nuclear power plants) – largely to ensure that those assets can be monitored and controlled from remote locations. For the defence industry, this has been vital for cost, legal and sociological reasons; modern armies cannot require missiles to be piloted directly by humans, for example! For the engineering and manufacturing industries, the main issues have been cost and safety. These kinds of system can require advanced user interfaces (particularly in military and defence applications); but universally they need to be robust, reliable and to perform to guaranteed levels. Technologies that provide these services are now moving into the mainstream.

The utility, retail and distribution industries have spent large sums of money developing and deploying mobile computing devices to reduce the cost of managing their supply networks. In most cases, mobile computers are used by employees 'in the field', to allow them to more accurately track the usage or movement of goods or services. Retail companies want to be able to track stock more accurately; utility companies want to read householders' electricity meters more easily; and distribution firms want to track the movement of their truck fleets more accurately. Technologies that provide these services are finding their way into data-centric cellular terminals and PDAs.

The consumer electronics industry has spent large sums of money using hardware and software technology to improve the sophistication of their products. Microprocessors are now embedded in cars, toasters, washing machines, VCRs, microwave ovens, home security systems, mobile phones and set-top boxes (among other things). The vast majority of these microprocessor-based systems are designed to run particular programs that are hard-wired into them; but the opening up of devices to enable them to run software that is not hard-wired into them has already occurred in games machines and is starting to happen with set-top boxes, cars and mobile phones.

The improvements that have been brought about by the consumer electronics industry are many: but games device manufacturers are at the forefront. Their devices have to be robust and reliable; but they must also be capable of rendering complex graphics and processing complex signals at very high speed. The improvements in signal processing and graphics rendering technology brought about by competition in this industry is now contributing to leading-edge user interface technology for interactive services, that is starting to be employed in set-top boxes, for example.

The interconnectedness of all things

Two major shifts in telecommunications are creating the fertile network-enabling environment that is so critical to the development of the pervasive computing concept:

- the creation of networks that can transmit packet data efficiently
- the increasing commoditisation of basic communication services.

Pervasive computing, by its very definition, involves more than just point-to-point fixed telecommunications networks – it also involves mobile telecoms networks, and terrestrial broadcast, satellite and CATV networks. Until recently, however, few of the operators responsible for maintaining any of these types of network had moved beyond providing analogue services. Analogue transmission of data is slow and error-prone; but there was little demand for anything more advanced, except within niche business communities.

However, the investment priorities of fixed-network operators changed with the widespread take-up by consumers of e-mail and Worldwide Web browsing over the Internet. The Internet has been the biggest catalyst for the creation and rollout of digital data transmission services on fixed networks by network operators, because these two most widely-used Internet applications have demonstrated to operators the colossal subscriber interest in interactive services, and the huge potential value of data services. A large number of broadcast network operators are now offering digital services; telecoms network operators are rapidly building out digital networks from the core (where the bulk are already high-speed digital networks) towards the local loop (where the availability of digital services varies widely between, and within, countries).

By contrast, the initial 'digitalisation' of mobile networks was introduced to improve call quality, rather than to enable enriched or interactive services. However, the widespread take-up of SMS, together with the rapid commoditisation of mobile voice services, has brought mobile network operators to the same conclusions as other types of network operator – that stimulating usage of data services on their networks is the way forward. Moreover operators' desire to stimulate data traffic over their networks is starting to force data tariffs downwards.

Data services have taken some time to be developed and launched, but simple IP-based wireless Internet and interactive TV services are now becoming widely available. Through their use of IP-based protocols, both these types of initiative take public telecommunications and television networks closer to the home territory of the fixed-Internet delivery channel.

B4.2 Where are we today?

Information delivery stovepipes are slowly being weakened

Historically, the computing and communications fabrics of the most developed countries, whilst broad and rich, have consisted of isolated delivery channels that were implemented by particular industry supply chains. In addition the content, services and applications they carry have been crisply partitioned – for example:

- the Internet carried Worldwide Web content and e-mail traffic between personal computers and corporate IT systems
- television (terrestrial, CATV and satellite broadcast) networks delivered audio-visual entertainment and information services to television receivers
- fixed and mobile public telecommunications networks carried voice calls and (in some cases) SMS messages between telephone handsets.

Figure B4.3 shows today's stovepipes.

Figure B4.3 **Today's stovepipes**

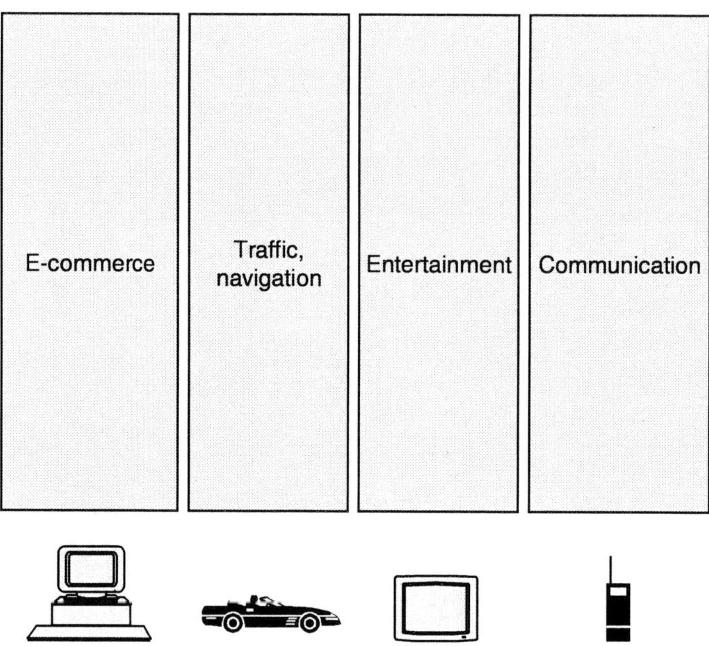

Source: Ovum (Pervasive Computing: Technologies and Markets/Chapter B)

As we enter a new millennium, we have seen a period of change that has started to blur the edges between these delivery channels. Today, it may seem as if computers, networks and the digital information they store, manipulate and show are everywhere. Certainly it is now possible to use your mobile telephone, your TV and your personal computer to carry out functions (such as personal banking) without interacting with anyone – whereas until recently you had to talk directly to a person or (possibly) talk to a person via a telephone. Other examples of blurred edges are illustrated through the availability of:

- e-mail and e-commerce on your TV
- web browsing on your mobile phone
- making voice calls using your PC and an Internet connection, rather than the PSTN.

But there is much more to come

These blurred edges represent the first small steps towards a world of pervasive computing. The number of companies delivering sophisticated, interactive services electronically over multiple networks, to multiple types of device, is very small – the cost and complexity of doing it is too great for most. Even where electronic services seem to be delivered universally, the reality is that today's computing and communications landscape is still a set of largely unconnected delivery channels dedicated to providing particular types of content, services and applications to particular types of device.

There is an important distinction to make between the availability of multiple similar-looking services through multiple channels, and the integrated delivery of services through multiple channels. Today, fledgling 'multichannel' services are very rarely actually single, unified services offered via multiple 'front-ends'. We are still a long way from the situation where content and applications can be created once, and offered to users via multiple delivery channels transparently.

B5 Introducing the pervasive computing players

The pervasive computing 'market' is, in fact, several markets that cross multiple rigid, well-established supply chains – including:

- mobile and fixed telecommunications services
- Internet services
- home appliances and services
- PCs
- business applications
- mobile personal computing
- automotive
- broadcast media.

Each of these industries is either already involved in the delivery of digital information; or is moving to a point where the delivery of digital information is a key part of the value of the products and services within it. Key suppliers in all these industries are already getting behind the idea of pervasive computing.

B5.1 Who are the key players, and what are they doing?

The three key supply chains that are playing major roles in early pervasive computing developments have similar structures. Supply chains across the Internet (PC), telecommunications (voice handset) and broadcast media (TV) industries comprise content and/or application providers, content and/or application aggregators, service providers, network operators, infrastructure providers and device manufacturers. Within each supply chain, companies occupying each major link all have opportunities to promote their strengths, and exert their influence over market development.

Leading players within the home appliances, automotive and mobile personal computing industries are in the process of understanding how digital information delivery services can enhance their value propositions; in many cases, they are forming technology partnerships with companies that have historically formed part of the Internet, broadcast media or telecoms supply chains, in order to kick-start their pervasive computing initiatives.

Many of the world's largest software infrastructure suppliers are starting to build bridges between the key supply chains. These companies are realising that interworking across these supply chains will be the key to enabling pervasive computing, and are busy expanding their spheres of influence accordingly. Companies such as IBM, Microsoft, Oracle and Sun Microsystems are investing heavily in building out capabilities in markets outside their traditional heartland of corporate IT.

In addition to the IT industry behemoths, a galaxy of smaller companies – some start-ups, and some mature software players – has started to capitalise on early interest from players at the tail of the supply chain and from service providers by providing point solutions that address some of the technology challenges of providing multichannel applications and services. Such companies include Aether Systems, Centura Software, Flextech, NetMorf, OpenTV, Phone.Com and WindRiver.

Figure B5.1 **Pervasive computing players and their strengths**

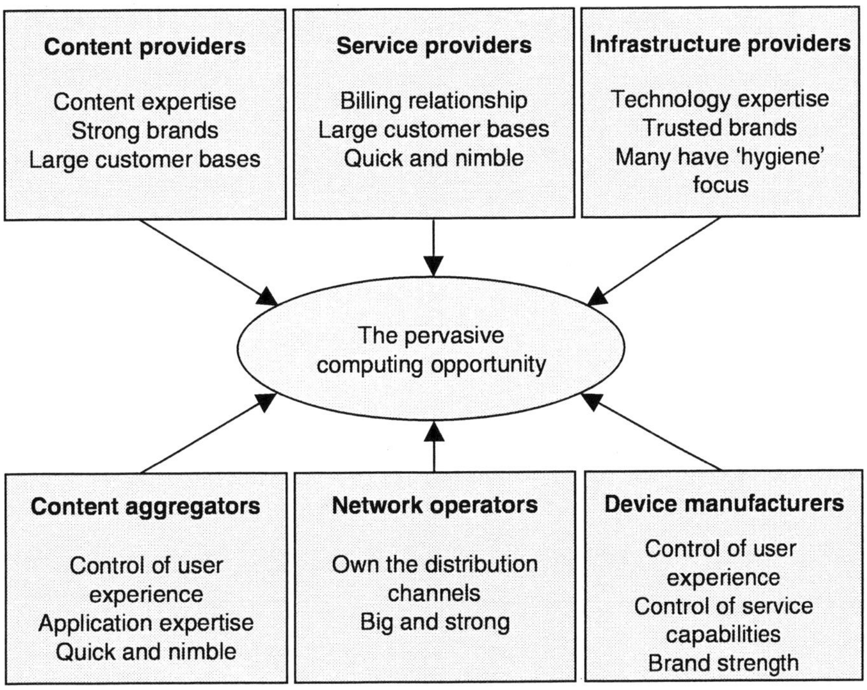

Content providers
Content expertise
Strong brands
Large customer bases

Service providers
Billing relationship
Large customer bases
Quick and nimble

Infrastructure providers
Technology expertise
Trusted brands
Many have 'hygiene' focus

The pervasive computing opportunity

Content aggregators
Control of user experience
Application expertise
Quick and nimble

Network operators
Own the distribution channels
Big and strong

Device manufacturers
Control of user experience
Control of service capabilities
Brand strength

Source: Ovum (Pervasive Computing: Technologies and Markets/Chapter B)

B5.2 Which players are best positioned?

The complexity and scope of the pervasive computing market means that it is impossible to single-out any one type of player within any particular supply chain(s) that has an advantage for anything more general than a particular service delivery example.

In general, branding strength lies in the hands of device manufacturers, service providers and content aggregators – but in terms of technology opportunities it is the large infrastructure (both software and network) vendors that have most expertise in providing the necessary solutions, as shown in *Figure B5.1*. They will have to bring these to market through partnerships with brand owners.

But technology alone will not enable pervasive computing. Service providers that can attain critical mass will have the potential to take-up positions of strength, by acting as brokers of service agreements and other commercial relationships.

B6 Realising the pervasive computing vision

B6.1 Pervasive computing infrastructure is the enabler

Pervasive computing *infrastructure* is the foundation for Ovum's definition of pervasive computing, so it deserves its own definition:

> Pervasive computing infrastructure is the range of software and communications products and services that together provide the 'glue' that enables multiple types of content applications and services to be delivered to multiple devices over multiple types of network.

Pervasive computing infrastructure enables delivery of true multichannel applications and services, as shown in *Figure B6.1*.

Pervasive computing infrastructure, just like enterprise middleware, utilises existing devices and networks, and provides sophisticated technical services throughout the computing environment that abstract away physical details of the environment. Pervasive computing infrastructure allows applications and services to be deployed to that environment without application developers or device users having to worry about physical environment details.

Figure B6.1 **Pervasive computing infrastructure enables true multichannel applications and services**

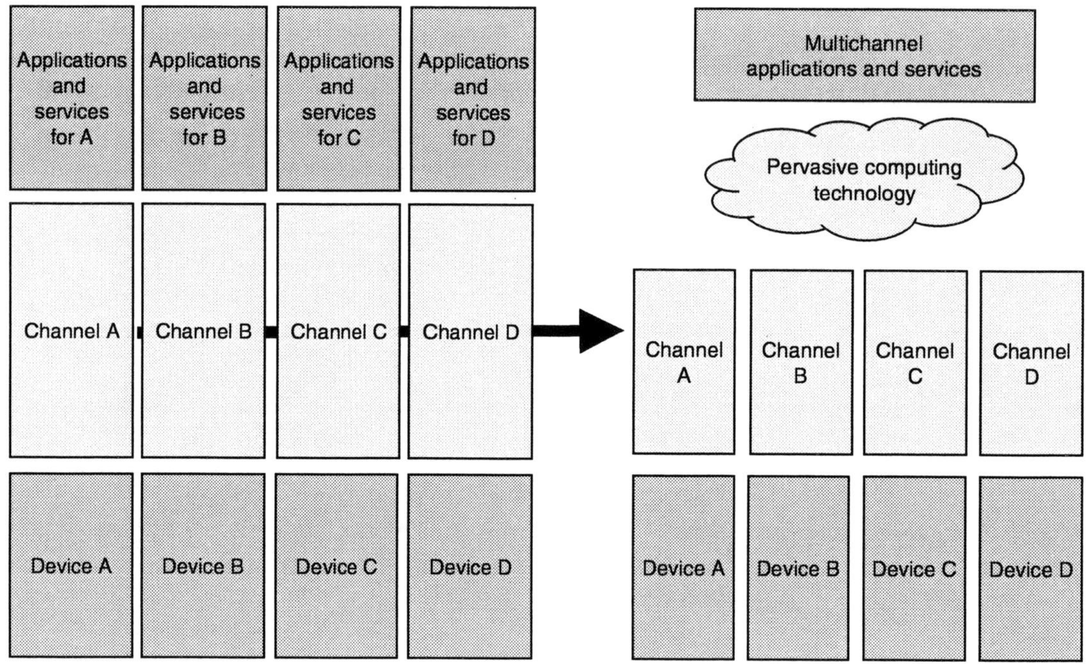

Source: Ovum (Pervasive Computing: Technologies and Markets/Chapter B)

B6.2 Three challenges – creating big opportunities

There are three main challenges in the path of the development of pervasive computing:

- outside the realm of the PC, today's digital information access platforms vary widely in their capabilities and therefore their suitablity for delivering certain types of application to users
- the majority of applications in use today are not deployed in a form that makes them suitable for delivery across multiple access platforms
- industries have been created and have matured around the delivery of particular types of digital information to particular types of device over particular types of network. These stovepipes make the level of industry interworking that will be required to deliver truly pervasive computing applications, very difficult.

Chapter C covers these three challenges in more detail.

In 2001, the market for software infrastructure to address these challenges will be worth under $2 billion worldwide. By 2006, the market will have grown to more than $20 billion. This investment in infrastructure technology will vastly increase the numbers and reach of multichannel applications delivered as network services. This increased use of network services, combined with the fact that much infrastructure technology will itself use networks to carry out its functions, means that in the same period the rise in pervasive computing will increase data traffic dramatically.

C Market overview

C1 Key messages

C1.1 Be realistic – hype is dangerous

Wireless networks are a core component of the fabric of pervasive computing, and they are the current focus of much of the hype in the IT and telecommunications industries. But third-generation mobile network services, WAP and Bluetooth are all being dangerously over-sold by suppliers eager to impress potential customers, venture capitalists and financial analysts. The result is confusion that can only serves to inhibit pervasive computing market development in the long term.

Third-generation mobile services will not deliver anything near to 2Mbit/s to mobile access platforms. WAP's future as a universal mobile applications platform is a fiction; nor can it directly be compared to i-Mode. Bluetooth technology will not deliver on its potential this year, next year or even the year after. Neither Java technology nor XML can solve the challenges associated with delivering applications to multiple devices over multiple networks, alone. All of these technologies will help to deliver pervasive computing – but there are no 'silver bullets' and no quick fixes.

Different information access platforms vary widely in their capabilities, due to constraints on battery technology, form factor, processing power and network connectivity. But variations will continue, even when (and if) the current technology constraints are removed. Today, hard constraints limit the capability of particular access platforms; tomorrow softer constraints – primarily, the usage contexts in which people like to use devices – will play much greater roles in determining particular platform capabilities and form factors. But many of today's constraints will remain. The most striking example is the continuing scarcity of bandwidth on mobile networks (comparative to that available through fixed networks).

C1.2 Practise pragmatism

The telecommunications industry in particular has been built around high-quality network & management infrastructure and processes, so that service levels can be absolutely guaranteed for customers. But the development of pervasive computing markets depends on a different, more pragmatic approach.

The most important developments that will take place in order to enable pervasive computing are those that make the widest-available networks and devices good enough to support the most widely-popular applications and services. Infrastructure providers that attempt to solve every possible shortcoming of every aspect of every access platform, will risk losing out to more time-to-market-focused players content to make platforms good enough.

C1.3 Market development revolves around the evolution of infrastructure

A key aspect of the trend towards pervasive computing is the evolution of the infrastructure 'glue' that will bind applications to users, regardless of the access platform that they use. This will transform current world of information delivery stovepipes and enable the vision of universal access associated with pervasive computing; rather than a new 'killer' software application, new type of network or device.

Pervasive computing infrastructure encompasses a myriad of software, hardware and communications components. The set of software components alone includes quality-of-service assurance, application integration, service management, content and application adaptation, service creation tools, data synchronisation, managed storage, and device operating systems. Together, though, these functions have one fundamental aim:

> *to help break the bonds that currently tie users to devices, devices to networks and applications to both of these; and to enable more direct relationships between users and applications, regardless of the device and network being used.*

C1.4 The new value is in context and its management

As more and more applications and services are made available through multiple channels, understanding of user requirements based on assumptions about environments and delivery channels, as it is currently achieved, will be very hard to maintain. As a customer of such a provider, if you can interact with an application or service using a mobile phone network, a broadcast TV network and a LAN, you do not want the application to treat you as three different people (one person for each channel). The application needs to recognise you, no matter how you arrive 'at the front door'. But it also needs to understand that the context in which you are interacting with it is different with each channel you use.

As applications, networks and devices become more pervasive, individual customers of information and communication services will play different roles in their lives – each of which might correspond to a different customer segment, and involve the use of multiple devices and networks. In other words, a different usage context. There is a lot of talk in the mobile telecommunications industry about the importance of mobile location services; but user location is just one aspect of usage context.

Usage context information, and the ability to let users manage and shape how that information controls the ways applications are delivered, will become a significant value point for service providers offering applications to multiple devices over multiple networks. 'Pull' everywhere is good, but 'push' everywhere is bad. The ability for users to access information and services wherever they are, at any time, is very appealing to many: but the ability for applications and services to access users at any time brings the danger of information overload and intense customer dissatisfaction.

C1.5 The death of the application, and of the device platform

By 2006, the implementation of pervasive computing infrastructure, in order to break the bonds between physical elements of digital information delivery channels, will in turn bring about two important shifts in information technology, broadcast media and communications:

- applications as we think of them today will no longer be built. Pervasive computing applications in 2006 will be collections of co-operating e-services that deliver personalised groups of functions to support users' own favourite activities, the way they like them
- new high-end devices will also be disaggregated, through the widespread use of Bluetooth technology. New modularised personal computing platforms, enabled by Bluetooth, will be composed and re-composed dynamically by users as they move between different locations and roles.

These two changes will create further challenges in managing complexity not only for device and application providers, but also for service providers. The complexity will not be in dealing with today's heterogeneity in technologies that are employed in delivering digital information; but in providing that information in a way that is specialised for each user – regardless of location, role, time of day or device used.

C1.6 Technology is not the whole answer

Delivery of new multichannel services brings complex challenges to industries. Increasingly, players (possibly from multiple industries) will have to co-operate online, possibly with competitors, to enable the services that users want. This online co-operation cannot happen without information sharing, thus making possible the sharing of revenues and responsibility for quality-of-service.

Technology has an enabling part to play in addressing this issue, but it is not the whole answer. There are many geographical and market issues that need to be addressed by suppliers; and suppliers can only address these issues through partnerships, potentially with companies they may think of as competitors, to fill gaps in their expertise and execution capabilities.

C2 Market drivers, challenges and opportunities

C2.1 Drivers: convergence, diversity and the desire for transformation

Since 1995, we have seen levels of innovation create a steady build-up of market pressure in information-delivery industries and device-manufacturing industries. This pressure is being relieved now, through those communities enabling delivery of more types of digital information to more types of device.

In other words, the pervasive computing vision is slowly becoming reality because multiple communities need it to happen. The three major trends of media convergence, device diversity and the desire for transformation (from products into services) are actually forming a virtuous circle, as shown in *Figure C2.1*.

Trend 1: Convergence of media types and industries

The Internet has become the major force for digital convergence between information technology, broadcast media and telecommunications. Internet technology is also the foundation for the pervasive computing vision.

Convergence of different types of digital information, and the industries that produce it, is stimulating diversification of information access. Convergence makes it easier and cheaper to build devices that can access a variety of content, applications and services.

Figure C2.1 **Convergence, diversity and transformation – the virtuous circle**

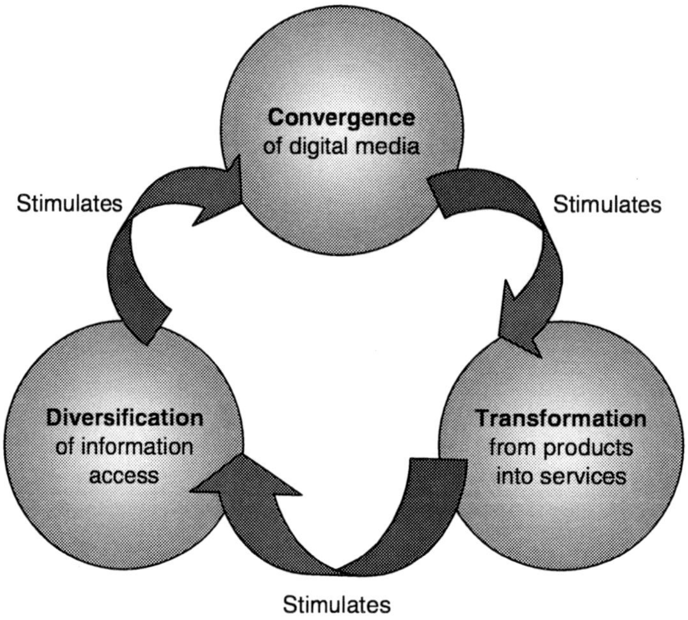

Source: Ovum (Pervasive Computing: Technologies and Markets/Chapter C)

Trend 2: Diversification of information access methods

Between 1995 and 2000, there have also been many advances in software and hardware technologies, so that a great deal of diversity in digital information access methods is possible – and indeed likely. Diversity in devices is stimulated by media convergence, and by manufacturers' desire to transform products into services. Moreover, the more different types of device that are able to access Internet-based content, the more the providers will want to provide the content – because (in theory) more diverse access means larger potential markets. Consequently, device diversity also stimulates convergence.

Not every device form factor will be a major winner, however. There will be many failures and many limited niche successes. But the overall universe of devices will be very varied.

Trend 3: Transformation of products into services

There has been a lot of talk about Internet technology revolutionising the software industry through the ASP movement – turning software products into services. But it is not just software companies that are looking to the Internet to transform their products into services; it is also happening in the automotive, home appliances and computing hardware markets. The desire to add value, and create more satisfying investment-revenue models, is leading companies to look for ways that product features can be dynamically enabled as services over networks, rather than as hardwired product functions. This desire for transformation is further stimulating diversity in access platforms, as more products have access platforms embedded in them to enable these services. Simultaneously, media convergence technology is stimulating the transformation of goods into services, by lowering barriers to entry.

C2.2 Areas of change: access platforms, applications and industry structures

The most visible changes in devices and applications are initially being driven by:

- application and content providers, looking to deliver their assets to increasingly diverse ranges of devices
- device manufacturers, looking to enable increasingly diverse ranges of information to be accessed by their products.

But very soon pressure to change will spill over into wider communities of suppliers – in particular, service-provider communities. Increasingly, service providers will need to interwork with providers from other communities in order to deliver the content, applications and services that users want and are willing to pay for.

C2.3 The technology: breaking and re-building relationships

Pervasive computing infrastructure, which is driving the development of pervasive computing and thus (at least temporarily) relieving market pressures, encompasses a myriad of software, hardware and communications functions. Together, these functions have one fundamental aim:

> *to help break the bonds that currently tie users to devices, devices to networks and applications to both of these; and to enable more direct relationships between users and applications, regardless of the device and network being used.*

Figure C2.2 illustrates this aim.

Figure C2.2 **Pervasive computing infrastructure – breaking bonds**

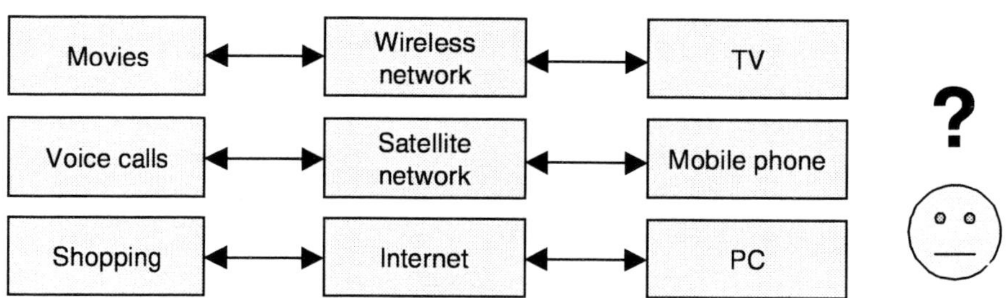

With pervasive computing technology...

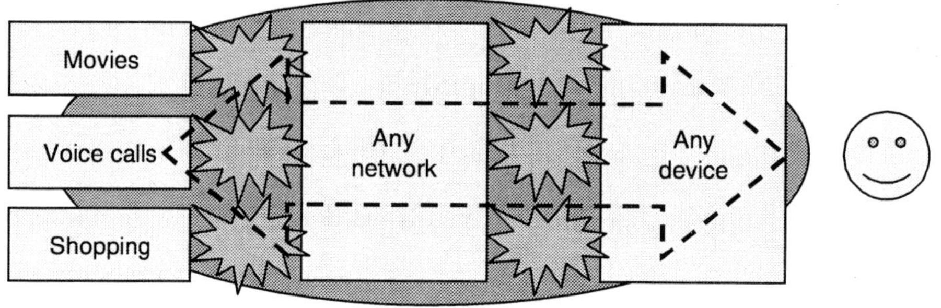

Source: Ovum (Pervasive Computing: Technologies and Markets/Chapter C)

Applications have to be deliverable to a diverse range of devices over multiple types of network – but neither the user nor the application developer should have to worry about the details of how it is done.

C3 The elements of the pervasive computing market

C3.1 Market development centres on infrastructure

Pervasive computing is about making applications, content and services available to many types of device and therefore enabling ubiquitous user access to things of value.

Key to the trend towards pervasive computing is the evolution of the infrastructure 'glue' that will bind applications to users, regardless of the access platform that they use. This will transform today's world of information-delivery stovepipes and enable the vision of universal access associated with pervasive computing; rather than a new 'killer' software application, type of network or device.

We concentrate our analysis on the requirements of important types of application, and the capabilities of important types of device and network – because they will influence demand for pervasive computing infrastructure – rather than on the market opportunities for new applications or content; or for new devices or networks *per se*.

The structures of the industries that have grown up around delivering today's major digital information types (the stovepipes of *Section B3*) also affect and are affected by the development of pervasive computing infrastructure. An understanding of the ways that industries, applications, devices and networks are likely to change over time is also crucial, so we cover these too.

Figure C3.1 shows the relationships between the main elements of pervasive computing market development.

Figure C3.1 **Infrastructure drives market development**

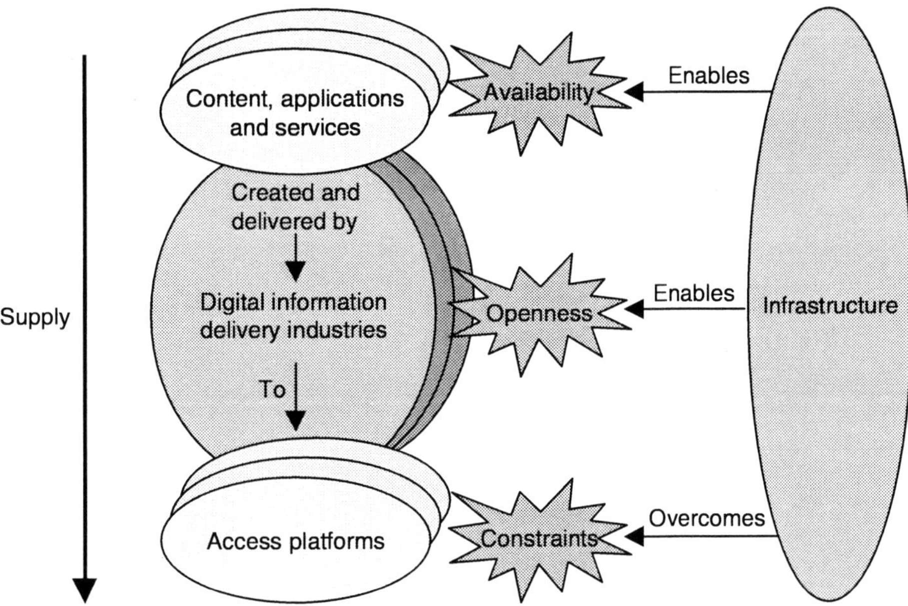

Source: Ovum (Pervasive Computing: Technologies and Markets/Chapter C)

C3.2 Pervasive computing applications

The development of pervasive computing revolves around the evolution of infrastructure; but without compelling applications, services and content across multiple access platforms, market development will be stifled. Without availability of these, the pervasive computing experience will be a frustrating one for both suppliers and users, involving access to fragmented services that are unsatisfying to use and expensive to build and maintain.

The most important activities that users will engage in (on which many variants will be deployed) are those based on:

- personal communications management applications, which provide a combination of voice communication management functions (such as voicemail, call-back, call screening and conference calling), e-mail, unified messaging (the provision of a unified inbox for voicemail, e-mail and fax messages) and instant messaging
- commerce applications – the execution of electronic transactions that result in the transfer of value in exchange for information, services or goods
- infotainment applications, which deliver digital information designed to inform and/or entertain users. This umbrella definition encompasses a wide range of applications, delivering different types of digital information in different formats (from text-only to full-motion video with stereo sound). Examples include news and weather information, navigation aids, and games
- corporate business applications, which utilise software applications that automate business processes. Examples include ERP (enterprise resource planning), salesforce automation and workflow/collaboration environments
- remote asset management applications, which allow the owner of an intelligent asset (or a designated third party) to remotely monitor and manage it.

The technology requirements of these applications bear strongly on the ways in which access platforms, in combination with infrastructure technologies, must be deployed to users. We discuss these types of application, their technology requirements and likely evolution in more detail in *Chapter D*.

C3.3 Pervasive computing access platforms

Access platforms are neither devices nor access networks, but combinations of the two. The capabilities and limitations of both devices, and the networks to which they are connected, contribute to the overall characteristics of a particular delivery channel for digital information.

Which are the important device types?

Over the long term, the only definite thing that can be said about the universe of devices that will be used to access information and services is that it will be very large and diverse. The same advances in hardware, networking and power technologies that are making devices smarter and more connected, will eventually enable much greater and cost-effective proliferation of device form-factors.

This report concentrates on PCs, data-centric handheld devices (PDAs), voice-centric handhelds (mobile phones and their smartphone cousins), set-top boxes, in-car computing platforms and networked home appliances – for the following reasons:

- they represent a set of the most commonly-used and well-understood computing platforms
- they are diverse in their capabilities, and in the contexts they are used
- they are the products of, or enabling technologies for, a diverse set of industries.

The capabilities of devices (or lack of them) will affect the delivery of the pervasive computing vision, and drive demand for infrastructure that enhances those capabilities. We examine these types of devices, and discuss their capabilities and likely evolution in much more detail in *Chapter E*.

Which are the important access network types?

A word about access networks

For efficiency, telecommunications networks are organised hierarchically, in a tree structure – with wide-area core networks forming the trunk of the tree, and (relatively) local-area networks forming the leaves at the ends of the branches. Switching at the branch points between the trunk, the branches and the leaves ensures that communication follows the most efficient route. In this report we focus the vast majority of our attention on access networks, rather than core networks – for the simple reason that access networks are currently, and will continue to be, the main bottleneck in any kind of data communication. Increasingly telecommunications regulators are forcing the operators that built the access networks to allow specialist third-party access service providers to offer services at the edges of their networks, directly to subscribers.

Access networks – the straw in the milkshake

The situation is like attempting to drink a very large, thick, tasty milkshake through a very narrow straw. It is a frustrating experience; the speeds with which particular types of 'straw' become wider will have a significant effect on the viability of the pervasive computing vision, and on the demand for infrastructure that can circumvent the shortcomings of access networks.

There is huge variety in the types of access network that must be employed to bring about a pervasive computing future. Private networks such as corporate LANs will have to be employed alongside broadcast networks (satellite and terrestrial broadcast), broadband access networks (cable and xDSL), narrowband fixed access network services such as PSTN over copper; and even personal area networks (PANs) such as those implemented through technologies such as Bluetooth. This report's market and technology analysis touches on all these types of network – for exactly the same reasons as those listed above.

We examine these network types, and discuss their capabilities and likely evolution, in more detail in *Chapter E*.

C3.4 Information delivery industries

There are three main industries involved in the delivery of particular types of digital information:

- the telecommunications industry, in which most activity has traditionally been focused on enabling voice communication across fixed and mobile telecommunications networks
- the IT industry, in which most activity has historically been focused on delivering applications to PCs
- the broadcast media industry, in which most activity is focused on delivering infotainment content to TVs.

However, the huge growth in use of the Internet and its protocol, in both business and consumer contexts, is fast dissolving the binds that have tied particular digital information delivery industries to particular applications, networks and devices. The proliferation of IP services is galvanising convergence between these industries, networks and applications – as shown in *Figure C3.2*.

We concentrate most of our analysis on the corporate IT (PC), public telecoms (voice handset) and broadcast media (TV) industries, and how they are converging. The rate at which these industries can increase their level of interworking will both affect and be affected by the use of multichannel content, applications and services.

Chapter F provides overviews of these industries, and examines the ways in which interworking is increasing between them. It also examines the potential structures of supply chains that are still forming to deliver content, applications and services over networks to our three other types of device – PDAs, cars and embedded devices.

Figure C3.2 **IP adoption is driving convergence**

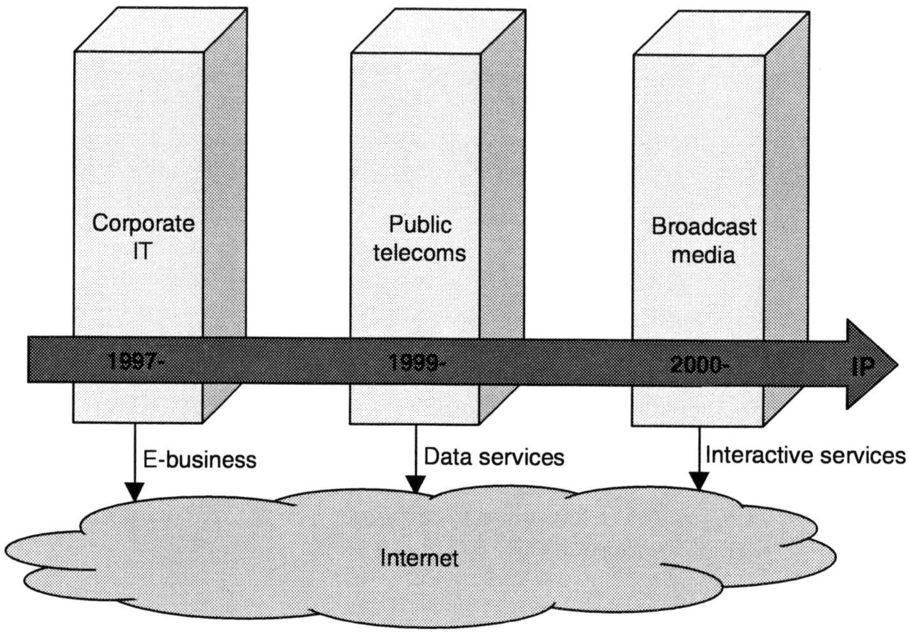

Source: Ovum (Pervasive Computing: Technologies and Markets/Chapter C)

C4 Four key market development themes

The evolution of pervasive computing infrastructure will drive market development. As shown in *Figure C3.1*, infrastructure will affect, and be affected by, four market development themes:

- the creation of multichannel applications, content and services to enable users to access them via multiple platforms
- the enhancement of access platform capabilities in line with the applications that users want
- the opening of industry structures and increasing interworking between providers, to enable true user mobility between applications, content, services, devices and networks
- the strategies and spheres of influence of leading infrastructure suppliers, as well as the creation and proliferation of technology standards.

Sections C5 to *C8* address these themes in turn.

C5 Applications: from uni-channel to multichannel

Today's 'uni-channel' applications will gradually be replaced by integrated multichannel applications. Despite the considerable investments on the behalf of service providers that are required to make this transition, there is considerable pressure from the application and content-provision communities, and device-manufacturer communities to move forward. Infrastructure vendors are starting to get behind this movement, but there are considerable challenges that they must help service providers overcome. Compelling, easy-to-use multichannel applications must:

- be designed to reduce the cost and complexity of supporting new access platforms
- take advantage of personalisation, localisation and device-specialisation technologies
- be delivered to appropriate quality-of-service levels
- scale to support many thousands, or even millions, of connections.

A precursor to this transition, however, is the provision of applications as services. This requires infrastructure support, of course, but service provision is about more than creating a web, WAP or TV front-end for the application. Issues such as quality-of-service, provisioning, customer support and billing are just as important.

C5.1 The current application landscape

Most applications are uni-channel

Today's applications are predominantly 'uni-channel' – they are designed for delivery to a particular type of device, probably over a particular type of network. The majority of what people traditionally think of as applications are designed to be delivered to PCs. *Figure C5.1* summarises the current situation.

Figure C5.1 **Main delivery channels for applications, 2000**

	Personal communications	E-commerce	Infotainment	Business applications	Device management
PC	2	2	3	3	3
Voice handheld	2	2	1	n/a	n/a
PDA	n/a	n/a	1	2	n/a
TV	n/a	2	3	n/a	n/a
Car	1	1	1	n/a	n/a
Home appliances	1	1	1	n/a	n/a

Key: 1 = possible; 2 = usable; 3 = easy and compelling

Figure C5.1 seems to contradict our assertion, by showing that almost all applications are already delivered to users through multiple channels. However, this is never done in an integrated way in practice – and it is integrated multichannel applications that are at the heart of our definition of pervasive computing.

In most cases the provision of a particular application is carried out by suppliers dedicated to one particular delivery channel. Even where a provider offers its application over multiple channels, it is highly likely that each delivery channel is served by a unique application instance that is tightly coupled to that channel.

Consequently, even where application functionality is available through multiple channels, applications are not truly multichannel.

Not all applications are delivered as services

In order for applications to be deliverable to users through a pervasive computing medium, they must be deliverable as services: digital delivery of content, applications and services is a key part of the pervasive computing definition. Of our five key pervasive computing applications, three – communications, e-commerce and infotainment – are already delivered in some circumstances to users as services, as opposed to products.

Whilst corporate business applications are not yet delivered as services by default, the hot application service provision (ASP) market is in the process of transforming corporate business applications from products into services – although not for all applications, and not for all users (Ovum's report *Application Service Providers: Opportunities and Risks* explains this in detail).

Remote asset management applications are certainly not delivered as services. In the market for technology management tools in general, there is an emerging shift from products to services in the area of system and network monitoring – in particular, the remote monitoring of e-business applications and websites. However, until now, market demand has not been great enough for management of software and hardware assets to be addressed by an ASP-type market. The proliferation of leased or service provider-owned access platforms, together with (in the longer term) smart, networked home appliances and home networks, will slowly build demand for these services.

C5.2 Drivers for change

Threats: high levels of competition and market over-supply

All five of our pervasive computing application types are delivered within very competitive markets. The actual providers of the content and applications that power these markets rarely make big margins on actual products. Suppliers' profits come from providing end customers or service providers with complementary services such as consulting, training and systems integration.

Particularly in the area of e-commerce, application providers face competition not only from other application providers, but also from service providers' own software development teams.

The high levels of competition experienced by application and content providers is being combined, in many areas, with creeping subversion of markets by the open-source software market. For several years, open-source infrastructure commodities such as operating systems and web servers have been available on the market – in 2000, the first open-source database management systems (DBMSs) are starting to appear. It will not be long before open-source e-commerce frameworks and e-CRM applications hit the market, forcing suppliers of proprietary products to work harder to differentiate their products on features, qualities or price.

Opportunities: access to new markets and re-use of existing assets

The creation of multichannel application and content assets that can be delivered to end users as services brings application and content providers opportunities to develop their businesses in the face of fierce competition on their 'home turf'. Furthermore, if they construct these in the right way, with assistance from infrastructure providers and technologies that promote re-use of assets across channels, growth of revenue from new delivery channels and markets will outpace the level of incremental investment that these providers will have to make.

C5.3 Challenges for the industry

From applications to services

E-business infrastructure products such as web development tools and application servers are helping companies 'turn the screen around' on their corporate business applications in order to allow customers, suppliers and partners to do business with them electronically. But 'turning the screen around' on an existing application by creating a new web-based user interface for it, is not enough to turn that application into a service.

The most important part of e-service provision is not presenting an electronic interface to an existing application or service; it is the implementation of the higher principles of service to what you are offering electronically. That is, implementing systems and processes to enable you to support a contract with a subscriber (which may be explicit or implicit). The ability to guarantee a particular quality of service, and provide channels for subscribers to report their problems, and have them resolved, are the hallmarks of true service provision – not a web-based application interface. The ability to offer these essential service wrappers requires much more technology infrastructure, and more personnel, than the creation of the core of the e-service functionality.

Figure C5.2 shows the elements of application service provision.

Figure C5.2 **The elements of ASP**

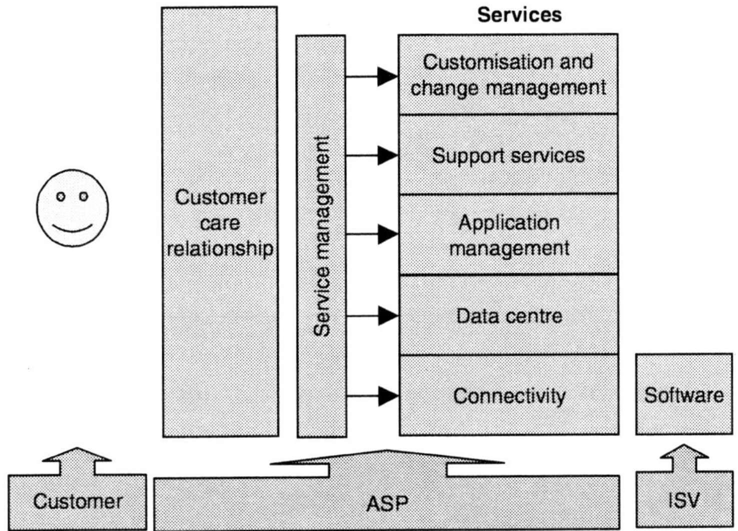

Source: Ovum (Pervasive Computing: Technologies and Markets/Chapter C)

Creating multichannel applications

If you implement a multichannel application or service, there are three things that are certain to occur:

- people will use those multiple channels to access the service or application at different times
- people will want to be able to commence an application or service session through one delivery channel, then switch to another channel at their convenience
- not all parts of your service or application will fit well in every delivery channel.

These three demand factors will have profound effects on the way that you will have to design, construct and deliver services and applications.

A multichannel service example

Consider an online bookshop service, available through the TV, PC and mobile phone. The service allows you to search for a book or just browse through other users' previous recommendations, then buy the book by entering your credit card details, and finally have the book shipped to you – once you have specified the delivery address.

Phones do not just have small screens – they also have very restrictive input capabilities. Typing characters is a real pain on most devices. Consequently typing in the name of a book to search for, and your delivery address will be very frustrating. Most people will not bother to browse the book catalogue on a $10cm^2$ screen. Most of today's TV set-top boxes do not come with full-size keyboards. Input of that same data will therefore be time-consuming.

The online bookshop decides that phones will undoubtedly be used to invoke e-commerce transactions, but it is unlikely they will be used for browsing. TVs are more likely to be used for browsing, but data entry on both types of device will need to be minimised to prevent user frustration. It therefore decides to store delivery and credit-card details for each subscriber, and allow users to call them up as default settings through entry of a code.

The online bookshop also decides to enable users to browse for a book through their TV or PC, and bookmark one or more selections that they can choose to buy later. If, at a later date, they access the service through any supported channel (including their phone), they can choose to buy one of their bookmarked selections.

Pervasiveness means personalisation

The restrictions of certain types of delivery channel mean that more functionality and interactivity can be delivered by some applications and services than can actually be supported on some delivery channels. Service providers therefore need a way of cutting down what is seen. They can do this statically, by unilaterally deciding which elements of the service will be provided on each supported delivery channel. But this approach takes no account of users' preferences and is likely to alienate users. More importantly (from a design point of view), it maintains strong links between application or service functionality and individual delivery channels, at the expense of building relationships between applications and actual users.

A much more flexible and value-added approach is to allow users to tailor elements of what they see on different types of device. This makes life easier for both service providers and users, by bringing the widely-understood benefits of personalisation (chiefly, increasing the 'stickiness' of customer relationships and reducing churn) to bear on what is as much a supplier problem as a user problem.

Certain elements of application or service user interfaces will need to remain solely under the control of the provider, in order to ensure that essential functions and other non-negotiable content (perhaps advertising) are always accessible, whilst other elements can be configured by users. Information tailored by providers is personalisation too, but it is enforced personalisation, rather than voluntary personalisation.

As an application or service provider you will probably not want to offer every function of your service through every channel. 'Any service to any device over any network' does not mean 'every aspect of every service to any device over any network'.

Pervasiveness brings segmentation through context, not channels

Companies of all types (including application and service providers) distinguish between segments of their potential customer bases – into businesses and consumers, for example. Application and service providers' business implementations of their segmentations are based on assumptions about the environments in which customers interact with their products and services – for example, by assuming that business users interact with a service at work, using a work computer and a work phone; and consumers interact with a service from home using a home computer and home phone.

But as applications, networks and devices become more pervasive, this rather artificial notion of customer segmentation by environment, starts bumping up against physical reality:

> *individual customers of information and communication services actually play different roles in their lives – each of which might correspond to a different customer segment and each of which involves using multiple devices and networks.*

As more applications and services are made available through multiple channels, understanding of user requirements based on assumptions about environments and delivery channels will be very hard to maintain. As a customer of such a provider, if you can interact with an application or service using a mobile phone network, a broadcast TV network and a LAN, you do not want the application to treat you as three different people (one person for each channel). The application needs to recognise that you are you, no matter how you arrive 'at the front door'. But it also needs to understand that the context in which you are interacting with it is different with each channel you use.

Usage context: from 'who?' to 'who, when, where, how and why?'

The notion of context information is not a new one; having to manage it is an important part of what makes a software application or an interactive service different from a static piece of information. But the evolution of pervasive computing will make the set of context information that needs to be managed, much larger and more complex. *Figure C5.3* summarises how the context information that applications and services have to manage is changing as we move to a pervasive computing environment. There is a lot of talk in the mobile telecommunications industry about the importance of mobile location services (as discussed in Ovum's report *Mobile Location Services: Market Strategies*), but user location is just one aspect of usage context.

Figure C5.3 **The evolution of context**

Type of application	User activity	Context information required
Static website	Browsing	Who are you? (subscriber ID)
Interactive service	Interacting Transacting	Who are you? What are you doing? (session state)
	Multichannel service access	
Multichannel application	Interacting across multiple channels	Who are you? Where are you? What are you doing? How are you interacting?

Source: Ovum (Pervasive Computing: Technologies and Markets/Chapter C)

Web browsing is an example of an application that requires very little context information to operate correctly. All the service provider needs to know in order to provide browsing services is an IP address for the user's machine, so that the web servers it operates know where to send requested web pages.

Interactive services, including games, e-commerce applications and personalised portals, present dynamic (rather than static) information to users. In order to present dynamic information to a user, an application or service must generate and render the information on-the-fly to users at runtime, rather than merely transmitting hard-coded information to users at runtime. In order to function at a particular point in time during a usage session, therefore, an interactive service needs not only a users' identity, but also knowledge of the current state of the session, in order to know what instructions to pass to its information-generation engine. This state information can be thought of as a memory of service for each particular user.

Context information becomes more complex when you try to offer an application or service to users through multiple delivery channels. As applications and services are offered through multiple delivery channels and as users begin enacting individual sessions across multiple channels, applications will have to depend on context information at runtime, in order to determine what is provided to whom, and how (as shown in *Figure C5.4*). In order to deliver the right information to each segment of one, the overall application or service may have to manage and act on the following information:

- the user's identity
- the application or service session state

- the channel through which the user is accessing the application or service
- the user's preferences for the way in which information is presented to them for that particular channel
- the physical location of the user and the device
- the time of day that the user is accessing the application or service (at that location).

In its ultimate form, context information is what enables (from the user perspective) relationships to be forged directly between applications and users, regardless of the devices, networks and service providers that sit in between them. Consequently the battle for management and ownership of context information will be one of the key landmarks in the history of pervasive computing.

Doing it right: separation of concerns

Individual content types, services and applications are uni-channel because their cores are tightly coupled with external interfaces that are associated with particular content delivery channels. For example, Amazon.com's shopping service is tightly coupled with web user-interface technology that dictates how people interact with the service.

This coupling conflicts with the notion of pervasive computing, but it is not necessarily the fault of application or content developers. Application architectures are increasingly mandated by popular software development platforms – so unless they choose to completely go it alone, applications end up conforming to infrastructure vendors' own computing architecture blueprints. Software development platforms clearly have some growing up to do. Luckily, the early signs are positive; for example, next-generation platforms such as IBM's WebSphere Everyplace Suite, and product strategies such as Microsoft's .NET and Sun's plans for its iPlanet infrastructure, are all pointing in the right direction.

Figure C5.4 **Pervasive computing context**

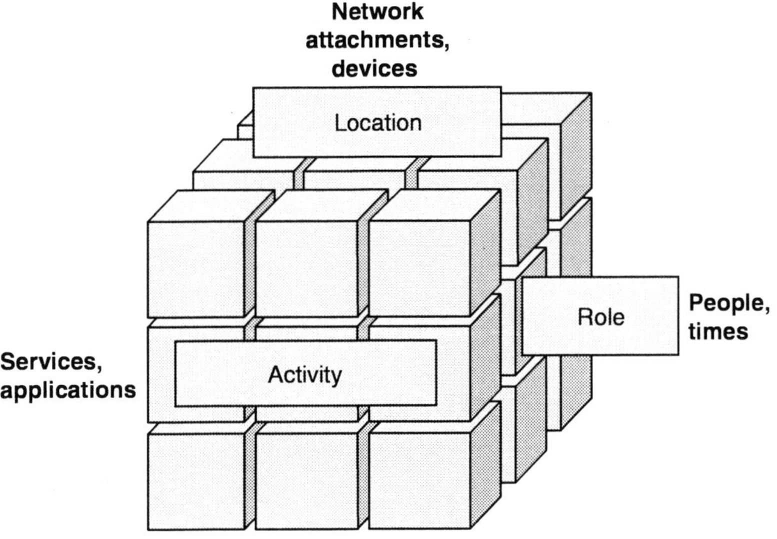

Source: Ovum (Pervasive Computing: Technologies and Markets/Chapter C)

Creating a multichannel application requires the concepts of application interfaces and application implementations to be decoupled, in order to allow service providers, content providers and content aggregators to deliver their products and services over multiple channels without 're-inventing the wheel' every time. But decoupling these concepts and implementing multichannel services cost-effectively will require suppliers to invest in new types of software infrastructure, and will not be possible without significant up-front investment in changing the ways in which applications and services are designed and implemented.

Do not re-invent the wheel – even if it is the easy option

There have been plenty of examples of 'wheel re-invention' over the past 20 years in the IT industry, which have led to many companies developing and re-developing their applications in line with the latest fashion.

Revenue flows between infrastructure & tool providers, and application & service providers, are becoming much more tightly linked and symbiotic. In the pervasive computing market, the companies building applications and services using new infrastructure technologies will be the ones providing the routes through which infrastructure investment will be recouped. If they suffer or fail in their endeavours to build compelling applications and services cost-effectively, infrastructure providers will fail too. The move towards pervasive computing cannot induce the same kinds of tremor in users' world views as have previous industry evolutions.

As an application or service provider, if you build a new version of your service or application for each new channel you want to serve, it is going to cost you a lot to build and manage – in both technology and business terms. Suppliers are interested in pervasive computing because it will help them reach new audiences, drive up service usage, and re-use their existing investments (and hence grow at a lower cost). There is an obvious conflict here.

Duplication of infrastructure and application or service functionality therefore has to be minimised. This will require a mature, measured approach to marketing and product development from both infrastructure and tool vendors, that encompasses two design philosophies sometimes overlooked in the quest for a quick profit: modularity and support for standards.

The cost of re-inventing the wheel

In the early 1990s, client-server computing started to gain popularity as a way to maximise use of new mid-range Unix and other proprietary systems that were starting to gain ground against the mainframes that had dominated the corporate computing landscapes. The argument at the time was that mainframe computing was too restrictive; certainly a handful of vendors had used their oligopoly to keep capital and maintenance costs high, and mainframes required skilled management. As the new wave of Unix crashed onto the corporate shores, the new breed of systems architects also undertook to replace mainframe systems' green-screen terminals with more attractive, interactive GUI systems. Client-server's proclaimed business benefit was the empowerment of lines of business; the sugar-coating was the cuteness of the new look-and-feel.

Client-server computing brought new requirements for application development. Structured information-engineering toolsets, which generated and managed vast tracts of Cobol code, were rejected and replaced with rapid application development 4GL tools that could make use of the new breed of transactional environment – relational database systems. Many companies were seduced into weakening their dedication to the mainframe, and developing all their new applications in line with the client-server architectures and principles.

By the late-1990s, however, it was increasingly accepted that the two-tiered model of many client-server applications did not deliver the flexibility or the scalability demanded of it; moreover, these applications were expensive and complex to manage. Some companies sent employees out to retrieve their dusty mainframe manuals from their dustbins. Meanwhile, development tool vendors had long been looking for a way out of the mess that was created. The most obvious thing to do was to migrate users towards thin-client architectural principles, which promised to increase flexibility and scalability, and decrease the cost and complexity of application management. But early attempts by client-server development tool vendors were based on proprietary runtime technology for both clients and servers, which proved very expensive for tools vendors to maintain – and which did not deliver a readily-understandable operational cost advantage to customers. They were not widely-adopted – but some leading-edge customers invested in re-building their applications once again.

Spurred on by a flurry of new market entrants, those tool vendors took up the challenge to reach a wider audience. They took advantage of the increasing universality of web clients to build thin-client application development tools, using standard web protocols and technologies. The current wave of interest surrounding application server products has been catalysed by the efforts of both new and existing tool vendors, with existing infrastructure vendors now working hard to get in on the act.

More and more companies are now basing their new applications on this architecture. Large companies are deploying IBM's S/390 systems as their application servers; others are using similar machines from Sun and HP – machines that look suspiciously like mainframes.

A very conservative estimate of the money that has been spent by companies on shifting from centralised computing principles to client-server and back again would be 2–3% of the overall worldwide IT expenditure since 1992 – between $65 and $100 billion. The real figure could well be three or four times as much.

Design rules for multichannel services

Three design rules must be followed in order to deliver a multichannel service cost-effectively:

- applications and services must be designed in such a way that logic that deals with the technology specifics of individual delivery channels is kept separate from the real application logic
- applications and services must be componentised, with each component implementing an individual element or function of the service/application – or a logical grouping of elements or functions
- context information that enables the application or service to keep track of user navigation and the state of transactions must be made available through all supported delivery channels.

The alternative is to replicate large chunks of functionality across multiple implementations of the product or service, each of which is specialised for a particular delivery channel. This route is more cost-effective in the short-term – but crippling in the long term, as shown in *Figure C5.5.*

Figure C5.5 **The cost of ignoring multichannel service design principles**

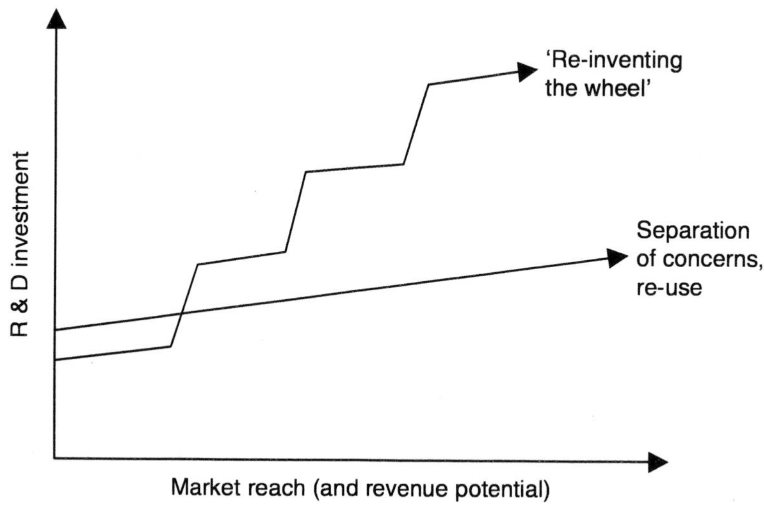

Source: Ovum (Pervasive Computing: Technologies and Markets/Chapter C)

C6 Devices and access networks: creating the right channels

The hype that surrounds the launch of new network and device technologies such as 3G and Bluetooth obscures the fact that different access platforms vary widely in their capabilities, and will continue to do so even when and if the current technology constraints are removed. It is hard constraints such as battery technology and access network bandwidth that currently limit the capability of particular devices. In the future, soft constraints – primarily, the usage contexts in which people like to use devices – will play much greater roles in determining the variation in device capabilities and form factors. Device manufacturers are very keen to increase the level of commonality between different device types, and improve accessibility to digital information over networks: many see this as a key differentiator in markets that are highly competitive. However, it is not guaranteed that network operators can remove differences in the capabilities of different kinds of access network.

Software infrastructure technologies will help bridge the gaps between access platform capabilities and the demands of applications, by implementing services that address the peculiarities of particular application platforms and provide suitable application-delivery environments. The most effective technologies will be end-to-end solutions that integrate the functions of application-server platforms, with infrastructure functions hosted on individual devices and in the network.

C6.1 The pervasive computing platform landscape

Wide variations in capabilities

Particular types of device – and particular types of network service connecting those devices to services, applications and other devices – have their own strengths and weaknesses. PCs, for example, are high-powered, general-purpose computing tools, but are too large to be truly mobile and too complex to use. Mobile phones, by contrast, are small and comparatively lightweight, but compared to PCs they are very limited in terms of their computing power and configurability. xDSL network services are (to varying degrees) capable of delivering high bandwidth data communication, but the upstream bandwidth is much smaller than the downstream bandwidth. PSTN services over the same wires offer lower bandwidth, but greater bandwidth symmetry.

Closed architectures

Closed architectures make it hard for large communities to address platforms. Unfortunately, the majority of today's devices and access networks (outside the world of the PC and the corporate network) suffer from closed architectures to varying degrees. In terms of pervasive computing devices, the PC is (perhaps perversely) the ultimate open platform. Most of the interfaces between PC components, and between software elements, are published and addressable through popular tools.

However, few other device types offer truly open platforms: the relative immaturity of the PDA and advanced voice-handset markets, for example, mean that there is a great deal more fragmentation, and a comparative lack of readiness to make platform-interface specifications freely available. The WAP group of standards is the first real example of an open application platform being made available, and widely adopted, outside the realm of the PC.

Physical constraints

Mobile devices suffer most from physical constraints. There are two main constraints that limit the capabilities of mobile devices today:

- physical size – mobile devices have to be small enough to prevent them from being inconvenient to carry
- battery life.

Between them, these place constraints on networking capabilities, processing power, secondary storage and user interfaces.

Hype

> *Third-generation mobile networks will provide data transfer rates of up to 2Mbit/s to devices.*

This has been stated in journals, newspapers, analyst reports, vendor literature and start-up companies' business cases worldwide over the past 12 months. But there are at least three things wrong with the statement:

- the theoretical maximum data rate of 2Mbit/s is only attainable if your device is fixed to a particular location
- the theoretical limit for devices on the move is 384kbit/s – but this is only attainable if there is no congestion in the cell that you are in
- the current fragmentation in 3G implementation standards and their adoption means that in order to deliver a 3G handset that can roam internationally, more processing power is required than can currently be fitted into a convenient-sized handset.

Third-generation technology is just one aspect of access platform technology that is in danger of being hyped to extinction. Bluetooth and WAP are two others. There is also a great deal of confusion about the potential of i-Mode, and of miniaturised Java implementations for mobile devices.

C6.2 Drivers for change in the device community

Threats: intense competition and creeping commoditisation

The 'innovator's dilemma' has hit many of the markets where the opportunities for pervasive computing are being scrutinised. Device manufacturers that have spent hundreds of man-years and millions of dollars creating innovative technologies have seen market share taken away from them by new competitors that have come to market using the technology advances that the innovators have stimulated, to deliver low-cost, entry-level devices.

This situation creates at least two problems for the innovators:

- high-volume market segments can more easily be dominated by the new competitors, which have built their companies around delivering low-cost devices, rather than innovating
- a high-value market segment is unlikely to sustain a large enough customer base, and a leading position will be difficult to achieve because prices are driven down and high sales volumes are unlikely.

Opportunities: value-added services and business model transformation

Many leading companies – such as Palm Computing (in the PDA market), Nokia (in the voice handset market) and Whirlpool (in the home-appliances market) – see the opportunity to bundle complementary value-added services, which increasingly involve connection to data networks, as a way of differentiating without excessive risky hardware innovation. These companies are betting that their market power will allow them to tie up deals with network operators and service providers and thus maintain a market lead beyond the life of any first-mover advantage they may gain.

For companies such as Palm and Nokia, the services enable infotainment and commerce applications; for companies such as Whirlpool, remote device management is more likely to be the 'killer' application that allows them to differentiate themselves from competition.

In more extreme cases, manufacturers of some goods (automobiles and computer servers, for example) are implementing technologies in their products that enable them to offer certain features and functions as remotely-enabled and disabled services. Hewlett-Packard, IBM and Bull have all announced 'computing power on-tap' features in high-end server products that allow customers to upgrade their hardware capacity simply by requesting a licence key from the vendor. The key switches on previously dormant or disabled processors, memory or disk volumes. In this way, manufacturers are not augmenting their products with services; they are actually transforming their products into services.

C6.3 Drivers for change in the access network community

Threats: declining voice revenues, and stiff competition

Although most operators and access service providers spend most of their marketing budgets extolling the virtues of their more exciting services, the majority of most operators' revenues is obtained from carrying voice traffic. But very high levels of competition in the fixed telecommunications market are forcing the cost of voice calls down faster than the call volume is increasing, and revenues from fixed voice services will start to decline worldwide within a few years. Few fixed telecommunications operators want to be stuck as providers of 'bit pipes'. Mobile access network providers' lives are easier, due to the aggressive growth currently occurring in the penetration of wireless handsets; but they too are looking to move to provision of value-added services in order to differentiate themselves against tough competition.

Opportunity: new markets

Network operators and access service providers see their major opportunities in pervasive computing revolve around the use of their central supply-chain role to carve out futures as service providers of various types. Service provision opportunities include e-commerce, content aggregation, application hosting, systems integration and (in the longer term, as applications become multichannel) management of usage context information. Network operators (such as BT, Vodafone, Deutsche Telekom and NTT DoCoMo) and access service providers (such as Cable & Wireless) are all moving in this direction – either by themselves or through partnerships with portal providers and content aggregators.

C6.4 Challenges for the industry

Avoiding the temptation to create small PCs

Pervasive computing takes applications and services, through networks, to devices that have not previously been seen as computing platforms, and to users who have not had extensive experience of using personal computers or any network, apart from their PSTN.

All of the devices we consider are smart versions of existing devices. The familiarity of pervasive computing devices is creating user expectations that infrastructure suppliers, device manufacturers and network operators are left to fulfil. If pervasive computing is to be successful, applications and services delivered to users via pervasive computing technology must live up to as many of these expectations as possible.

In order to meet user expectations, infrastructure suppliers, device manufacturers and network operators must work together to deliver high levels of reliability, performance and security – and just as importantly, deliver these characteristics as transparently as possible to users.

Making information delivery good enough

Two types of quality

In addition to addressing the basic 'hygiene' factors that make each type of pervasive computing device and access network usable, the supplier community will have to ensure that delivery of content, applications and services to these devices is carried out in a suitable way.

Applications and services have differing requirements, which place different demands on networks and devices. For example, e-commerce transactions must be secure but need not be performed in absolute realtime; whilst voice communication need not necessarily be secure, but must occur in 'real-enough-time' so the participants do not notice any delay.

The main ways in which applications and services differ in their technology requirements are:

- security (user authentication and encryption)
- reliability
- availability
- user interactivity and data dynamism.

These requirements are often over and above those that device manufacturers and network operators must provide to deliver the 'hygiene' factors that make their products and services usable. The gaps between the capabilities of devices and access networks, and the technology requirements of different types of applications and services, must be bridged by infrastructure technologies. But infrastructure technologies need capable device platforms on which to run. Device manufacturers must therefore deliver access platforms that are capable enough to run software that can improve the quality-of-service of application delivery – whilst working with software providers to ensure that their powerful systems are not open to the same malicious abuses and accidental misuses that PCs so often are.

End-to-end infrastructure is the only solution

Major aspects of quality-of-service are dependent on the activity the user is engaging in, and different devices will continue to have differing capabilities. This means that quality-of-service of application delivery will not be assured through one universal solution; different device platforms will require different approaches. Software infrastructure that resides on devices to optimise quality-of-service of application delivery will therefore have to co-operate and negotiate with software infrastructure that resides in the network and with the service provider's context-management infrastructure in order to provide the right kind of environment for each user's activity. Consequently end-to-end quality-of-service assurance solutions are the only way in which a wide variety of devices can access a wide variety of application types cost-effectively.

The 80:20 rule

Can infrastructure technology enable delivery of every application to every device? The short answer to this question is no.

However, this is not as unsatisfactory as it might seem – because in practice it is very likely that the application-channel combinations that are infeasible are not going to be the ones that are most important. There will be demand for some applications to be available for every type of device – personal communication and remote management applications and services will be the most pervasive. But neither of these applications places particularly heavy demands on networks or devices.

The most important developments that will take place in order to enable pervasive computing are those that make the widest-available networks and devices good enough to support the most widely-popular applications and services. In other words, the perennial 80:20 rule will come into effect with respect to bringing channels and applications closer together in terms of their suitability for each other.

C7 Industry structures: breaking the stovepipes

Moves at both the tops and bottoms of the main supply chains that are contributing towards the pervasive computing movement – IT, public telecommunications and broadcast media – are enabling service providers of all kinds to consider developing and delivering multichannel services. However delivery of these new services brings complex challenges to industries. Increasingly, players (possibly from multiple industries) will have to co-operate online, possibly with competitors, to enable the services that users want.

This online co-operation cannot happen without information sharing, to enable the sharing of revenues and responsibility for quality-of-service. Technology has an enabling part to play in addressing both these issues, but it is not the whole answer. There are many geographical and market issues that need to be addressed by suppliers: and suppliers can only address these issues through partnerships, to fill gaps in their expertise and execution capabilities. Suppliers moving from a position of strength in one supply chain will not be able to rely on that strength translating to their target market. Successful ventures will be built from partnerships between what may seem at first to be unlikely bedfellows: for in many cases partners will compete in some areas.

Just as people going to work in a foreign country must abide by local customs in order to prosper, moves from one stovepipe to another will work best when the immigrant plays by the incumbent's rules. Incumbents, as a rule, understand 'local customs' such as ownership and content regulation, customer segmentation, user-interaction paradigms, platform peculiarities and users' likes and dislikes. Immigrants ignoring these local customs, and bypassing the potential value to be gained from working with existing services providers, will find life very difficult.

C7.1 The industry landscape

Within the multichannel landscape of pervasive computing, we are seeing changes in supplier dynamics. Some suppliers are starting to look for revenue opportunities outside of the channels with which they are traditionally associated, and in many cases suppliers are looking to form partnerships across industries to enable them to participate in multiple channels, or to expand their presence via acquisitions or taking shares in other companies.

Recently there have been several high-profile mergers and acquisitions between content providers and network companies, the largest of which is currently AOL's merger with Time Warner (still pending). This kind of merger is a good example of the desire by large organisations to control as much of the supply chain as possible across as many channels as possible. If it succeeds, the AOL-Time Warner merger will see a major content aggregator with a background in the PC/Internet industry combining with an organisation with a significant delivery channel associated with broadcast media (Time Warner's cable network). However, mergers and acquisitions of this kind are facing increasing levels of scrutiny from industry regulators, which are starting to realise the market-power potential of such cross-industry giants.

Partnerships, rather than takeovers, are likely to form the backbone of the cross-industry moves that are breaking the stovepipes. A good example is the partnership between Vivendi and mobile operator Vodafone to form Vizzavi, a new venture seeking to develop an infotainment portal to be accessed from PCs, TVs and mobile phones.

Pervasive computing is also bringing about relationships between organisations that have not had much involvement with each other in the past. For example both automobile and home-appliance manufacturers are now working with software companies, network operators and content providers to enable the delivery of applications and services to vehicles and domestic appliances respectively.

C7.2 Drivers for change

Device manufacturers and network operators (at the heads of digital information supply chains, and the content and application providers (at the tails) are being influenced to promote pervasive computing. They are being influenced both by negative aspects of their current positions, and by exciting opportunities to reach larger communities and add more value to their customers.

As shown in *Figure C7.1*, the market moves that are occurring at the heads and tails of digital information supply chains are allowing service providers to 'go multichannel'.

Chapter F examines the drivers of the different supplier communities in different industries in more detail.

Figure C7.1 **Everyone is pushing for multichannel services**

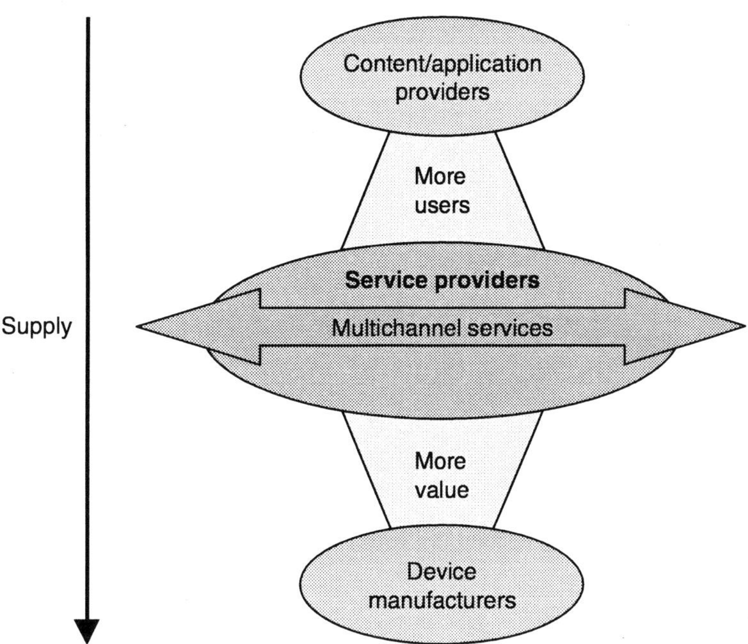

Source: Ovum (Pervasive Computing: Technologies and Markets/Chapter C)

C7.3 Challenges for the industry

One of the key features of the pervasive computing vision is that it enables users to move between delivery channels in a single application or service-usage session. The evolution of context information discussed in *Section C3.1* is concerned with enabling this transfer of session context between delivery channels.

What is going to be much harder to deal with is the fact that moving between delivery channels potentially introduces the possibility of users moving between service providers, unaware of the transfer of responsibility for service delivery.

A good example of this would be if a user is watching a programme on digital TV and 'clicks through' to begin surfing the Internet. When the user clicks through to start surfing the wider Internet, they may move from their digital TV service provider to an Internet service provider – but if the environment is built correctly, this transfer will be transparent to them. This invisible responsibility transfer gives rise to two major business issues for service providers:

- who is responsible for quality-of-service?
- how can revenue flows be protected?

Quality-of-service responsibility

Service providers act as aggregators of relationships to provide the user with a single point of contact for customer service and billing. Consequently, in the event of a problem occurring whilst the user is surfing the Internet through their TV, they will assume their TV service provider is responsible – even though they may be supported by a different service provider.

Whither revenue flows?

The ability of users to move transparently between delivery channels creates revenue-collection problems for service providers – particularly where they rely on advertising revenue.

Advertising revenues are traditionally paid to a service provider based on 'eyeballs' (the number of people who actually see the advertisement). When users are able to navigate freely between service providers, it becomes much trickier to actually monitor how many users see particular adverts. For example, if whilst watching an advertisement on interactive TV, a user clicks on a web link to take them to the company's website, the user is unlikely to see the advertisements shown after that particular one.

C7.4 What can service providers do?

Walled gardens – preventing the problem

A solution – and one which is already being tested in the integration of Internet services into TV broadcast and mobile data networks – is to create walled gardens, which only allow users to navigate through confined collections of content, applications and services that are either provided by one primary service provider, or by that service provider and a small number of its closest partners with whom it has revenue-sharing agreements and quality-of-service agreements.

This approach is unlikely to be viable over the long term – competition will force providers to bring more content, applications and services to users.

Service providers may instead provide 'rose gardens', which make clear distinctions between validated content, applications and services (which are easy to find) and other untested content, applications and services (which are much more difficult to navigate to). This approach gives the service provider the opportunity to circumvent the quality-of-service issue by showing a disclaimer, informing users that the content they wish to view is not approved, and therefore any problems fall outside its responsibility. It does not help with revenue-flow issues, however.

Information sharing – enabling transfer of revenue and responsibility

Revenue tracking and sharing could be enforced through regulation, as in the interconnect agreements used in international telecommunications. Interconnect provides a framework whereby operator A pays an amount to operator B in order for operator A's traffic to be carried over operator B's network. Something similar could be devised to allow service providers to bill one another when users migrate between them, but the question remains of who would actually be the regulator. Different industries have different regulatory bodies and it is not immediately obvious who would be best placed to undertake this task.

An alternative to regulation is for service providers to voluntarily establish commercial agreements with each other and with advertising network providers across different delivery channels. These agreements will require significant information sharing to take place between providers, however, in order for them to bill each other and track users' activities and service usage as they navigate around the digital universe.

This is a big leap that will require service providers to invest in new technologies, as well as forging commercial agreements. The technology problems are eminently solvable – it is the commercial ones that form the larger barrier. Due to the current emphasis on owning the customer, and the reluctance of many organisations to share information that they have invested significant time and money in gathering, substantial changes in business models are likely to be required in order to enable delivery of pervasive computing applications where the free exchange of information between service providers is required.

C8 Disaggregation of applications and platforms

C8.1 The delivery of information is going to get a lot more complex

As market development challenges start to be addressed by infrastructure vendors, application and content providers, service providers, network operators and device manufacturers, the changes that are induced in application architectures, application platforms and industry structures will have a profound effect on the focus of both the technology providers and implementers.

It would seem at first glance that these changes will make delivery of digital information to wide varieties of devices easier. After all, more networks will support packet delivery services and the IP protocol; and there will be more similarity in access platform capabilities.

However (as is always the case) the complexity is not going to disappear – it will just move elsewhere:

- as applications become multichannel, personalisation and specialisation functions will lead to the demise of the software application as we now know it. What will exist in their place is groups of co-operating software services that support personalised sets of user activities over a network
- as devices become more capable, their diversity will not be as a result of technology limitations; it will be as a result of the ways in which people like to use different access platforms in different environmental contexts. Moreover, Bluetooth will disaggregate device functions into modules that may be composed in different ways, according to the context in which they are used.

By 2005, the focus of leading-edge software, hardware and communications technologies will have transferred from their current position – dealing with complexity brought about by technology heterogeneity – to dealing with complexity brought about by the need to specialise services for individual users, according to their identities, preferences and locations. This is shown in *Figure C8.1*.

Figure C8.1 **Complexity – from heterogeneity to specialisation**

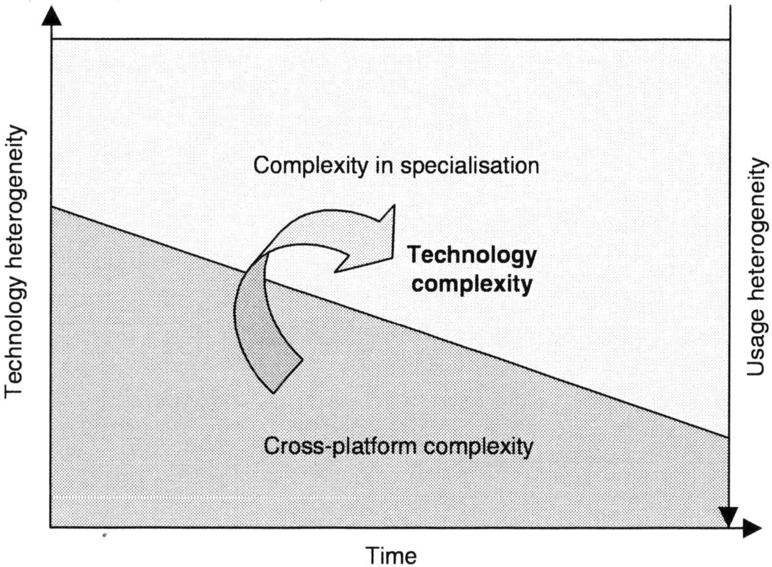

Source: Ovum (Pervasive Computing: Technologies and Markets/Chapter C)

C8.2 From applications to activities

As applications become multichannel, cost-effective service implementation dictates that elements of applications become more clearly separated into individual layers, each of which is dedicated to dealing with a particular set of problems. Furthermore, as multichannel usage increases, not all aspects of every application will be delivered to each type of access platform. Limitations of particular platforms will dictate specialisation of application presentation on a per-delivery channel basis.

In order to deal with increasing levels of specialisation, applications will have to become increasingly decomposed into atomic functions that can be composed in many different ways, to suit particular users and usage contexts. With applications that are componentised in this way comes enhanced flexibility, application quality and (hopefully) user satisfaction.

Service providers will start to deliver highly 'personalisable' sets of services to individual users, so that the services one user receives may bear little resemblance to the services received by their friends, families and colleagues. Software applications as we currently think of them (sets of software functions) will not exist at all in this world. Users will instead interact with personalised collections of software functions that let them carry out their own favourite activities, in their own way.

C8.3 The Bluetooth effect

Today's most popular device is the PC, which (in most configurations) is an aggregation of a processing unit with some associated primary storage (RAM), some secondary storage (a hard disk drive), support for temporary storage media (CD-ROM and floppy-disk drives), video output and a keyboard and mouse for input. All these things are connected together by an internal network or bus. But Bluetooth's ability to create wireless personal area networks (PANs), in combination with the ever-decreasing costs in hardware components and software platforms, is creating a trend towards disaggregation of computing functions.

Ideally, we want to be able to carry out certain computing and communication functions whilst walking, whilst in our cars, and at home and for certain functions in the office. It is impractical to have one device for each usage context; it is not practical to look at a video-screen whilst driving your car, for example. But what if we could modularise the capabilities of our ideal platform, and use different modules as and when we need to? Bluetooth technology has the potential to enable this. *Figure C8.2* illustrates this with an example.

In the medium term (five or more years), there will be significant numbers of these modular personal computing platforms in use. Not everyone will use them; and not every user of such a platform will use only that platform. But their convenience and potential fit to executive lifestyles, in particular, will make them popular high-end solutions.

Figure C8.2 **Modular personal computing platform usage scenarios**

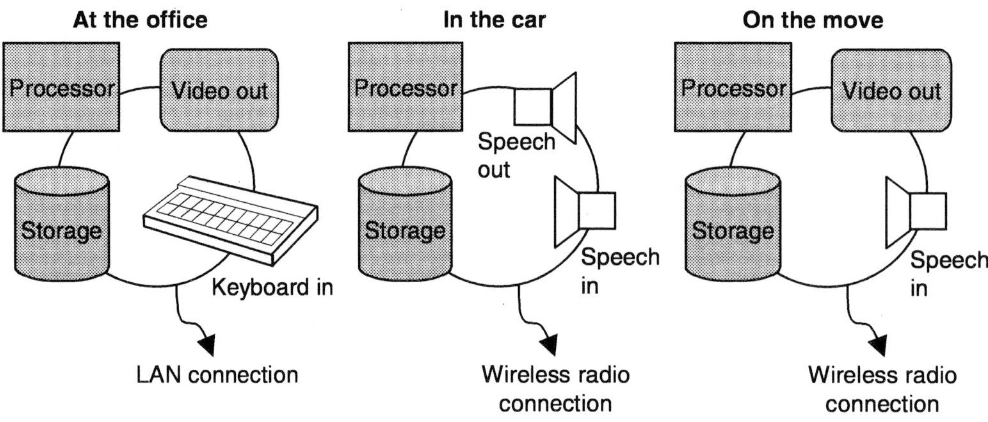

Source: Ovum (Pervasive Computing: Technologies and Markets/Chapter C)

C9 Infrastructure supplier strategies and standards

C9.1 The infrastructure supplier community

IT giants

The majority of the heavyweights in the IT industry – Microsoft, Sun Microsystems, Hewlett-Packard, IBM and Oracle – are currently evoking their own pervasive computing visions, and working on strategies. Microsoft's .NET strategy is the most high-profile of these; its vision is to 'empower people through great software any time, any place, anywhere'. In keeping with its ethos of empowerment, the company's strategy is to bring capable clients to the Internet and to create a universe of peer-to-peer collaboration between devices and services.

The other giants are investing significant amounts of time and money, too. Sun's strategy builds on its vision – 'the network is the computer'. As the company continues to increase the influence it has over the iPlanet co-venture it runs with AOL/Netscape, Sun is finally in a position to bring an integrated, end-to-end hardware and software infrastructure stack to market – and it is working hard to extend iPlanet technology to enable application and content delivery to non-PC platforms.

Hewlett-Packard's e-speak and Chai technologies form the foundation of its attempt to deliver on its vision of 'chapter two of the Internet' as a universe of co-operating e-services. Its recent purchase of Bluestone Technologies (a supplier of Java-based development tools and application-server technology) marks a departure from its usual hardware-centric approach and shows that the company is starting to consider competing seriously with companies such as Microsoft and Oracle, as well as IBM for mind- and market-share.

IBM started a dedicated Pervasive Computing Business Unit in 1999. Since then it has worked hard to seed the market with early versions of server infrastructure technologies, and has also worked to bring its myriad of middleware and development tool offerings under one banner – WebSphere. WebSphere Everyplace Suite, an extended solution bundle, is specialised for delivering content and applications to multiple kinds of mobile device, as well as normal web clients: and it has recently released a version of the suite aimed specifically at network operators.

Oracle hitched itself firmly to the Internet-based computing bandwagon considerably earlier than most of its major competitors. It has made much of the fact that all its corporate business application software is now designed on an Internet computing model. It claims that because it uses these applications, it saves $1 billion annually on infrastructure. The latest directive from Larry Ellison (chief-executive officer) is that every development project within Oracle that produces a software product, must produce it so that it can be hosted by an ASP as a service. Oracle's pervasive computing pedigree is much weaker than this core activity might suggest, however. It has project teams developing infrastructure solutions for interactive TV and mobile Internet, but these are not considered first-class objects within the Oracle business plan. Oracle's announcements are now putting flesh on the bones of its pervasive computing vision.

Device and network infrastructure manufacturers

Device and network infrastructure manufacturers are looking to Internet-based services as ways to differentiate themselves. Motorola has perhaps the broadest strategy, and it is beginning to galvanise the far-flung corners of its empire in line with this. 'Digital DNA' is Motorola's take on the pervasive computing vision, and the company has projects underway to further develop its expertise in mobile data application platforms (through a partnership with Sun Microsystems), in-car systems (through work with specialist embedded software platform suppliers such as QNX), home entertainment (with the acquisition of General Instrument) and data network infrastructure. Motorola views pervasive computing as a vehicle to transform itself from a hardware component manufacturer, into a computing platform vendor.

Nokia is building itself a pervasive computing infrastructure platform via its mPlatform solution, which is initially designed (unsurprisingly) for provision of mobile Internet services and targeted at mobile network carriers. However, the solution's foundation is a more generic platform that offers a secure, high-availability runtime environment together with pre-built provisioning, billing and monitoring functions for IP-based applications and services.

As the market-leading supplier of IP routers and switches to the corporate IT and data communications industry, Cisco is a key player in the development of pervasive computing infrastructure. The company is a champion of 'IP everywhere' as the foundation of next-generation networks, and has a strategy in place to take its IP infrastructure technologies beyond the enterprise to carrier networks (both fixed and mobile), as well as home networks. For home networks, it has formed partnerships with Toshiba and Echelon to build a residential gateway product, based on Echelon's LonWorks, called i.LON 1000.

Palm Computing has two aspects to its strategy:

- to improve the capability of its core device platform (the company is currently investing in speech recognition and synthesis, and other advanced technologies)
- to broaden its market penetration in the PDA market, through offering value-added services (via its Palm.net ISP and portal offering) and also by licensing its PalmOS operating platform to third-party device manufacturers.

Meanwhile, Psion is concentrating its efforts on broadening its range of wireless-connected PDA and notebook devices. Its new netBook is notable for the fact that its EPOC operating system runs a Java virtual machine environment, and contains software technology from IBM (MQSeries Everyplace queuing software and the DB2 Everyplace DBMS).

LG Electronics and Whirlpool are both keen to forge and maintain leadership positions in the emerging networked home-appliance market. LG Electronics has already launched an Internet-enabled refrigerator that provides recipes and home-shopping applications, and a washing machine that automatically downloads specialised washing programs for particular types of wash load. In October 2000, LG announced a strategic patent and intellectual property-sharing partnership with Intel. The companies will work together to deliver digital TV, home networking and Internet-appliance products.

Whirlpool's Integrated Home Solutions Initiative is creating a whole range of networked appliances. Electrolux is also in the game; it recently formed a partnership with ICL to deliver its own Internet fridge product.

Infrastructure platform providers

Increasing numbers of infrastructure platform providers that made their names selling technology for traditional corporate computing solutions view pervasive computing (or at least its early stages) as a major market opportunity to sell their core technologies to new markets. BEA, for example, believes that service providers are a key market for its technology – and that they will want to treat all delivery channels as extensions of a single e-services infrastructure back-end. Consequently, it is turning its core WebLogic application server platform into a common platform foundation for multichannel service delivery. In line with this strategy, the company has forged a co-development and co-marketing partnership with Nokia, which is taking it into the mobile application platform market. BEA's WebLogic Mobile Commerce Solution is one output of this partnership; the use of BEA technology in Nokia's mPlatform is another.

Inprise/Borland is another infrastructure platform provider that sees great potential in pervasive computing. It is starting to address corporate interest in the use of PDAs and voice handsets for mobile intranet and corporate application use; and is applying its Java platform and tools expertise accordingly. Inprise/Borland already ships an add-in for its JBuilder tool that allows developers to build Java clients that run on PalmOS.

Centura now develops and sells the db.star DBMS (formerly sold by Raima as a specialised DBMS for embedded systems). It has coupled this platform with its own lightweight messaging middleware, called eSNAPP, which it sells as a client-side application platform for mobile business applications. More than most, the company aims to be operating system-neutral – it has already produced implementations for PalmOS, Pocket PC, Windows CE, Linux, NT, and Unix, as well as a range of embedded RTOSs such as QNX Neutrino.

Tivoli's IBM parentage is pushing it to apply its device and service management products to pervasive computing. It now sells specialised management solutions for:

- service providers. The Tivoli Internet Services Manager and Personalised Services Manager implement device management, subscription management, provisioning and provide billing interfaces
- corporate customers (through extensions of Tivoli Enterprise platform for handheld device management).

Specialised technology providers

Quite apart from the more mature infrastructure providers with broad technology solutions, there is a very large number of specialised technology providers coming to market with infrastructure solutions targeted at serving particular delivery channels or delivering particular applications.

NetMorf's SiteMorfer is a development and deployment environment that allows service providers and corporates to build specialised interfaces to existing applications, which present them over wireless networks to limited-capability handsets. The new version of the technology includes a context-management technology the company calls m-logic, which is a framework that allows the platform to determine device, location and user information, and use this to tailor the content delivered to each user.

Aether Systems is not afraid to say that its mission is to become 'the Microsoft of the wireless world'. It is a wireless ASP (WSP) that also owns Aether Software, which develops and sells the software platform and tools used by the ASP. The company's ScoutWare platform consists of a wide range of software components to enable mobile computing. The company has already built on this solid foundation and now offers North American customers a wireless ISP service (which includes rental of a PocketPC device), and a content adaptation service (in partnership with AlterEgo Networks). At the back-end, the company has formed a partnership with Tibco, the integration middleware vendor owned by Reuters, to provide a set of integration technologies to make it easier to link ScoutWare solutions to existing business applications and content. It is also working with First Data to design money transfer and bill payment applications for wireless devices – building on an earlier partnership with Visa to develop standards for implementation of mobile e-commerce applications.

RealNetworks, the largest streaming media technology specialist player, has an important role to play in the development of pervasive computing – as an enabler of the convergence between Internet content and TV content. The company has more than 750 partnerships with organisations from a variety of industries, including terminal providers such as Nokia, and broadcasters and content providers such as the BBC and AOL. It intends to use these partnerships, together with its large user base (there are more than 130 million licensed RealPlayer users) and its dedicated media streaming network, to remain as the leading rich-media middleware provider – whether the media client is a PC, a Unix machine or a Nokia handset. The company has recently formed a partnership with Sony, to include its RealPlayer and RealJukebox technology in Sony's Vaio notebooks and portable music devices; in return, it has licensed Sony's compression and digital copyright-protection technologies.

Phone.com, which as Unwired Planet sold wireless Internet middleware to wireless carriers, has broadened its market offering considerably. The foundation platform has been broadened to include push notification, subscriber-identity management, a fax server and a content translator, which now supports WAP/WML, as well as Phone.com's proprietary HDML and HTML. Additionally, the company now sells a suite of wireless applications, including e-mail, PIM and web browsing; and a wireless portal framework called MyPhone.

Phone.com has built an impressive partner roster – including:

- e-commerce players, such as Amazon and TicketMaster Online
- content providers, including ABC News, AirFlash, Bloomberg and Webraska
- application and content management providers, including Vignette, 724 Solutions, Business Objects, Lotus and Plumtree Software

- tools providers, including Allaire, Edify, OnDisplay and Argo Interactive
- consultants and systems integrators, including Aether Systems, Attachmate, Razorfish and Cross Systems.

Its recent merger with Software.com (which provides unified messaging infrastructure) has the potential to transform Phone.com into a powerhouse wireless platform player.

New entrants

A small but growing number of vendors are coming to market with infrastructure solutions specifically targeted at pervasive computing. Their approaches have the potential to induce fundamental shifts in the computing landscape.

InterX is a UK-based technology company that builds and sells BladeRunner, a content management and application development environment that has been designed specifically for the creation of multichannel applications. The technology started life as a web-development environment; but the current version of the product suite is focused on the delivery of e-CRM functionality, provided on top of a platform that explicitly separates core business functions from software components, and functions such as presentation and navigation that are unique to particular delivery channels.

Amino Communications is a technology company that licenses its intellectual property to device manufacturers. Its market offering is a modular device architecture that allows suppliers to build new types of device, and device upgrades and patches, in very short timescales. The architecture core is a high-speed ATM-like network architecture that links modules within a device, and provides high-level interfaces between modules that allow modules to be added, removed and changed without extensive electronic testing needing to be carried out. The architecture also allows manufacturers and service providers to remotely monitor and manage device modules in a high-security environment. The company's core markets are e-commerce, automotive and application-specific video devices (such as set-top boxes, games consoles and seat-back entertainment consoles).

C9.2 The role of standards

Java

Java has been widely adopted by developers and platform providers as a device-independent application platform. It is quickly becoming influential across the whole range of delivery channels we consider in the scope of this report, and is also being specified as a core component of standardisation efforts within individual device markets – for example, digital TV (via the DVB-MHP standard) and networked home appliances (via the OSGi's home network gateway specification). Deployments are limited, but its penetration in these markets is set to grow over time.

Bluetooth

Bluetooth has tremendous potential as a shaper of the devices of tomorrow, and it has already achieved significant investment and backing from within the computing and telecommunications sectors. However, its widespread adoption is not a foregone conclusion: there are still several factors that could conspire to hamper its spread. The cost of Bluetooth technology is a major issue, but we expect this to fall to commercially-viable levels by 2003/2004.

Perversely, a greater threat comes from the popularity of the technology. The sheer size of the Bluetooth SIG has affected the speed at which applications are being developed. The large membership means that it is taking longer for new designs to be approved for manufacture. Delivery uncertainty will also serve to affect the market's attitude toward the technology, and missing launch dates will increase negative attitudes towards Bluetooth products. Suppliers will also need to ensure that they educate customers up-front about the support functions they will provide. A perceived lack of support for what is fundamentally an untested technology will affect long-term acceptance of the technology.

Bluetooth competes with several other technologies, including the wireless LAN standard IEEE 802.11b, and HomeRF. All operate in a similar frequency range and have the potential to interfere with one another when used in close proximity. It is still far from clear which standard will dominate and even less clear whether they will be targeting similar customer groups. The IEEE 802.11 technology appears to be heading towards a corporate and SME solution whilst HomeRF, by its nature, will probably target the SoHo and residential market segments. Bluetooth, due to its ubiquitous nature, will most likely tap into all major market segments. Bluetooth champions will have to communicate a clear value proposition (the pervasiveness of the technology) or risk it being overlooked in favour of its more specialised competitors.

XML

XML has immense potential for providing a common approach to the interchange of data. Its self-describing nature makes it attractive as a technology foundation for integration between systems that were not designed to work together – making it valuable for enabling pervasive computing applications. XML documents can easily be transported across networks using existing web protocols, so a communications and security structure is already in place for anyone with web access.

It should be no surprise, therefore, that XML has become an important weapon in every pervasive computing infrastructure player's armoury. Two of the highest-profile areas in which suppliers are using XML technology is in the creation and transmission of device-independent content; and in the encoding and transmission of information that describes a device's capabilities to server platforms, in order that they can adapt content for it accordingly.

XML is not a 'silver bullet', however. In order for two systems to share XML data, the systems must share common knowledge of the data being sent; this normally requires domain-specific document type definitions (DTDs) to be specified and agreed between suppliers in advance. But the value of XML to vendors means that everyone wants a piece of the action. As a result, many potential applications of XML are being hamstrung by a proliferation of competing DTD standards being promoted by different parties within a particular application domain. Moreover, XML and other related technologies (such as XSL and XSLT) are not powerful enough tools, by themselves, to cope with some scenarios that occur in real-world integration projects – proprietary tools are still required in many cases. Automatic interworking between applications, infrastructure and devices, enabled by the exchange of XML data, is still a fantasy.

IP

IP technology is a crucial element of pervasive computing infrastructure. As the core technology of the Internet, the development of which is driving many players' expectations of pervasive computing, the degree to which IP is supported in access platforms and application-server platforms in particular will have a major effect on the speed of development of pervasive computing. IP is also one of the candidate technologies for operators to use as the basis for rolling out unified next-generation core networks – but the speed of adoption in core networks has less direct effects on the overall development of pervasive computing.

Strangely, one of the main challenges facing IP is its ubiquity in corporate IT and enterprise networking. Many infrastructure suppliers from this background assume that either IP is already a universal piece of communications fabric, or that its introduction as such is straightforward. The telecommunications community understands, though, that this is not the case. There are several key challenges that IP technologies must overcome in order to become truly universal – not least, the addressability of devices, IP quality-of-service and IP mobility.

D Towards pervasive applications

D1 The road from uni-channel to multichannel

D1.1 Application delivery needs

Successful multichannel application delivery initiatives require strategies that are driven by a hybrid IT/communications view. Without input from both perspectives, service providers will fail to deliver compelling services.

There are three critical success factors that service providers must address in order to deliver multichannel applications to users:

- implementation of practices and technologies that facilitate true service-based, rather than product-based, application delivery
- implementation of a multichannel application architecture that allows cost-effective deployment of the application to new access platforms
- implementation of infrastructure that enhances the overall quality of service of application delivery, which is implemented throughout the delivery environment (not just on the access platform).

All three factors depend on the implementation of technologies and practices to maximise the quality of service of application delivery. These technologies and practices are the domain of different types of supplier, but they must be aligned to work together.

D1.2 There will be three waves of pervasive application development

Application providers, software infrastructure providers and service providers will engage in three distinct types of multichannel development activity, which will come to market in three distinct waves:

- construction of new platform-specific extensions to existing applications
- construction of new applications that are designed to be multichannel applications from the outset
- re-engineering of older applications and integration of these with new applications that are designed to be multichannel applications.

The first wave has already begun. It is the result of a short-term strategy to get multichannel capabilities to market quickly, involving a 'top-down' approach to multichannel application architecture. The need for a strategy that enables quick time-to-market will be stimulated by the steady advances in transformations of application products into network-based services that are already occurring and will continue to occur over the next three years.

The second wave is starting now, and is largely the preserve of new-entrant service providers, working in partnership with innovative software infrastructure providers and systems integrators to deliver multichannel applications that are designed that way 'from the ground up'.

The third wave will start in earnest in around 2002, as cost and profitability pressures on established players, brought about by competition from new entrants, force them to analyse their ongoing investments in infrastructure and platforms and find new ways of deploying services that are more cost-effective.

D1.3 Application personalisation, granularity and convergence

By 2006, new pervasive computing applications will be very different to today's applications. Many will be highly granular and highly personalised; the lines between different kinds of application will be blurred. The eventual transformation of the application from monolithic product to personalised, granular set of network-based services is an inevitable consequence of the subsuming of Internet technology into application infrastructure technologies, and into different markets. E-commerce, infotainment and personal communications applications will be the most affected.

We are already starting to see convergence between e-commerce, infotainment and personal communications applications. For example:

- the introduction of 'avatars' (software simulations of people) and personalised content mean that infotainment and personal communications are starting to merge
- advanced merchandising services are blurring the boundary between infotainment and e-commerce
- innovation in call-centre, computer telephony and customer relationship management (CRM) technologies is bringing together e-commerce, e-marketing and personal communications applications.

D1.4 Application delivery channels, 2001–2006

Figures D1.1, D1.2 and *D1.3* show how availability of application access will evolve between 2001 and 2006. By 2006, e-commerce and infotainment applications will be the most compelling and easy-to-use across the widest range of access platforms, followed by personal communications applications that provide unified interfaces to communications functions, such as e-mail, fax and voicemail. Business applications and remote asset/device management applications are key to market development, but access to these will continue to be easiest and most compelling on the PC platform.

Figure D1.1 **Application delivery channels, 2001–2002**

	Personal communications	E-commerce	Infotainment	Business applications	Device management
PC	2	2	3	3	3
Voice handheld	2	2	1	n/a	n/a
PDA	n/a	n/a	1	2	n/a
TV	n/a	2	3	n/a	n/a
Car	1	1	1	n/a	n/a
Home appliances	1	1	1	n/a	n/a

Key: 1 = possible; 2 = usable; 3 = easy and compelling

Source: Ovum (Pervasive Computing: Technologies and Markets/Chapter D)

Figure D1.2 **Application delivery channels, 2003–2004**

	Personal communications	E-commerce	Infotainment	Business applications	Device management
PC	3	3	3	3	3
Voice handheld	3	2	2	2	2
PDA	2	2	2	3	2
TV	2	3	3	1	1
Car	2	1	2	1	n/a
Home appliances	1	2	1	n/a	n/a

Key: 1 = possible; 2 = usable; 3 = easy and compelling
Source: Ovum (Pervasive Computing: Technologies and Markets/Chapter D)

Figure D1.3 **Application delivery channels, 2005–2006**

	Personal communications	E-commerce	Infotainment	Business applications	Device management
PC	3	3	3	3	3
Voice handheld	3	3	3	2	3
PDA	2	3	3	3	3
TV	2	3	3	2	1
Car	2	2	2	1	1
Home appliances	2	2	2	n/a	1

Key: 1 = possible; 2 = usable; 3 = easy and compelling
Source: Ovum (Pervasive Computing: Technologies and Markets/Chapter D)

D1.5 Pressure on supply chains

Application convergence will pressurise players in today's channel-specific supply chains to work together much more effectively. The 'stovepipes' – the supply chains that have grown up around the delivery of particular types of information, to particular types of device over particular types of network – will eventually be broken down for two reasons:

- delivery of multichannel applications requires service providers to partner with multiple network operators and device suppliers working in multiple channel-specific markets
- application convergence means that, increasingly, no single service provider will be able to supply all the services that every user will want to access. Service providers will therefore have to partner with their peers working in other channel- and application-specific markets.

Chapter F looks at the deconstruction of today's industry stovepipes in more detail.

D1.6 Pressure on access platforms and software infrastructure

The personalisation, granularity and convergence of application types will not happen smoothly – and will not happen at all without significant evolution in access platforms and software infrastructure.

Today's devices are evolving from application-specialised objects into general computing platforms. However, in the short term at least they will not be sufficiently capable to support converged application environments. Broadcast access networks are today used to deliver infotainment and, increasingly, e-commerce applications, but as these applications become more granular and personalised, broadcast starts to become an inefficient application delivery model. Broadcast delivery in this environment can only work if personalisation and aggregation functions are provided by access platforms, rather than by central application-serving platforms. This distributed computing arrangement brings its own set of infrastructure challenges.

Another factor that will inhibit application convergence is that the software infrastructure that is used today, in supporting quality of service of application(s) delivery, either does not support multichannel applications, or is highly proprietary and therefore less easy to promote across multiple supply chains.

D2 Critical success factors for multichannel applications

There are three critical success factors that must be addressed in order for a service provider to deliver a multichannel application:

- service-based delivery of the application
- implementation of a high-quality, multichannel application architecture that allows cost-effective deployment of the application to new access platforms
- implementation of infrastructure that enhances the overall quality of service of application delivery, which is implemented throughout the delivery environment (not just on the access platform).

Quality of service assurance is a theme running through these factors. It requires the co-ordinated enlistment of the service provider's operational management services, the infrastructure underpinning the network-based application, and the access platform itself.

Today, such an undertaking is difficult: the infrastructure platforms that confer high quality of service to applications do not promote the types of design principle that underpin the cost-effective delivery of multichannel applications. If you try to design a multichannel application you will get little support from 'off-the-shelf' infrastructure products.

In any case, the co-ordination of end-to-end assured delivery quality requires service providers that want to offer multichannel applications to form technology and implementation partnerships with infrastructure providers, application and content providers, network operators and device manufacturers.

D2.1 Applications as services

Delivering an application as a service entails a lot more than just bolting an XML-enabled interface on the front of it. If you want to deliver an application as a service, you must provide a number of 'wrapper' services in order to offer assured levels of quality to your customers. These include:

- customer care – the issuing, signing and management of a service-level agreement (SLA) that forms the basis of the contract between the service provider and the user
- service level management – the monitoring and management of service levels in terms of the performance, availability and reliability of the overall service (including not just the actual application, but any other wrapper services that interact with the customer)
- application support services – support and training
- application management services – daily administration tasks associated with 'feeding and watering' applications, managing and testing upgrades, and so on
- data centre services – management of the hardware, operating systems, DBMSs and other application-serving infrastructure elements that underpin the application
- connectivity services – management of the connection to the network(s) over which the application is delivered to the customer.

The difference between commercial and private service provision

The degree to which individual services are likely to be implemented depends on the context in which the application is being delivered. Over time, many companies will offer multichannel access to certain corporate business applications; these companies will be much less concerned than commercial service providers with delivering formalised customer care, service level management and change management services. The reason for the discrepancy is that few companies view their own IT departments as true service providers and users within that context do not expect commercial-grade service provision.

Many companies that want to offer multichannel access to their corporate business applications will implement the requisite services in partnership with a commercial network service provider. Few companies can justify investment in delivering wireless connectivity services, for example. In these situations, the service provider partner has opportunities to deliver service 'bouquets' that help the company integrate its existing applications with the required channel-specific infrastructure – as well as simply providing a 'bit pipe'.

D2.2 Multichannel application architectures

In *Chapter C*, we introduced the concept of an ideal architecture for multichannel applications, and highlighted the danger of ignoring the potential value of such an architecture in reducing the investment required to deliver multichannel applications. In this section, we expand on what our 'ideal architecture' involves.

The core principle of the architecture is the separation of 'business logic' from implementation details that are specific to individual access platforms. 'Separation of concerns' is a well-understood software design principle – because it reduces the impact of changes to those implementation details, and hence the cost of adapting software in line with those changes.

If the software that handles the user interfaces for an application or service is cleanly separated from the channel-independent part of the application or service then, in theory, adding support for a new delivery channel, or changing the way in which a supported delivery channel is handled, will not require any changes to the core application or service. This is shown in *Figure D2.1*.

Designing a service or application so that it can be operated independently of the user interface is not just a case of 'tearing off' the user interface and creating multiple new interface variants. This is because different channels employ devices with different form factors and network services with different characteristics. Particular channels do not just require translation of a user interface to allow it to fit onto a smaller screen, for example; designers have to consider the ways in which users will want to interact with the service through different channels.

It is therefore not just the presentation of the service that must be designed specifically for individual delivery channels, but also the user navigation and access protection rules that determine the aspects of the service that are available on each delivery channel.

Figure D2.1 **Insulating applications and services from delivery channel specifics**

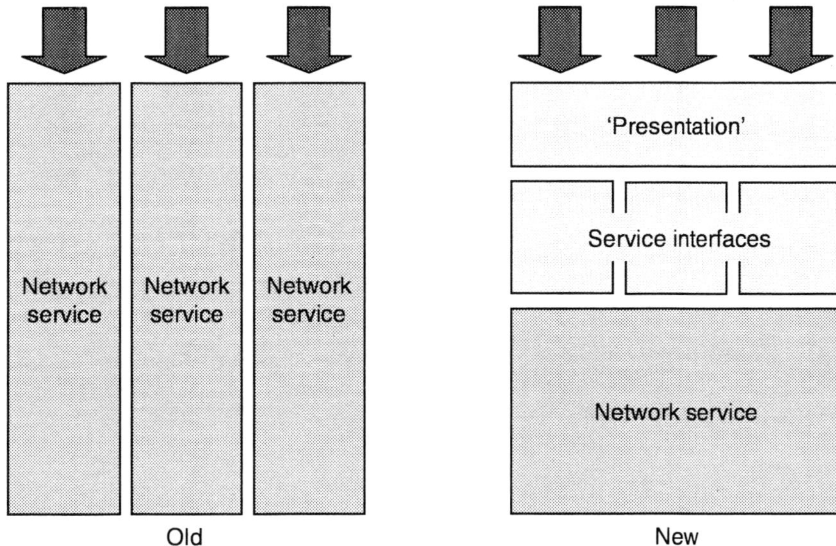

Source: Ovum (Pervasive Computing: Technologies and Markets/Chapter D)

Componentising applications and services

In order to make varying sets of service features available via particular delivery channels, it must be possible for a service provider to associate individual service feature functions, or logically-associated groups of functions, with access that is restricted to particular interfaces.

Componentisation of applications and services is the primary process through which this software modularisation is carried out. However, taking a 'bottom-up' approach to componentisation by re-developing a monolithic service or application as a set of components is complex, expensive and risky. The other way of componentising applications and services – 'top-down' componentisation – is to create multiple interfaces that reference functions within the monolithic service, but hide the monolithic implementation from the outside world. *Figure D2.2* shows the differences between these two methods.

Figure D2.2 **'Bottom-up' versus 'top-down' componentisation**

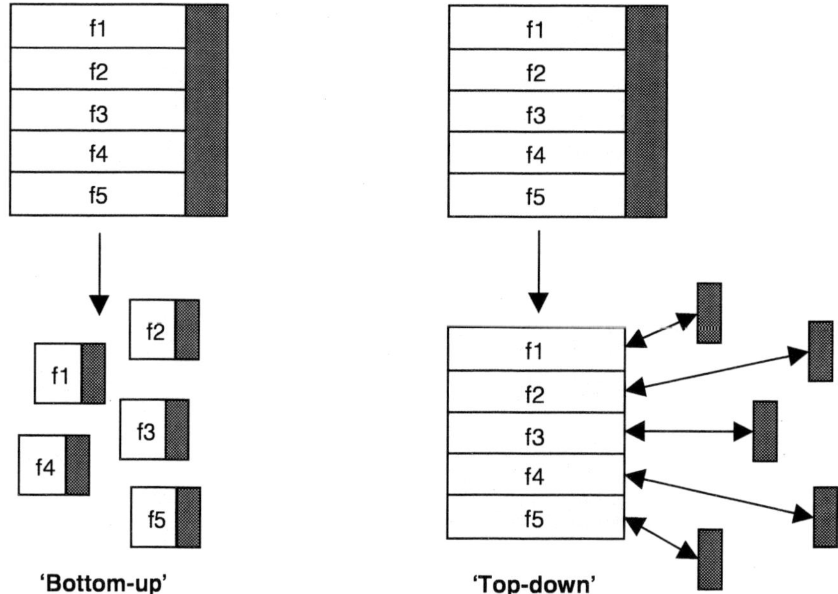

Source: Ovum (Pervasive Computing: Technologies and Markets/Chapter D)

Of course, carrying out a 'top-down' virtual componentisation of a monolithic service or application is only straightforward if the implementations of the functions within the application or service are neatly delineated. Many applications and services are developed to very tight timescales, however, and time pressure conspires against a sufficiently 'clean' application implementation.

By interposing interfaces between the outside world and the application or service, you are then at liberty to re-engineer the application or service at your leisure – the interfaces hide any changes in implementation, so long as the interfaces do not change.

Managing context across multiple channels

Context information must represent, for each active application session, the user's identity and the delivery channel they are using to access the application. It may represent other application-specific information (such as the geographical location and time of day they are accessing the application), in order to help the application understand more about the context in which the user is working, or the 'role' that they are carrying out.

In order to enable all the other things that are desirable in pervasive computing applications and services – personalisation, modularisation, separation of core application logic from delivery channel specifics – context information must play a central role in managing how the application or service operates for each user:

- it must determine the ways in which a user can access different application or service functions, and how they can navigate between them

- it must determine the ways application user interfaces and data are presented to each user through every supported delivery channel.

Clearly, in order to make a service or application that functions in this way cost-effective to develop and operate, the infrastructure that underpins the application or service must be able to access one single store of context information, regardless of the delivery channel for each individual user session. This is much easier if the information is stored and managed separately from:

- delivery channel specifics
- the core service application logic
- service or application interfaces.

It is also much easier if access to the information is provided using standardised interface technologies.

Figure D2.3 shows the central role that context information management plays in the operation of a multichannel application or service, and how it fits in with the other software layers that comprise such a piece of software.

Developing services and applications with a clear separation between context information management, delivery channel specifics, service interfaces and application logic requires a different approach to that taken in most of today's web applications – from which many of tomorrow's multichannel applications and services will evolve.

Figure D2.3 **Where does context information management fit?**

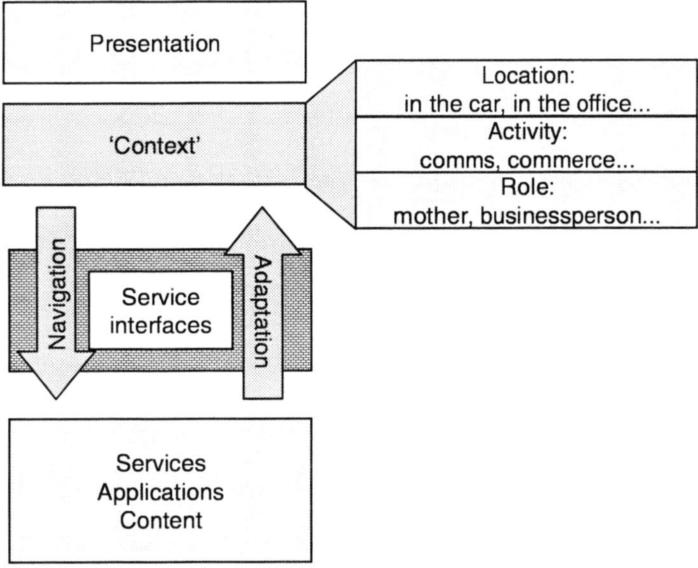

Source: Ovum (Pervasive Computing: Technologies and Markets/Chapter D)

Context management in web applications

Web applications are interesting because, by necessity, they separate the specifics of the delivery channel (the Web – that is, HTML and HTTP) from the core application logic, but context information tends to be tied into the implementation of the delivery channel. This is not surprising, because web applications suffer from a particular drawback that arises from the design goals of the web protocol (HTTP).

In order to make the protocol efficient, the designers decided to make it 'stateless'. This means that, when an HTTP server receives a request from a client (a web browser), the server has no notion of the context of the request. Each new request is treated in complete isolation – the HTTP server has no inherent 'memory' of what may have gone before. This approach makes for very scalable middleware – but means that the protocol by itself is not enough to support the implementation of an interactive service or application. In order to implement such a service, management of session state has to be carried out explicitly between the web server and the application server.

In web applications, application state tracking tends to be implemented through the use of 'cookies' or specially encoded URLs. Both these mechanisms use web technology in ways the protocol designers never intended, to get around 'problems' that the protocol was never intended to address in the first place.

D2.3 Infrastructure for enhancing the quality of application delivery

Where an application is delivered from a central point over a network to a remote access platform, the overall application delivery quality is constrained by:

- the quality of the application itself
- the quality of service offered by the access platform
- the ability of the service provider to monitor and optimise service quality.

Figure D2.4 shows these three aspects of application delivery quality.

This section highlights some of the infrastructure technologies that are already helping suppliers provide the appropriate kinds of application delivery environment to their subscribers.

Figure D2.4 **The three elements of end-to-end quality of service assurance**

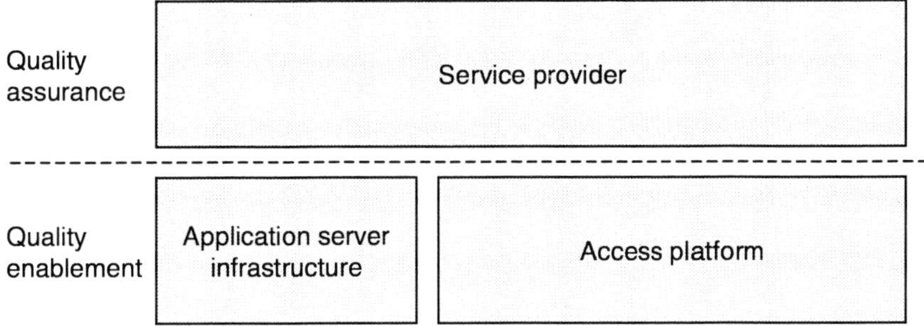

Source: Ovum (Pervasive Computing: Technologies and Markets/Chapter D)

A wide variety of application technology requirements

Our five types of application make widely differing demands on delivery channels, by virtue of their requirements in four areas:

- security – whether the application or service requires user authentication, authorisation frameworks and data encryption
- reliability – whether the application or service requires facilities that guarantee that information will not be lost or corrupted
- availability – whether the application or service requires facilities that guarantee that, even if problems occur, the overall application or service will remain available for use
- user interactivity and data dynamism – whether the application or service, or the data it manages and presents, change rapidly over time.

Figure D2.5 provides a summary of the technology requirements of our five application types.

The variations in requirements, when coupled with the variations in the capabilities of networks and devices, give rise to requirements for different types and degrees of software infrastructure to 'bridge the gap' between platforms and applications.

Figure D2.5 **Summary of applications' technology requirements**

	Personal communications	E-commerce	Infotainment	Business applications	Remote asset management
Security	Low–medium	High	High	High	High
Reliability	High	High	Medium	High	High
Availability	High	Medium	High	High	Medium
User interactivity and data dynamism	Medium	Medium	High	Low–medium	Low

Source: Ovum (Pervasive Computing: Technologies and Markets/Chapter D)

The requirements of personal communications and infotainment applications are largely due to the transfer of users' expectations from the physical world – users already experience these services, either from existing analogue communication services or from physical media such as newspapers.

E-commerce's requirements are mainly due to the need for trust in any transaction involving money, and the requirement for 'wrapper' services (such as merchandising) for high degrees of user interactivity and data dynamism.

Business applications' requirements arise largely from their business criticality as IT applications become increasingly important facilitators of business, and from the need to protect commercially sensitive data and functions from unauthorised access.

Remote asset management applications have unique requirements due to the fact that they are generally designed to interfere as little as possible with the correct functioning of the assets that they are designed to manage (as to do otherwise would be counter-productive).

Assuring reliability and availability

Most reliability and availability problems in computing platforms arise from software system problems, rather than hardware failures. It is, therefore, the responsibility of device operating system suppliers, communications infrastructure providers and application infrastructure providers to maximise system reliability and availability.

High-end middleware platforms provided by companies such as BEA and IBM fulfil many potential service providers' criteria with regard to assuring quality of application provision. They do this by implementing advanced distributed computing schemes to facilitate software component replication and other features – but these infrastructure products must themselves be monitored and managed to ensure that they confer maximum availability and reliability on the applications they serve. The suppliers of these platforms have not yet made it a priority to provide tools that work with their platforms, in order to facilitate development of multichannel applications.

Maximising the reliability of data transmission over a network requires a slightly different approach, but it still involves the implementation of middleware products. 'Message queuing' middleware products improve the reliability of network communication – at the expense of a small degradation in overall system efficiency.

Assuring security

Until recently, person-to-person services were conducted 'face-to-face' between supplier and consumer; when business services started to be delivered over the telephone, people were initially sceptical and wary of conducting business in such a way.

Pervasive computing applications will have to overcome the same wariness, because many potential subscribers to new applications delivered through new delivery channels will not be 'Internet savvy'.

Information security is the key here. Security must be delivered through trust – the security of the application delivery environment must be proven. This has already been demonstrated in the area of 'regular' web-based applications. Telling a potential subscriber 'oh, it's secure – don't worry' will not work the majority of the time. What will work much better is saying 'it's secure – and Brand X (which you've trusted for many years – your bank, for example) can confirm that for you'. In fact, implementing these trust relationships is the focus of most Internet security innovation occurring today.

Public key infrastructure-based security frameworks, which are installed on both access platforms and central application server platforms hosted by service providers, are already providing solutions in the fixed Internet – the leading players from this market (such as Entrust, VeriSign and Baltimore Technologies) are already being courted by wireless device and network infrastructure suppliers. TV service providers and device manufacturers have implemented their own encryption technologies in order to control access to content.

Enabling interactivity

There are two aspects to application interactivity:

- the degree to which information flows from the central application server to the access platform, to be passed to the application user
- the degree to which information flows from the application user (usually in the form of requests for information or for execution of a particular function) to the application server.

Interactivity requires two-way communication

In order to enable both these aspects, we need a two-way communication channel – something which users of PCs and the Internet take for granted, but which is missing from satellite and terrestrial broadcast networks.

Where a satellite or terrestrial broadcast network is employed for 'downstream' communication (from the central application server to the access platform), service providers and device manufacturers have to facilitate a separate, upstream communication channel – an additional complexity that adds to the cost of devices and services.

In almost all applications, the amount of downstream bandwidth required is much greater than the upstream bandwidth required. This is a good thing, because the amount of per-user upstream bandwidth is highly limited in almost all types of access network. *Chapter E* discusses this issue in more depth.

High levels of interactivity involve high volumes of data

Our five types of application differ widely in the degree to which their data changes over time. E-commerce and infotainment applications in particular may involve a high degree of interactivity and require the rendering of large amounts of data on the access platform over short intervals.

However, it is vitally important not to automatically equate the requirement for large volumes of data with a requirement for high network bandwidth. The reason for this is that pervasive computing access platforms will not just be windows onto remote network-based applications. Pervasive computing may emphasise information access over information processing, but platforms do have (and will continue to have) processing and storage capabilities, as well as network connections. If access platforms are sufficiently open, suppliers can install software infrastructure components on them that maximise the performance of highly interactive applications over restricted bandwidth connections.

The actual software infrastructure technology that is suitable is a function of:

- the volume of data that needs to be transferred
- the predictability of the data that is transferred.

Figure D2.6 summarises the techniques that are suited to particular combinations of data volume and predictability.

Figure D2.6 **Infrastructure options for supporting interactive applications**

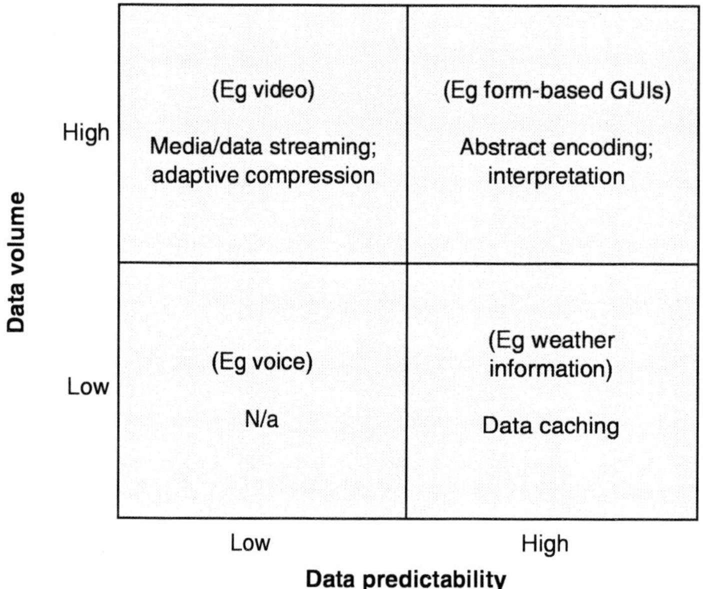

Source: Ovum (Pervasive Computing: Technologies and Markets/Chapter D)

D3 Personal communications applications

D3.1 What are personal communications applications?

We define personal communications applications as applications that provide unified interfaces to one or more of the following functions:

- voice communication management functions – for example, voicemail, call-back, call screening and conference calling
- e-mail
- unified messaging – the provision of a 'unified inbox' for voicemail, e-mail and fax messages
- 'instant' messaging.

We do not include basic telephony in our definition of personal communications applications.

Personal communications applications do not carry out one particular task, but enable users to manage their 'communications lives'. They do this by helping their users to access and use the personal communication services that are available to them more easily. A core capability of personal communications applications is that they are made available to users through high-level, easy-to-use interfaces – for example, via voice-activated 'personal assistants' for users accessing services via telephones, and via simple GUIs for those accessing services through data-centric devices.

D3.2 The state of the market

The market for personal communications applications is still in its infancy. Even though the first 'personal assistant' offering was launched by Wildfire in 1995, subscriber numbers increased slowly, due to a combination of technology expense and immaturity, and lack of initial demand (which was in turn due to the markets into which it was sold being immature and fast-growing themselves). This is now changing.

Personal communications application vendors are already moving towards supporting multiple delivery channels for their applications, through user interface extensions that are bundled together to form 'personal communications portals'.

Within a personal communications portal, individual interfaces, application functionality and additional information and services are selected and combined to meet the requirements of each user. Leading-edge personal communications portals are starting to support multiple delivery channels, and include:

- voice user interfaces (VUIs), which enable interaction with communications management services via a voice channel using interactive voice response (IVR) technology
- GUIs, which allow users to view a graphical (or multimedia) representation of their personal communications application from any web-enabled device
- cellular terminal microbrowsers, which enable interaction with communications management services via text-based menus.

D3.3 Application characteristics

Figure D3.1 shows the technology requirements of personal computing applications.

Security

Mainstream personal communications applications are unlikely to require very high security from either networks or application infrastructure. Once users have authenticated themselves through entry of a PIN or password, most applications then provide open access to communications management functions.

Reliability

Personal communications is the area where users have least tolerance to outages and technical problems. When people decide they need to communicate with others, they want to do so now. Interfaces to personal communications applications must therefore be highly reliable.

Not all elements of personal communications applications have to provide highly reliable infrastructure end-to-end, however. One of the benefits of e-mail systems (one of the applications within the domain of personal communications) is that they tend to cope well with unreliable environmental conditions.

Availability

As for *Reliability* above.

User interactivity and data dynamism

Few personal communications applications are highly interactive – interactions with them tend to be limited to brief 'conversations' (whether voice or data), and the information presented to users only changes when messages or calls arrive or are initiated/sent. Individual changes are unlikely to result in changes to large amounts of data – for example, voicemail playback generates only approximately 1.8kbit/s of data. However, users expect communication to be immediate.

Figure D3.1 **Personal communications applications – technology requirements**

Security	Low–medium
Reliability	High
Availability	High
User interactivity and data dynamism	Medium

Source: Ovum (Pervasive Computing: Technologies and Markets/Chapter D)

D3.4 Personal communications application delivery, 2001–2006

Today, personal communications applications are delivered both as products and as services. Many corporate implementations of unified messaging, for example, are implemented as PC-based products, whereas personal assistant and unified inbox applications are delivered as services to voice handsets over mobile networks and also to PC-based consumers over the Internet.

Availability of personal communications applications is currently limited to PCs and voice handsets, but, as shown in *Figure D3.2*, we expect that availability will increase over the next five years to include all the access platforms that we consider. However, applications will continue to be easiest to use on PCs and voice handsets.

By 2006, vendors and service providers will move towards delivering products and services that implement much tighter integration between different types of personal communications application through personal communication portals, including voice and data, realtime communications and store-and-forward messaging communications. In addition, leading portal suppliers will expand their personal communication portals to include provision of complementary services, such as calendaring and address book management, e-commerce and advertising.

Figure D3.2 **Personal communications applications, 2001–2006**

	2001–2002	2003–2004	2005–2006
PC	2	3	3
Voice handheld	2	3	3
PDA	n/a	2	2
TV	n/a	2	2
Car	1	2	2
Home appliances	1	1	2

Key: 1 = possible; 2 = usable; 3 = easy and compelling
Source: Ovum (Pervasive Computing: Technologies and Markets/Chapter D)

D4 E-commerce

D4.1 What is e-commerce?

Ovum defines e-commerce as:

The execution of electronic transactions that result in the transfer of value in exchange for information, services or goods.

This definition ignores the value of the 'wrapper' services that are starting to be offered, however – much of the value in e-commerce offerings to customers today resides in the ways in which products are packaged. Support services such as the information provided to the customer pre-sale (merchandising) and post-sale (support), customer service and personalisation are all examples of ways in which wrapper services provided by sellers can help to ensure a better match between buyers' requirements and sellers' abilities to meet them.

D4.2 The state of the market

Provision of an e-commerce application is perhaps the most heavily sold Internet opportunity. However, the business-to-consumer e-commerce market in particular is at a delicate stage – the combination of a vast influx of venture capital, poured in with the expectation of handsome returns, and overpowering levels of marketing hype, have brought the market to the edge of serious deflation. Venture capital and investment attention has moved on from web-based e-commerce ventures to mobile e-commerce ventures, leaving many dot.coms to fend for themselves without adequate financial support; there is now a significant likelihood that the mobile e-commerce market will also be hyped to the point of destruction. Few 'pure' e-commerce ventures have thus far managed to build self-sustainable businesses from their activities, but the dream is still far from over for the majority of business pioneers looking to provide e-commerce applications. Everyone still believes they can invent the 'killer application'.

The mobile e-commerce market is currently the area where there is most activity – but the market is still immature. The low cost of entry (relative to deploying an e-commerce application in a digital TV environment) and the increasing availability of most of the required base-level infrastructure is stimulating rapid growth in the number of mobile e-merchants and services providers. In these early stages of mobile e-commerce market development, most successful applications need to be easy to use and sufficiently compelling that they become a substitute to existing services in the market – despite the limitations of most current mobile data-capable devices.

Currently, successful mobile e-commerce applications fit most of the following criteria:

- the application is of high value to the player
- a low media output is required (for example, text messaging versus media streaming)
- low complexity of transaction and/or a minimal number of players involved in launching the service
- low security is required for a successful transaction.

Ovum estimates that the value of e-commerce transactions worldwide (through all mobile and fixed channels) will be $2.7 trillion by 2005.

D4.3 Application characteristics

Figure D4.1 shows the technology requirements of e-commerce applications.

Security

Transactions that involve the electronic transfer of money need to be protected by sophisticated security services. The actual need for data security and access security is proportional to the frequency or 'size' of transactions, but more important is the reassurance that security brings to application users. Consequently, the presence of user authentication and data encryption services is a prerequisite.

Reliability

E-commerce applications need to be highly reliable to be viable business tools. Applications that crash halfway through processing thousands of financial transactions may well leave thousands of customers unhappy and needing recompense.

Availability

Whilst e-commerce applications must be highly reliable, users' sensitivity to application availability may be less of a problem – certainly in comparison to personal communications applications, for example.

User interactivity and data dynamism

E-commerce transactions do not themselves make onerous demands on infrastructure due to their interactivity or the dynamism of the information they present. Service wrappers surrounding transactions, however, may make heavy use of animation, video and audio – all of which are data types that require large amounts of data to be presented to users in short periods of time.

Figure D4.1 **E-commerce applications – technology requirements**

Security	High
Reliability	High
Availability	Medium
User interactivity and data dynamism	Medium

Source: Ovum (Pervasive Computing: Technologies and Markets/Chapter D)

D4.4 E-commerce delivery, 2001–2006

In 2001, business-to-consumer e-commerce applications are principally delivered as network-based services rather than as applications. However, most suppliers of business-to-business e-commerce applications deliver product components within their solutions. The vast majority of business-to-consumer e-commerce applications are delivered within websites, through the fixed Internet to PCs. In some countries, business-to-consumer e-commerce applications are delivered as part of interactive TV services; limited business-to-consumer e-commerce applications are also being deployed to mobile cellular terminals.

As shown in *Figure D4.2*, we expect the availability of e-commerce applications to broaden across every access platform by 2006. However, research published in Ovum's report *Ovum Forecasts the Internet and E-commerce* indicates that the vast majority of this broadening of e-commerce access will be in the business-to-consumer domain, with the PC remaining the principal access device for business-to-consumer e-commerce applications.

The market for e-commerce applications is developing at different speeds in different geographical territories, for regulatory and business reasons as well as technology reasons.

The mobile e-commerce market, for example, will develop in three major waves, with the second wave (2000–2003) due to improved terminal capabilities and the third wave (2002–2005) due to improved network capabilities. 'T-commerce' (television e-commerce) will also develop in three waves, largely for the same reasons. In both these areas, security capabilities (and customers' increasing awareness of them) will enable the second and third waves of growth.

Figure D4.2 **E-commerce applications, 2001–2006**

	2001–2002	2003–2004	2005–2006
PC	2	3	3
Voice handheld	2	2	3
PDA	n/a	2	3
TV	2	3	3
Car	1	1	2
Home appliances	1	2	2

Key: 1 = possible; 2 = usable; 3 = easy and compelling

Source: Ovum (Pervasive Computing: Technologies and Markets/Chapter D)

D5 Infotainment

D5.1 What is infotainment?

'Infotainment' applications deliver digital information designed to inform and/or entertain users. This definition encompasses a wide range of applications, delivering different types of digital information in different formats (from text-only to full-motion video with stereo sound). Examples include:

- news and weather
- sports scores
- navigation aids
- games
- pre-recorded music
- passive entertainment – including soap operas, movies and radio plays.

Some people refer to infotainment applications as interactive services, but this is misleading – the range of infotainment applications includes some that demand a lot of user interaction and some that require none at all. The term 'interactive services' reflects the passive nature of the environment in which some of them operate – broadcast TV. In a 'traditional' broadcast context, such applications are distinguished from the other services provided because subscribers can choose whether and when to invoke them.

D5.2 The state of the market

There is no single infotainment market. Infotainment applications are the output of multiple media industries – with each industry geared around a particular 'physical' delivery channel (such as newspapers, movies, radio, music or TV). However, we are at the start of a media industry revolution, enabled by the growth of the Internet.

Media players specialise in producing and delivering information. In the physical world, the only way to cost-effectively deliver information is to broadcast it – so that everyone who is interested in the information receives the same thing. This is true today of all traditional media. However, the Internet – a global (almost) public digital network with lots of electronic media-reading devices attached to it – does three things to revolutionise traditional media industries:

- it makes information delivery very cheap
- it makes narrowcast and unicast delivery of information much more straightforward – and not much more expensive than broadcast delivery
- it stimulates evolution of computing platforms that make it easier and cheaper to produce the information in the first place.

These three things are lowering barriers to entry considerably, and are allowing new players to deliver more personalised applications than has so far been possible. Everything that media industries have historically held as vital assets are now commodities – bar the ability to produce high-quality content.

The evolution of digital media devices also means that media delivery channels are becoming smarter and more general-purpose, which in turn means that they are becoming less tied into delivering particular types of media. This poses both opportunities and challenges for many media owners – in fact, the challenges facing media companies represent a more focused version of the general challenges of pervasive computing.

Media players are only now starting to realise how important this is. They are dealing with it in two ways:

- the vast majority of players across different media delivery channels are looking to the Internet as a new delivery channel for *their* type of content
- large players (or consortia) are starting to buy into positions of power across multiple media delivery channels.

Ovum forecasts that, by 2006, there will be more than 260 million fixed broadband network connections worldwide, all of them capable of delivering complex multimedia entertainment applications. There will be more than 1.5 billion Internet terminals in use by this time – all of them capable of accessing some kind of infotainment application.

D5.3 Application characteristics

Figure D5.1 shows the technology requirements of infotainment applications.

Security

Delivery of infotainment applications requires the presence of information security services for one reason – to ensure that only people who are meant to receive and use a particular application or piece of content, do so.

Security technology implements control mechanisms that must be put into place for the following reasons:

- commercial – only people who have paid for the service can use it
- regulatory – only people over a particular age limit can use it (if the application contains adult content)
- legal – only people resident in a particular country can use it (if the application contains images that are banned in certain countries).

Figure D5.1 **Infotainment applications – technology requirements**

Security	High
Reliability	Medium
Availability	High
User interactivity and data dynamism	High

Source: Ovum (Pervasive Computing: Technologies and Markets/Chapter D)

Reliability

In comparison to e-commerce applications, infotainment applications do not need to be highly reliable. If some data is lost during transmission of a video stream over a network, for example, very little of the value of the service is lost to the consumer. Persistent reliability problems in most infotainment applications will be annoying to users, but will not affect them in any major way. There are exceptions, of course. Navigation applications that provide realtime directions to vehicle drivers, for example, will lose much of their value if data transmission is unreliable.

Availability

As with personal communications, users' expectations of infotainment applications transfer from the 'physical' world. In order for new network-based digital services to be adopted, they must be delivered in line with people's expectations. Outages of TV and radio broadcasts are rare and newspaper delivery is reliable; whilst service downtime in these analogue media are not likely to be life-threatening, people's expectations of service availability are high.

User interactivity and data dynamism

Information that is static, and applications that do not require interaction, tend not to be particularly informative or entertaining. The majority of infotainment applications either demand significant levels of user interactivity or present dynamic data to users. However, the volume of data changes that these characteristics entail depends on the type(s) of user interface being employed.

Some types of infotainment application (text-based ones in particular) do not generate large volumes of data to be rendered at the user interface. However, games and other types of application that make heavy use of animated graphics, high quality sound and full-motion video require large volumes of data to be rendered on a device every second. For example, a CD-quality stereo sound playback requires a device to render approximately 170kbit/s, and playback of a digitally sampled broadcast-quality PAL TV signal requires a device to render around 130Mbit/s.

D5.4 Infotainment delivery, 2001–2006

Infotainment applications are delivered to users through a wide range of delivery channels. Historically, most applications were delivered as products – the multimedia industry was founded and grew on the back of the CD-ROM product format. However, infotainment applications are leading the way in the transformation of applications from products to services: of all the types of infotainment application that are widely in use, the only type that is still delivered principally as a product is interactive gaming.

In general, the more interactive the application, the more restricted its availability. For example, information-based applications such as news, sport and weather are delivered (in different formats) through TV, radio, PCs attached to the fixed Internet, and mobile cellular terminals connected to digital wireless networks; most interactive games are today restricted to a smaller range of channels (most notably, dedicated games consoles and PCs).

Figure D5.2 **Infotainment applications, 2001–2006**

	2001–2002	2003–2004	2005–2006
PC	3	3	3
Voice handheld	1	2	3
PDA	1	2	3
TV	3	3	3
Car	1	2	2
Home appliances	1	1	2

Key: 1 = possible; 2 = usable; 3 = easy and compelling
Source: Ovum (Pervasive Computing: Technologies and Markets/Chapter D)

By 2006, pressures on media industries, combined with the greater reach of the Internet and improved capabilities in devices and access networks, will bring infotainment applications to more access platforms, via service rather than product delivery – as indicated in *Figure D5.2*. This increased penetration will be driven by three significant changes in the nature of infotainment applications:

- they will become more granular, due to pay-TV and pay-per-view service frameworks that are easier to buy and manage, and content that is easier to produce
- they will become more personalised, driven by increased ease of narrowcasting together with the commercial advantages of close customer targeting (principally for marketing and advertising reasons)
- they will blend increasingly with business-to-consumer e-commerce applications as they are used as 'hooks' to pull users into commerce services, and as increasingly granular payment schemes and programming become more widespread.

D6 Business applications

D6.1 What are business applications?

Ovum defines business applications as:

software applications that automate business processes.

Many business applications are business-critical; consequently, they are 'owned', operated and managed either by trained departments within businesses themselves or by trusted third parties.

The business-critical nature of these applications, together with the data that they manage, means that the blending of pervasive computing with business applications is not resulting in these applications being distributed out to different types of device; rather, *access to* these applications and data is being distributed. Consequently, applications tend to be partitioned into server software, which remains centrally managed, and client software, which is distributed to employees. Client software is delivered either statically (application client software is installed on employees' own devices) or dynamically (client software is downloaded on demand when application access is required, but does not reside on devices).

Some business applications are 'horizontal', in that they automate business processes that are common across multiple industries. Examples include salesforce automation, customer relationship management (CRM), accounting and human resources processes. Others are specialised within individual industries (for example, extraction simulation applications in the oil and gas industries).

Business applications that are being deployed in this way automate four types of business process:

- information publishing and distribution – for example, management reporting
- informal collaboration – for example, project management and knowledge management
- transaction-based – for example, customer service or helpdesk, order processing and payroll
- formal collaboration – for example, product design.

D6.2 The state of the market

In the world of business applications, the 'thin client' is king. Suppliers and customers of packaged business applications in particular fell foul of the client-server revolution of the early 1990s, which freed them from the confines of the mainframe computer, but tied them to inefficient, unmanageable installations of expensive computers. The Internet was seen as a facilitator of a standards-based renaissance of the centralised model of computing, and to some extent this is becoming more true. Most of the market-leading packaged business applications are now thin client applications that can be invoked from within a web browser.

The trend for thin client applications has also enabled another key trend – the application service provision (ASP) model of application delivery. ASP is still a relatively small part of the market, but its popularity is growing fast – particularly for relatively uncomplicated, but essential business applications, such as informal collaboration applications.

Of the four process types listed in *Section D6.1* that could be automated by business applications, formal collaboration processes are the least widely automated in practice. This is despite the wide availability of enabling technology – and is mostly due to negative perceptions of the complexity of the technology, and of the potential organisational impact that might be required. However, there is currently a resurgence of interest in the automation of formal collaboration processes, under the guise of business-to-business collaboration.

D6.3 Application characteristics

Figure D6.1 shows the technology requirements of business applications.

Security

Many business applications manage highly sensitive data on behalf of companies – consequently, external access to business applications needs to be tightly restricted. The need for user authentication and data encryption services is therefore strong.

Reliability

The importance of the data managed by many business applications means that not only must application access be tightly controlled – but that the integrity of application data must be protected by ensuring that the overall 'state' of the application does not get corrupted at any point. Whenever data is transmitted from one application component to another, data must not be lost or corrupted; when data is read from or written to a database management system (DBMS), these actions must also be carried out reliably. Corrupt or incomplete data has a habit of proliferating and making applications behave in unexpected ways.

Figure D6.1 **Business applications – technology requirements**

Security	High
Reliability	High
Availability	High
User interactivity and data dynamism	Low to medium

Source: Ovum (Pervasive Computing: Technologies and Markets/Chapter D)

Availability

Delivery of business applications is one area where expectations from the 'physical' world are not imposed. Users of business applications tend to be inured to occasional crashes, brown-outs and so on. However, the increasing penetration of e-business into the world of mainstream corporate IT means that existing business applications are increasingly forming the foundations for companies' own e-business operations. In this context, guaranteed application or service availability is a key competitive differentiator – and availability problems can mean business failure.

User interactivity and data dynamism

Business applications tend not to demand the same degree of user interactivity or data dynamism as infotainment applications. The overall set of data managed by an application may change rapidly if it manages a large set of data (for example, a flight reservation system), but in these cases it is unlikely that every user of the application needs to be appraised of every change to the data. Consequently, even though application data may change rapidly, application users do not see the majority of the changes as they happen. On the contrary, users of most business applications only see data that they explicitly request.

D6.4 Business application delivery, 2001–2006

The primary delivery mechanism for horizontal business applications is as a product delivered through PCs via a corporate LAN or WAN. However, innovation in vertical industries is increasingly driving out general availability of all types of business application to other types of delivery channel – in particular, to PDAs and mobile cellular terminals. The emerging ASP movement is starting to transform the delivery of certain types of business application from product-based to service-based models.

As shown in *Figure D6.2*, by 2006, access to business applications, driven by early adoption in certain vertical industries, will have broadened. Access via voice handheld devices and PDAs will be commonplace. Access will be available through other platforms, but use of these access platforms will be limited to tightly constrained usage contexts. The ASP model will thrive, and will also see increased take-up as a follow-on market from the increased corporate use of wireless network access service providers, which will help companies extend their applications to mobile devices.

Figure D6.2 **Business applications, 2001–2006**

	2001–2002	2003–2004	2005–2006
PC	3	3	3
Voice handheld	n/a	2	2
PDA	2	3	3
TV	n/a	1	2
Car	n/a	1	1
Home appliances	n/a	n/a	n/a

Key: 1 = possible; 2 = usable; 3 = easy and compelling
Source: Ovum (Pervasive Computing: Technologies and Markets/Chapter D)

D7 Device management

D7.1 What is remote asset management?

Ovum defines a remote asset management application as:

> *a software application that allows the owner of an 'intelligent' asset, or a designated third party, to remotely monitor the status of the asset, and remotely carry out management tasks on it when necessary.*

Some delivery channels (such as digital TV) employ devices that are required to enable applications and services, but which are not owned by application or service subscribers. In these cases service providers, rather than application subscribers, manage the devices. In cases where customers own the device, they may choose to manage it themselves or they may pay a service provider to manage it remotely for them.

Remote management of mobile cellular terminals and set-top boxes is a hot topic for wireless network operators and digital TV service providers respectively. However, there are other, less obvious targets for remote asset management. These include:

- vending machines
- cars
- people
- home security systems
- ticket machines
- EPOS (electronic point-of-sale) systems.

We exclude assets that operate in safety-critical environments and concentrate on 'mainstream' pervasive computing devices and home appliances.

D7.2 The state of the market

The remote asset management market is still in its infancy. Remote management of corporate IT networks and computer systems is widespread, but because 'smart' home appliances are still rare, the remote management of 'non-IT' smart assets is still the preserve of certain vertical industries rather than a general business consumer proposition. Even where the devices being managed participate in the delivery of consumer applications and services, it tends to be service providers in the telecommunications and digital broadcasting industries that manage the devices.

D7.3 Application characteristics

Figure D7.1 shows the technology requirements of remote asset management applications.

Figure D7.1 **Remote asset management applications – technology requirements**

Security	High
Reliability	High
Availability	Medium
User interactivity and data dynamism	Low

Source: Ovum (Pervasive Computing: Technologies and Markets/Chapter D)

Security

The prospect of insecure remote asset management raises the unattractive idea of anyone being able to monitor or manage something you own. Security is thus critical to remote asset management, both in terms of user authentication and authorisation frameworks, and encryption over the network (to ensure that commands are not hacked in transit by malicious third parties).

Reliability

As well as being highly secure, remote asset management applications must be highly reliable – application users cannot be faced with a situation where a management command becomes corrupted or lost in transit, or is erroneously processed.

Availability

High availability is less important than reliability and security in remote asset management applications. A temporary outage is unlikely to have any long-term material effect on the asset.

User interactivity and data dynamism

User interactivity and data dynamism within remote management applications will be low. The effect of high interactivity or high data dynamism on the overall performance of the device being managed (and the network that that connects the user to it) is too great to consider implementing such features for this type of application.

D7.4 Remote asset management delivery, 2001–2006

The primary delivery channel for remote asset management applications today (to the degree that they exist) is as software products that are hosted on servers, and accessed via LANs on PCs. Management products themselves use many different networks for communicating with individual remote assets – many use fixed IP networks, but wireless networks are increasingly being used. We are starting to see a trend away from management applications being delivered as products, towards their delivery as services. Management service providers (MSPs) are an emerging category of ASPs dedicated to providing technology management services. These services are typically delivered as web applications, over the fixed Internet to PCs.

As *Figure D7.2* shows, the widening availability of interactive websites will bring access to remote asset management applications to these places – in particular to PDAs and mobile cellular terminals. Remote asset management will be available on other access platforms, particularly management of consumer devices and other consumer-owned assets. However, the bulk of the activity – and the bulk of the innovation – will continue to be made available to the principal business tools of today and tomorrow – the PC, the voice handheld device and (to a lesser extent) the PDA.

The remote management of pervasive computing devices and other assets is set to become a very hot topic over the next three to five years. With worldwide deployment of set-top boxes estimated to reach more than 130 million worldwide by 2006, service providers in this segment alone will face significant operational challenges if they cannot monitor and manage their assets remotely. Systems management vendors are already delivering the first components of frameworks that will enable service providers and customers to manage their assets remotely, but even they recognise that demand for these products is not yet high. Suppliers are developing prototype solutions for pilot projects with service providers, but widespread deployment of solutions amongst service providers is unlikely before 2002.

Adoption of remote asset management solutions by end customers will be tied into purchases of new, 'smart' consumer products; whilst some products now reaching the market fit into this category, product replacement cycles (even in the context of hype-fuelled high-tech home appliance markets) dictate at least a 12-month lag before measurable demand occurs.

Figure D7.2 **Remote asset management applications, 2001-2006**

	2001–2002	2003–2004	2005–2006
PC	2	3	3
Voice handheld	2	3	3
PDA	n/a	2	2
TV	n/a	2	2
Car	1	2	2
Home appliances	1	1	2

Key: 1 = possible; 2 = usable; 3 = easy and compelling

Source: Ovum (Pervasive Computing: Technologies and Markets/Chapter D)

E Access platforms

E1 From dedicated to multi-purpose – a slow but steady evolution

Access platforms consist of the client device hardware, and networks, which provide the basic access infrastructure for pervasive computing applications. Access platforms are the 'seeds' of pervasive computing; they require the presence of other things to grow.

Access platforms have a symbiotic relationship to pervasive computing applications and services. Without the widespread deployment of some type of access platforms, applications and services cannot be delivered; but widespread take-up of access platforms will not occur unless compelling applications and services are readily available.

This chapter examines the access networks and devices that will be employed throughout the development of pervasive computing in the foreseeable future. It highlights important characteristics of those networks and devices that will contribute towards fulfilling application requirements; and it shows how the capabilities of devices will change over time.

E1.1 Access platforms: different, but becoming more similar

Whilst fixed networks and 'traditional' computing devices form highly capable access platform combinations, there is considerable variation in the capabilities of device and network components across the entire spectrum of pervasive computing access platforms – with mobile devices and networks providing the greatest challenges. The main factors that are limiting the capabilities of individual access platforms today are:

- the capability of wireless networks to support data services
- the fundamental limitations of broadcast networks
- the slow evolution of battery technology (relative to the pace of mobile device innovation).

Common technology issues in supporting applications

The variety that we see in access platform capabilities does not manifest itself in differences in platforms' suitability to particular applications. For when it comes to platforms' suitability to the delivery of particular applications, there are two almost universal issues that are not wholly addressed by platforms themselves – issues that can therefore only be addressed through the implementation of software infrastructure:

- controlling access to applications and data through security frameworks
- ensuring the reliability of transmission of application data and functionality across networks.

Differences in access platform capabilities do, however, affect the ways that the gaps between platform capabilities and application-technology requirements can be addressed. The more restricted the access network, the more information bandwidth must be optimised; but the more restricted the device, the less dynamic optimisation can be performed. The suitability of software infrastructure solutions to enhance quality-of-service is therefore highly dependent on the details of the access platform.

For example, reliability and security issues are being dealt with by implementations of the relatively lightweight WAP set of protocols (WTP, WSP and WTLS) in mobile wireless access platforms today; but reliability is being addressed in a more proprietary but heavyweight fashion by IBM (with its MQSeries Everyplace messaging middleware) on PDA platforms. Third-generation technology will bring significant mobile access speed improvements, but specialised streaming media and compression technologies will still need to be employed if subscribers are to be able to view the video clips that operators so often talk about.

Device differentiation: from technology limitations to usage contexts

The wide variation in access platform capabilities will continue, even when the current technology constraints are removed. Today, it is 'hard' constraints such as battery technology that limit the capability of particular devices; tomorrow it will be 'soft' constraints – primarily, the usage contexts in which people like to use devices – that will lead to variation in device capabilities and form factors. Device manufacturers are particularly keen to increase the level of commonality between different device types, in order to improve accessibility to digital information over networks. Many see this capability as being a key short- to medium-term differentiator in markets that are highly competitive.

Converged applications: there is no such thing as the specialised device

Many manufacturers talk of their pervasive computing devices as specialised appliances: but application convergence means that such an approach has fundamental limitations in the long term. Slowly but surely, devices are evolving from application-specialised objects into more open computing platforms. But as infotainment, e-commerce and personal communications applications in particular converge, device manufacturers will have to look to the overall requirements of the converged application space to determine the capabilities that next-generation devices must have.

The challenges are significant. The fact that broadcast networks work best when every subscriber wants the same information, means that devices used in conjunction with broadcast networks in particular must be designed to shoulder increasing degrees of the overall application-processing burden. When everyone gets everything, the delivery of specialised, aggregated sets of converged application components requires the bulk of that work to be carried out post-transmission, rather than pre-transmission.

E1.2 The danger of the open platform

Local personalisation is one example of a situation where significant processing has to be carried out on a device. There are others – for example, the implementation of software infrastructure that can enhance the quality of application delivery. These situations will be common in the deployment of pervasive computing access platforms over the coming years, and they present a tricky challenge for device and operating system manufacturers. Avoiding the problems of the PC platform is not just a matter of making devices easier to use: unless certain system features are 'locked down' in new devices, beneficial software infrastructure (such as a Java runtime environment, or a piece of streaming media middleware) may not work. We have already seen, with the PC, that where there is openness, users can configure their machines in ways that prevent certain types of application and content from being deployed.

E1.3 The road to network convergence

Carriers are set to gradually replace today's spaghetti mass of core network infrastructure with unified, IP-friendly, multiple class-of-service fibre backbones. That much is well-understood. But a similar, less dramatic shift is also coming to pass in access networks. This shift makes converged applications easier to deliver to users.

The increasing penetration of digital services over broadband access networks is allowing existing cable and copper infrastructure to be used much more efficiently. More and more, operators are installing infrastructure that allows them to deliver voice, data and video over the same wires (or through the same area of RF spectrum). Moreover, applications are converging in their use of transmission schemes. For example:

- rich-media Internet applications are slowly moving from unicast to multicast protocols
- sophisticated interactive TV services are bringing requirements for certain data to be unicast to particular subscribers, in tandem with other common elements broadcast.

The convergence of voice, video and data through digital network transmission is not the same thing as the emergence of uniform availability of broadband transfer speeds, however. In particular, increasing numbers of mobile operators are starting to move the development of broadband mobile services down their agendas. They fear that the high prices that they have paid for operating licences, might preclude the requisite infrastructure spend.

E1.4 Partnerships in access platform delivery are key

Software infrastructure technologies will help bridge the gaps between access platform capabilities and the demands of applications, but the most value will come from end-to-end technology solutions that are specialised to optimise quality-of-service for particular access platforms, and that integrate the functions of application server platforms, with infrastructure functions hosted on individual devices and in the network.

Success requires access platform suppliers to forsake the temptation to develop proprietary infrastructure solutions, and to work with best-of-breed solutions. This in turn means manufacturers must ensure that their products are open enough to stimulate partnerships – with the biggest and best. If standards are involved then all the better.

E1.5 Do not believe the hype

Two common misperceptions need to be debunked. The truth is as follows:

- the pervasive computing revolution will *not* kill the PC platform

  PCs are very widely deployed the world over and users are not about to get rid of them. Pervasive computing embraces many new types of computing platforms, but such platforms are not going to lure PC users into throwing away their investments overnight. In contexts where PCs are widely used, they will continue to be a hub around which other devices fit. Digital TV sets and varieties of voice-data hybrid handheld terminals will be the killer non-PC computing platforms over the next five years. But they will not replace the PC. Rather, it is likely that innovation in smart appliances will transfer to the PC community, making PCs more reliable, more secure and easier to use

- third-generation networks will bring only one-tenth of the data transfer speeds to mobile devices that are widely reported

  radio technology is not sophisticated enough to allow a 3G radio to be housed inside a traditional-sized handset – especially as it is highly likely that in order to provide true 3G capabilities (including roaming) a handset will have to employ multimode radio units.

E2 Access platform characteristics affect application availability

In *Chapter D*, we examined the applications that will play a key role in the development of pervasive computing, and highlighted the fundamental characteristics of those applications that drive technology requirements:

- reliability
- availability
- security
- user interactivity and data dynamism.

The characteristics of both the device and access network elements of access platforms bear on their ability to support applications' technology requirements. *Figures E2.1* and *E2.2* provide a summary of the key characteristics and way that they fulfil (or subvert) applications' requirements.

Figure E2.1 **Important device characteristics**

Characteristic	Description	Effects
Capability	Some combination of processing power, memory capacity and secondary storage (disk) capacity	Interactivity Ability to deploy infrastructure services
Battery life	Only important for devices that must carry their power around with them	Availability
Connectivity	For example, wireless data, LAN or PSTN	Interactivity
Openness	Is it easy and cheap for third parties to build applications that address the device?	Availability of applications Reliability (negative) Security (negative)
Security	Facilities within the device for securing access to data and functions	Security
Cost	Cost per device unit	Take-up

Figure E2.2 **Important network characteristics**

Characteristic	Description	Effects
Data transfer speed	The sustained data transfer rate that the network can offer, in real-world deployment, per application session	Interactivity
Symmetry	The degree to which the network can support symmetrical data traffic (the same volume of data passing from A to B as from B to A in the same period)	Interactivity
Reach	The percentage of a country's population that can access the network	Availability Reliability
Openness	The level of support for IP data traffic	Interactivity
Cost	Cost to user or service provider of sending data	Interactivity Take-up

E2.1 How do device characteristics affect application availability?

Device capability

The capability of a particular device is a measure of the capacity of the device for receiving, processing and rendering digital information. Obviously the processing capability of a device depends on more than the clock speed and complexity of the CPU itself; the amount of RAM, and the secondary (non-volatile) storage capacity of the device are also important.

Without a certain degree of capability, devices will not be able to support highly-interactive applications. There are trade-offs, of course. Improvements in device capabilities all tend to have negative effects on device power usage, form factor and cost.

Device battery life

Battery life is only important where devices are mobile and do not have any external power source. Importantly, however, devices operating under these constraints are likely to become the most common computing platforms over the next five years. Unfortunately, battery technology is not improving as fast as device innovations and their demands for power.

The more processing a device does, the faster the battery drains. Implementations of user interfaces are particularly power-hungry – as are wireless radios. If battery-powered devices run out of power, they cannot deliver applications to users.

Device connectivity

The type(s) of network that any given device can connect to will dictate the types of application that it can support, since network characteristics place important constraints on applications (see *Section E4*). For example, if a device can only connect to circuit-switched networks, highly-interactive applications are likely to require additional support from software infrastructure service to ensure that the time taken to create a data connection does not affect the application.

Device openness

If a particular device is 'closed', it does not freely expose interfaces that allow third parties to take advantage of its features. Conversely, an 'open' device can be targeted by third-party software and hardware companies, without those companies having to pay high prices for access to private, proprietary interfaces. Device manufacturers implementing open interfaces are more likely to garner third-party support than manufacturers of closed devices – unless the latter are very powerful companies with large market share, in which case third parties will bow to commercial pressures, even if the technology indicates otherwise.

The unwelcome downside of a truly open device is the increased risk of application unreliability and security problems, due to accidental interactions between installed software components, and the possible introduction of viruses. An open device makes it easier to write any kind of software – not just benevolent software.

Device security

Devices can directly fulfil applications' security requirements – to some extent. Security is about much more than encryption of data prior to its transmission over a network; it also includes the ability to prevent unauthorised access to device functions.

Device cost

End users may not have to pay for devices themselves: in some cases (as with mobile phones in certain countries) devices are subsidised by network operators or service providers; in other cases (as with set-top boxes in some countries) devices are owned wholly by service providers. However, high unit costs will always inhibit take-up of a device; even if a service provider buys the device, they will need to recoup that capital investment through some other route – most likely through increasing subscription costs for users or through increased use of advertising (which may provoke negative user responses).

E2.2 How do network characteristics affect application availability?

Network data transfer speed

Data transfer speeds are one of the most misreported and misunderstood areas of network technologies – particularly when it comes to wireless and mobile networks. Theoretical data transfer speeds quoted for particular network technologies are never reached. In some cases the real transfer speed achieved may be less than 10% of the theoretical maximum. In our discussions of different network technologies and services, we emphasise likely real-world data transfer speeds, rather than theoretical maxima. We focus on the speed of downstream data transfer; our discussions of symmetry offer an idea of upstream capacities.

The faster the rate at which a network can transfer from one host to another, in real-world deployment, will determine the level of user interactivity that can be supported within applications running over that network. The more dynamic the data that is presented by an application, the more important data transfer speed becomes. Even if rich media are not employed in an application user interface, data throughput may be high. For example, an application might refresh certain data for each user every tenth of a second.

Rich-media interfaces are likely to be the prime swallowers of data capacity, however. It takes vastly differing volumes of information to represent different types of application user interface:

- telephone-quality voice playback utilises 1.8kbits/sec of information
- CD-quality stereo-audio playback utilises 170kbits/sec of information
- PAL-format video playback utilises 130Mbits/sec of information.

Software infrastructure technologies such as adaptive compression can reduce the data transfer rates that are required to deliver audio and video – but they will only work on devices that have sufficient processing capacity.

Network symmetry

Different applications make very different demands on networks downstream (central application host to device), than they do upstream (device to application). An important element of application interactivity is the degree to which users must drive changes in application behaviour and in the information managed by the application; consequently the more interactive an application, the more network symmetry becomes a requirement.

Network reach

We consider the reach of a type of network as a measure of the proportion of a target population that it can reach. The reach of a particular type of network will dictate its suitability for certain types of application. Reach (or coverage) is particularly important when delivering applications over mobile networks. If a mobile application user moves to a location with poor radio reception during an application session, data could become corrupted or lost en route – and even though network protocols may detect and correct these errors, the act of error detection and data re-send slows the real-world achievable data transfer rate.

Network openness

By openness, we mean the degree to which a particular network supports IP traffic. In keeping with this definition, a network is completely open if it can support IP transmission without a service provider having to layer any specialised bridging protocols onto the basic network service in order to support IP traffic. The more layers of protocols that need to be interposed, the less open the network is.

Openness has an indirect effect on the levels of user activity and data dynamism that a network can support in any given application. The more additional protocols that are required to support IP, the more handshaking that will need to occur – which means longer IP connection times, and slower IP packet transmission.

Network cost

The cost of sending or receiving data over a network will be a significant determinant of that type of network's adoption as a vehicle for pervasive computing. The simplistic view is that transmission costs are directly related to of the original network-build cost and the ongoing operational cost of the network – because operators must be able to recoup their investments (and more) if they are to continue to provide services. However, increasingly, public network operators are looking to other sources of revenue, as competition is forcing down the prices they can charge for data transmission.

This argument works for public networks, where operators can charge their customers for other higher level services such as portals, and also charge advertisers for space on those portals (for example) – but the same does not apply to private networks, which are bought and operated by end-user companies. Here, cost is cost – it cannot be recouped by charging third parties or by subsidy through advertising.

E2.3 There is wide variety in access platform capabilities, but...

Particular pervasive computing access platforms – combinations of devices and networks – have different sets of characteristics, which strongly influence the types of application that they can support. However, the degree of variation in access platforms themselves does not create huge variation in the applicability of a range of common access platforms to our range of pervasive computing applications. The capabilities of individual access platforms will dictate that the implementation details of how they can be made to be suitable for delivery of particular applications will be widely varied; but the key issues are broadly universal.

To illustrate, *Figure E2.3* maps the current capabilities of some common access platforms (as set out in *Sections E4* and *E5*) to the technology requirements of our range of applications. It highlights three important technology challenges:

- the requirement for application security is almost universally not met by access platforms. The exception is access platforms that use set-top box devices. These devices are designed to implement access control mechanisms that control access to certain broadcast programmes, which are encrypted for transmission (pay-TV and pay-per-view events)

- access platform support for applications that demand high reliability is also almost universally poor – principally due to one of two factors: the openness of some devices; and the current unreliability of mobile networks as data bearers
- satellite and terrestrial broadcast networks cannot, by themselves, support interactive applications – there is no 'return path' to allow upstream communication.

Figure E2.3 **Examples of current gaps between platforms and applications**

	Personal communications	**E-commerce**	**Infotainment**	**Business applications**	**Remote asset management**
PC/xDSL	Reliability Security	Reliability Security	Security	Reliability Security	Reliability Security
Voice handset/ wireless mobile	Reliability Availability Interactivity	Reliability Availability Security Interactivity	Reliability Availability Security Interactivity	Reliability Availability Security Interactivity	Reliability Availability Security
Set-top box/ satellite	Interactivity	Interactivity	Interactivity	Interactivity	Interactivity
PDA/ wireless mobile	Reliability Availability Interactivity	Reliability Availability Security Interactivity	Reliability Availability Security Interactivity	Reliability Availability Security Interactivity	Reliability Availability Security
Car/wireless mobile	Reliability Availability Interactivity	Reliability Availability Security Interactivity	Reliability Availability Security Interactivity	Reliability Availability Security Interactivity	Reliability Availability Security
Network consumer goods/cable	Reliability Security	Security	Reliability Security	Reliability Security	Reliability Security

E3 Critical success factors for access platforms

There are three critical success factors that must be addressed by device manufacturers and network operators in order for access platforms to play as a 'first-class citizen' in the pervasive computing revolution:

- a reliable, secure platform foundation
- sufficient capability on the device to host, and device openness to, third-party infrastructure software
- a focus on developing partnerships with software infrastructure providers, not application/content providers.

E3.1 Creating reliable, secure platforms

Access platforms must address two main 'hygiene' factors – reliability and security – in order for users to persevere. Without a baseline solution that is reliable enough and secure enough, an access platform will never become popular.

Pervasive computing takes applications and services, through networks, to devices that have not previously been seen as computing platforms, and to users who have not had extensive experience of using personal computers or any network apart from their PSTN. Access platforms must therefore behave more like household appliances than computers.

The familiarity of pervasive computing devices is creating user expectations that infrastructure suppliers, device manufacturers and network operators are left to fulfil, including:

- when I supply power to a device, it will immediately be ready to carry out work for me
- it will not go wrong too often
- when it does go wrong, I will detect an outwardly physical symptom of the problem (a burning smell, for example)
- if there is a danger that it has been tampered with, I will not use it.

If pervasive computing is to be successful, applications and services delivered to users via pervasive computing technology must live up to as many of these expectations as possible. It is not just platforms themselves that contribute to addressing these issues, however: the software infrastructure that runs on devices has to conform to users' reliability and security expectations.

Device designers must walk a tightrope. They must replicate the positive characteristics of PCs, in order to make devices smart enough to deliver multiple applications and services; but they must address users' concerns over security and reliability too.

Moreover, these concerns can only be addressed through partnerships with the right software infrastructure suppliers, which can implement functionality that helps avoid problems of complexity and unreliability.

One of the problems of delivering applications to PCs over the Internet is that PCs' openness and complexity makes it almost impossible for an application provider or service provider to determine what kind of software infrastructure resides on the client. Moreover, users can choose not to allow new capabilities to be downloaded – even if they are required to boost the quality-of-service. Device designers must therefore make new devices as smart as PCs, but they must also ensure that certain vital software infrastructure facilities can be secured, so that they can be guaranteed as always available.

What are suppliers providing?

The primary software layer through which platform reliability and security are delivered is the operating system. Some device operating systems are more reliable, and confer more high-reliability services on applications, than others. Companies such as QNX and WindRiver specialise in delivering highly-reliable, small-footprint embeddable realtime operating systems that are suitable for pervasive computing access platforms. Symbian too claims that its EPOC system is highly reliable. However, the highest-profile platform player – Microsoft – is in an interesting situation because the market perception of its products is that they are not particularly reliable, secure or simple in their construction.

Many of the more 'heavyweight' operating systems that are suitable for pervasive computing access devices are starting to be shipped with optional security libraries that can be installed if required (the PalmOS platform is one notable exception here). There is also an emerging trend in the embedded operating-system market (driven by the capabilities of the Java runtime platform) to have software libraries (such as security libraries) downloadable to devices at runtime.

E3.2 Hosting software infrastructure

Applications' technology requirements that cannot be fulfilled by devices and basic access network services must be fulfilled by software infrastructure services that can improve the quality-of-service of application delivery; otherwise some applications will not be supportable on particular platforms. Of course, for this route to be viable, devices must have enough capability to run the kind of software infrastructure components that can enhance the delivery quality of applications.

Few operating systems address some applications' requirements for high levels of application reliability, however. Most operating system suppliers seem to believe that if they implement TCP correctly, their job is done. Infrastructure vendors such as IBM, Oracle, Sybase and Centura (in the business application domain) and OpenTV, RealNetworks and Liberate (in the infotainment domain) provide software components that work with popular platforms of different kinds, to improve application reliability; but these can only work where access platforms have a certain degree of capability. Thus far, the vast majority of voice handsets are excluded from this community.

Infotainment, e-commerce and personal communications applications in particular are starting to converge; consequently, the technology requirements that access platforms must fulfil in order to support users' activities are becoming supersets of those of individual applications – as shown in *Figure E3.1*.

When we combine this trend with the understanding that the capabilities of different access platforms have profound effects on implementation details, we see that the range of techniques that the software infrastructure supplier community must implement (and which device manufacturers must build support for) is set to broaden considerably.

E3.3 Partnerships with infrastructure suppliers

It is software infrastructure platforms, which span the application delivery channel from application server to access platform, that will form the operating environments for pervasive computing applications; not raw access platforms themselves. But no single device manufacturer has enough market power to dictate that application and service providers use its own proprietary software infrastructure solutions.

Indeed, the drivers for pervasive computing legislate against such power being wielded. If device manufacturers try to force application and service providers to use their own proprietary infrastructure solutions, then users of access platforms based on those devices will only be able to access subsets of applications that are sanctioned by the device manufacturer. The application providers will have to develop their assets to work with multiple software infrastructure solutions, in order to reach the widest possible audience. It is therefore in neither community's interests to pursue the proprietary infrastructure route.

Figure E3.1 **Converging applications means tougher technology requirements**

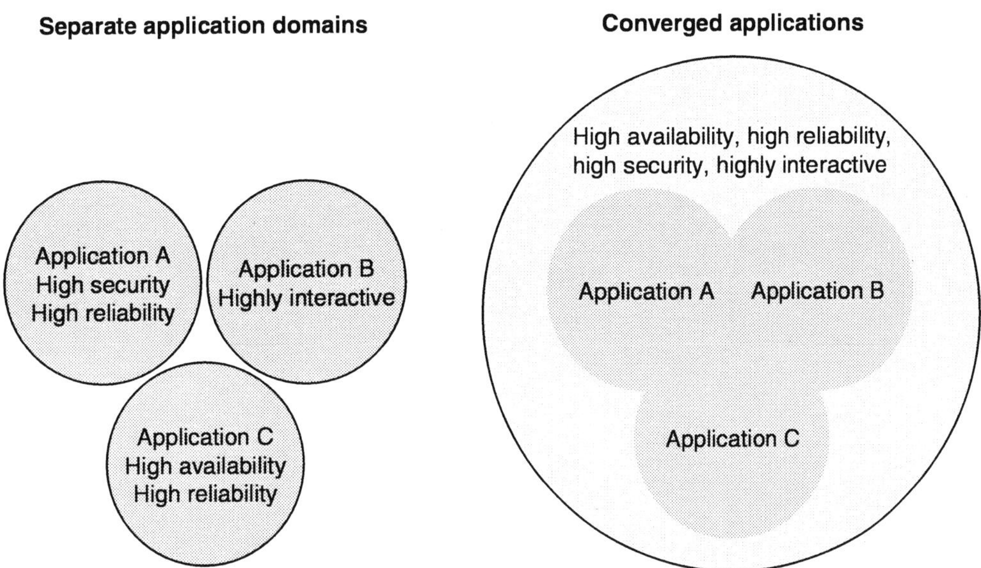

Source: Ovum (Pervasive Computing: Technologies and Markets/Chapter E)

As well as making devices capable enough to run quality-enhancing software infrastructure, therefore, device manufacturers also need to engineer a certain level of openness into their products, to encourage the porting of best-of-breed infrastructure solutions. Devices that are not capable of hosting software infrastructure components, or that are too closed to stimulate third-party innovation, will be marginalised from the pervasive computing revolution.

Device manufacturers must not adopt 'build it, and they will come' market positions, however. Palm Computing, as the undisputed market-leading PDA manufacturer, is perhaps the only device manufacturer that can currently afford that kind of attitude. Software infrastructure vendors such as IBM and Oracle have been queuing up to port their products to the Palm platform. Still, RealNetworks has resisted a Palm port of its market-leading streaming media infrastructure thus far, claiming the platform is not yet capable enough.

Software infrastructure suppliers have plenty of potential partners to choose from in the device manufacturer community; the development of the pervasive computing market means that the truth is much more like 'partner aggressively, or they will go elsewhere'.

E4 Computing devices, 2001–2006

Device and appliance manufacturers are being driven to innovate by intense competition and creeping commoditisation – and the chief way in which they are doing so is by making their products smart and connected, so that they can deliver value-added e-services.

Quite apart from market development factors concerning the availability of compelling applications and software infrastructure, there are three key 'local' factors that will affect the development and uptake of pervasive computing devices between 2001 and 2006:

- the current maturity of the device market
- the ability of battery technology to maintain pace with the desire of device manufacturers to innovate
- the desire of service providers to subsidise the cost of devices to end users.

The PC market is already mature; we consequently expect relatively little change to occur in this market – apart from incremental increases in device capability. However the markets for voice handsets (particularly smartphones), connected PDAs and set-top boxes are still in their infancy – and the market for networked home appliances is only now being created with the launch of a few early, expensive and functionally limited products.

The capability and evolution of battery technology is a major issue for manufacturers of personal mobile devices that must have their power sources attached. Motorola has created a next-generation fuel cell technology that promises to vastly improve battery capacities; but we anticipate that this will take at least three years to come to market. Until then, we anticipate that the capabilities of personal mobile devices will be constrained by battery technology. Innovation in this sector is likely to actually reduce battery lives during 2002 and 2003.

Low-end devices that are already associated with the delivery of particular network services (particularly voice handsets and digital TV set-top boxes) are prime candidates for end-user cost subsidisation by service providers. However, through ongoing device manufacturers' innovation, we are already starting to see two-tier business models being created in these markets:

- low-end models are provided wholesale to service providers, which then subsidise the cost to end users
- high-end models are increasingly sold to consumers direct, or through retailers – because they cost too much to make subsidy an attractive proposition for service providers.

This mixed model creates challenges for device manufacturers if they want to take part in the pervasive computing revolution. In order to sell high-end devices that are capable of accessing multiple applications (and certainly converged applications), they will have to create compelling value propositions for their high-end products that justify the cost to the consumer.

Figures E4.1 to *E4.3* provide a summary of how the capabilities of major device types will change between 2001 and 2006.

Figure E4.1 **Computing device capabilities, 2001–2002**

	Capability	Battery life	Connectivity	Openness	Security	Cost
PC	5	N/A	3	5	1	1
Set-top box	3	N/A	4	3	4	4
Home appliance	2	N/A	2	1	1	1
Voice-centric handheld	1	4	3	2	3	4
PDA	2	3	1	2	1	3
In-car system	3	N/A	2	2	1	2

Key: 1 = very poor; 2 = poor; 3 = medium; 4 = good; 5 = very good
(For cost, a higher score means a lower cost)

Figure E4.2 **Computing device capabilities, 2003–2004**

	Capability	Battery life	Connectivity	Openness	Security	Cost
PC	5	N/A	4	5	1	3
Set-top box	5	N/A	4	3	4	3
Home appliance	3	N/A	3	2	1	2
Voice-centric handheld	3	3	4	3	4	4
PDA	4	3	3	3	2	3
In-car system	4	N/A	3	3	1	3

Key: 1 = very poor; 2 = poor; 3 = medium; 4 = good; 5 = very good
(For cost, a higher score means a lower cost)

Figure E4.3 **Computing device capabilities, 2005–2006**

	Capability	Battery life	Connectivity	Openness	Security	Cost
PC	5	N/A	4	5	1	3
Set-top box	5	N/A	4	4	4	3
Home appliance	4	N/A	3	3	2	4
Voice-centric handheld	3	4	4	4	4	4
PDA	4	4	4	4	2	3
In-car system	4	N/A	4	3	2	3

Key: 1 = very poor; 2 = poor; 3 = medium; 4 = good; 5 = very good
(For cost, a higher score means a lower cost)

E4.1 Fixed devices

PCs, DTVi set-top boxes and networked home appliances have two important common attributes:

- device size is not an issue
- neither is power consumption.

A lack of constraints on form factor and power consumption means that device manufacturers are free to make their devices as sophisticated and capable as they like.

PCs and networked home appliances differ from digital TV set-top boxes, in that PCs and networked home appliances tend to be used by one person at any one time, whereas digital TV reception equipment will tend to have more group-oriented usage patterns. But this usage difference is largely due to the types of application that have been delivered on the different devices, rather than any particular attributes of the devices themselves. Moreover, design considerations that arise from these usage differences tend to affect the operating system and user interface software deployed on devices, more than device hardware.

PCs

Personal computers are the most widely-used form of computing device – Ovum estimates that there are approximately 400 million PCs in use worldwide. They have evolved from their introduction in the early 1980s to be high-powered, multipurpose computing tools. However, they are clearly not suited to everyone and every type of activity: the flip-side of their sophistication is a high degree of complexity in use, and a lack of reliability.

Capability

A typical high-specification PC includes a 700MHz CPU, 256MB of primary storage (RAM), and perhaps 10GB of secondary storage (on SCSI-connected hard disks). Many will also ship with powerful video accelerator cards that can render enormously complex graphics at upwards of 30 frames per second, and drive sophisticated digital audio subsystems into the bargain. Some desktop PCs are more powerful than the supercomputers of ten years ago.

Moore's Law (the doubling of transistor density every 18 months) has held true for the development of PCs over the past 15 years. This has not led to a correspondingly exponential growth in overall processing capability, however. In today's mainstream CPU architectures, each innovation brings more design complexity and less improvement in capability. In the short-to-medium term, however, PC capabilities will continue to advance at least as fast as software companies can think of ways of using up the available power.

Battery life

Not applicable.

Connectivity

Few new PCs now ship to consumers without pre-installed 56K analogue modems for connecting to a PSTN, or to business users without 100MB Ethernet LAN connectivity cards. More currently exotic connectivity options (such as cable modems) are possible, but not generally provided out-of-the-box by PC manufacturers.

Cable modems are available today, but they are insecure and expensive. xDSL connectivity requires an Ethernet card to be installed in the PC, but these are cheap compared to cable modems.

Openness

Modern PCs are open, in that PC hardware is entirely independent of the services and applications that run on them. The separation between hardware and applications is provided by an operating system layer, implemented in software. Applications and higher-level services are also implemented in software. Consequently, almost every behavioural aspect of a PC is dictated by configurable, upgradeable software, rather than a pre-built, static hardware platform.

With respect to developing applications for the PC platform, there are no cross-industry supported *de jure* standards to speak of (Java comes close, but in truth its support is not universal). However, the Microsoft/Intel standard has become the *de facto* standard system architecture for PCs. Development tools for Microsoft/Intel systems in particular are readily available – in some cases for no cost. Such is the market position of Microsoft.

Since the early 1990s, IP has been the networking *lingua franca* of the PC platform. All Microsoft's operating system flavours implement full IP stacks.

Security

Mainstream PC hardware units themselves are not engineered to be secure; they are engineered to be open, and implementation of security features is left to software infrastructure suppliers. This is unlikely to change.

Cost

It is possible to buy the typical high-specification PC outlined above for approximately $2,000. Bulk orders often attract significant discounts.

Competition is, and will continue to be, fierce in the PC manufacturing industry – which is resulting in improved price:performance ratios of PC systems. Moreover, the same technology advances that have enabled recent improvements in system performance, have enabled budget PC manufacturers to come to market with less high-powered (but still very capable) systems for approximately $500.

Set-top boxes

Set-top boxes are rapidly evolving from simple receivers for digital TV signals into full PC-like computing platforms. A simple set-top receiver acts rather like a combination of a modem and a video adapter, decoding and rendering digital audio and video signals on analogue CRT systems. It contains the following components:

- a decoder, which decompresses incoming digital signals, and splits them into audio, video and control data streams
- digital-to-analogue conversion modules, which control the actual screen and audio amplification equipment
- a conditional access module, which ensures that only certain signals can be decoded at any particular time by a particular receiver – mostly to ensure that only subscribers that have paid to access a particular service or piece of content, get to access it.

In simple digital TV receivers, all these modules reside in hardware. However the new generation of set-top boxes are more like PCs, in that they are based on distinct software-based operating systems that enable enhanced TV and truly interactive applications and services to be dynamically deployed to subscribers. Moreover, advanced set-top boxes employ secondary storage in order to cache content and applications.

Capability

Set-top boxes are not designed to be multipurpose computing tools. However, they are rapidly becoming as powerful as PCs. For example, Motorola/ General Intrument's DCT-5000+ 'Advanced Interactive Digital Consumer Terminal' has a 300+ MIPS processor, 32-bit 2D/3D graphics processor, and integrated DOCSIS-compliant cable modem, 14+MB of primary memory storage and an optional 1GB IDE hard disk drive. The box can also ship (if a service provider so desires) with PCMCIA-based smartcard interface for conditional access authentication, a Firewire port and many other interesting extras.

Set-top boxes are only going to become more capable over time. What will constrain their capability is the design goal of ensuring device reliability and availability – and hence restricting the complexity of application or service installation; and the level of access that applications and services will have to hardware facilities.

Battery life

Not applicable.

Connectivity

Set-top boxes are generally shipped with built-in connectivity to one kind of network – whether cable, satellite, xDSL or terrestrial broadcast. Increasingly, however, set-top box manufacturers are designing modular products that isolate network connectivity and demodulation functions from other device capabilities.

Openness

API standardisation efforts for set-top box operating systems have been restricted to particular geographical regions. Consequently, we have ATSC and ATVEF in North America; DVB in Europe and ARIB in Japan. However HTML and Java technologies are both making inroads into the strategic plans of operating-system manufacturers. By 2002/2003, we will see widespread availability of JavaTV implementations within set-top boxes – with the exception of Microsoft's implementations, which are likely to remain 'Java-free zones'.

Thus far, the interactive digital TV application and service market has been too specialised and niche to interest mainstream development tool vendors; consequently most application development is still done without the aid of sophisticated automated tool support and without high-level, standardised APIs. Companies such as 4DL and OpenTV are attempting to change this; but Microsoft's strategy of supporting the same languages, tools and architectures across all of its platforms means that despite the proprietary nature of its solution, development skills for set-top box platforms are likely to become widely available from the Microsoft camp before they become widely available elsewhere.

Security

Set-top boxes' conditional access modules provide potentially generic data and function security frameworks. They are currently employed to impose access controls on encrypted broadcast programmes, but there is nothing to stop an application supplier working with conditional access infrastructure suppliers to enable their applications to use set-top boxes' inbuilt security features.

Cost

Oracle states that in order to run the kinds of software required to support fully interactive services, advanced set-top boxes cost between \$500 and \$600. Consequently the cost to the consumer tends to be subsidised (to varying degrees) by the interactive services provider.

Costs are likely to continue on a steep path downwards. Service providers have high expectations of investment returns gained from transaction royalties and advertising revenues from 't-commerce' (television e-commerce). In addition, manufacturing costs will fall as volumes ramp up.

Networked home appliances

'Networked home appliances' is an umbrella term for home appliances that are connected to some kind of network in order to deliver information services and software applications to their users. Examples of these already exist: LG Electronics' Internet fridge and Internet washing machine may sound fanciful but they are already being sold in Korea; and Whirlpool and Electrolux are both rolling out network refridgerators too.

Suppliers envisage networked home appliances as platforms that offer value-added e-services along with basic products.

Capability

The computing devices that are embedded in networked home appliances are, and will continue to be, based on existing devices that are designed for delivery of interactive applications into the home. Manufacturers are primarily building their devices using embedded PDA and PC technology; however there is no reason why, in future, these devices cannot be based on set-top box technology.

Battery life

Not applicable.

Connectivity

There are many ways in which manufacturers can connect networked home appliances to the Internet. Most are building strategies that involve communication via a central home network gateway – a device that acts as a router for a local network of home devices, and as a combined firewall/ network server to enable access to the 'outside world'. LG's Internet washing machine, for example, currently connects to the Internet via a PC using a serial link. However, the company has its own home network gateway product in development. Connectivity to home network gateways is being developed along three paths:

- wireline Ethernet
- Bluetooth and other wireless LAN technologies
- powerline connectivity.

Openness

The first wave of networked home appliances is highly proprietary and closed. However, a major driving force in this emerging market is the Open Services Gateway Initiative (OSGI) – a supplier consortium advocating a Java-based home network gateway platform based on an open specification, that provides two-way interfaces to individual appliances.

Security

Early indications suggest that networked home appliance manufacturers are addressing security issues in two ways:

- firstly, by being cautious in the degree to which they make their device platforms open
- secondly, by mandating only indirect Internet connectivity (via some kind of intermediate home network gateway).

Security will become more of a focus for manufacturers as they make their products more capable and open.

Cost

Networked home appliances are barely beyond the concept-demonstrator stage. The proprietary nature of a lot of the technology in today's generally-available devices, combined with the lack of competition, means that manufacturers are selling them at considerable premiums over their 'regular' products.

E4.2 Mobile devices

PDAs, voice-centric handhelds and in-car systems have two important common attributes:

- a tension between the need for capability and the form factor/user interfaces that are viable, due to the contexts in which these devices will be used
- a need for connectivity to remote content, applications and services via wireless mobile networks.

Battery life is a key issue for PDAs and voice-centric handhelds, in which power supplies must be integrated with the devices themselves. However it is much less of an issue for in-car systems, where power is essentially 'on tap'.

PDAs

Personal digital assistants (PDAs) are data-centric (rather than voice-centric) handheld devices, optimised for delivering data applications to users via a screen (for output) and either a miniaturised keyboard or a touch-sensitive pad (for input).

Form factor is highly important in the PDA market. Screen size and resolution are key differentiating characteristics with respect to other types of mobile handheld device. Current PDAs do not incorporate voice communication functionality, although there is a general move in that direction. For example, Nokia's Communicator integrates data capabilities with voice communication. The big players in this market such as Palm and Psion are not yet incorporating voice.

Capability

The bulk of PDAs currently in use are limited-function, specialised devices optimised for delivering PIM applications. However, PDAs are evolving rapidly – driven by improvements in hardware, battery and display technology. Leading-edge PDAs are much more like full-function PCs in terms of capability. For example, Compaq's new iPAQ handheld computer uses a 200+MHz Intel StrongARM RISC processor, a colour display capable of rendering 4096 colours, 32MB of RAM and 16MB of secondary ROM storage on flash memory (from which the operating system boots).

Battery life

Battery lives of PDAs vary widely, depending on the sophistication of the hardware that is implemented. Restricted-function PDAs (Palm V devices, for example) forsake advanced multimedia features in order to minimise power consumption – certainly, batteries on these devices can last more than 12 hours between recharges. Other devices (such as the Compaq iPAQ) implement those advanced multimedia features – at the expense of battery life. Some users report batteries lasting fewer than five hours on devices utilising advanced multimedia features.

Over the next two years, increased deployment of integrated wireless connectivity is likely to degrade, not improve, the overall battery life of PDAs. This situation will be remedied by 2004–2005; but only if poor battery performance of new devices does not invoke a user backlash in the meantime.

Connectivity

Network connectivity in the PDA market is a 'patchwork quilt' of options and availability. For example:

- most deployed PDAs connect to other devices and external information sources via a serial link connected to a PC or via an infra-red link
- Palm Computing's Palm VII ships with integrated wireless connectivity, but this is hardwired to BellSouth's mobile network and therefore does not work outside major metropolitan areas of the US
- new devices from companies such as Compaq – and new peripherals from other vendors such as Palm – provide wireline data connectivity via add-on PSTN modems, and wireless connectivity via add-on wireless modems.

During 2001/2002, network connectivity (both wireline and wireless) will become much more widely deployed with PDAs. Cradle-based and infra-red data connectivity will continue to be provided, however, as transfer speeds through these conduits mean that they continue to offer the most sensible way of downloading relatively static applications, content and services to these devices. Wireless connectivity in particular is likely to be used to enable applications, content and services to be refreshed periodically with more dynamic elements.

Openness

Despite the increases in PDA capabilities. The majority are far less open than PCs. For example, in many of the most sophisticated PDAs, the operating system and core application suite is burned into ROM – which means that an operating system or core application upgrade requires a new flash memory card.

Security

There are no mainstream PDA devices that implement security features by themselves. PDA manufacturers work in partnership with software infrastructures to provide access control and data encryption features. For example, Microsoft's PocketPC PDA operating system can provide users with a rudimentary username/password challenge on device start-up. PDAs that utilise wireless networks use SIM-card security to obtain access to network services.

Cost

PDAs cost between $100 and $700 per unit. There are very few examples of service providers offering subsidised PDAs to consumers. However, this type of scheme is undergoing trials by large retail brands in some countries, in order to enable easier home shopping and (in many cases) to tie customers into the retailers' complementary financial services portfolios.

Voice-centric handheld terminals

Devices are characterised as voice-centric if they are designed primarily for voice communications. The form factor of these devices is optimised for voice communications – they have an integrated speaker, microphone and a small screen, and they are suitable for lifting up to the face and speaking into. They also have a keypad to dial numbers.

Today's voice-centric devices are characterised by 2G handsets. However, we are rapidly moving towards more segmented voice-centric handheld device types, with widely differing data-centric capabilities:

- basic handsets – voice-centric devices represented by the majority of 2G phones. Data transmission is typically limited to SMS
- 'feature phones' – voice-centric devices but which contain a microbrowser for accessing remote information services and data applications
- smartphones – devices in which voice-centric functions govern the form factor, but which also offer many of the features and functions traditionally associated with PDAs.

Basic handsets are widely available, and feature phones are becoming so – with Japan leading the way with NTT DoCoMo's iMode service and iMode-capable handsets. Ericsson and Nokia are in the midst of launching their first smartphone devices in the European market.

Capability

Basic handsets are pretty stupid devices. Their functionality is limited to initiating and receiving voice calls, storing phone numbers and in some cases sending and receiving short data messages (through SMS). The capability of this kind of device is unlikely to improve; the manufacture of basic handsets is a commodity business and will continue to be so. Manufacturers are engineering all their product differentiation into feature-phones and, increasingly, smartphones.

Early smartphones are already perfectly capable (from a processing point of view at least) of performing most mobile-office functions. For example, the newly-launched Nokia 9110 Communicator has (as well as voice capabilities) fax, SMS and e-mail capabilities, plus calendar, contact database, calculator, world-time clock and notepad applications pre-installed. The terminal uses a 32-bit AMD IA-486 processor, and utilises Nokia's own GEOS operating system on top of the hardware.

Over the next five years, smartphone developments will drive the capability of all types of voice-centric device beyond basic handset models, which will remain commoditised and so will take on new features much more gradually (only when implementation cost is very low). The introduction of 3G networks will also force further innovation in device capability; 3G radios are currently too large and power-hungry to be installed inside a normal-sized handset.

Battery life

The battery life of a voice-centric handheld device depends on a combination of the features installed in the device, and the way in which it is used. Voice-centric terminals of any type can currently achieve between six and 12 hours of interactive operation (either of voice communication or of data application usage) with a new battery. However, battery life degrades quite sharply as the battery gets older. As with PDAs, battery technology is improving; however, on top of the addition of PDA-like functions to voice-centric terminals, the introduction of 3G wireless networks is set to increase terminals' demand for power further. It is very likely that by 2002/2003 we will see a marked decrease in the battery life of the most capable terminals.

Connectivity

Voice services within mobile voice-centric terminals are provided over 2G digital networks such as GSM, which are capable of data transmission but only through the layering of additional protocols. 2G mobile networks are circuit-switched, whereas data communication works best over a packet-switched medium. However, the introduction of packet-switched wireless mobile networks will start soon and these will bring much higher data transfer speeds.

Smartphones and feature phones tend to provide additional connectivity options to allow the functions and data that they store to be shared with other devices. The Nokia 9110, for example, ships with an infra-red port for wireless line-of-sight communication with other phones and devices, and an RS-232 port for serial wireline connectivity to a PC.

Openness

Few deployed mobile phones have open architectures. Functions in basic handsets are hardwired into the device hardware – only the data content within the 'phone book' of such devices is alterable. Feature phones offer microbrowser functionality that executes in standard computer memory, but more often than not, that functionality is burnt directly into ROM, rather than held in re-writable secondary storage.

The newest smartphones are based on proper software-based operating systems. Symbian, a consortium of terminal vendors, is particularly active in the areas of specifying a widely-used operating system and set of open APIs for voice-centric terminals.

Higher-capability voice-centric handheld terminals will become more open over time – but it is unlikely that this same opening of devices will occur for low-end commodity handsets. The additional complexity and manufacturing costs associated with deploying a handset with an open operating system layer is not worth the effort for such limited-function devices.

Security

There are inbuilt security mechanisms in today's voice handsets; but these are present because of the way voice handset devices are tightly integrated with particular network services. The SIM card in a voice handset today identifies the handset (and, by implication, the service subscriber) to the network service provider. Consequently, the security is highly proprietary to a particular type of network service. But smartcard technology is now at the point where SIM cards can be augmented to widen their security remit and make SIM-card security more application-specific. Modern smartcards have their own operating systems, and can even host functions and data on behalf of multiple applications (such as security, billing and payment applications).

Cost

Voice-centric handheld terminals – particularly low-end models – are sold as part of service packages and the cost of these devices is therefore heavily or completely subsidised by the service provider. More capable devices such as high-end feature phones and smartphones are more niche propositions, which make them unattractive ways of locking subscribers into service packages. These types of device therefore tend to be only lightly subsidised – or not subsidised at all. High-end devices such as these can be purchased for anything up to $500.

Prices at the high-end will drop during 2001/2002 as manufacturing costs decrease and as sales start to come in higher volumes – but it is unlikely that smartphones will ever become the heavily-subsidised commodity items that today's basic handsets are.

In-car systems

Many cars (particularly 'prestige' cars) already include lots of computers that deal with local management issues. Evolutions of micro-controlled servos, 'powertrain' (engine, gearbox and clutch) management, and electronic seat control are examples.

In-car systems are different from these. Advanced in-car systems will play multiple roles:

- a conduit for delivery of remote interactive content, applications and services into the car
- a server for the local network of devices embedded within various parts of the car (such as powertrain management)
- a secure gateway between that local in-car network and one or more public communications networks.

There are some in-car systems on the market today – Clarion's AutoPC is an example – but the vast majority of systems focus on playing the first role while eschewing the second two. This is set to change however, with initiatives from Motorola and Infineon, for example. By 2006, the majority of prestige cars will include systems that fulfil all of these functions.

Capability

Early in-car systems are already capable computing platforms. Clarion's AutoPC, for example, functions as an AM/FM radio and CD player; but it also provides several 'mobile-office' functions (including a phone address book, a memo pad and e-mail), which are accessible through speech recognition and artificial speech synthesis interfaces.

AutoPC is based on a Hitachi SH3 32-bit RISC processor, with 16MB RAM and 8MB ROM. Its secondary storage capacity can be expanded through a Compact Flash card. As well as providing speech user interfaces to its functions, the device comes with an eight-colour TFT Active Matrix LCD display.

Battery life

Cars (and therefore the systems within them) come with a handy power supply – the engine. It is unlikely that in-car systems will ever require power levels that will significantly affect fuel consumption, compared to the power consumed by the activity of propelling the car itself.

Connectivity

The mobility of a car means that connectivity to public content, applications and services has to be through wireless mobile networks. In the few instances where in-car systems are being deployed today, those systems either use 2G mobile technology or they do not connect to any network at all. The current version of the AutoPC, for example, only provides one function that requires connection to a remote service – a navigation function that uses GPS.

Whilst cars are generally not shipping with inbuilt wireless network capabilities, other types of vehicle (notably, trucks and tractors) already provide these facilities for fleet and asset management purposes. Ovum's report *Mobile Location Services: Market Strategies* discusses these applications in more detail.

Interestingly, automotive manufacturers might adopt and implement 3G technology before mobile handset manufacturers. The current state of handset and radio hardware means that 3G connectivity cannot be realistically embedded in the handset. However the power consumption, form factor and cooling issues that give rise to this problem are less relevant in the context of a car.

Openness

As in-car systems start to become widely deployed, they will be based on software-based upgradeable operating systems. The major ongoing development efforts are already based on such platforms (Windows CE and QNX's Neutrino are the most popular choices). These platforms will enable service providers to deliver upgradeable and flexible services & applications to vehicles and their users. Moreover as systems start to link into vehicles' own networks of devices it will become possible for those service providers to sell functions of those vehicles as services that can be switched on and off remotely, rather than as optional extras.

Security

Current in-car system devices do not directly address security issues. This will change significantly by 2006, as platforms become more capable and more open, and as their connectivity to the outside world becomes more widespread.

Cost

In-car systems are expensive, luxury items in 2000. The AutoPC, for example, costs from $1,000 – and this is without wireless data network connectivity. However, by 2004, sophisticated in-car systems will be offered as subsidised options on prestige vehicles, just as in-car audio systems are today.

E5 Access networks, 2001–2006

Access network operators are being driven to innovate by a decline in their core business (voice traffic) and intense competition. The main way in which they are doing so is by using their central supply chain role to carve out futures as service providers of various types. Most operators' current service provision aspirations, however, rely on the widespread availability of access networks that support data transmission, and therefore data services.

Quite apart from market development factors concerning the availability of compelling applications and software infrastructure, there are three key 'local' factors that will affect the development and take-up of data services over access networks between 2001 and 2006:

- the cost of those services to end users
- the data transfer speeds realistically attainable
- the ability of access networks to provide basic infrastructure for interactivity.

End-user cost of access services is, of course, masked by the degree to which service providers subsidise costs. The current situation, which arises from this common subsidy model, is that Internet access services through broadband access networks are much more expensive than, for example, broadcast TV and radio services. This is because there is little that service providers can currently do to achieve a high ARPU on basic Internet access services. Overall, though, access costs to users are set to decrease steadily between 2001 and 2006, particularly in countries with high teledensities, as three things happen:

- competition between access networks increases as their capabilities improve
- competition between providers increases, due to local loop unbundling
- more sophisticated transmission protocols are implemented, which makes it easier for multiple media types to be transmitted simultaneously, and therefore makes service bouquets easier to deliver.

Attainable network transfer speeds are an area of extreme hype – particularly concerning mobile networks. For example, 3G mobile technology is often associated with transfer rates of 2Mbit/s: but this is pure fantasy. The truth will be much closer to one-tenth of that figure – where there is not much network congestion. This is not purely because of technology constraints; the high prices that many operators have had to pay for operating licences is forcing them to scale back plans for delivery of services that require the rollout of large amounts of expensive high-speed infrastructure.

Not all networks are suitable bearers for interactive applications. Broadcast networks in particular suffer here, as neither satellite broadcast nor terrestrial RF broadcast networks provide upstream communication channels. Moreover terrestrial RF broadcast does not even benefit from the main upside of satellite broadcast – huge downstream data transmission capacity. In the future, satellite broadcast technology will remain the best option for mobile or isolated users and will play a large part in the backbone distribution of data – but it will not be a mainstream access network technology.

Figures E5.1 to *E5.3* provide a summary of how the capabilities of major access networks will change between 2001 and 2006.

Figure E5.1 **Network capabilities, 2001–2002**

	Speed	Symmetry	Reach	Openness	Cost
PSTN	1	2	5	2	4
xDSL	5	3	3	5	2
Cellular data (2G+)	1	2	2	4	3
PAN	4	5	1	5	2
Terrestrial broadcast	4*	1	5	2	3
Satellite broadcast	5*	1	4	2	4
Cable	3	3	4	3	4

Key: 1 = very poor; 2 = poor; 3 = medium; 4 = good; 5 = very good
For cost, a higher score means a lower cost
For speed, 1= 0+ kbit/s; 2 = 250+ kbit/s; 3 = 500+ kbit/s; 4 = 2,000+ kbit/s; 5 = 5000+ kbit/s
**Data transfer speeds of broadcast networks can be misleading, as the available capacity must be shared between multiple users if personalised, point-to-point services are being delivered.*

Figure E5.2 **Network capabilities, 2003–2004**

	Speed	Symmetry	Reach	Openness	Cost
PSTN	1	2	5	2	4
xDSL	5	3	4	5	4
Cellular data (3G)	2	2	2	5	3
PAN	4	5	2	5	3
Terrestrial broadcast	4*	1	5	3	4
Satellite broadcast	5*	1	4	2	5
Cable	4	3	4	3	5

Key: 1 = very poor; 2 = poor; 3 = medium; 4 = good; 5 = very good
For cost, a higher score means a lower cost
For speed, 1= 0+ kbit/s; 2 = 250+ kbit/s; 3 = 500+ kbit/s; 4 = 2,000+ kbit/s; 5 = 5000+ kbit/s
**Data transfer speeds of broadcast networks can be misleading, as the available capacity must be shared between multiple users if personalised, point-to-point services are being delivered.*

Figure E5.3 **Network capabilities, 2005–2006**

	Speed	Symmetry	Reach	Openness	Cost
PSTN	1	2	5	2	5
xDSL	4	3	4	5	5
Cellular data (3G)	2	2	3	5	5
PAN	4	5	2	5	5
Terrestrial broadcast	4*	1	5	3	5
Satellite broadcast	5*	1	4	3	5
Cable	4	3	4	4	5

Key: 1 = very poor; 2 = poor; 3 = medium; 4 = good; 5 = very good
For cost, a higher score means a lower cost
For speed, 1= 0+ kbit/s; 2 = 250+ kbit/s; 3 = 500+ kbit/s; 4 = 2,000+ kbit/s; 5 = 5000+ kbit/s
**Data transfer speeds of broadcast networks can be misleading, as the available capacity must be shared between multiple users if personalised, point-to-point services are being delivered.*

E5.1 Fixed networks

The only fixed narrowband network service type we examine is PSTN over copper local loop – in other words POTS (plain old telephone system), used in conjunction with analogue modems to enable dial-up data connections.

Broadband network services such as xDSL and cable have two common characteristics:

- they suffer from high levels of signal attenuation, which limits the distance that the access network can span
- this distance limitation means that in order to achieve good coverage, network providers have to build out more network infrastructure – which makes the networks more expensive than narrowband networks.

PSTN

Access network operators are focusing their new infrastructure investment on broadband services, and delivering fibre and wireless access to the home: but the copper-based PSTN service will continue to be a significant installed access network to the home for the next few years – particularly in Europe.

Data transfer speed

Transfer of data over an analogue PSTN connection, using an analogue modem, gives a current maximum transfer speed of approximately 56kbit/s. The effective data transfer speed possible on a PSTN local loop will increase slightly over the next five years – but this will be due to advances in analogue modem compression schemes, rather than improvements in the underlying network service.

Symmetry

Improvements in analogue modem standards are making normal analogue PSTN data connections much more symmetrical than they have historically been. The new V.92 standard, for example, allows an analogue modem to achieve up to 48kbit/s upstream, as well as 56kbit/s downstream – just not simultaneously, of course.

Reach

PSTN services are available almost universally worldwide. Access services that can offer 56kbit/s analogue data transfer speeds are limited in their availability, however – because they require service providers to install the right kind of modem. Global availability of 56kbit/s+ access services is likely to improve significantly by 2004. Analogue modems based on the V.90 standard are fast becoming the default mechanism for consumer Internet access globally.

Openness

The vast majority of consumer PSTN services are analogue, circuit-switched network services that are not well suited to IP data traffic. This is unlikely to change – instead, xDSL technologies will provide the conduit for high-bandwidth data communications over the PSTN local loop.

Cost

With local loop unbundling, PSTN is increasingly a commodity and charging for local access usage is quickly moving to fixed-price, unmetered schemes in many developed countries. Increasing competition within the local loop will force prices down much further during 2001/2002 – particularly in developed countries with high teledensity, where free local access over PSTN is a real prospect (as it already is in the US).

xDSL

DSL (digital subscriber line) uses ordinary copper telephone lines to bring high bandwidth data to consumers, SoHos and SMEs. xDSL is used to refer to different variations of DSL, such as ADSL (asymmetric DSL which provides more bandwidth downstream to the customer than upstream from the customer) and VDSL (very high data rate DSL, which will deliver much higher data rates over relatively short distances). An xDSL line can carry both data and voice signals, and the data part of the line is continuously connected. It is a point-to-point technology.

Data transfer speed

ADSL can achieve downstream transfer speeds of 6Mbit/s point-to-point, and this is set to improve steadily as compression technologies improve. This capability makes ADSL a significant competitor to cable and satellite, for delivery of interactive services into the home. Plus, xDSL lines are dedicated to particular subscribers so performance is not affected by the number of users on the network.

Importantly, however, xDSL technologies introduce a service latency when carrying interactive services that is not present in cable or satellite networks. This is because xDSL is a point-to-point medium, where only one channel is offered to any one subscriber at any particular point in time – in contrast to cable and satellite, where all channels are provided right to the set-top box. Consequently while channel switching is carried out at the set-top box on cable and satellite networks, changing channel on an interactive service over xDSL requires switching remotely, at the central office.

Symmetry

Different xDSL variants provide for different degrees of symmetry. A good example, though, is full-rate ADSL, which allows the customer to download data at up to 6Mbit/s and to send upstream data at up to 640kbit/s.

SHDSL, which is still under discussion, is intended to provide symmetrical data communications over a single loop at over 2Mbit/s in both directions. This will be much more suitable than asymmetrical DSL for many business applications.

Reach

xDSL installations began in 1998 and will replace ISDN in many areas, as well as compete with cable data services. xDSL is already starting to make inroads into the home (as well as SMEs and SoHos) as a replacement for narrowband dial-up Internet services. However, its reach is limited by the fact that the end user has to be within a certain distance of the central office (or local exchange) – approximately four kilometres in the case of ADSL, and one kilometre for the higher bandwidth VDSL. The downstream xDSL data rate falls off sharply from around 2.7 kilometres, depending on circumstances. Current estimates suggest that this leaves 30% or more of US telephone subscribers out of xDSL range, for example, although the situation is generally better in Europe.

Openness

xDSL provides a digital data transmission network that shares the same wires as a PSTN local loop service, but is encoded and switched entirely separately from the circuit-switched voice service. xDSL data services provide packet-switched, digital networks, so subscribers do not require modems.

Cost

xDSL is a high-cost home access network option. However competition from cable services will drive the cost down quite rapidly, where both are available. In countries where local-loop unbundling has occurred, competition between xDSL service providers will be another factor in cost reduction to the end user.

Cable

Cable networks originated in the US in the 1950s to provide clean TV signals to customers in areas where reception was difficult. The cable network typically has a tree and branch structure, and initially both the trunk and local distribution networks were constructed from coaxial cable, used for its efficiency in carrying signals with little attenuation. Despite this efficiency, attenuation of the signal and the ingress of external electrical noise into the system meant that a series of amplifiers had to be used to maintain signal levels. Operators have now taken advantage of the benefits of introducing fibre into their networks (fibre is now no more expensive to implement in the trunk network than coax), and are upgrading them to produce hybrid fibre-coax (HFC) networks. This upgrade offers significant advantages to the operators, and has aided the delivery of broadband communications. Most of the available spectrum is used for downstream transmission of TV signals – simply because this it what the networks were originally designed to do. Many operators now offer telephony services, as well as distribution of TV signals to homes.

Data transfer speed

Typically, a current cable modem system can deliver 27Mbit/s in a single 6MHz channel once error correction and other overheads have been accounted for. The 8MHz channels in European networks allow for slightly higher data rates.

However, cable networks share bandwidth between multiple termination points, so the theoretically attainable downstream transfer rate is never likely to be experienced by any one user. On the basis that one user in ten is likely to be online to the Internet at peak times (which is a rule of thumb often used by ISPs), a cable head-end installation with 500 cable modem customers on a single TV channel will have to share 27Mbit/s between 50 simultaneous users, giving them 540 or 720kbit/s each. The real situation is more complicated but this illustrates the orders of magnitude involved.

These data transfer speeds arise from fundamental limitations of the architecture of cable networks. Any kind of improvement in transfer speeds will therefore have to come from improved encoding and compression technologies.

Symmetry

Typically, the spectrum reserved for upstream traffic in a cable network is a small portion of the frequency plan at the lower end of the spectrum. Cable modem implementations use this for the return path, although it is possible to use the standard telephone network for upstream traffic if the cable network has not been upgraded to support two-way traffic.

This area of the spectrum is relatively sensitive to 'ingress noise' (from passing traffic on roads above the cable). Given an appropriate coding scheme and channel frequency, upstream data rates of between 320kbit/s and 10Mbit/s are obtainable.

Reach

North America leads in cable modem service availability, although there are a growing number of deployments throughout the world. However, the current level of penetration is still well short of the levels expected when cable modems were first launched. A few years ago, particularly during 1996/1997, cable modems were widely tipped to undergo massive growth in a very short space of time and establish themselves in the market before xDSL. Despite the recent acceleration of growth in the US, this has clearly not happened.

Europe has had a disappointing start compared to expectation, with only Austria, France and The Netherlands having a significant installed base by late 1999.

Openness

In order to enable IP communication over a cable network, client devices need a cable modem and PPP (point-to-point protocol). Cable networks were not designed for point-to-point digital data transmission. This situation is unlikely to change materially; cable networks will continue to be convenient conduits for broadband data services where they are deployed – but they are not sufficiently suitable to be deployed as a preferred option for data service.

Cost

Cable modem services are relatively cheap where they are available. For example, the current model for cable modem services in North America is to have a single all-inclusive price – typically between $30 and $50 per month for connection to the network and a basic basket of services, which usually includes unlimited access to the content provided by the cable company and to the Internet as a whole. This commonly includes the cost of renting a two-way cable modem, although some of the cheaper options are for telephony-return modems or even consumer purchase of the modem. The cost of cable modem services will continue to fall, as competition from xDSL increases.

For the operator wanting to offer digital cable services, there are high infrastructure costs involved in setting up a cable network with good household coverage. The costs of 'passing' a household vary principally with population density, hence urban areas are more attractive. Cable is therefore the obvious choice for enhancing bandwidth in heavily populated urban areas, but in rural areas the cost of connection per user is prohibitive.

E5.2 Mobile networks

Mobile networks have one main characteristic in common – interference in real-world deployments is likely to drastically reduce the data transfer speeds or the network-operating reach promised by the technology vendors.

Cellular data networks

Today's second-generation (2G) mobile environment provides digital wireless radio networks that are optimised for two-way voice communications. There is huge interest in mobile networks within the context of pervasive computing, due to the imminent widespread availability of 2G+ networks, which are packet-switched, rather than circuit-switched (as are the current 2G networks). Interest in third-generation mobile network technology is also high as the 3G standards adopted by the ITU promise broadband data transfer speeds. But the 3G vision is wider than just delivery of broadband data – 3G mobile systems will also:

- increase the capacity available to mobile operators, as a result of more spectrum being made available and through greater spectral efficiency
- enable users to take their service profile with them when they roam.

A successful implementation of a third-generation mobile system will enable a user to receive a consistent quality-of-service and coverage for voice, data, graphical and video-based information, independent of the access network. This means that flexible bit-rate services will be available on wide-area mobile, local area cordless and satellite networks.

Data transfer speed

Rollout of 2G+ networks (GPRS in Europe) will start to become widespread in 2001. GPRS will raise the downstream data transfer speed to approximately 28kbit/s from the 9.6kbit/s theoretical maximum available through today's 2G networks (like GSM). Moreover 2G+ networks will bring an 'always on' data connectivity environment to mobile devices, which will make a tremendous difference to the end-user appeal of mobile data applications and services.

The 3G family of standards adopted by the ITU will, in theory, enable mobile devices to obtain downstream data transfer speeds of 144kbit/s on the move, and 2Mbit/s when stationary. However this is highly unlikely in practice. A more realistic speed for a 3G-capable mobile device in 2004 (when networks start to become widespread) is 64kbit/s – not much higher than will be available through a 2G+ system such as GPRS.

Symmetry

2G+ mobile data standards split the available data communications bandwidth 4:1 (downstream:upstream). Third-generation networks will eventually provide more symmetrical data communications environments, but it is unlikely that there will be any material change before 2004/2005.

Reach

Early rollout of 2G+ networks are already taking place. Many industrialised nations will have at least one nationwide 2G+ network in place at some point during 2001. 3G networks are much further down the line – unlike 2G+ networks they require the installation of new infrastructure. We do not expect to see widespread international deployment of 3G networks until 2004.

Openness

2G mobile networks are lousy environments for packet data transfer. They are digital media, but they are circuit-switched for voice traffic (which is what they are designed for). Consequently, a data connection must be explicitly established over a 2G network, just as a dial-up connection is made from your home PC to your ISP every time you want to connect to the Internet. Data connections can take anything up to 30 seconds to establish.

All this will change with 2G+ network technologies such as GPRS, which are packet-switched data networks and are 'always on'. This means that data connections are pretty much instantaneous. 3G networks employ the same 'always on' technologies.

Cost

Auctions for 3G operation licences have taken place in many countries – and (with few exceptions) the operators have paid high prices (in the UK, for example, some operators paid more than £5 billion). On top of this outlay operators will have to spend significant sums to rollout 3G infrastructure – approximately $100 million to upgrade their 2G networks for packet data and higher data speeds, and then a further $1 billion on a 3G network. Furthermore, 3G terminals will also be expensive to produce. In order to stimulate consumer demand, operators will have to (at least initially) subsidise the cost.

All these costs will have to be recouped from combinations of user subscriptions and advertising. Consequently 3G mobile connectivity, when it finally arrives in 2003/2004, will be expensive.

PANs

Personal area network (PAN) is a label for a short-range wireless network that is designed to allow personal computing devices and peripherals to communicate and collaborate in a peer-to-peer fashion. There are three potential PAN technologies vying for industry interest – Bluetooth, IEEE 802.11 and HomeRF. We concentrate most on Bluetooth, because it has the widest applicability and also because it is the most talked-about of the options.

Bluetooth is a short-range wireless networking specification being developed by the Bluetooth Special Interest Group (SIG). The idea originated in 1994 when Ericsson Mobile Communications initiated a study to investigate the feasibility of a low-power, low-cost radio interface between mobile phones and their accessories, with the aim being to eliminate cables between mobile phones and PC cards, headphones and desktop devices. The Bluetooth specification, which is distributed freely to companies wishing to build Bluetooth compatible devices, is comprised of two main technologies – the radio transmitter/receiver, which allows devices to communicate with each other, and the underlying network logic, which makes the communication meaningful.

IEEE 802.11 is another standard for wireless local area networking that is already commonly available in implementations. It operates in the same area of radio spectrum as Bluetooth, which presents something of a problem because IEEE 802.11 signals are actually significantly more powerful than those of Bluetooth, resulting in the scrambling of Bluetooth signals when the two are used together. Engineers are tackling the problem from both ends, but until a solution becomes available, the problem could constrain the adoption of IEEE 802.11, Bluetooth or both.

Data transfer speed

Bluetooth devices can support three voice channels operating at 64kbit/s, or one data channel operating at up to 1Mbit/s. Bluetooth devices can be set to either transmit their own availability and capabilities ('master'), or just listen for other devices ('slave'). Typically, devices that have a permanent power connection such as a Bluetooth-enabled Internet router or PC will transmit their availability, as they do not have the power constraints of mobile devices such as phones and PDAs.

A group of computers communicating over an IEEE 802.11 LAN can communicate at speeds of up to 11Mbit/s, and whilst companies with wired networks offering better connection speeds are unlikely to wish to switch to 802.11, it does provide a simple, wireless networking alternative in new offices or for smaller companies. The technology is also being pitched as an attractive option for home networking for those not wishing to install a hardwired network such as Ethernet.

Symmetry

Both 802.11 and Bluetooth are capable of supporting applications that have symmetrical data transfer requirements.

Reach

Bluetooth devices can transmit and receive over a distance of approximately 10 metres, although this can be boosted to up to 100 metres by an amplifier. A group of devices communicating within a 10 metre range of each other is known as a 'piconet'.

Apple Computer's 802.11 based AirPort wireless LAN system enables wireless connectivity between Macs at distances of up to 30 metres. Several companies are manufacturing 802.11 adapters for use with PCs.

Openness

Both Bluetooth and 802.11 implement packet-switched protocols over a digital data transmission technology. The Bluetooth protocol stack is based on a protocol that 'hides' the RF wireless implementation, and is explicitly designed to support IP-based transmission protocols (such as UDP and TCP) and application protocols (such as HTTP and WAP).

Cost

It currently costs approximately $30 to enable a device with Bluetooth, and this is too high for the technology to become a commodity. In order for this to happen, the price has to fall to at least $5 per device.

IEEE 802.11 technology is costly, and therefore current implementations tend to be limited to corporate use.

E5.3 Broadcast networks

Terrestrial RF broadcast (normally associated with digital TV transmission) and satellite broadcast networks are only now becoming interesting access network propositions, as they evolve first towards digital transmission of information, and then to ATM-based packet transmission of multiple media types. However, neither network type (in general use at least) provides an upstream communication channel.

Terrestrial digital TV broadcast

With terrestrial television, services are transmitted from radio towers situated at strategic sites. The more populated areas use the main transmitters, and less populated ones use relay transmitters. Many broadcasters are using the same overall RF bandwidth range as they use for analogue transmission; and are 'piggy-backing' on analogue transmission infrastructure.

Delivering digital television via terrestrial technology currently offers the most viable solution to gaining universal acceptance – many consumers with TV sets in the home already have the aerial required to receive digital services.

Data transfer speed

Terrestrial transmission capacity is determined by national governments that allocate the frequency spectrum among broadcasters, mobile phone operators and for military and police use. Transmission involves encoding schemes that have the potential to deliver high data-transfer speeds. However, most countries have restricted the RF bandwidth ranges in which broadcasters can transmit TV signals, which means that the overall data capacity of terrestrial broadcast networks is lower than cable and satellite substitutes.

Symmetry

Terrestrial broadcast transmission provides no upstream communication channel.

Reach

Digital terrestrial broadcast networks have the potential of near universal reach. Transmission infrastructure can 'piggy-back' on existing analogue radio masts, which are almost universal through the industrialised world.

Openness

Terrestrial RF broadcast is not a particularly open medium for transmission of IP packet data.

Cost

Digital terrestrial television has the lowest cost-delivery system at national aggregate level. However, as with satellite and cable television, the cost of developing a set-top box for reception is the largest part of the system outlay. Modulation and coding of terrestrial services on interactive TV require more processing and a more expensive set-top box than is the case with cable or satellite transmission.

Satellite

Advances in satellite communications technology resulted in the arrival of several direct broadcast satellite (DBS) systems implemented during the late 1990s, each delivering about 200 television channels to subscribers with a 46-centimetre dish antenna and a set-top converter, similar to those used for CATV. DBS networks are used to deliver broadcast media output to TVs throughout the world. However, DBS implementations are not ideal components of access platforms – despite their wide reach, they provide no upstream communication channel, which means that support for interactive applications requires employment of a separate network.

Data transfer speed

Satellites and fibre-optic cables can convey a huge number of digital television channels. The main advantage of satellite technology is its high transmission capacity. In Europe, approximately 350 analogue TV and radio channels in more than 20 languages are available via satellite; digital transmission greatly enhances these numbers.

Symmetry

As with terrestrial broadcast, broadcast satellite networks provide no upstream communication channel.

Reach

The advantage of satellite transmission is that it provides instant infrastructure – once available in one location, the signal can be received at any location that can see the satellite.

Openness

Digital broadcast satellite transmission is increasingly becoming packet-switched, making it a much more suitable bearer for IP traffic than it has historically been. Packet-based transmission protocols are set to become widespread as digital TV applications themselves become more widespread; Lockheed-Martin plans to start deploying satellites that implement ATM, in order to support simultaneous voice, video and data transmission.

Cost

Broadcast media service providers generally subsidise two major costs, which must be passed onto subscribers (to a degree) through subscription charges: the first and largest cost is rental of transmission capacity; the second is the cost of set-top boxes. However the cost of transmission has fallen more than 90% with the arrival of digital, as a result of the increasing capacity of channels on a transponder. This is due to digital compression of the information transmitted, allowing eight to ten channels on a single transponder. Low-end set-top boxes are also becoming cheaper. Whether or not cost savings will eventually be passed onto subscribers depends on substitution competition from xDSL and cable operators.

F Breaking the stovepipes

F1 Introduction

Central to the notion of pervasive computing is the idea that applications and services will be delivered to users through many different channels. This implies breaking out of today's 'stovepipes' – the supply chains that have grown up around the delivery of particular types of information, to particular types of device over particular types of network.

There are three very well-established stovepipes at work in the delivery of digital information:

- the PC stovepipe, which traditionally focused on delivering the whole gamut of applications – business applications, e-commerce, infotainment, personal communications, and also remote management applications – to PCs owned by consumers and businesses
- the telecommunications stovepipe, which traditionally focused on delivering one type of application – realtime voice communication – over multiple types of network, and considered anything that hung off the end of a network as an 'anonymous terminal'
- the broadcast media stovepipe, which historically focused on delivering audio-visual content over various types of broadcast network to TV and radio receivers.

Pervasive computing allows companies to break out of these rigid supply chains and either enter the other stovepipes, or construct new supply chains around the delivery of content, applications and services to new types of smart, connected device.

Migration of suppliers from their traditional stovepipes brings them into contact with suppliers they have never previously had to form partnerships with or compete against. For example, both car and home-appliance manufacturers are now working with software companies, network operators and content providers to enable the delivery of applications and services to vehicles and domestic appliances respectively.

F2 The slow dance of the elephants

F2.1 Vertical industry disintegration – major battles

Convergence of the major digital information delivery industries is in many ways the 'engine' behind the development of pervasive computing. Migrations of suppliers across the major digital information supply chains will be the pioneers of multichannel service provision. Over the next five years, events that are just starting to play out across these industries will unfold dramatically – resulting in fundamental changes to the computing, telecommunications and broadcast media landscapes of 2006.

Figures F2.1 to *F2.3* summarise the major ways in which content and applications, networks and devices currently tied together within stovepipes will be interwoven between 2001 and 2006, to create an environment where applications are delivered over multiple networks, to multiple types of device.

The major migrations of suppliers that will enable this weaving will occur around four events:

- the maturation of the wireless Internet trend, during 2001 and 2002
- the popularisation of digital interactive TV services, during 2001 and 2002
- the widespread availability of broadband point-to-point access services to the home, during 2003 and 2004
- the widespread availability of broadband access speeds in mobile networks, during 2005 and 2006.

As these events play out, we will also see a degree of access platform substitution and the growth in importance of new types of smart, connected device – the connected PDA, car and home appliance.

Figure F2.1 **Major migrations, 2001–2002**

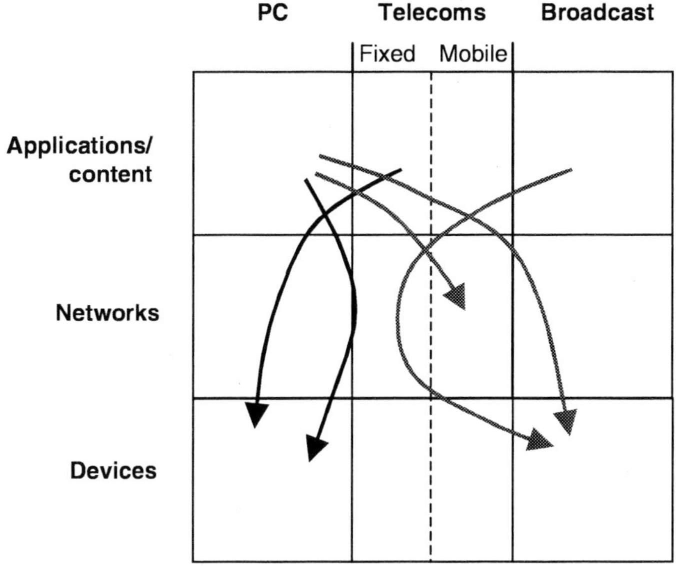

Source: Ovum (Pervasive Computing: Technologies and Markets/Chapter F)

Figure F2.2 **Major migrations, 2003–2004**

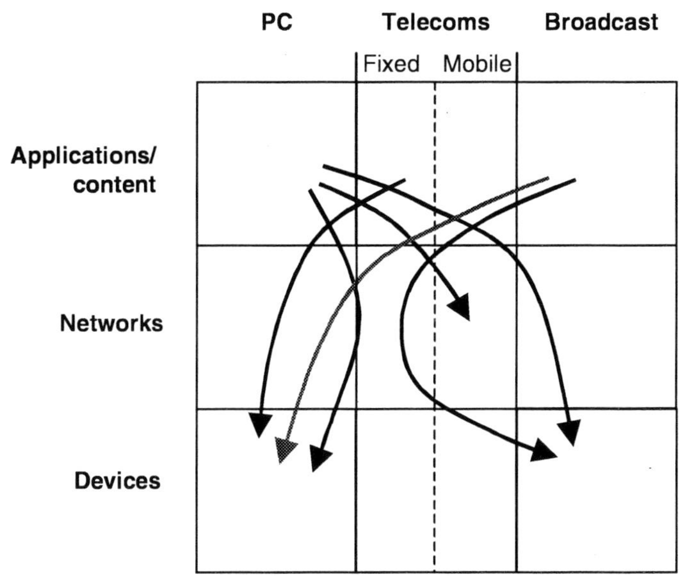

Source: Ovum (Pervasive Computing: Technologies and Markets/Chapter F)

Figure F2.3 **Major migrations, 2005–2006**

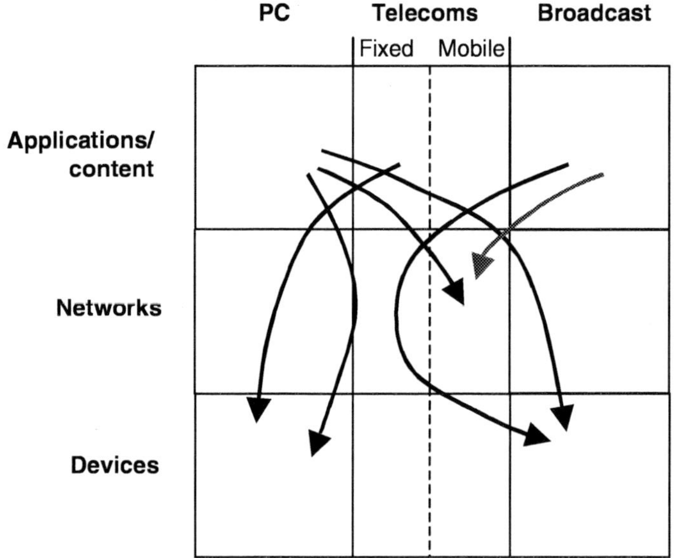

Source: Ovum (Pervasive Computing: Technologies and Markets/Chapter F)

Wireless Internet

The evolution of wireless mobile networks towards packet-based digital networks, and eventually to broadband capacities, is luring business application providers, as well as infotainment providers (web-based content providers and aggregators) into the provision of content, applications and services for mobile access platforms. Part of the reason that the current level of supplier interest is so feverish, is that the transformation of mobile networks into data bearers potentially brings a whole new dimension of opportunity: the delivery of content, applications and services that are mobility-aware. In 2001 and 2002, there will be a huge degree of market movement in this area – primarily because mobile network operators are very keen not to pass up the opportunity to play a major role in the development of mobile networks as application access platforms.

Broadband goes point-to-point – TV on the Internet

The increasing availability of point-to-point broadband access networks into the home, primarily through the introduction of xDSL services (combined with the rapidly increasing amount of access bandwidth available to businesses) is starting to attract content providers from the broadcast media industry to the PC delivery channel. Today the first 'baby steps' are being taken through the use of streaming media technology by big providers such as CNN and the BBC, and also through the *ad hoc* streaming of live events by niche suppliers. Significant market development of interactive digital services through this route requires telecommunications, broadcast media and PC-centric application and content suppliers to work together in several ways – despite the fact that they will also want to compete.

Interactive services – Internet on your TV

Early rollouts of 'Internet on your TV'-style interactive services by cable operators and satellite-based content aggregators are piquing the interest of the web content aggregator community; and, to a lesser extent, the personal communications application provider community (particularly providers of e-mail services). In many ways, this is a reflection of the broadband invasion of the PC stovepipe. Content aggregators such as AOL, Vizzavi and Yahoo! are starting to forge partnerships that enable them to provide TV portals, bringing web content and web-based applications, and improving the breadth of interactive TV services. The bulk of activity in this area will occur in 2001/2002.

As well as enabling digital interactive services by the TV-on-the-Internet route, the introduction of xDSL telecommunications networks also provides fixed-access operators and service providers with an opportunity to play roles in the provision of Internet on your TV. Furthermore, satellite-based interactive service providers must enable a return path for upstream communication; otherwise, there can be no interactivity. Where their infrastructure provides the path for interactivity, telcos have the potential to manage the valuable information that passes through their doors – enabling more efficient advertising, billing and customer-management services than the broadcaster could provide alone.

Mobile goes media-rich

The widespread availability of higher-speed access services on mobile networks in 2004/2005 will bring broadcast content providers and aggregators (along with their broadband content assets) into the wireless Internet fray. The resulting battles are unlikely to wreak the same degree of industry havoc as earlier wireless Internet-induced market shake-ups – market and technology constraints will dampen the fireworks – but a new type of supplier will be introduced to the supply chain.

Device substitution

Device suppliers are keen to provide substitutes for consumer use of PCs. The evolution of digital TVs, games consoles and new types of connected home appliances are starting to transform all of these device types into competitors to the PC in its consumer usage context. Similarly, suppliers of PCs and those same suppliers of games consoles and new types of connected home appliances are keen to provide substitutes for television sets.

Beyond the PC, TV and phone

The creation of new supply chains for delivery of digital information to new device types will not result in tomorrow's stovepipes. Many existing content providers, aggregators, service providers and network operators have opportunities to play significant roles in the promotion of PDAs, in-car systems and networked home appliances to the 'premier league' of pervasive computing access platforms.

However, the lack of rigid information delivery stovepipes does not mean that the supply of digital information to these new access platforms will be generic. All of these three new types of smart, connected device are becoming so to add value to them as devices, rather than to create general digital information conduits. Supply chains that enable the introduction of these new smart, connected devices to the pervasive computing market will consist of familiar players, but be skewed towards adding value to the applications and usage contexts of the devices.

F2.2 After the battles, the supplier melting pot

By 2006, numerous market, technology and geographical issues will have transformed digital information delivery stovepipes into a 'melting pot' of suppliers, forming partnerships to offer complete, compelling solutions to subscribers, as summarised in *Figure F2.4. Figure F2.5* shows the resulting 'melting pot'.

Figure F2.4 **Today's stovepipes**

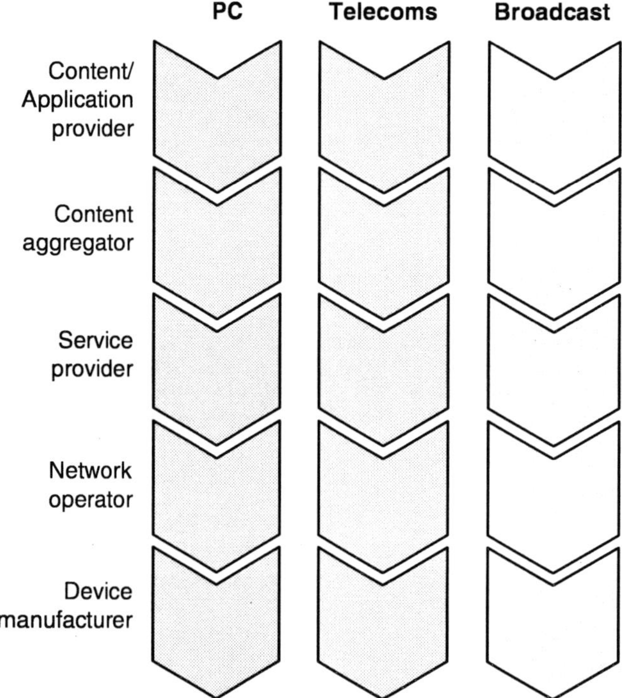

Source: Ovum (Pervasive Computing: Technologies and Markets/Chapter F)

Figure F2.5 **Tomorrow's supplier 'melting pot'**

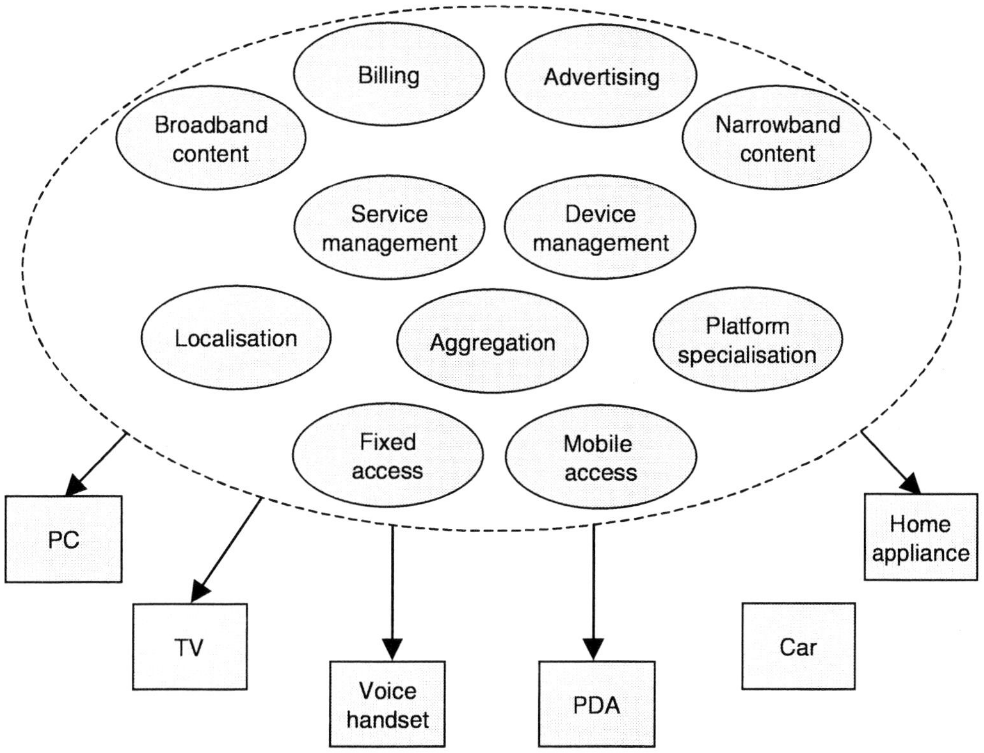

Source: Ovum (Pervasive Computing: Technologies and Markets/Chapter F)

F2.3 Market issues

You play in my park, you play by my rules

The major migrations of suppliers that characterise the development of the pervasive computing market over the next five years have one major thing in common – in order to succeed, suppliers moving from a position of strength in one supply chain will not be able to rely on that strength translating to their target market. Successful ventures will be built from partnerships between what may seem at first to be unlikely bedfellows – in many cases, partners will compete in some areas.

Just as people going to work in a foreign country must abide by local customs in order to prosper, moves from one stovepipe to another will work best when the immigrant plays by the incumbent's rules. Incumbents, as a rule, understand 'local customs' such as ownership and content regulation, customer segmentation, user-interaction paradigms, platform peculiarities and users' likes and dislikes. Immigrants ignoring these local customs, and bypassing the potential value to be gained from working with existing services providers, will find life very hard.

For example, in the development of broadband applications for mobile access platforms, mobile network operators understand the nature of mobility and how it affects the delivery of information – but they do not have the expertise or tools to produce high-quality broadband content and applications. Broadcasters know how to produce and distribute great broadband content and applications, and also know about content localisation – something that potentially adds significant value when targeting mobile users.

The value of information is changing – but not as you expect

A corollary of the last point is that in the pervasive computing world, a strange thing happens to the value of information. Rather than information being a concept that has intrinsic value, information (specifically, information about content, applications and services, and their delivery to users) becomes more valuable, the more it is shared.

This change in the nature of the value of information brings major changes in the relationships that service providers must have with their customers, and with the information that they hold about those customers, in order to succeed as a pervasive computing player.

There are three factors inducing this major change:

- the delivery of content, applications and services across multiple channels, which is forcing service providers to form partnerships with providers from other industries to offer compelling propositions
- the requirement for compelling content, applications and services to be reliable, secure and of high quality, which requires an end-to-end approach to quality-of-service delivery
- the convergence of different application types – particularly, infotainment, e-commerce and personal communications applications – which will bring disparate supplier communities closer together.

In order to provide seamless, high-quality services to subscribers in an environment where these three factors hold true, service providers will have to share all sorts of metadata, as users navigate around their personalised universes of content, applications and services. The evolution of context information (discussed in *Chapter C*) is central to this transfer of information about information. Without such metadata exhanges, the pervasive computing vision is a Dantesque one for suppliers: there will be no simple subscriber billing, no interactive advertising, and no open access to the Internet, to name a few examples.

Sharing for profit (and blame avoidance)

Information sharing models have the potential to overcome two of the thorniest issues facing pervasive computing service providers:

- how can they afford to provide open access to other providers' applications and services. Does this mean that revenues will stop flowing to them and start flowing to those other providers?
- how can they support a user (and avoid blame) if a problem occurs somewhere in a third party's delivery of a service?

Walled gardens can only be a stop-gap solution. The implementation of the other option – information-sharing models – brings much more significant cultural challenges for providers than it does technical challenges.

Revenue tracking and sharing could be enforced through regulation, as in the interconnect agreements used in international telecommunications. The biggest issue here is who would be the regulator? Different industries and countries have their own regulatory bodies and it is not immediately obvious who would be best placed to undertake this complex task.

An alternative to regulation is for service providers to voluntarily establish commercial agreements with each other and with advertising network providers across different delivery channels. These agreements will require significant information sharing to take place between providers, however – in order for them to bill each other and track users' activities and service usage as they navigate around their own digital universes. This is a big leap and will require service providers to invest in new technologies, as well as commercial agreements.

The technology problems are eminently solvable, though – it is the commercial ones that form the larger barrier. Due to the current emphasis on ownership of the customer and the reluctance of many organisations to share their information, substantial changes in business models are likely to be required for some pervasive computing applications where the free exchange of information is important.

The last (and most radical) scenario involves customers themselves owning and controlling access to the information held about them. In such a scenario, customer information might be hosted and managed by particular trusted service providers, and tightly bound to context information, which is also held and managed by those providers. This scenario, whilst perhaps far-fetched, also has potential benefits for advertisers, merchants and other providers: they will be able to tell who is interested in their services, rather than having to find out through targeted marketing and advertising – because customers themselves will tell them.

F2.4 Technology issues

Dealing with specialised quality-of-service infrastructure

We have already ascertained that the development of pervasive computing depends on the availability of access platforms and applications that are secure, reliable and that perform well. However, pervasive computing application infrastructure must support cost-effective deployment of applications to multiple access platforms.

Furthermore, (almost by definition) software infrastructure that optimises the quality-of-service of application delivery is specialised for particular access platforms. This presents a major challenge for the software providers that are trying to build next-generation infrastructure products that host multichannel applications. On top of providing platforms that must help providers build multi-channel assets (and potentially scale to millions of users), significant chunks of the software must be specialised and rigorously tested for each access platform supported.

The scale and complexity of this challenge means that there can only be relatively few serious players in this market. Since many variations in access platforms are peculiar to particular regions, only companies with very significant multichannel experience, international operations and product development budgets can afford to attempt to build such a platform and support it properly.

Facilitating information sharing

Information sharing is at the heart of enabling interconnection between service providers – just as it is a key part of the regulations that allow interconnection between telecommunications carriers. There are three broad targets that need to be considered:

- usage information. In order for providers to support open access to other providers' applications, services and delivery channels, revenue must be able to flow between them. But the amount of revenue that flows must, in some way, be related to patterns of user activity. It is relatively straightforward (from a technological point of view) to identify when a user moves from one provider's 'universe' to that of another; what is required is for this information to be correlated with usage information for each user that is collected by each provider
- operational management information. Users see their 'primary' service providers (those that bill them) as the parties responsible for problems in delivering paid-for services. This will be their view even if the actual problem occurs within another service provider's domain. Service assurance is therefore a very thorny issue; primary service providers become responsible for the quality of services and infrastructure that they do not own or control. Consumers in particular – and especially those users who have not experienced the reliability and performance problems that regular PC users have come to expect – will demand high levels of service performance and reliability. Competition between service providers will force greater pressure on the providers to deliver high-quality services. Primary service providers will therefore need to have confidence that the third-party-operated applications, services and infrastructure that they allow their subscribers to access, is being managed to a high standard
- context information. Session context information identifies user sessions and what and whom those sessions actually involve. It therefore makes sense that these should be the foundation of the information processing that individual providers have to carry out. However, the promotion of session context information to being something that is shared not only between components of an application or service, but also between providers, brings further technology challenges.

Security and privacy

One of the main technology challenges that must be addressed in order for information exchange to be viable is targeted at allaying providers' concerns. That is, that information must be shared in a tightly-controlled manner that prohibits unauthorised viewing or editing of the information.

Data-privacy laws, combined with the need to prevent unauthorised access to information, mean that there are three main aspects of electronic security that providers must consider when planning information sharing initiatives:

- information to be transmitted electronically between companies must be secure in transit. This ensures that no unauthorised person or system can read or tamper with the information as it passes from one party to the other

- once received, shared information must only be readable by a tightly-controlled set of systems and people. This ensures that no unauthorised person or system can read or tamper with the information once it has arrived at its destination
- any changes to the rules that govern who, or what, can read which information, must be logged. This ensures that any investigation into breaches of data privacy (where, for example, information is shared with a third party not consented to by the customer) can be carried out effectively.

Translation

The second main technology challenge arises from the fact that different companies very rarely have precisely the same ways of storing and managing information. The third challenge arises from the possibility that each provider may (over time) build many commercial relationships that require sharing of usage and operational information to some degree.

The ways in which companies go about doing business is not standardised. Now that IT systems are increasingly used to support business processes, the ways that companies go about doing business affect the ways that companies store and manage electronic information about business processes.

So when companies decide they want to share information, they must find a way to overcome the differences between their own terms of reference. If two providers decide that they will share usage information, for example, in what format should date and time information – essential information – be represented?

There are three paths to satisfaction:

- both parties agree to adopt a widely-recognised set of standardised information representations
- the more powerful party imposes its own terms of reference on the weaker one
- both parties stick to their own terms of reference, but employ a translation service, which automatically ensures (based on information that both parties have given it) that each party receives something that it can understand.

Whichever path is chosen, translation software will be employed somewhere. Without translation software, the public standards option and the 'do what you are told' option require one or both parties to change the ways that their systems work. The difference between these paths from a technology point of view, therefore, is who implements the translation software and whose rules are used to configure it.

Management of information sharing

Where a provider has commercial relationships with third parties that all require some degree of usage and/or operational information sharing, just managing the information sharing processes and underlying infrastructure may become a significant undertaking. Providers will have to ensure that they make adequate provision for effective management of processes and infrastructure, or commercial relationships may very soon crumble under the weight of delayed payments or commercial negotiations.

F2.5 Geographic issues

Some say that we live in an age where national boundaries no longer matter. The truth, unfortunately, is nothing like that. Quite apart from differences in penetrations of particular types of application and access platform, matters of geography create widely differing environments, which affect the ability of suppliers from particular markets to migrate to other positions in other markets. The considerable variation that exists across national boundaries brings yet another dimension to the need for suppliers to form partnerships with incumbents when they consider migrating from one position to another.

Application and content issues

The chief geographical variations concerning the provision of applications and content are:

- cultural attitudes towards, and regulation of, content – including sex & violence, profanity, religious content and advertising
- requirements for content localisation – the Internet and the Worldwide Web have developed as largely English reservoirs of information. Broadcast content and telecommunications services, by contrast, are created or adapted specifically for local markets
- consumer protection regulation.

Service-provision issues

The main geographical variations concerning the provision of network-based services to particular access platforms are:

- regulation that restricts ownership of media channels
- regulation that restricts which types of company can set up as a network service provider and bill subscribers for network services
- requirements for the localisation of service wrappers such as portals, customer-service information and online bill payment.

Device issues

The chief geographical factor affecting the successful (or otherwise) provision of devices is the degree of cultural variation that exists, particularly in the consumer market, when it comes to who spends time doing what. In countries where particular family members spend a lot of time in the kitchen, Internet refrigerators are not such a far-fetched idea as in countries where most adults work away from the home. In addition, in some cultures 'traditional' computers are seen to be intimidating – and there is correspondingly greater opportunity for networked home appliances.

F3 The PC stovepipe

F3.1 Supply-chain overview

The PC stovepipe is a device-centric set of supply chains that deliver business applications, personal communications applications, e-commerce and infotainment to PCs.

In 2001, we already see the PC as a platform for convergence. Many consumer users of PCs utilise public telecommunications networks to connect to the Internet, in order to interact with web-based e-commerce and infotainment applications. In the business segment, personal communications applications, traditionally the preserve of the telecommunications supply chain, are provided to PCs through computer-telephony integration (CTI) technology.

The Worldwide Web is already delivering infotainment applications (traditionally associated with broadcast media supply chains) to PCs – for example, the plethora of radio stations now 'webcasting' their programming.

The markets associated with delivery of PCs are maturing – particularly in the corporate sector. The rise in popularity of Internet-based e-commerce and infotainment services is providing some content, application and service providers with healthy revenues, but the rich vein of gold has so far failed to materialise for the dot.com miners. Moreover it is questionable how much capacity for growth there is in the PC market.

Device and platform vendors, as well as content, application and service providers are therefore starting to pursue new opportunities both within their own supply chain, and outside of the fixed-Internet world. For device and platform vendors this means building portals and services around those, and developing new devices such as PDAs; for content, application and service providers this means attempting to move into the mobile networks and services, and broadcast media supply chains. For example, some ISPs are diversifying into new types of service, such as interactive TV content. UK-based ISP Freeserve has recently announced details of its new TV portal service offering.

How did we get here?

The birth of the PC stovepipe came with the introduction of the PC in the early 1980s. PCs quickly became a corporate computing proposition, and over the next ten years stimulated the growth in LAN technology and the client-server computing paradigm. Now, however, the corporate market segment (which is focused on the use of PCs for business applications) is saturated; and most of the industry's growth comes from the consumer segment, where PCs are mostly used for infotainment and (increasingly) e-commerce. Most of the device innovation is targeted at the consumer sector too (for example, the introduction of DVD players and sophisticated graphics cards).

In 2000, there are approximately 400 million PCs and this figure will grow to nearly 900 million by 2006 – which explains why delivering services to PCs represents a very attractive proposition for broadcasters and telecommunications companies.

Many PC manufacturers have their products in the handheld and consumer appliances markets and are keeping PC development in step with these products and those of partners. Since there is still a great deal of uncertainty about which devices and applications are likely to be successful in the pervasive computing space, manufacturers remain cautious about abandoning the PC just yet.

The PC supplier community

Figure F3.1 shows the PC application supply chains.

The PC supplier community can be summarised as follows:

- device manufacturers, which provide the PC hardware. This includes companies such as Compaq, Dell, IBM and HP, as well as organisations that supply important PC components, such as Intel and AMD
- fixed network providers, which operate the network infrastructure over which the consumer segment connects to the Internet to access infotainment and e-commerce applications. Most of the suppliers in this group are large telcos. However, cable network operators are starting to open up their home cable networks to data transmission through cable modems – particularly in North America. BT, Cable & Wireless, US West, NTL and Time Warner Cable Network are examples of this type of company
- ISPs, which provide the access services that enable both consumers and corporate users to connect their home PCs or corporate LANs to the Internet. As well as the many dedicated ISPs found across the world, ISP services are offered by virtually all the big telcos. There is an enormous amount of competition in the ISP market in both the consumer and corporate sectors. Examples of this sort of company include AOL, BT, Colt, Freeserve and T-Online

Figure F3.1 **The PC application supply chains**

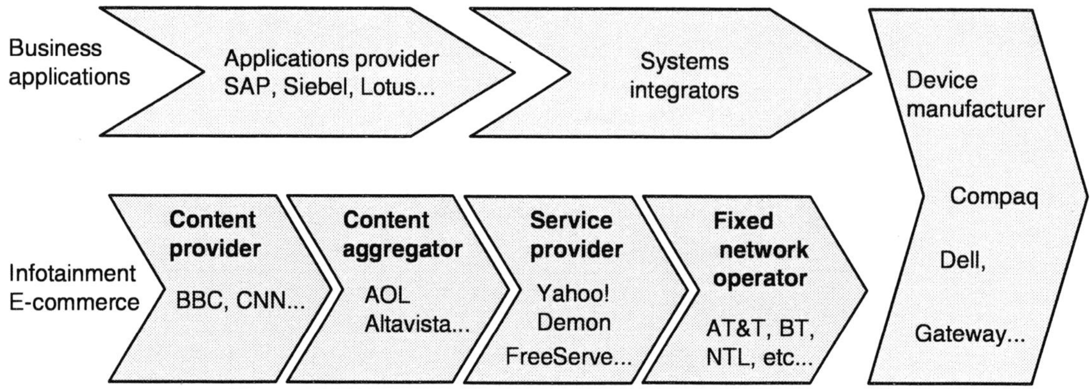

Source: Ovum (Pervasive Computing: Technologies and Markets/Chapter F)

- web content aggregators/portal providers, which collect content and present it to both consumer and corporate users through a single service or interface. In some cases (such as AOL), ISPs play this role. Other examples include AltaVista and Vizzavi (which also aggregates content for mobile devices)
- application software companies, which provide business applications for LAN-based (and increasingly Internet-based) access by PCs. This market category contains a huge array of software companies, including large corporations such as Microsoft, Oracle, SAP, Siebel, Lotus, Computer Associates, right through to the smallest companies providing software packages and tools specialised for vertical industries and niche markets
- web content providers, which provide (and in some cases charge for) access to web-based content and services. Examples include BBC, CNN, Reuters and Time Warner.

Powerbases

In both the consumer and corporate PC market segments, power lies with the brokers that make it possible for PC users to access and interact with applications and content. In the market of delivering business applications to PCs, the power principally resides with Microsoft and its close partners. Within the consumer domain, where infotainment and e-commerce are the principal applications and the Internet is increasingly the access medium, it is the Internet content aggregators that wield the bulk of the power. The reason why most power is in the hands of the aggregator role, rather than the ISP role, is twofold:

- the Worldwide Web is a colossal, confusing universe of content
- low barriers to entry for content creators means that much content is of dubious quality or not suitable for many people.

Consequently the role of content aggregator, categoriser and filter is a highly valued one.

F3.2 What is breaking down the walls?

Web-based content providers & aggregators, portal providers and business application suppliers are keen to follow other potential opportunities, as well as exploit the expanding user base of PC owners. The bulk of the remaining growth of the PC market is in non-English-speaking consumer markets, and many of the successful web content providers lack the expertise to really attack these. They are looking to see if moving sideways might be an easier and cheaper way for them to increase their revenues.

Immigration: the broadband invasion

The increasing availability of point-to-point broadband access networks into the home, combined with the rapidly increasing amount of access bandwidth available to businesses, is starting to attract content providers from the broadcast media industry to the PC delivery channel. The first 'baby steps' are being taken through the use of streaming media technology by big providers such as CNN and the BBC, and also through the *ad hoc* streaming of live events by niche suppliers. Thus far, however, despite encouragement from the fixed network operator community, the market issues are less close to being addressed than are the technology issues. We expect the main bulk of activity to occur between 2003 and 2004.

Drivers

Broadband content providers and aggregators, currently residing in the broadcast media stovepipe, are looking for opportunities to leverage their key asset – the ability to produce high-quality broadband content – on the PC platform. Many of them have high-profile broadcast media brands, which they see as powerful aids in their competition with existing narrowband content providers to produce media assets that will make broadband Internet applications compelling.

Fixed network operators are keen to stimulate this re-use of broadband content and applications. Their view is that the more compelling broadband content and applications there are, the more data traffic will flow over their broadband networks – bringing welcome revenues.

Inhibitors

The arrival of broadband content will not be inhibited by protectionism from the PC stovepipe. The short-term inhibitor of the broadband invasion is a technological one: the availability of broadband access networks, and the resulting requirement that existing broadband content be adapted for delivery to PCs – which requires new skills and potentially devalues the content.

In the longer term, however, broadcast service providers themselves may be inhibited from growing businesses in providing TV on the Internet – by competition from existing ISPs and portal providers, including fixed network operators, which want to provide broadband interactive services themselves.

In addition, the re-use of content providers' and aggregators' assets over the Internet depends on the resolution of three uncertainties regarding protection of revenue streams:

- how can providers apply rights management controls to content distributed over the Internet, to ensure that piracy is minimised? (the recent problems of Napster.com highlight media owners' concerns here)
- what is the best way to make money when broadband content is delivered over the Internet? Is the answer interactive advertising, pay-per-view, or both?
- how can pay-per-view models be implemented?

Immigration: PC substitution

Device suppliers are keen to provide substitutes for consumer use of PCs. The evolution of digital TVs, games consoles and new types of connected home appliances are starting to transform all of these device types into competitors to the PC in its consumer-usage context. We discuss the potential role of networked appliances in more detail in *Section F6*.

Drivers

Manufacturers of potential consumer PC substitutes (digital TVs, games consoles and networked home appliances) are driving Internet connectivity to web-based infotainment and e-commerce applications (albeit at different rates) chiefly through the desire to differentiate themselves in what are extremely competitive markets.

Inhibitors

There are two main inhibitors to the substitution of the PC by other devices:

- many households in industrialised nations already own some combination of TVs, games consoles and home appliances. All the potential PC substitutes require consumers to replace existing devices with new ones
- the PC is a multi-function device that even residential users employ for different tasks. For example, many are used not only for playing games and surfing the Web, but also accounting, budgeting, e-mail and word-processing. For many people, the interactive services offered through other access platforms do not yet provide the full range of functions that they need.

Emigration: TV portals and interactive services

Early rollouts of digital interactive services offered through the TV by cable operators and satellite-based content aggregators are piquing the interest of the web content aggregator community and, to a lesser extent, the personal communications application provider community (particularly providers of e-mail services). In many ways, this is a reflection of the broadband invasion; here, we have content aggregators such as AOL, Vizzavi and Yahoo! starting to forge partnerships that enable them to provide TV portals that bring web content and web-based applications, and improve the breadth of interactive TV services. Most of the activity in this area will occur in 2001 and 2002.

Drivers

Threats and opportunities are both contributing to the desire of web-based content aggregators and personal communication application providers to break out of the PC stovepipe:

- the difficulty of growing PC-related markets in geographies where PC penetration is still low, because of the cost of setting up new sales and marketing channels, and localising content
- the opportunity to re-use existing assets and technology expertise, and to leverage existing brands, in accessing new markets that are not addressable through the PC platform.

Inhibitors

The primary inhibitors to web-based content aggregators and personal communication application providers moving into delivery of interactive services in the broadcast media stovepipe are:

- competition from interactive electronic programme guides (EPGs) and TV portal services built by existing broadcast players and partnerships
- the need to invest in building relationships with new service providers, which are already active in delivering broadcast media applications and content
- the expense and risk of building multichannel applications
- the need to localise both content and services. Much of the content served through the Worldwide Web is in English; but TV programming is almost universally either adapted (through subtitling or subbing in video) or specially authored in local languages for particular audiences.

Emigration: wireless Internet

The evolution of wireless mobile networks towards packet-based digital networks, and eventually to broadband capacities, is luring business application providers, as well as infotainment providers (web-based content providers and aggregators) into the provision of content, applications and services for mobile access platforms. Part of the reason that the current level of supplier interest is so feverish is that the transformation of mobile networks into data bearers potentially brings a whole new dimension of opportunity – the delivery of content, applications and services that are mobility-aware. In 2001/2002, there will be a huge degree of market movement in this area, primarily because mobile network operators are keen not to pass up the opportunity to play a major role in the development of mobile networks as application access platforms.

Drivers

For business application and infotainment suppliers, the drivers that are pushing them towards the wireless Internet platform are clear:

- the very large installed base of mobile voice handsets brings huge new opportunities for owning customers
- there is very significant demand for new mobility-aware applications from network operators, which are very keen to stimulate the growth of data traffic over their networks
- provision of content, applications and services brings providers an opportunity to position themselves as multichannel players and thus differentiate themselves from their competitors.

Inhibitors

The main inhibitors that are holding back the tide of emigration of application and content providers into wireless Internet relate to technology, skills and experience:

- mobile network operators understand the mobility concept and its effects, and are desperate to play significant roles in the development of mobile applications. Their approach to building and deploying applications is very different from that used by providers used to working with the PC platform
- many providers used to working with the PC platform lack the technology skills required to build applications that are deliverable as network services over the wireless Internet
- multichannel applications require new approaches and considerable investment in infrastructure and application-hosting platforms.

F3.3 How open are the main technologies?

Much of the drive towards standardised content representation and application middleware technologies is coming from players in the PC stovepipe, keen to make their assets applicable to other access platforms. There is increasing pressure from software infrastructure providers on the application and content provider communities, to use open standards such as Java and XML.

The melding of Internet technology with the mechanisms for delivering all kinds of application and content to the PC platform is what is driving the opening of important application delivery technologies:

- most of the available application servers, which host network-based application components and serve them to access platforms using web technologies, now encourage development of applications using Java – and there is a trend towards better support for XML-based content too
- content management tools, which help content providers manage the process of authoring and assembling content, are moving towards XML technology as the foundation of content representation.

However, software infrastructure technologies, which enhance the quality-of-service of application delivery to PCs, have evolved to be specialised for the PC platform. Furthermore, the PC stovepipe has a unique problem regarding the use of this infrastructure in the future. The wide variation in PCs, together with the fact that users can install or remove software components very easily, makes it very hard for any supplier wanting to deliver an application to PCs using Internet technology to anticipate what facilities will be in place on the client platform. Some PCs have the Java runtime installed, for example, whereas others do not. Some users configure their PCs so that no software components can be downloaded by browsers; others do not. Consequently, use of Internet technology to deliver applications to PCs can preclude the use of software infrastructure to enhance the quality of application delivery – since using such technology will invariably exclude many PC users whose machines are not configured correctly. This problem is much less likely to occur in other access platforms – at least in the short term.

Moreover, content and application authoring tools, which enable organisations to rapidly generate and maintain content, lag behind deployment platforms in promoting the creation of cross-platform assets.

F4 The telecommunications stovepipe

F4.1 Supply-chain overview

The telecommunications stovepipe's history is as an application-centric and delivery-centric industry – the focus of the industry was to deliver voice applications through telecommunications networks. Until recently, handsets were considered as 'terminals' – just the things at the ends of a network that allow people to use the service.

The telecommunications stovepipe actually consists of two distinct supply chains (there are more, but we focus here on the provision of access networks, and of services over those access networks) that historically dealt with:

- delivery of voice over fixed access networks
- delivery of voice over mobile access networks.

As with the PC stovepipe, however, the telecommunications stovepipe is also starting to be broken down. Since the arrival of the Internet as a mass phenomenon, the PC stovepipe has been 'piggy-backing' on the fixed telecommunications supply chain, in order to provide consumer PC users with local access to the Internet. Many telcos have responded to this threat by creating their own ISP businesses. And computer-telephony integration (CTI) technology has already brought interfaces to corporate personal communications applications to the PC platform.

Fixed networks

Fixed network operators, under increasing competition from cable substitutes in many countries, are now rolling out new residential access network services that bring broadband data transfer speeds to homes. Most of this new capacity is being delivered through xDSL. In the corporate environment, fibre-to-the-building (FTTB) rollouts are bringing huge data capacities to offices, capitalising on the massive build-out of metropolitan, national and international fibre between 1990 and 2000.

Mobile networks

Mobile network operators are now feverishly building out new packet data services over their networks. This, in many ways, is a paradigm shift in mobile networks.

A good analogy is parenthood. For the mobile operators, this move to packet networking is like having a first child. It completely changes the way in which they work, from the partnerships, service development and portfolio mix, through to customer support and billing. Anything that follows from that, in terms of further upgrades or a move to third-generation networks is more of the same – more opportunities, more hassle, more complexity. But the fundamental change has been made with the move to packet.

In Japan, NTT DoCoMo's proprietary packet-prepared PDC network has already been in place for some time. Its success as a revenue generator for NTT has 'sounded the gong' for mobile data and is pulling network operators in other countries to move ever faster in rolling out 2G+ technologies such as GPRS, and then to delivering broadband capabilities with 3G technology.

How did we get here?

Fixed networks

The 'piggy-backing' of PC-Internet connectivity on the fixed telecommunications supply chain has long since pushed the telecommunications community into providing data carriage services – whether they knew it or not.

Now, however, voice revenue in fixed networks is declining in many countries as teledensity reaches saturation point, and as voice services over fixed lines become a commodity. This process is accelerating as new entrants utilising voice-over-IP (VoIP) technology route voice calls over the Internet backbone for free and undercut incumbent operators using legacy networks.

Operators are not about to stop delivering voice communication; but they are looking for alternative revenue sources. Packet data transmission and the provision of value-added applications based around data services are seen as the major opportunities.

Mobile networks

Since the development of digital cellular networks in the late 1980s and early 1990s, the launch and development of mobile networking has been both dramatic and seemingly inexorable. Starting from 1990, when the penetration of mobile phones was a relatively low percentage of the overall population in most countries, we have now reached the point where the population of mobile phones exceeds that of fixed lines in many areas. Penetration rates of over 60% are not unusual.

This growth has been particularly noticeable in Europe and Asia-Pacific, where the choice of common networking standards based on GSM have boosted adoption. In North America, the failure to adopt a common cellular networking standard across the region has resulted in a lot of fragmentation, which has left its mark on the scale of adoption.

The supplier community

Figure F4.1 shows the telecommunications supply chains.

Figure F4.1 **Telecommunications supply chains**

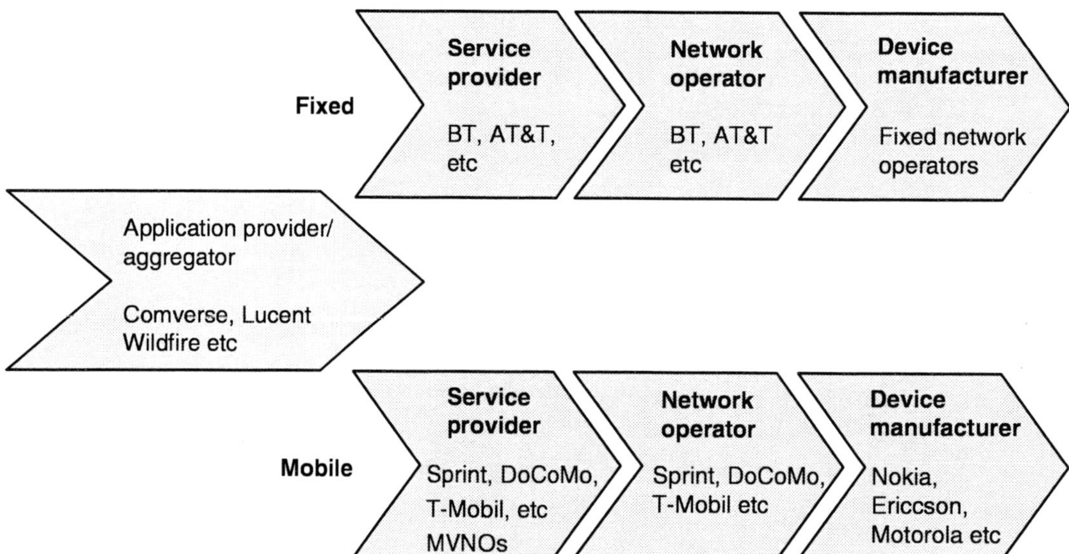

Source: Ovum (Pervasive Computing: Technologies and Markets/Chapter F)

Bearing in mind our focus on access networks, we summarise the telecommunications supplier community as follows:

- fixed network operators, such as BT, Deutsche Telekom and AT&T, which also sell telephone handsets
- fixed service providers, which have historically been the same organisations as the fixed network operators. However, this is changing with local loop unbundling and other deregulation activities, which is allowing other utilities such as gas and electricity providers to offer telecommunications services
- infrastructure manufacturers, which provide the transmission and switching infrastructure and mobile voice handsets to mobile network operators. These companies include Nokia, Ericsson, Motorola, Siemens, Nortel Networks, Alcatel and Lucent
- mobile network operators, such as T-Mobil in Germany, BT Cellnet in the UK and Sprint PCS in the US
- mobile service providers, which until fairly recently, as in the fixed telecommunications supply chain, were businesses run by the same parent companies that operated the networks. However, the creation of mobile virtual network operator businesses has challenged the *status quo*. Banks, retailers and other well-known brands integrate several functions, such as the issuing of SIM cards, billing and the provision of enhanced services. In some countries it is a regulatory requirement that service provision cannot be carried out by a mobile network operating company

- application providers, such as Comverse and Lucent, which offer packaged personal communications applications to network operators and service providers.

Powerbases

Fixed networks

Historically, the positions of power in fixed-access network markets undoubtedly lay with the incumbent network operators. However, as deregulation has swept through national telecoms industries, competition from new entrants has grown rapidly. Increasingly, the opening of markets to other utilities and consumer brands has further increased competition, which has been greatest in international, long-distance and the highly profitable business sectors. The last bastion of regulated hegemony for the incumbent operators has been the residential local loop, and that is now crumbling in the face of the Internet.

Competition in fixed telecommunications is a matter of price and quality-of-service. Telephony-related network services are all but commodities. The very mature nature of the fixed telecommunications markets in all industrialised nations means that power, at the moment, lies more with national regulators than anyone else.

Mobile networks

The rapid development and huge scale of the development of second-generation mobile networks has led to a dramatic increase in importance and power of two types of player in the mobile market:

- the operators, which derive their power from two major sources – their subscriber base (in absolute terms or relative to that of their competitors) and the range of their activities (in terms of the breadth of their service portfolio or their geographic operation). Vodafone is a prime example of an operator that has extended the geographic scale of its operations through acquisition
- the infrastructure vendors, such as Ericsson, Nokia and Motorola, which have built a large portion of their business on selling infrastructure and handsets for the second-generation digital networks around the world.

Both these power bases are under threat. The operators face competition from new virtual competitors, as the early, comparatively unregulated years of operation in the mobile market give way to more open competitive scenarios. The vendors face a situation where the second-generation networks are due to be replaced by the next generation of mobile technology. It is by no means certain that the vendors that succeeded so spectacularly in the second generation will maintain their pre-eminent position in the third. The second-tier vendors, particularly those in Asia-Pacific, see the emergence of the third generation as their opportunity to take a share in the spectacular growth of mobile, missed during the 1990s.

F4.2 What is breaking down the walls?

Immigration: wireless Internet

The wireless Internet phenomenon is already with us. Success from an early packet-switched wireless network implementation by Japan's NTT DoCoMo has galvanised both the supplier community and the venture-capital community to roll out packet-switched 2G+ mobile networks worldwide. The importance of utilising the unique aspect of mobile networks – the mobility of the users – in the applications that are deployed is already widely understood. Mobile network operators are already developing such applications.

However, application providers and web content providers & aggregators from the PC stovepipe are also making inroads into the market for mobile data services. The term 'wireless Internet' is an indication that the PC world has already made its mark. Most of the activity will occur in 2001 and 2002, as suppliers from the two stovepipes compete, form partnerships and acquire each other.

Drivers

The high levels of competition in the mobile service provision market are driving network operators and service providers to build new applications and services quickly, in order to reap early-mover rewards and construct platforms for future growth. However, the mobile-network supplier community is keen to boost the breadth and depth of applications and content available to mobile network subscribers. In theory, more compelling content and applications means more network traffic, and more revenues to the operator. However, mobile operators and service providers do not have the skills and resources to build all the assets themselves. This means bringing in suppliers of web-based content and applications.

Inhibitors

Mobile network operators and service providers' skills and resources are focused on delivering network services based around voice. Web content providers & aggregators and business application providers' skills and resources revolve around the provision of assets that work on the PC platform. Neither community has all the answers, and both must work together to develop the right kind of solution.

Confusion and competition in the application platform market is also having an inhibiting effect on application deployment. Without the right infrastructure, applications will not scale, but the level of competition in providing the platforms for these applications is actually clouding the issues for operators and service providers. Leading infrastructure providers from both the software community (such as BEA, IBM and Microsoft) and the network community (Nokia) together with new entrants (such as Aether and Phone.Com) are all vying for pole position, and bringing the hype more often associated with dot.coms to the proceedings.

It is tempting to draw a comparison from obvious successes such as i-Mode in Japan, where the level of adoption and use of non-voice services have quickly reached levels that make operators elsewhere salivate. This is dangerous. There are many cultural issues that make translating this success elsewhere difficult. Most importantly, i-Mode runs on a well-established packet network in a country where fixed-Internet penetration is low.

Immigration: rich-media mobile applications

The widespread availability of higher-speed access services on mobile networks in 2004/2005 will bring broadcast content providers and aggregators, along with their broadband content assets, into the wireless Internet fray. There are two factors that will colour the nature of the ensuing battle:

- the degree to which content is produced with multichannel distribution in mind
- the capability of the wireless mobile access platforms – including the access networks in use.

It is unlikely that, by 2005, broadcast players will add value by producing or adapting content specifically for mobile (or indeed any particular type of) access platform. Streaming media technology is already playing that content-adaptation role, in a broadcaster- and increasingly platform-independent way. Broadcasters are therefore already losing access to that possible value point. Consequently, it is likely that partnerships between content providers and service providers will occur in a climate of balanced power, and revolve around a free market for commercial rights agreements, as they do in television.

There is a lot of uncertainty over precisely what level of sophistication will be offered to mobile network users, as 3G technology becomes widespread. What is almost certain, however, is that bandwidth will continue to be much more constrained in mobile-access platforms than it is in fixed-access platforms – and therefore the ability to adapt content specifically for transmission over constrained mobile networks will be a powerful value point for someone.

Drivers

As with the broadband invasion of the PC stovepipe, the chief driver for this immigration into the telecommunications stovepipe will be the desire of broadband content providers and aggregators to leverage their key asset – high-quality broadband content – on mobile access platforms.

You might consider that the level of PC stovepipe penetration in the wireless Internet market by this point would inhibit the entry of broadband players. But broadband content providers and aggregators from broadcast backgrounds have a sizeable lever that they can use to gain entry – their ability to produce localised content and applications, which at the moment is sorely lacking in many of the web-centric players.

It is unlikely that the market for broadband applications on mobile access platforms will be inhibited by service providers. On the contrary, it is highly likely that service providers will want to stimulate the provision of more compelling interactive services to users in the race to compete for customers and retain them.

Inhibitors

The most important inhibitor to the delivery of broadband content to mobile access platforms is the fact that even broadband mobile networks will have limited bandwidth to offer individual subscribers. There is no historical precedent to support the notion that a high-bandwidth application is inherently better than a low-bandwidth one. What is most important is the delivery of compelling services; the restriction on bandwidth will mean that suppliers will have to continue taking steps to conserve network resources.

In order to receive and display rich-media applications, mobile access platforms will have to become highly capable computing environments – indeed, some of the more advanced platform models available come close to what is required. But that capability is highly likely to be won at the expense of control over platform openness, which means that the same issues will inhibit the delivery of broadband content to mobiles as those that inhibit broadband's invasion of the PC stovepipe. That is, concerns over revenue protection:

- how can providers apply rights management controls to rich-media content distributed over the Internet, to ensure that piracy is minimised?
- what is the best way to make money when rich media-content is delivered to mobile access platforms? Is the answer interactive advertising, pay-per-view or both?
- how can pay-per-view models be implemented?

Emigration: Interactive TV services

Cable operators and satellite-based content aggregators are starting early rollouts of broadband interactive services on TV. The development of xDSL services operating over normal copper telecommunications networks provides fixed access operators and service providers with an opportunity to compete in this area. Furthermore, satellite-based interactive service providers must enable a return path for upstream communication, otherwise there can be no interactivity. Where telcos provide the upstream channel for broadband interactive services, they also see an opportunity to offer 'bouquets' of operational services. Where their infrastructure provides the path for interactivity, telcos have the potential to manage the valuable information that passes through their doors – enabling more efficient advertising, billing and customer-management services than the broadcaster alone could provide.

Drivers

For fixed telecommunications providers, the opportunity to play a role in the delivery of interactive services has a powerful lure – the combination of increased traffic flowing over their networks, with the possibility of using their existing skills and assets in service management and billing to enhance broadcasters' service offerings.

For service providers using satellite broadcast transmission, the driver for telco involvement is obvious: without the employment of a return path, there can be no interactivity and therefore no interactive services. In many countries PSTN is the most attractive return path option because it is practically universal (in contrast to cable). Its low cost is also a major factor.

Telcos may be able to play primary broadband service-provider roles, by turning the traditional view of interactive digital services on its head – and building on existing portal services to deliver TV on the Internet, rather than the Internet on TV.

Inhibitors

The major market inhibitor for telco involvement in the delivery of interactive services is (perhaps perversely) the increasing openness of the infrastructure used to deliver interactive services. The increasing pressure being applied to incumbents to provide fair, non-discriminatory access to not only the conditional access infrastructure within set-top boxes, but also set-top box middleware APIs, electronic programme guides (EPGs) and content & application authoring tools, means that barriers to market entry are being lowered considerably. Telcos wanting to pursue the Internet-on-TV route to interactive services, in partnership with broadcasters, are increasingly facing competition not only from cable operators, but also from dedicated interactive services providers and from dedicated ISPs and web content aggregators entering the market.

F4.3 How open are the main technologies?

In the fixed-access network sector, the IT industry has already – by virtue of its historic 'piggy-backing' on PSTN for Internet access – come to grips with enabling narrowband applications, content and services to be delivered over fixed-access networks. The move to broadband access networks will certainly be no harder for data services players: in fact, the situation will be markedly improved, since xDSL services are designed to enable broadband data applications.

There is much more to be said in the area of mobile networks and their enablement as bearers of data applications. Certainly 2G+ and 3G network services, being packet-switched rather than circuit-switched, are open. Moreover, the widespread availability of WAP technology brings service providers a true (if limited) application platform.

But WAP is designed to make best use of voice-centric handsets' capabilities – therefore WAP-based applications are not inherently portable. Indeed much of the 'new' content, applications and services arriving on WAP services are re-written or adapted specifically for the mobile channel. Furthermore:

- WAP is not universally supported – it has gained most market influence in Europe, but in Japan the market has gone a different route
- individual infrastructure providers' implementations of the WAP specifications are not always compatible.

As voice-centric handsets become more capable, they are becoming more general-purpose computing platforms with true software operating systems that can manage the execution of multiple software programs simultaneously. They are also becoming part of a continuum of mobile devices that brings together phones and PDAs. Microsoft, Symbian and PalmOS are all attempting to become suppliers of popular cross-platform operating systems that play along this continuum; furthermore, they compete with the infrastructure providers, which continue to deploy proprietary operating systems in many of their handsets.

In one fundamental way, the openness of individual technologies in mobile-access platforms is irrelevant in the consideration of such platforms as just another delivery channel. The very mobility of mobile voice-centric handsets brings opportunities for content, applications and services that are mobility-aware – and these are already being built. Consequently, in order for mobile voice-centric handsets to be considered as just another delivery channel, it is the addition of location information to other access platforms that will bring the pervasive computing vision nearer.

IPv6 technology has the potential to provide the foundation for this evolution, by enabling each and every device to be given a unique, permanent address that is compatible in format with every other – something that is not possible using today's addressing schemes. But the steady implementation of IPv6 throughout networks and devices is far from a certainty. We look at IPv6 in more detail in *Chapter G* and the *Appendix*.

F5 The broadcast media stovepipe

F5.1 Supply-chain overview

The broadcast media stovepipe is a content- and device-centric set of supply-chains. But as broadcast media go digital, the industry's device-centricity is disappearing. The cost of both broadcasting and reception is decreasing: and the circuitry required to receive and decode broadcast content can easily be fitted onto a PC expansion card – or even encoded in software. Increasingly, streaming media technology is also enabling broadcast content to be adapted and delivered over the Internet.

Broadcast industries in the developed world are mature ones. In many industrialised countries, markets for TVs and radios are saturated. In addition, the Internet and streaming media technology are challenging the business models of many established players. Historically, most broadcast service providers' strengths lay in the delivery of media, and control over the airwaves. With the possibility of distribution of rich media by the Internet, much of the broadcasters' power may be destroyed – leaving only their ability to produce compelling rich-media content.

Against this background, the television broadcasters in particular have chosen to take up the fight and pursue not only web-based delivery strategies for the PC community, but also to deploy interactive services through digital TVs. Many broadcast content providers, aggregators and service providers are now amongst the most fervent advocates of multichannel application and content delivery. However, provision of interactive services requires significant investment commitments from broadcast players, as well as innovative use of technology to obtain revenues from multiple sources. In today's environment, where each service provider cannot expect to deliver services to one or two million subscribers, they must aim to obtain annual ARPUs of $2,000 or more in order to recoup their investment and earn profits in satisfactory timescales.

Fortunately, the 'digital revolution' means that in addition to the passive entertainment offerings that they were confined to under analogue, broadcasters are now able to offer more interactive infotainment applications, e-commerce and personal communications applications – all of which have multiple revenue-generating possibilities attached to them.

There are two variations on digital interactive services that the players are aiming to provide:

- television programming is the dominant medium, and web-based interactive content, applications and services are accessible through the TV – the Internet on your TV
- the Worldwide Web is the dominant medium, and broadcast video programming is accessible through web-based portals – TV on the Internet.

How did we get here?

Until recently, the broadcasting industry's supply chain was very much restricted to the delivery of information and entertainment services to TVs and radios. This was a result of the limitations of the analogue broadcasting network. The advent of digital TV has caused a huge revolution in the broadcasting industry. In principle, it is now possible to deliver content to practically any digital device (not just TVs), and use the TV to deliver other types of content and services previously only accessible from other devices, such as PCs.

The potential market for interactive services delivered through TVs is huge – because of the near-total penetration of TV devices worldwide. This delivery channel is particularly interesting to providers of mass-market consumer services, because of the familiarity of the TV to people who do not want to use more traditional service access devices; and in territories where PC-based Internet access penetration is low (such as China and Japan).

The supplier community

Figure F5.1 shows the broadcast TV supply chain.

Digital TV suppliers fall into four main groups:

- transmission infrastructure suppliers, which provide transmission infrastructure, set-top box infrastructure (to receive and decode transmissions) and conditional access systems (which secure broadcast data from all but paying subscribers). These suppliers include Pace, General Instrument/Motorola, NDS, OpenTV (which now also owns Spyglass), Liberate, Microsoft, SECA (owned by CanalPlus) and Oracle. Microsoft is a very active player: it has teamed up with Pace, DirecTV and Thomson Multimedia
- network providers, which provide the 'pipes' for the services through xDSL, cable or satellite network services. These include Astra, AT&T Broadband, DirecTV, NTL and Telewest. Some provide broadcast networks, others provide point-to-point services
- content providers, which provide programmes and charge for their broadcast. These include Carlton, CNN and Time Warner. Companies such as Reuters may become content providers in the future

Figure F5.1 **The broadcast TV supply chain**

Source: Ovum (Pervasive Computing: Technologies and Markets/Chapter F)

- broadcasters, which 'own' the broadcast bandwidth, buy and aggregate content into channels, and may (depending on their business model) sell advertising space within those channels' schedules, and sell subscriptions to those channels. These include ABC, BBC, CanalPlus and Sky. Future content aggregators may include players such as AOL and Yahoo!

However, the introduction of interactive services brings three new supplier groups into the industry:

- new interactive services providers, which will compete with partnerships between incumbent broadcasters and network operators
- fixed telecommunications network operators, which provide return paths that are not inherent in the terrestrial broadcast or satellite networks
- networked home appliance and games console manufacturers, which will compete with set-top box manufacturers.

Powerbases

Regulators play significant roles in all broadcast media (of which digital TV is a segment) worldwide – although, of course, individual regulators' powers tend to be limited by particular country boundaries.

Historically, terrestrial TV broadcast networks have been technologically open (anyone can develop a TV set) but regulators make it difficult to enter – broadcasters have to work hard to gain and keep their licences. Consequently, the real power in the digital TV market will start with those that already have licences, and that are providing the money to develop interactive services – the current broadcasters.

F5.2 What is breaking down the walls?

Immigration: Interactive services

The introduction of the first interactive TV services in Europe is attracting the interest of major players from both the PC and telecommunications stovepipes. These two communities, together with broadcast service providers, all have value to bring to the introduction of interactive services. During 2001 and 2002, we will see feverish activity in this area as new companies emerge – and established players form partnerships with them, compete with them or acquire them.

Broadcasters are doing most of the driving towards interactive digital TV services. Commercial broadcasters are particularly keen to use digital broadcasting as a way of remaining competitive, and see interactive services as a way to pay for new digital content, and lock subscribers into their services. The main players are looking to 'commerce-enabled infotainment' delivered to mass-market consumer audiences, as the main revenue generator for their services.

Drivers

Threats and opportunities are contributing to the desire of web-based content aggregators, personal communication application providers and fixed telecommunications providers to break out of their stovepipes:

- the difficulty for PC-based application providers of growing PC-related markets in areas where PC penetration is still low, because of the cost of setting up new sales & marketing channels and localising content
- declining voice revenues for fixed telecommunications providers in many markets
- the opportunity for web-based players to re-use existing assets and technology expertise, and to leverage existing brands, in accessing new markets that are not addressable through the PC platform
- the opportunity for fixed telecommunications providers to increase traffic flow over their networks, and to use their existing skills and assets in service management and billing to enhance broadcasters' interactive service offerings.

Inhibitors

The primary inhibitors to immigration into the broadcast stovepipe from the PC and telecommunications stovepipes arise from suppliers' lack of experience in delivering broadcast media services, which:

- have particularly demanding quality-of-service and ease-of-use requirements, due to the nature of the TV medium
- are regulated in ways that the delivery of telecommunications services, and the Internet, are not
- are frequently localised for regional and national markets in ways that Internet content in particular is not.

Both types of player have something to offer, but they must form partnerships with or acquire broadcasters in order to get to market – and the acquisition route may be closed off in some territories due to media ownership rules.

Immigration: TV substitution

Suppliers of PCs, games consoles and new types of connected home appliances are keen to provide substitutes for televisions. The evolution of these devices into smart, connected access platforms, capable of delivering rich-media applications (especially with the assistance of streaming media technology) is starting to transform all of these device types into competitors to the TV. This situation is in many ways the flipside of the device substitution trend that the PC stovepipe is starting to grapple with.

Drivers

Manufacturers of potential consumer TV substitutes (PCs, games consoles and networked home appliances) are driving Internet connectivity to rich-media content and applications – primarily related to infotainment and e-commerce – mainly in order to differentiate themselves in what are extremely competitive markets.

Inhibitors

There are two main inhibitors to the substitution of the TV by other devices:

- many households in industrialised nations already own some combination of PCs, games consoles and home appliances. All the potential TV substitutes require consumers to replace existing devices with new ones
- in many households, the TV is a device that is used in a community concept, where usage is shared between a group of people. PCs, in particular, are designed for use by one person at a time. Most have comparatively small screens, and require users to interact with them at close quarters via a keyboard or a mouse.

Emigration: Use of point-to-point networks

The rise in availability of residential broadband access services is bringing together the telecommunications, broadcast media and PC stovepipes. There are many ways in which these communities need to interact in order to deliver services that customers might want, and (more importantly) want to pay for. Telcos have roles to play in the delivery of all types of interactive service – but because of the power that existing broadcasters have in the broadcast media stovepipe, telcos wishing to pursue the dominant service provider role are most likely to gain success through the TV-on-the-Internet model of interactive services.

Drivers

Broadcast suppliers have two reasons for pursuing the delivery of interactive services and digital TV through point-to-point fixed networks:

- it gives them an opportunity to re-use their chief remaining asset – high-quality broadband content production – in a new delivery channel, and thus potentially reach new markets
- point-to-point networks provide a transmission medium that is particularly suited to the delivery of interactive services. The fact that each subscriber has a dedicated connection to the service provider brings greater security than is perceived on cable networks; and, unlike satellite networks, both downstream and upstream communication can be effected through the same channel.

Inhibitors

The chief inhibitor to broadcasters wanting to move into providing interactive services to residential customers through point-to-point networks is competition from existing ISPs and portal providers. These players – many of whom will be operated by the telcos that are operating xDSL services – are very keen to broaden their own service portfolios, and want to restrict the role of the broadcaster to a content provider. (Broadcasters, on the other hand, would rather network operators stuck to carriage and left the service provision to them.)

Each type of player needs the other – but forming partnerships with companies that you intend to compete against is tricky. Unless both parties can offer something of value to the other, effective, compelling services will not be delivered.

Whichever player provides broadband interactive services through the Internet and xDSL access to PCs, it will have to deal with payment and revenue protection issues.

In addition, the re-use of content providers' and aggregators' assets over the Internet depends on the resolution of three uncertainties regarding the protection of revenue streams:

- how can providers apply rights management controls to content distributed over the Internet, to ensure that piracy is minimised?
- what is the best way to make money when broadband content is delivered over the Internet? Is the answer interactive advertising, pay-per-view or both?
- how can pay-per-view models be implemented?

Emigration: Rich-media mobile applications

The widespread availability of broadband mobile services in 2004–2005 will bring broadcast content providers and aggregators, along with their broadband content assets, into the wireless Internet fray.

Drivers

As with the broadband invasion of the PC stovepipe, the chief driver for this immigration into the telecommunications stovepipe will be the desire of broadband content providers and aggregators to leverage their key asset – the ability to produce high-quality broadband content – on mobile access platforms. Players from broadcast backgrounds can use their ability to produce localised content and applications, which at the moment is lacking in many of the web-centric players, to gain entry to the wireless Internet market – which will be very crowded by 2005.

Inhibitors

The market for broadband applications on mobile access platforms will be stimulated by service providers, looking for ways to implement more compelling, interactive applications – but the entry of broadband application service providers will be met with intense competition. Existing service providers in the mobile market will, by 2005, be very familiar with wireless Internet users' preferences, platform peculiarities, the effect of mobility on interaction paradigms, and quality-of-service infrastructure. Broadcasters will come to the market without such experience.

As well as the usual revenue protection issues that they must deal with, broadcast players must therefore look to build partnerships with existing wireless service providers, rather than usurp them.

F5.3 How open are the main technologies?

Digital TV and analogue cable TV are closed, proprietary information conduits. The infrastructure vendors have built proprietary conditional access systems and set-top boxes, and have done so in partnership with the broadcasters. Thus far, digital TV is going the same way.

However, the arrival of interactive services has been controlled by regulators, which are pressurising broadcasters into doing two things:

- operating the interactive part of what they do as a separate business entity
- offering fair, non-discriminatory access to their set-top and conditional access infrastructure and 'return path' to third-party interactive services providers.

Regulators are also considering introducing new rules that force the infrastructure suppliers to provide equivalent levels of documentation and customer support to all service providers that want to develop services using their products. In this area, however, the openness of technology is improving with the increasing maturity of interactive service middleware platforms, and the gradual implementation of middleware and API standards.

Middleware technology providers such as OpenTV and Liberate (in the Internet-on-TV market), RealNetworks and PacketVideo (in the TV-on-the-Internet and the mobile rich-media markets) and Microsoft (with feet in all camps) are all competing to produce the most sophisticated, easy-to-use infrastructure platforms on which service providers can base their interactive services offerings. The level of competition is 'raising the bar' for both richness and openness.

Moreover, infrastructure suppliers on the TV-centric side of the market are now engineering support for digital TV and interactive service standards:

- DVB-MHP, which is a specification for a set-top platform with interactive service capabilities implemented in Java and/or HTML, is championed by Liberate, OpenTV and Philips (which has already implemented the standard and is licensing its implementation to other players) and has been adopted by ETSI
- ATVEF, which is a set of HTML-based standards for interactive services, is championed by the ATSC and Microsoft, among others
- ISDB, which is a set of high-definition and interactive services standards championed by Japan's ARIB.

As the old saying goes: 'the great thing about standards is that there's so many to choose from'. All these standards utilise MPEG-2 encoding of digital TV programming, but they differ in their specifications of the interactive services themselves.

F6 Supply chains for new, smart, connected devices

F6.1 New pervasive access platforms – new stovepipes?

The creation of new supply chains for delivery of digital information to new device types will not result in tomorrow's stovepipes. Many existing content providers, aggregators, service providers and network operators have opportunities to play important roles in the promotion of PDAs, in-car systems and networked home appliances to the 'premier league' of pervasive computing access platforms.

However, the lack of rigid information delivery stovepipes does not mean that the supply of digital information to these new access platforms will be generic:

- the primary value in connecting PDAs to the rest of the pervasive computing universe is in delivering mobile business application and intranet connectivity, and enabling mobile personal communication applications
- in-car systems are being developed to differentiate brands of car – so the most broadly-appealing and compelling services will be the ones that truly add value to the car. That is, applications that improve the navigability, reliability, comfort, ease-of-use and security of the vehicle
- similarly, the evolution of networked home appliances is being driven by the desire to differentiate home-appliance brands – so the first delivered services to be successful are likely to be those that help to deliver the functions of the appliance in more appealing, easy-to-use and innovative ways. When you open the door to your refrigerator, you are more likely to be thinking about what you can cook with its contents, for example, than about filing a tax return.

Supply chains that enable the introduction of these new smart, connected devices to the pervasive computing universe will consist of familiar players, but be skewed towards the applications and usage contexts of these new access platforms.

F6.2 Personal digital assistants (PDAs)

Market overview

Although PDAs have been available for several years, the phenomenon of the PDA as a true pervasive computing device is still in its infancy. Up until quite recently, PDAs have not enjoyed wireless connectivity and have only had any kind of wider network connectivity whilst connected directly to a PC through a cable, cradle or infra-red link. Third-party applications enabling the caching of content on PDAs for viewing at a later date have also been popular. AvantGo for the Palm range of PDAs is perhaps the best example of this kind of application. Also available are a range of application development tools from various vendors to allow applications to be rapidly developed for PDAs and other mobile devices.

The PDA market is enjoying significant growth at present. The market is most established in the US with Europe and Asia-Pacific lagging some way behind. Palm holds the greatest market share in the US and Europe, whilst Psion, although more established in Europe, is still to make significant in-roads in the US market. More and more vendors are entering the market now, and increasing numbers of terminals are shipping with variations of Microsoft's Windows CE operating system technology – the third major PDA operating system alongside Palm OS and Symbian's EPOC.

How will the supply chain develop?

Once PDAs are connected to wireless networks, users become truly mobile, and the supply chain opens up much more. Wireless network operators now become involved since they must carry the traffic to mobile PDAs – and of course, they have the opportunity to resell devices as part of service packages, just as they currently do with voice services today. For many existing wireless portal and service providers, connected PDAs provide an opportunity to target their content at a device that has less-restrictive resources than those of a mobile phone.

Most wireless connectivity to PDAs will be used for mobile access to business and personal communications applications. Consequently, opportunities will also appear for organisations wishing to produce and/or host applications and services that can be remotely accessed from PDAs, and also for those companies offering software to extend corporate applications so they can be accessed from PDAs. In addition the availability of software and services to support the management of remote PDAs will become much more important.

However PDAs differ from voice-centric handsets in two vital ways:

- they have always been relatively smart, and users interact with them differently than they do with voice-centric handsets
- particularly in corporate usage contexts, they can have Internet connectivity without the visible intervention of a network service provider. The ISP lies several links away – behind a serial link to a PC, and a PC connection to the corporate LAN.

Corporate users can therefore gain access to specially adapted, relatively latency-insensitive infotainment and personal communications applications, without a service provider playing a major role. This means that the opportunity for an existing wireless service provider to automatically play a major role in PDA connectivity and other network services, is not a foregone conclusion. Partnerships with service providers that provide or enable PDA services over fixed links (for example, Aether, AvantGo and OmniSky) will be more successful.

Drivers

The transformation of the PDA from executive toy to mobile corporate application access platform is not only being driven by device manufacturers keen to differentiate themselves and offer value-added services at a premium. Mobile network operators are keen to increase data traffic volumes over their networks; and existing web content providers and aggregators, which see the PDA market as an extension of the wireless Internet market, are keen to increase their profiles as multichannel players.

Inhibitors

There are several factors that could constrain the development of the PDA market. On the technology side, the usability of PDAs, and the practical extent to which they can connect to wireless networks, is currently constrained by battery technology. This is set to hinder further development of PDAs much more than the development of voice-centric handsets.

Another possible constraint on the PDA's transformation to fully-fledged pervasive player is the threat from smartphones offering all the built-in functionality of PDAs but with the addition of voice communication. If users are offered the ability to do everything that they can do on a PDA but with a phone, this could provide PDAs with some serious competition. There are already some smartphone terminals, such as the Nokia 9000I, which compete directly with some of the existing PDAs in terms of functionality.

Important technologies

The activities of several suppliers operating in different parts of the supply chain are shaping the development of PDAs. Since one of the most important applications for PDAs is the ability to use them to access corporate business applications, software that can optimise application reliability, availability, performance and security is highly significant. Companies that traditionally play in this market (such as IBM, Oracle, Microsoft and BEA Systems) are extending their software infrastructure platforms to allow devices such as PDAs to access enterprise systems and business logic. Other organisations, such as Aether Software and Centura, are also entering this market.

Those organisations developing synchronisation technology are also important to the market for PDAs. As well as traditional methods of synchronising data by direct cable or infra-red connections, there is increasing demand to be able to synchronise whilst 'on the move' over the wireless network. The SyncML initiative looks to address this by developing a standard approach to wireless synchronisation, and enabling this synchronisation is providing new opportunities for both established and new software suppliers.

There is at least as much variety in PDA for factors as there is in voice handsets. Furthermore, the chief suppliers of PDA operating systems are implementing different content representation technologies, and pursuing standards at different rates. Consequently, if you want to deliver content, applications or services to the gamut of future PDAs you will not be able to do so economically without using a content adaptation product or service – particularly in the short term.

F6.3 In-car systems

Market overview

The market for in-car (information and entertainment) systems is very immature. Car manufacturers are looking to the provision of these systems as a way of differentiating their products but, thus far, actual services and deployments are pretty thin on the ground. Modern cars are already dependent on electronics for controlling various functions – from engine management, climate control, and braking systems to rain-activated windscreen wipers. GPS technology is already built in to some high-end vehicles as standard, and is available in a standalone unit, which can be fitted to others. At present, however, there is very little integration between the various electronic systems found in vehicles.

The next step is to integrate all the in-car electronics on a vehicle intranet. This will not only serve to connect all in-car electronics to a simple, integrated network or single wiring loop, but it will also connect the vehicle to the Internet. This will allow access to a whole range of information and entertainment services, as well as enhanced GPS-based navigation systems, effectively integrating the vehicle with the wider information infrastructure that the Internet provides.

It is hard to estimate the total electronics content in vehicles, as the figure changes between manufacturers. It is likely that electronics content will continue to grow in all cars for the foreseeable future. Figures released by Siemens Automotive predicts that the value of electronics as a percentage of the total cost of a mid-sized passenger car built in North America in 2002 will be 15%, rising to 19% by 2007. More than half of the in-vehicle electronics is likely to be employed in mobile multimedia systems, and it is these systems that are of most interest to us in the scope of this report.

Car manufacturers are already forming partnerships with semi-conductor companies (for example, Volkswagen's work with Motorola on the in-car electronics for its future models), and software companies (for example, Wireless Maingate working with Volvo to provide GSM- and GPS-based navigation systems).

The kinds of application and service likely to become available in cars are quite varied. As well as services obviously targeted at drivers (such as traffic information, mapping services linked to GPS positioning, and even automatic fault reporting), there is also likely to be demand to be able to access office systems and business applications, as well as the kinds of PIM functions found in other mobile devices. Some manufacturers are also looking at enabling rich multimedia and broadcast services that can be accessed by passengers on the move.

How will the supply chain develop?

The in-vehicle information systems that have reached the market have taken advantage of GPS technology, but not been connected to wireless data networks that enable them to send and receive information on the move. But once this happens, the in-vehicle market represents a lucrative opportunity for many types of supplier. Until the cost of systems halves, however, the market will not develop significantly. And until one manufacturer deploys systems in volume, of course, system suppliers will find it hard to lower their prices.

Most large software vendors are not waiting, though. They are already carefully watching the market and many have initiatives already underway; for example, Microsoft with the AutoPC platform (a joint project with Clarion), which is based on Windows CE 2.0, and is designed to fit in the space normally reserved for a car radio.

Overall, however, it is the vehicle manufacturers that hold the balance of power in this market. They will ultimately decide what does and does not go into their vehicles, and although they do not have all the necessary expertise to be able to enable a full range of in-car applications and services themselves, there is no shortage of companies that do. Automobile manufacturers can afford to pick and choose who they partner with in order to provide the necessary hardware, software and network infrastructure to enable applications and services to be delivered to their vehicles.

Wireless network operators have significant opportunities in this market as wholesale providers of access services. It is unlikely that vehicle manufacturers will successfully exploit their strong market position to become wireless network operators themselves – they are much more likely to buy network access wholesale from existing operators, and rebrand with bundled information services and applications. This is because network connectivity itself is not the value point; it is the provision of information services and applications that run over wireless access networks that will add value to the vehicle.

Drivers

The market for in-car systems is being driven mainly by a desire by car manufacturers to integrate all in-car electronics onto one simple network – the vehicle intranet, and also because manufacturers regard offering additional value-added features and services (such as wireless connectivity and GPS) as a way of differentiating their products from those of other manufacturers.

The worldwide car market continues to grow and is showing no signs of slowing down in the short term, which means there is pressure on the manufacturers to continually release new models. As the cost of the electronics required to enable in-car systems continues to fall, manufacturers are beginning to introduce these systems across their whole range, rather than just in the high-end models.

Inhibitors

Much of the technology involved in delivering applications and services to vehicles is very similar to that required to deliver applications and services to mobile phones or connected PDAs in that it is necessary to use some sort of wireless network. Therefore, like any other mobile devices, in-car data rates to in-car systems will be governed by the data capacity of the network used. Unlike mobile phones and PDAs however, in-car systems are not constrained by factors such as battery life since systems can be powered directly from the car battery. Similarly there are not the same constraints on screen size and display quality as there are on other mobile devices, as these can be designed specifically to fit into the vehicle's dashboard.

The most significant inhibitor to deployment of sophisticated in-vehicle information systems, at least in the short term, is one of cost. Systems can cost from $1,000 – and at this price their value as a differentiation point is marginal.

Important technologies

Whilst mobile networks are perhaps the most obvious mechanism by which applications and services can be delivered to cars, it is not the only one – although it is the only one that provides a return path. Some manufacturers are working on using the digital TV broadcast network as a means of transmitting content to moving vehicles, others are examining the possibility of using digital audio broadcasting (DAB).

Since a car can basically be regarded as just another type of mobile device, a lot of the technology required to enable applications and services to be delivered to cars is the same as that required to deliver similar applications and services to other devices, such as mobile phones and PDAs. As screen size is not as much of an issue in cars as it is on a mobile phone, redesigning and formatting Internet content for restricted displays may not be so much of an issue. Indeed, passengers may be able to view content on screens of a reasonable size and quality. Some manufacturers are even investigating the possibility of deploying head-up displays (HUDs) similar to those found in fighter aircraft.

Applications developed for drivers must include a safe and non-distracting user interface. Companies are generally looking to provide very simple touch-screen interfaces or voice-controlled input for applications aimed at drivers, and it is voice control in particular that is likely to play an increasingly important role in the vehicles of the future.

Mobile location technologies are important because they enable a range of services especially applicable to vehicles on the move such as route planning and mapping services. GPS is not the only solution, and indeed it is not usable in many areas of cities – which ironically is where a lot of people get lost. Location services that 'piggy-back' on the use of mobile networks offer good alternatives, but the technology is still evolving.

Another area of technology that is already being implemented is in the area of fault diagnosis. In the latest Volvo, any faults detected by an internal detection and diagnosis system automatically generate and send an e-mail to the owner notifying them of the problem. This system can also be used to automatically notify owners when their vehicle requires servicing, and can even be configured to automatically contact a service centre or repair shop as necessary. This self-diagnosis of problems is also a technology being deployed in networked consumer goods.

F6.4 Networked home appliances

Market overview

The rapid growth of the Internet in recent years, coupled with developments in consumer electronics, has paved the way for networked home appliances to be technically feasible. We are already seeing the first fruits of manufacturers' labours.

How will the supply chain develop?

The desire for differentiation between suppliers will bring networked home appliances to market. However, unless consumers can be convinced that there are significant benefits to actually connecting the units to the outside world, service take-up will be slow. Once penetration starts to ramp up, however, there are significant opportunities for network operators and infrastructure providers.

It will certainly be necessary for white goods and networked device vendors to form partnerships with organisations that provide the means to IP-enable their products. The recent announcement from Whirlpool and Nokia is a good example of this kind of partnership.

Networked home appliances, like PCs and TVs, will connect to public network infrastructure through fixed residential access networks, rather than wireless cellular networks. Digital cable and xDSL services are likely candidates, as they both provide 'always on' connectivity. Consequently, incumbent telcos and cable network operators have the opportunity to play the access provider role to the networked home-appliance market.

However, it is unlikely that these providers will have the chance to play the role of content aggregator or portal provider. In the short term at least, the role of portal provider is much more likely to be played by the device manufacturer, which will have the expertise to deliver content and applications tailored for its own devices. Appliance manufacturers are network-enabling their products primarily to enhance their value as goods; not to create new conduits for general infotainment, for example. The most important online services in this context are therefore more likely to be skewed towards finding recipes, or watching cookery demonstrations, for example, rather than playing games.

The market for home networks is becoming established in the US, but consumer demand for the technology in other parts of the world is uncertain. Manufacturers of white goods are likely to network-enable their products in a way that is transparent to the end user. It is also important that any network-enabling technology included in devices does not significantly raise the cost. If both of these conditions are met, it is likely that manufacturers will be able to sneak network-enabled devices into the home without the consumer even being aware of the benefits on offer, until they get the unit home.

Drivers

The market drivers for home networking are centred on the provision of compelling applications for consumers, utility companies and other residential service providers. The market is chiefly being driven by home-appliance manufacturers, keen to differentiate their products through provision of value-added services.

The vision of many appliance manufacturers is of completely wired homes, in which every smart appliance is connected to every other smart appliance, and to the public Internet via a home network gateway. Certainly, technology that allows home-owners to remotely monitor and control services delivered by their appliances has immediate appeal to many – but utilities themselves are interested in remote management too. Power companies, for example, with the right access to your home's services, could ensure that demand for power is smoothed at peak times by forcing certain of your appliances to switch into power-saving modes if they are not in use.

Quite apart from remote monitoring and management, there is the possibility of using certain networked home appliances to access infotainment and e-commerce applications – in which case they act as PC or TV substitutes. Internet-connected refrigerators supplied by Whirlpool and LG Electronics already provide this function.

Inhibitors

There are three main inhibitors to the proliferation of networked home appliances:

- the demand for home automation functions and for PC/TV substitutes is still largely undetermined: many manufacturers' early efforts are more positioning statements, aimed at gaining mindshare, rather than serious revenue-generation attempts
- the immaturity of the technology. Existing technologies that are used in corporate networks are not necessarily suited to be used in home appliances, due to the 'hygiene' factors associated with consumer appliances
- networked home appliances work best in environments where networks are already installed. But few home-owners are prepared to install LANs in their homes, and wireless LAN technology and powerline network technologies are still expensive and immature.

Important technologies for networked home appliances

There are several competing standards, including:

- Bluetooth and IEEE 802.11, which are both wireless LAN technologies
- HAVi, which is a wireline appliance networking and middleware standard promoted by leading audio-visual appliance manufacturers.

The Open Systems Gateway Initiative's home network gateway specification, and Universal Plug & Play, which seek to provide a standard implementation for home networks will also play important roles in the development of the networked home.

G Infrastructure technologies, trends and suppliers

G1 Introduction to pervasive computing infrastructure

G1.1 The role of infrastructure in pervasive computing

Underpinning the trend towards pervasive computing is the evolution of the infrastructure 'glue' that will bind applications to users, regardless of the access platform that they use. This will help to transform today's world of information delivery 'stovepipes' and enable the vision of universal access associated with pervasive computing.

Pervasive computing infrastructure encompasses a myriad of software, hardware and communications functions. Together, they have one fundamental aim:

> *to help break the bonds that currently tie users to devices, devices to networks and applications to both of these and thereby enable more direct relationships between users and applications, regardless of the device and network being used.*

This is a grand statement of ambition for the role of infrastructure – but what does it mean? 'Breaking the bonds' involves addressing three main challenges:

- the majority of applications in use today are not deployed as network-based services, nor are they designed to be suitable for delivery to multiple types of access platform
- outside the realm of the PC and the corporate LAN, today's digital information access platforms vary widely in their capabilities – and therefore their suitability for delivering certain types of application to users
- industries have been created and have matured around the delivery of particular types of digital information to particular types of device over particular types of network. These 'stovepipes' make the level of industry interworking that will be required to deliver truly pervasive computing applications, very difficult.

Figure *G1.1* shows the central role that infrastructure plays in the development of pervasive computing, by addressing these three challenges.

We saw in *Chapters D* and *E* that, in order to enable pervasive computing, infrastructure technology has to deliver end-to-end solutions. It must play a central role in supporting:

- the creation of content, applications and services that can be delivered to multiple access platforms
- the creation and optimisation of access platforms for particular applications
- the delivery of content, applications and services to access platforms.

Given the diversity of technologies required and the scale and scope of even one of these supporting roles, it is clear that no single infrastructure supplier will be able to supply everything that the market needs. Without standards that can enable interworking between different 'islands' of infrastructure, market development could be severely constrained.

G1.2 Which technologies and why?

A large number of technologies have a potential role in supporting pervasive computing. *Figure G1.2* shows the pervasive computing technology 'jigsaw'.

Figure G1.1 **Infrastructure drives market development**

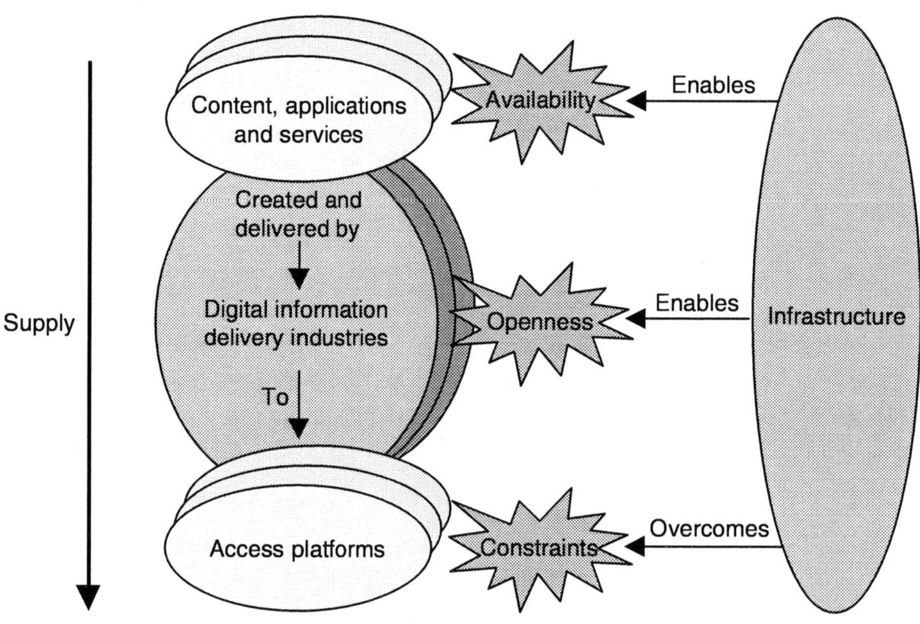

Source: Ovum (Pervasive Computing: Technologies and Markets/Chapter G)

Figure G1.2 **The pervasive computing technology jigsaw**

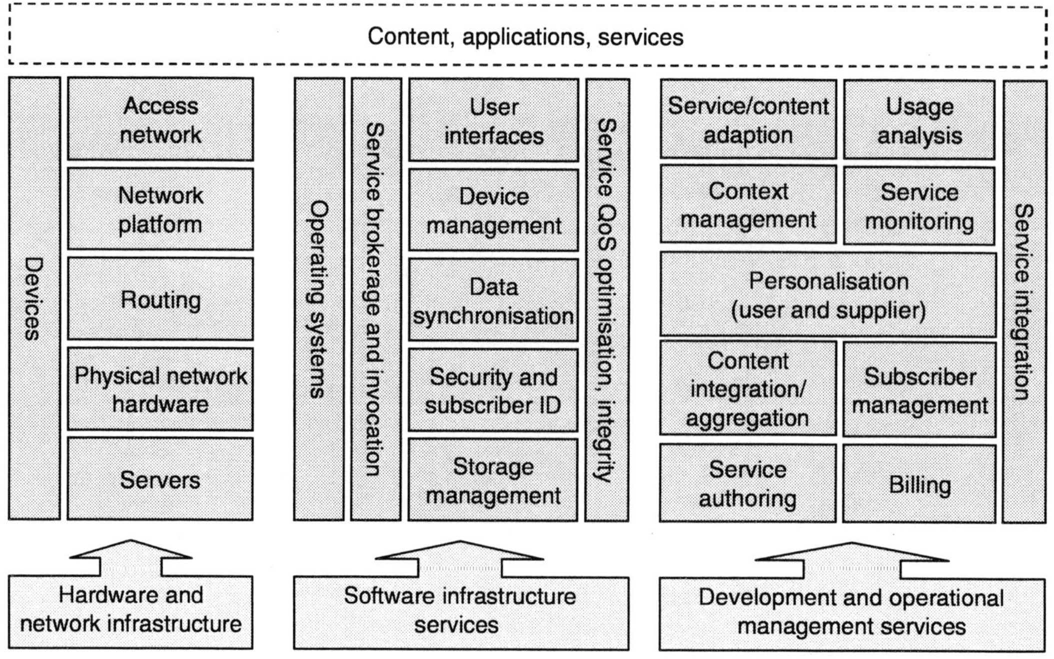

Source: Ovum (Pervasive Computing: Technologies and Markets/Chapter G)

The main technology groupings are:

- hardware and network infrastructure
- software infrastructure
- development and operational management services.

Between them, the technologies provide a complete 'living environment' for pervasive computing activity.

In order to be successful, different types of infrastructure service must work in concert. *Figure G1.3* shows the relationships that need to be implemented through integration between infrastructure elements.

Hardware and network infrastructure

Hardware and network infrastructure elements provide the raw elements of pervasive computing access platforms, and also the structural foundation for delivery of network-based content, applications and services. However, by themselves, they only provide the 'seeds' – smart, connected devices – from which pervasive computing can grow.

The four major components of pervasive computing hardware and network infrastructure are:

- client devices
- servers
- access network infrastructure
- core network infrastructure.

Figure G1.3 **Relationships between infrastructure elements**

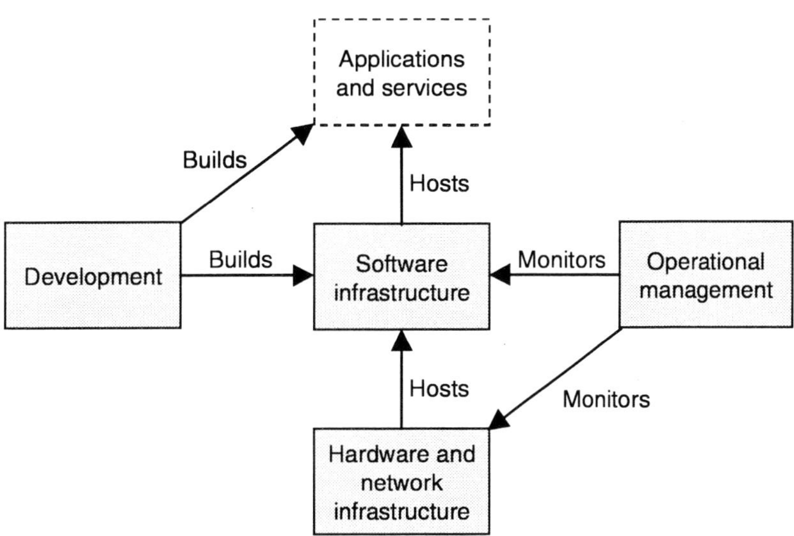

Source: Ovum (Pervasive Computing: Technologies and Markets/Chapter G)

Software infrastructure

Software infrastructure plays a role in addressing all three of the major technology challenges identified in *Section G1.1* – enriching access platforms, creating multichannel applications and opening industry structures. They enhance the foundation environment that servers, client devices and access networks provide by:

- making it easier to build and use pervasive computing content, applications and services
- hosting and managing applications and services to maximise reliability, availability, performance and security – even where the underlying devices and networks do not provide those qualities.

Pervasive computing software infrastructure includes the following technology functions:

- client operating systems
- service brokerage and invocation functions
- user interfaces
- storage management
- security and subscriber ID functions
- data synchronisation
- device management
- quality of service optimisation and integrity assurance.

Client operating systems

Client operating systems form a low-level abstraction layer on computing hardware that hides hardware details from, and manages access by, application programs when they need to use system resources such as memory, permanent storage and user input/output channels.

The main players in this area are Microsoft, Symbian, Palm Computing, QNX and Wind River, Sun Microsystems (with its Java platform) and OpenTV.

Service brokerage and invocation functions

Service brokerage and invocation functions 'hide' the network that separates client and server hardware and software components by enabling programmers to write distributed client-server software without recourse to network programming. In advanced cases, functions also enable dynamic service discovery, by searching for services that can process a particular request at runtime and connecting one of them to the requester.

The main players are Microsoft (with SOAP and UPnP), Sun Microsystems (Jini and RMI), Phone.Com (UP.Link), Hewlett-Packard (e-speak) and OpenTV.

User interfaces

User interfaces provide the conduits through which a device and its user communicate information to each other. In the realm of pervasive computing, user interfaces must be driven by the form factor of a given device, together with the context in which it will be used. For example, speech input and output interfaces are more viable for in-car systems than a keyboard and a GUI.

The main players are RealNetworks, OpenTV, Microsoft, Sun Microsystems and Lernout & Hauspie.

Storage management

Storage management functions manage the storage of information and allow multiple software programs to read and write to information stores in a co-ordinated fashion, which ensures that the information always remains consistent. Storage management functions are important on servers that host remote applications and services that 'live in the network', and also on client devices – particularly where application data needs to be cached locally to improve performance over limited network connections.

The main players are Oracle, Sybase, IBM and Centura.

Security and subscriber ID functions

Security and subscriber ID functions are responsible for:

- identifying the application user to network and application software components (authentication)
- ensuring that a particular user can only access applications and services that they are authorised to (through a set of centrally administered authorisation rules)
- ensuring that data that travels over the network is protected from unauthorised access or tampering in transit (through data encryption)
- protecting applications and services, and their runtime environments, from unauthorised access – and detecting and preventing the spread of malicious code (such as viruses, trojans and worms)
- ensuring that a user or software service cannot 'deny' that a particular communication took place (non-repudiation)
- auditing any application or service interaction that might need to be proven at a later date.

The main players include Entrust, SmartTrust, Network Associates, McAfee, Symantec, NDS and RSA Security.

Data synchronisation

Data synchronisation functions enable information stored on a (usually mobile handheld) client device to be synchronised with an information store held at a remote location.

The most widely used data synchronisation offerings transfer data both ways between a PDA and a PC over a direct serial link. However, the technology is starting to play a much wider role in the synchronisation and management of personal information across multiple devices – not just PDAs. The technology now underpins device management functions and also enables mobile business applications by allowing device-resident storage management software to propagate changes to central data stores (and vice versa).

The main players are AvantGo, Aether Systems, Starfish, PumaTech and the SyncML initiative.

Device management

Device management is becoming an important facility as access platforms grow smarter. Where pervasive computing devices are owned and operated by individual consumers, users have to be able to manage their devices, and the information and services presented by those devices, as straightforwardly as possible. Where pervasive computing devices are owned by network operators or enterprises, the operator or enterprise must be able to monitor and, if necessary, control from remote locations the configuration and operation of devices it owns.

The main players are Tivoli, Computer Associates and Aether Systems.

Quality of service optimisation and integrity assurance

Quality of service optimisation and integrity assurance functions enhance the operational environments in which applications execute by:

- maximising application reliability and availability
- maximising application performance
- ensuring that the integrity of the application is maintained.

The main players are IBM, Oracle, BEA, OpenTV and RealNetworks.

Development and operational management services

Development services

Development services help providers build applications and services that follow appropriate design principles for multichannel services. They include:

- building an 'engine' that can store and manage usage context information in order to tailor application behaviour for each individual user session, regardless of the delivery channel being used
- separating core application logic from delivery channel specifics, and supporting the implementation of 'layered' application architectures in general (which maximises adaptability and reduces the cost of coping with change)
- composing applications and services from sets of components, rather than building them as large, monolithic lumps of software.

The following technologies provide development services:

- application/service authoring tools
- content integration/aggregation tools
- personalisation frameworks
- context management frameworks
- service/content adaptation tools.

Development services relate to infrastructure services, in that they generate applications and services that use infrastructure services at runtime, in order to optimise quality of service and to maximise usability and manageability.

Operational management services

The following technologies provide operational management services:

- billing systems
- subscriber management systems
- personalisation runtime engines
- service monitoring tools
- usage analysis tools.

Operational management services should work closely with 'instrumented' infrastructure services, which allow other software to monitor the reliability, availability, performance and security of applications and services and their usage, and manage them as appropriate.

Using instrumented infrastructure services rather than directly monitoring application software means that developers are not required to explicitly build 'hooks' into those applications. This in turn means that core application functionality is clearly separated from code that deals with management instrumentation – making both of these easy to change in line with evolving requirements.

Service integration

Service integration infrastructure facilitates the sharing between suppliers of usage and operational information, as provided by operational management services.

Chapter F showed that a solution to the information-sharing challenge must address the following requirements:

- information translation – where suppliers have different ways of representing key operational information
- security and privacy – to ensure that access to information can be tightly restricted
- relationship management – to simplify the sharing of information with multiple suppliers, each of whom may have their own peculiar requirements regarding information transmission and formatting.

These services are not provided by any 'off-the-shelf' products today. However, there are many possible sources of technology that could be used to build these services. The most promising of these is enterprise application integration (EAI) technology. Many EAI tool suppliers are now addressing issues associated with business-to-business integration, through the use of IP, web protocols and XML-based technologies to transmit, describe and transform messages.

G2 Trends in infrastructure supply

G2.1 Market forces, not philanthropy, are the drivers

Infrastructure – and the way that it develops – is fundamental to the development of pervasive computing. Often, technology companies give the impression that it is their desire to improve society's lot that is driving them to spend their hard-earned profits (or venture capital) on developing new products. However, unless there are real market forces pushing suppliers along, their bold initiatives rarely produce results.

In this case, though, it is market forces, not the desire to make the world a better place, that are driving innovation in the areas that matter to the development of pervasive computing. The signs are therefore good that infrastructure products and services will, over time, fulfil the main requirements of all the different stakeholders – device manufacturers, network operators, service providers, aggregators, content and application suppliers. These requirements are:

- creation of a common network protocol
- increasing the commonality between the infrastructure technologies used across different digital information delivery industries
- implementation of services to improve the quality of service of application delivery
- implementation of services that make applications and services easier to develop and deploy
- reduction of the cost and risk of delivering applications and services to users.

Competition is forcing infrastructure suppliers to explore these issues. *Sections G2.2* to *G2.5* look at each issue in turn, examining the trends that are pushing infrastructure suppliers to address them.

G2.2 Sowing the seeds – the penetration of IP

A common network protocol is the essential foundation for end-to-end pervasive computing infrastructure, because it eases interworking between infrastructure elements from different suppliers. The software industry has chosen its champion – IP, the Internet protocol. However, the network infrastructure community is still divided over whether IP should be a core infrastructure element, or whether its implementation should be up to operators and service providers.

Pervasive computing will be extremely complex to implement without a common network protocol foundation, as without a common network protocol all infrastructure suppliers will have to 'back several horses' in order to enable multichannel application delivery. The resulting products will be too expensive and too complex for most potential service providers to consider. In contrast, widespread availability of a common protocol lowers the barriers to entry to pervasive computing, and therefore stimulates innovation in access platforms, applications and service provision through competition between suppliers.

It is interest in the Internet that is driving device manufacturers to make their products networkable, and it is interest in the possibilities of e-commerce and interactive advertising that is driving the telecoms and broadcast media industries to open their stovepipes to enable interactive data services. It makes sense, therefore, that IP should be the common network protocol throughout the IT, telecoms and broadcast media industries.

One of the main challenges facing IP's evolution into a universal protocol occurs because of its ubiquity in corporate IT and enterprise networking. Many infrastructure suppliers from this background assume either that IP is already a universal piece of communications fabric, or that its introduction as such is straightforward. However, there are several key challenges that IP technologies must overcome in order to become universal – such as the addressability of devices, quality of service and mobility.

Infrastructure suppliers in the telecommunications community, which are the providers of the networks that need to underpin pervasive IP, understand the challenges. However, until all parties – not just infrastructure suppliers – recognise the scale of the challenge, there is great scope for suppliers to set unrealistic expectations.

The speed with which implementations of IP will evolve to solve current problems is hard to determine due to the distributed nature of the community that directs Internet technologies. The IETF (Internet Engineering Task Force) makes technology recommendations, but what the IETF recommends is not necessarily implemented by the industry (as in the case of SNMP). In the commercial sphere there are many powerful network infrastructure players behind IP as core infrastructure – Cisco is perhaps the most high profile supporter. However, there are other approaches and Cisco, while powerful, is not yet in a position to 'call the shots' for the whole network infrastructure market.

G2.3 Cross-industry partnerships

Cross-industry partnerships between infrastructure suppliers and service providers are vital to the development and deployment of compelling, successful pervasive computing applications.

High levels of competition between infrastructure services, and between service providers, is already leading to such partnerships being created. The relationships between BEA and Nokia (for the provision of wireless Internet application platforms) and between Oracle and Sky Corp (for the provision of the Open Interactive application platform) are two examples.

G2.4 Value creep in software and network infrastructure

The low barriers to entry and innovation that have been brought about by the opening of network and software platforms, have led to high levels of competition in the hardware, network infrastructure and software markets. Suppliers are responding by adding more layers of technology to their offerings. These innovations are shifting the boundaries between applications, software infrastructure and network infrastructure, as shown in *Figure G2.1*. The shifts in boundaries are themselves generating more competition for suppliers and further increasing the pace of innovation. Many infrastructure suppliers are using their own visions of pervasive computing as a focus for their own innovation programmes.

Figure G2.1 **Boundary changes between applications, software infrastructure and networks**

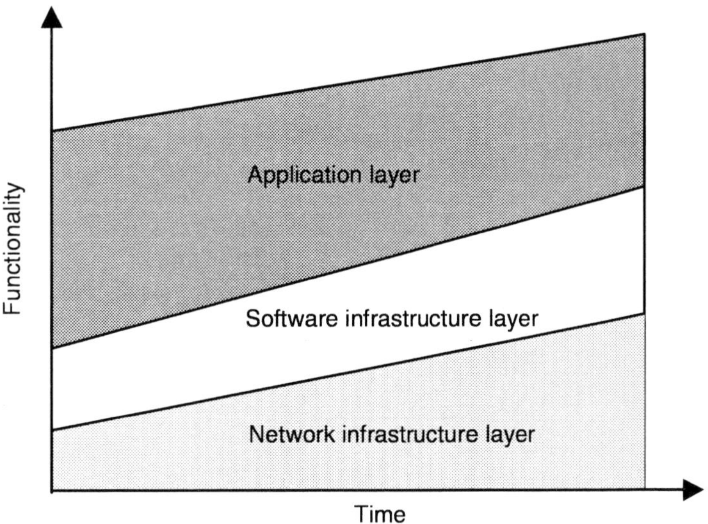

Source: Ovum (Pervasive Computing: Technologies and Markets/Chapter G)

Quality of service optimisation – from software infrastructure to networks

As network infrastructure suppliers start to deliver network elements that 'understand' the transmission of packet data, rather than just passively carrying data over voice circuits, providers are in a position to implement functionality in the service and routing layers of their networks that can recognise and act on characteristics of particular data packets.

Active optimisation of data transmission in the network is now possible not only in corporate networks, but also in next-generation IP-aware public telecommunications networks. Switches and routers, together with server-based solutions that integrate tightly with these network elements, are starting to implement functions such as:

- data caching
- load balancing and failover
- traffic prioritisation according to class of service
- network security.

A whole category of products – enterprise middleware – was created by IBM, Digital and Siemens to implement these functions. These functions are now being subsumed into networks, leaving enterprise middleware product suppliers to look for new opportunities.

Application frameworks – from applications to software infrastructure

The subsumption of low-level middleware functions into network infrastructure is a major driver pushing software infrastructure suppliers to add value to their products. The other major driver is suppliers' desire to offer solutions with obvious business value that can be sold to line-of-business or board-level management, as opposed to 'geek sell' products whose value is only appreciated by IT strategists.

Enterprise middleware vendors have exhausted this 'geek sell' market. The market is very restricted because, in order to recognise that the solution to one's problems requires an invisible, expensive piece of technology, one needs to have very large and complex problems and very astute and influential technical staff. Most companies that satisfy these criteria have already bought middleware products – and because reducing prices is rarely an attractive option, middleware suppliers have set about increasing the visibility of their technology.

Within the IT stovepipe, there are two more driving forces:

- the rise in popularity of software infrastructure products developed using an 'open source' process, by loose communities of developers – which tend to be very cheap or even free
- the strategy of Microsoft, which has historically been to bundle key software infrastructure components with its operating systems for very little incremental cost.

Software infrastructure suppliers such as IBM, BEA, Sybase and Oracle – and Microsoft itself – are responding to these drivers by delivering solutions that offer functionality previously only associated with packaged applications. Some examples include:

- portal infrastructure and pre-built components
- application integration tools
- application development tools and pre-built components
- service management frameworks.

G2.5 E-infrastructure services – the ASP model applied to infrastructure

Service providers no longer have to build and own all the infrastructure required to operate a network-based service. The infrastructure community is starting to respond to its customers' increasing interest in e-business, together with uncertainties regarding e-business implementation (in the case of many 'bricks and mortar' businesses) and fragile business conditions (in the case of many dot.coms). It is doing this by offering some infrastructure functions as network-based services that can be paid for through a service subscription rather than a large up-front product investment.

Elements of service management, application integration, content aggregation, content adaptation and storage management are starting to be offered by innovative new providers of e-infrastructure services. The trend is particularly likely to offer value to customers in the domain of pervasive computing, where complexity and diversity in access platforms conspire to make service provision costly and risky. In this context, e-infrastructure service providers can take responsibility for addressing some elements of complexity, and share the risk of bringing pervasive computing applications to market.

Companies such as Aether Systems already offer their solutions as products and also as e-services through an ASP model. Committed product-centric suppliers such as IBM and its Tivoli subsidiary are tracking the market for e-infrastructure services, to determine when and how they should make their products more 'ASP-friendly'.

G3 What are infrastructure suppliers doing?

We have held discussions with a range of suppliers whose activities are likely to have a significant impact on the development of infrastructure for pervasive computing.

Figure G3.1 looks at major digital information delivery stovepipes, provides a summary of the major themes in suppliers' activities, and highlights where today's biggest players are making the greatest impact.

Figure G3.1 **Major themes in infrastructure suppliers' current activities**

	IT	Telecoms	Broadcast media
Hardware	Wireless connectivity Processing on tap	Enabling for data services	Opening platforms to enable interactive services
Major innovators	Hewlett-Packard, IBM, Palm, Psion and Sun Microsystems	Ericsson, Motorola and Nokia	Motorola, Pace and Philips
Access networks	'Broadband everywhere'	'Packet everywhere'	n/a
Major innovators	Cisco	Cisco, Ericsson and Nokia	n/a
Software infrastructure	Extending web applications to wireless access Use of Internet as middleware (SOAP, UDDI, e-speak) Portal infrastructure for Web and wireless	Creating wireless Internet application platforms Early implementations of streaming media technology	Creating interactive services platforms Remote device management
Major innovators	Aether Systems, BEA, IBM, Hewlett-Packard, Microsoft and Sun Microsystems	Nokia, Oracle, Phone.Com, Sun Microsystems and RealNetworks	Microsoft, OpenTV, Oracle and Tivoli
Development and operational management	Content adaptation for mobile access platforms	Content adaptation for mobile access platforms	n/a
Major innovators	Aether Systems, IBM, Inprise and NetMorf	Phone.Com	n/a

Source: Ovum (Pervasive Computing: Technologies and Markets/Chapter G)

Figure G3.1 shows that wireless Internet is the area where most infrastructure supplier activity is focused. Most innovation in the use of Internet connectivity is currently being carried out within the corporate IT supply chain.

There is little innovation in optimising the quality of service of application delivery to different platforms. The little activity that is occurring is the result of partnerships between media streaming technology suppliers and device manufacturers.

The software infrastructure community is most active in driving the development of pervasive computing. However, while many of the most influential infrastructure players have a pervasive computing 'story' to tell, few know what lies beyond the second page. There is a real danger that, apart from a couple of notable exceptions (IBM being the main one), the software infrastructure community will ignore the quality of service issue, leaving it to the network infrastructure community to deal with.

G4 IT thought leaders

The companies are given in alphabetical order.

G4.1 Hewlett-Packard (HP)

Hewlett-Packard (HP) is a public company, founded in 1939. The company has grown from its original market (electronic test and measurement equipment) into computing products and services, which now account for more than 80% of its business.

Since May 1995, HP has seen considerable restructuring. It set itself up to accommodate Windows NT alongside its traditional HP-UX operating system, to exploit opportunities in the Internet space, to resolve internal competition between Unix and NT divisions, and to present a single, unified sales interface to its corporate customers. In 1999, HP realigned itself into two independent companies – HP itself and Agilent Technologies, which consists of HP's test-and-measurement, semiconductor products, chemical analysis and healthcare solutions businesses.

HP wants to be recognised as a company that is able to support the delivery of new Internet applications and services to a variety of device types over a robust software infrastructure. HP's corporate strategy is based around the company positioning itself at the centre of three 'vectors':

- information appliances
- 'always on' infrastructure
- e-services.

Information appliances

HP considers an information appliance to be any device that can be connected to a network (principally the Internet). The term encompasses a range of device types, including PDAs, cellular phones, set-top boxes, home network gateways, games consoles and connected 'white goods'. The company believes that it is well placed to address this market since it has worked with embedded systems for years as a core part of building peripheral devices such as printers, EFTPOS terminals and calculators. It points out that developing embedded applications is considerably different from conventional application development and feels that its considerable in-house expertise, built up over many years, differentiates it from some of the newer players in the embedded systems market.

HP's embedded software platform for information appliances, Chai, represents an effort by HP to package its expertise in embedded systems design in a user-friendly manner. Its commitment to this is emphasised by the fact that in June 2000 HP created a new division, Embedded and Personal Systems, reporting directly to the CEO with Chai as its key focus.

'Always on' infrastructure

HP's infrastructure division focuses on providing a solid back-end, usage-based infrastructure for supporting pervasive computing applications to ensure the availability and security of services. This division concentrates on the marketing of HP's range of high-end NT, Linux and Unix server boxes, aimed at supporting e-business applications.

E-services

HP launched its e-Services initiative in 1999. It defines e-services as 'a superset of e-business that also includes service entities available to customers'. The company's vision is based around this notion of e-services as being modular and combining with each other to solve problems, complete transactions and generally make life easier. E-services will be available on websites, but others will be delivered via TV, phone, pager, car, e-mail inbox, or nearly anything containing a microchip. This concept is central to HP's vision of what it calls 'the second chapter of the Internet'.

The strategy hinges around the provision of a software standard to allow services to communicate and combine. This is delivered through the e-Speak product, which provides an open source software specification and reference implementation to this end.

Infrastructure offerings

Figure G4.1 indicates the current coverage of HP's products in terms of our technology map.

e-Speak is an open source software platform designed to enable the development, deployment and intelligent interaction of e-services. The company claims that it allows any e-service to discover any other e-Speak enabled e-services anywhere on the Internet and link up with them on-the-fly in order to satisfy the original request. HP is pitching e-speak at application or e-service providers, as a way of enabling their products to be dynamically linked to complementary offerings and thus enhance their value.

Figure G4.1 **HP's offerings**

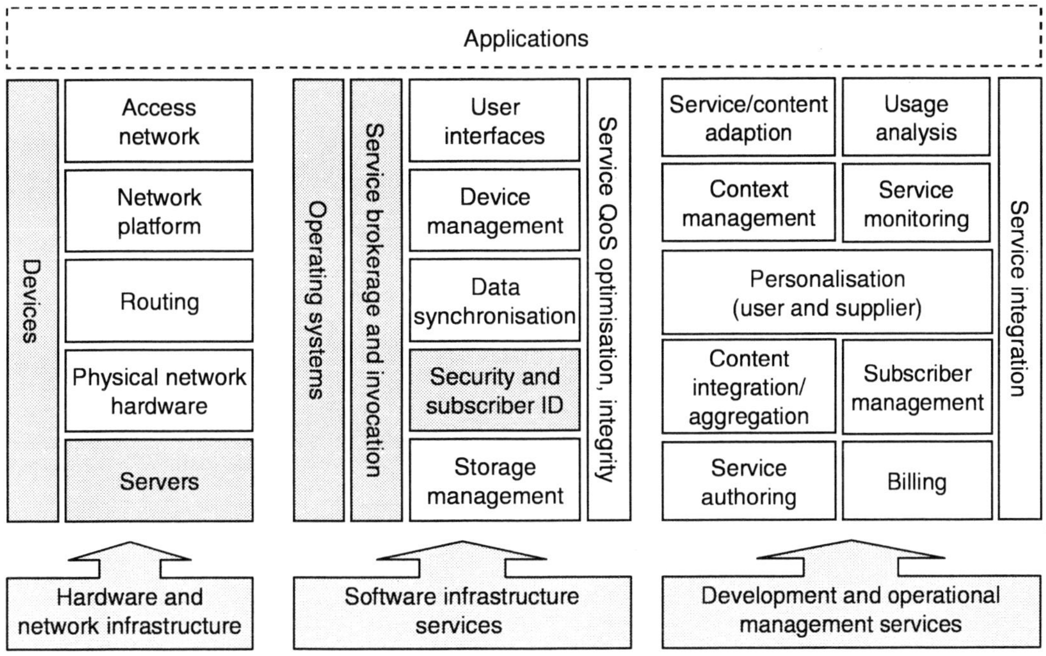

Source: Ovum (Pervasive Computing: Technologies and Markets/Chapter G)

Chai is a Java-based embedded software platform, designed to power memory-constrained intelligent appliances. Chai provides a way to extend e-services from enterprise systems on down to information appliances, and its modular architecture allows for applications to be developed and modified quickly. Chai is targeted at content and application providers as a way of making their existing assets suitable for deployment on new types of device.

OpenView is HP's network and application management software and provides the cornerstone for the management of the company's 'always on' infrastructure.

As well as being an 'arms supplier', the company also plays in the handheld market, manufacturing the Jornada range of PDA devices in a variety of form factors, including 'clam shell' designs (similar to Psion's range of PDAs) and 'Palm-style' devices. The Jornada range runs Microsoft operating systems (PocketPC) and their processor and memory specifications position them at the high end of the PDA market.

Sphere of influence

Figure G4.2 shows where HP's influence is greatest in the major digital information delivery 'stovepipes'.

Figure G4.2 **HP's influence**

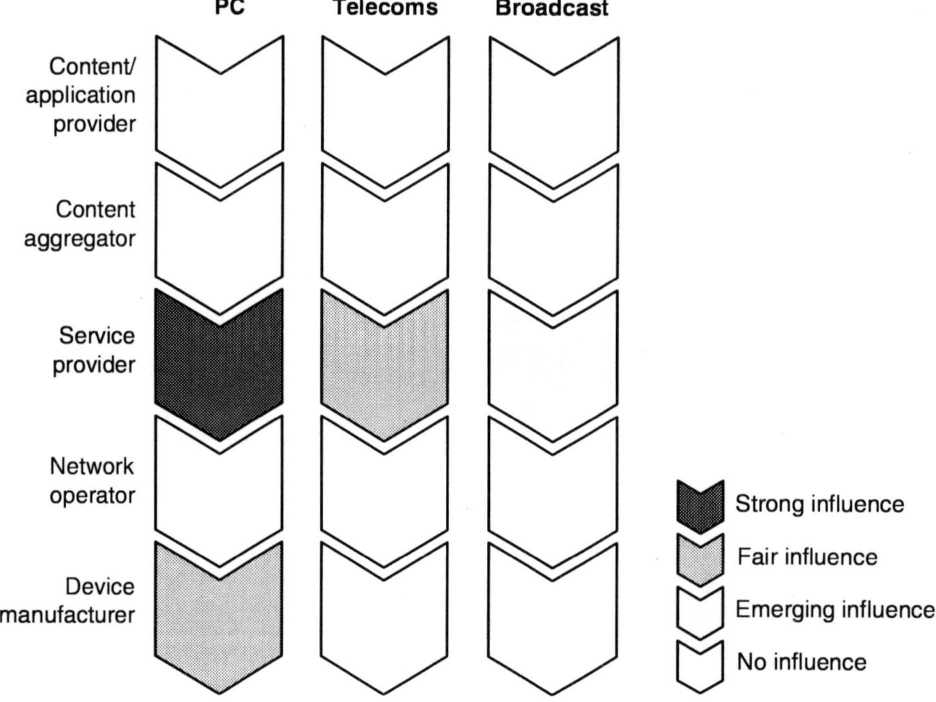

Source: Ovum (Pervasive Computing: Technologies and Markets/Chapter G)

HP's server hardware already gives it a degree of influence with content and application providers – particularly with 'bricks and mortar' enterprises. However, the company hopes that its e-speak and Chai technologies will significantly increase its influence in this area.

HP has some influence with network operators, through deployments of its widely established OpenView product. More than 400 partner companies have integrated their software products with OpenView, including network infrastructure providers such as Ericsson, Cisco and Lucent.

By virtue of its combined strengths in hardware and network management, HP has long been recognised as a leading technology supplier to service providers. The company sees the quality and reliability of back-end infrastructure as being critical to the success of pervasive computing, where applications are often literally in the hands of the consumer, and must always be secure and available. HP is now marketing its server products heavily to the service provider community, under a high availability banner that guarantees customers up to 99.999% availability – five minutes of downtime per year. The company claims that sudden variations in demand for applications can be accommodated via its 'Instant Capacity on Demand' solution, whereby additional processors are fitted but switched off in their server boxes, and can be activated by a command from within software when extra capacity is required, without the need to wait for new hardware to be installed. The customer is then billed for the use of this extra capacity.

In order for Chai to succeed, HP believes that it must introduce it into devices. To this end it intends to announce new alliances with major terminal manufacturers. Recently announced deployments include Delphi Automotive (the General Motors spin-off) and Hitachi, which will deploy components of the Chai platform in its Home Internet Controller – a device that connects domestic appliances such as burglar alarms to the Internet.

G4.2 IBM

IBM is by far the world's largest computer systems and solutions company, with total revenues in 1999 of $87.5 billion. It offers IT services and middleware and business connectivity solutions, as well as computing hardware. IBM's recent success has been in part due to acquisitions, key ones being Lotus, Tivoli, NetObjects, Sequent, Dascom and Mylex.

IBM wants to leverage its strong position as an e-business infrastructure provider to move into the pervasive computing space. It asserts that pervasive computing is an extension of e-business – whether you are a consumer, a business customer or a service provider. Furthermore, the company believes that the attributes that its software products, services and corporate brand promote – scalability, reliability and security – are vital to pervasive computing. It now understands that it does 'databases and transactions' – and wants to use those strengths to address the challenges of this market.

IBM is currently enjoying the benefits of an Internet-based renaissance. The software division of the company is (along with Sun Microsystems and HP) one of today's e-business 'thought leaders'.

IBM Software began its transformation into an e-provider in earnest in 1999, with the launch of its WebSphere brand. It has since developed a coherent vision for e-business – the weaving of Internet technologies into every business process that companies carry out. The company sees tremendous opportunities for growth if it can supply the engines for driving this wave of business transformation.

The company believes that transparent mobility and immediacy of information access are the key drivers for pervasive computing applications. It believes that it can provide both of these by ensuring that its customers (and ultimately, service consumers) never have to think about 'plumbing'.

IBM sees three distinct market opportunities for its pervasive computing offerings, at different points in the supply chain:

- extending the e-business applications of its existing customers, to allow them to deploy services to new devices
- providing IBM expertise and infrastructure to wireless carriers
- extending its infrastructure, tools and hardware expertise into the smart, connected device market through OEM relationships.

IBM is keen to point out that, unlike its competitors, it will not compete with its customers – which means, in essence, that IBM will not itself become a content provider. It wants to make money as an 'arms supplier', not a combatant. It is also adamant that it will avoid a revenue model that involves revenue sharing – it believes that transactions and conversations need to be as cheap as possible, otherwise market development will be stifled. Instead, the company will sell capacity-based runtime licences.

IBM's Tivoli subsidiary has its own major pervasive computing initiatives underway. Tivoli has decided to focus its efforts on specific technology areas, and has created two separate business units to address them:

- the Pervasive Management Business Unit, which concentrates on providing systems management solutions for business devices such as ATMs, EFTPOS terminals, broadcast network infrastructure, phones and PDAs
- the Service Provider Business Unit (SPBU), which has the same broad strategy as the Pervasive Management Business Unit, but which focuses on the management of infrastructure not owned by its customers.

Tivoli believes that its value proposition as a systems and device management solution provider will not come to fruition until the pervasive computing market takes off and there is a much greater penetration of devices and services than there is today.

Infrastructure offerings

The WebSphere Everyplace Suite (WSE) is the central component of IBM's pervasive computing infrastructure offering. WSE is a portfolio of pre-existing and new infrastructure products, and implements the following functions:

- application serving (through the core WebSphere application server)
- caching and load balancing (WebSphere Edge Server)
- content adaptation (WebSphere Transcoding Publisher)
- WAP support (the Nokia WAP stack)
- store-and-forward client-server message passing (MQSeries Everyplace)

- client-side data storage (DB2 Everyplace)
- network data synchronisation (a new SyncML implementation)
- subscription management (through the Tivoli Subscription Manager)
- open interfaces to service management applications (such as billing and provisioning).

IBM also ships a superset of this suite called the WSE Portal framework. It offers all the above functionality, together with functions to implement personalisation, location-based services and unified messaging applications.

IBM does not believe that thin-client architecture is the only way to implement pervasive services and applications. It takes the view that applications will drive computing configurations – and wants to ensure that application developers have a full range of options at their disposal. The WSE Device Edition is an attempt to provide this range of client options. IBM already sells some client-side software infrastructure (in particular, DB2 Everyplace and MQSeries Everyplace). However, WSE Device Edition is an embedded version of a broader set of elements of the server suite, implemented in Java and supported on QNX, EPOC and Embedded Linux systems. IBM is currently designing a set of reference platforms for WSE Device Edition, which it intends to license to OEMs.

IBM is committed to selling its own range of smart, connected client devices – for selling to its largest, most loyal customers (who it believes may buy these in bulk).

IBM also offers a range of application development tools via its VisualAge portfolio, supporting coding in Java and C++, RAD and information engineering. Tools in the VisualAge portfolio can be used to design and build applications to be hosted on WSE.

Tivoli has two business units that support its pervasive computing efforts – the Pervasive Management Business Unit and the Service Provider Business Unit. The Service Provider Business Unit is of particular interest, as it is focusing its efforts on providing software that helps service providers manage service subscriptions, service provisioning and billing associated with service access from multiple types of platform. It also sells device management software products.

Figure G4.3 indicates the current coverage of IBM's products in terms of our technology map.

Figure G4.3 **IBM's offerings**

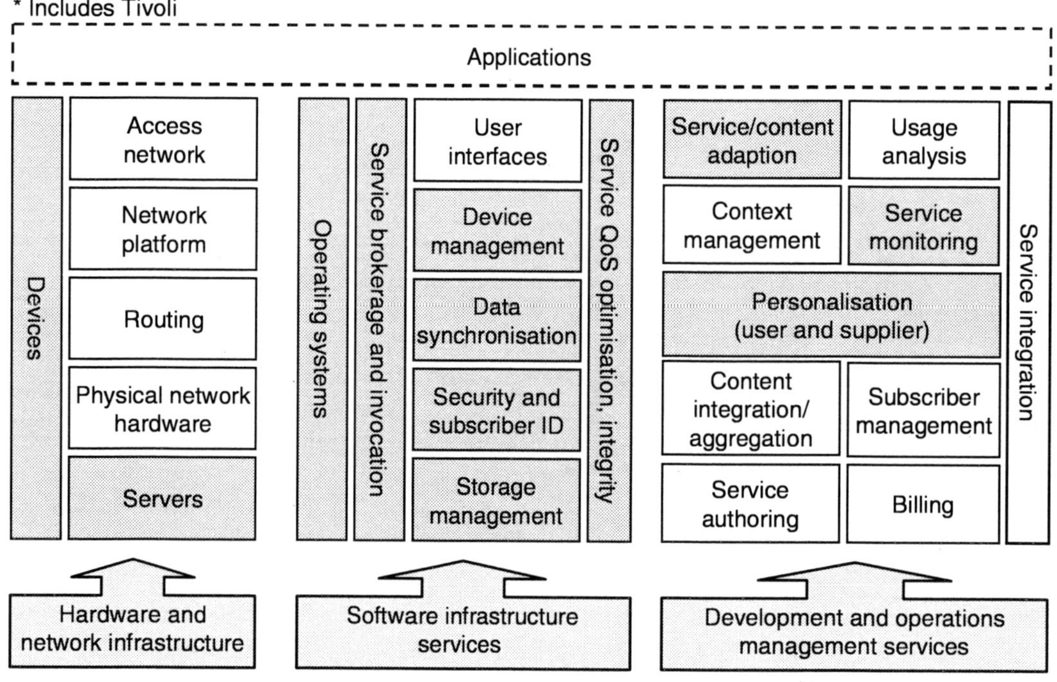

Source: Ovum (Pervasive Computing: Technologies and Markets/Chapter G)

Sphere of influence

Figure G4.4 shows where IBM's influence is greatest in the major digital information delivery 'stovepipes'.

IBM is a major influencer of the content and application provider community – in particular, its heartland of 'bricks and mortar' players, where its high-end hardware platforms, software infrastructure products and global consulting services operations have shaped the ways that many of these companies now use IT.

IBM's offering to service providers is its WebSphere Everyplace Suite (WSE) and the WSE portal framework. The company claims that it has carried out more than 400 implementation engagements using technologies that are now bundled in WSE.

The sheer size and industry influence of IBM means that it can capitalise on its extensive, established installed base of enterprise infrastructure software and extend this to include new devices. This is evident from the WSE portal framework, which extends the basic WSE functionality to implement personalisation, location-based services and unified messaging, and the WSE Device Edition for which IBM is developing a range of reference platforms to be licensed to OEMs.

Figure G4.4 **IBM's influence**

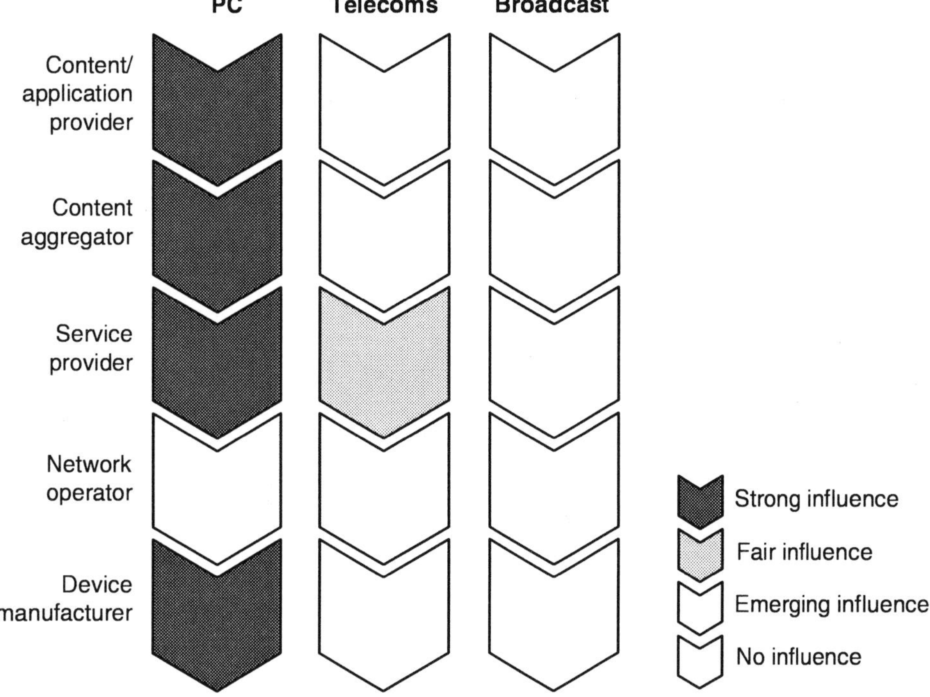

Source: Ovum (Pervasive Computing: Technologies and Markets/Chapter G)

IBM is committed to selling its own range of smart, connected client devices. In many cases, however, IBM may just re-brand another vendor's device – it has already done this with its WorkPad palmtops, which are re-badged Palm III devices. Its ability to sell its products – even if they are just re-badged – into the enterprise community means its influence cannot be underestimated.

G4.3 Microsoft

Microsoft is the world's largest independent software vendor, enjoying annual revenues in the order of $20 billion. Microsoft is focusing on the Internet – and its development as a computing platform – as the foundation of its plans for future growth.

Central to Microsoft's efforts in this is the '.NET' strategy. This strategy represents an attempt by the company to control the technologies that people use to access the Internet. .NET is all about pervasive computing. Even before the launch of Windows, Microsoft's platform play has been about rich clients, interactivity, ease of use and user control. The .NET strategy overlays these attributes on the network-centric world view that is becoming widely promoted in the Internet community.

Microsoft's overall market strategy has always been to provide easy-to-use, functionally rich platform and application software to as many people as possible. As its customer base has penetrated large businesses it has invested in building increasingly sophisticated server infrastructure and development tools, but with the emphasis still on ease of use and mass-market appeal.

To this end, Microsoft has fostered a very large, very loyal developer community. The company makes a great effort to ensure that these developers' skills are applicable to any new platform or infrastructure innovation it releases. By doing this, and by selling its own range of applications that are tightly integrated with Microsoft platform technology, the company has been able to ensure that new platforms are accompanied by compelling applications and other software.

Internet strategy

Microsoft calls what it is doing now the 'third generation' of the Internet (the first generation being the presentation of simple, static information and the second being the presentation of simple thin-client applications using web technology). This third generation consists of three extensions to today's web technologies:

- taking interactivity beyond the browser, to make Internet communication and interaction two-way. In other words, to create an environment in which systems act as peers rather than as smart servers and thin clients
- providing fine-grained user control over the presentation of content, the sharing of data and access to network services
- transforming today's constellation of web 'islands' into web services that can be linked together in order to share data and collaborate in fulfilling user requests.

The .NET strategy is large and complex. However, there are four key parts:

- enhanced services for client devices

  with future releases of its various client OS technologies, Microsoft will seek to move towards providing a single environment that can adapt content and services so that whichever environment a user is working in, user interaction occurs in the most 'natural' context. The aim is for this client platform, with its adaptive interface, to work independently of client device form factors, network bandwidth and so on. This strategy includes the integration of handwriting and natural language, voice processing and speech synthesis technologies into the user interface, and the creation of text completion and 'user assist' technologies, based on IntelliSense technology, to make user input easier

- an enhanced server platform

  the Microsoft .NET platform is intended to support the deployment of e-services. The Microsoft .NET architecture uses XML-based protocols as the means to describe messages and assemble service requests, which the company claims will enable any capable client to request the invocation of a .NET service from any location, without the need to employ any complex middleware 'on the wire'. The core protocol is called the Simple Object Access Protocol (SOAP)

- a developer framework for building .NET web services

  the important area for Microsoft over the past ten years has been its developer community – a roadmap for existing Microsoft-friendly developers is therefore key to the .NET strategy. Microsoft has been very clever about the tooling technology it has provided to its developers over the years; so much so that existing developers' skills can be applied to the .NET architecture with relatively little effort. Surprisingly, the company has already given 7,000 software companies pre-release versions of its new .NET-enabled tools to help them construct .NET services

- a set of 'building block' services to help developers build rich network-based services and applications

  Microsoft's .NET building blocks are designed to add value to the core .NET platform by providing out-of-the-box services that Microsoft believes need to be present in most network-based applications.

Infrastructure offerings

The .NET vision is not yet a reality – but the company already ships a wide range of technologies that are playing roles in the development of pervasive computing solutions.

Figure G4.5 indicates the current coverage of Microsoft's products in terms of our technology map.

Figure G4.5 **Microsoft's offerings**

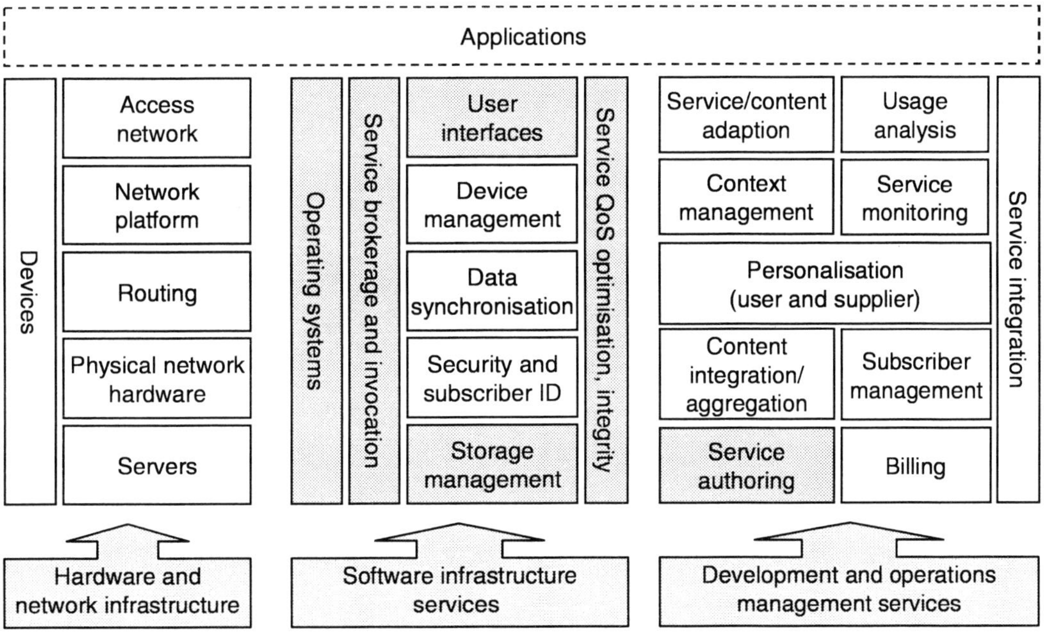

Source: Ovum (Pervasive Computing: Technologies and Markets/Chapter G)

Microsoft sells a portfolio of mainstream development tools called VisualStudio. The company also ships eMbedded Visual Tools, a toolset that includes IDEs for Visual Basic and C++, and which allows application developers to write applications for any Windows CE-based operating system. The tool ships with three reference platform SDKs – PocketPC, Handheld PC and Palm-size PC.

Microsoft's current strategic server operating system is Windows 2000. For client devices, it offers a range of reference platforms to OEMs that are built on the core Windows CE system for the development of personal mobile devices such as smartphones and PDAs. It also offers specialised client platforms for phones (Mobile Explorer), set-top boxes (the TV platform), smart cards (Windows for Smartcards) and embedded systems (Windows NT Embedded).

Other infrastructure products include:

- a mobile version of the SQLServer DBMS
- numerous application server technologies, based around the value-added services offered with the Windows 2000 server, which optimise the quality of service of running applications
- the SOAP XML-based RPC standard that both Microsoft and IBM are implementing and contributing to.

Sphere of influence

Figure G4.6 shows where Microsoft's influence is greatest in the major digital information delivery 'stovepipes'.

Microsoft serves content and application providers and aggregators across the PC, telecoms and broadcast supply chains through its hugely popular range of developer tools. Its tools are particularly favoured in Internet and corporate application development, but the increasing penetration of the Windows NT/ Windows 2000 platform and the degree of coupling of its tools and client platforms, mean that its influence in the broadcast supply chain is set to increase.

Microsoft has great influence in the Internet and fixed e-commerce service provider community through the widespread deployment of the Windows NT/ Windows 2000 platform; it now has a burgeoning interest in serving the mobile network service provider community. During 2000, Microsoft has started a major push to provide core elements of service providers' management and application infrastructure, via a set of purpose-built products built on Windows 2000 Server, Exchange 2000 and SQLServer 2000, and a new wireless application server product called Mobile Information Server 2000.

Microsoft is keen to see its operating systems employed in as many different types of device as possible, and has licensed its technology to a wide range of equipment manufacturers that want their products to run on a Microsoft platform. South Korean electronics giant Samsung was the first company to commit to manufacturing a 'feature phone' on a Microsoft platform, although other mobile terminal manufacturers have also licensed the Mobile Explorer technology, including Ericsson.

Figure G4.6 **Microsoft's influence**

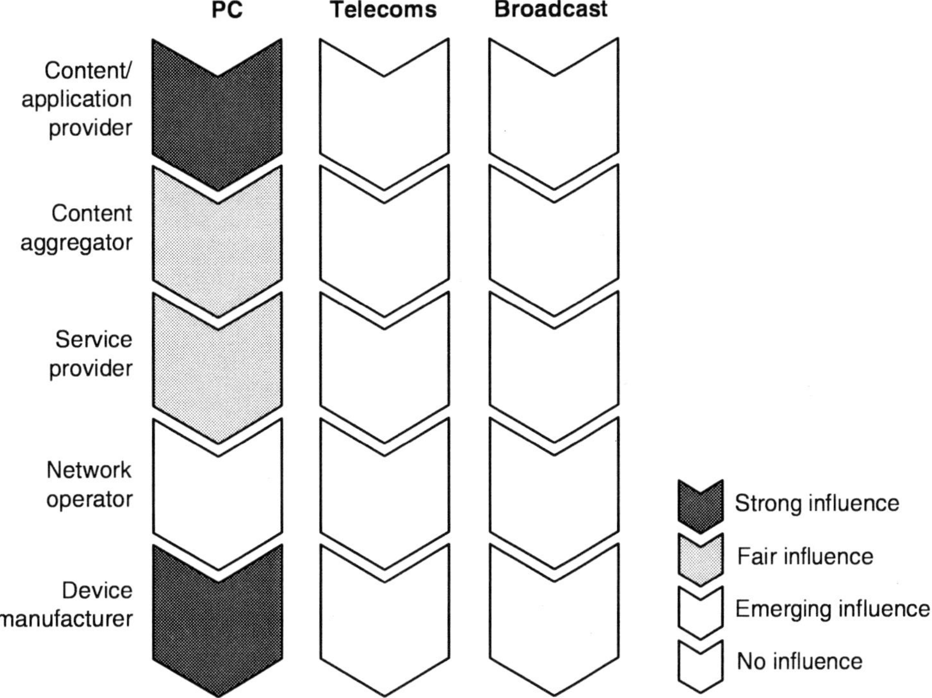

Source: Ovum (Pervasive Computing: Technologies and Markets/Chapter G)

Microsoft is keen to see the widespread use of its TV platform in set-top boxes. In May 2000 it announced partnerships with the UK-based set-top box manufacturer Pace, and with Motorola and AT&T Broadband in the US, to work on the evolution of its Microsoft TV Advanced Client software. However, as Microsoft has been aggressively purchasing stakes in a number of cable TV operators in Europe and elsewhere, it is running the risk of attracting the attention of regulators.

Microsoft's AutoPC initiative for in-car systems, developed in partnership with vehicle electronics company Clarion, has been taken up by several manufacturers. In addition, the company recently announced an initiative to work with five Japanese companies, including Clarion, to develop in-car systems based on Windows CE for Automotive, Microsoft's operating system for vehicles, which focuses on enabling hands-free communication, Internet access and the ability to summon emergency services and roadside assistance.

G4.4 Oracle

Oracle Corporation was founded in 1977 and was the first company to market a commercial RDBMS based on SQL. The company is now a global supplier of RDBMSs for a wide variety of platforms. In addition to its database offering, Oracle markets a set of development tools focused strongly on the Oracle RDBMS and a range of packaged applications. Application sales, including Oracle Financials, account for more than half of Oracle's consultancy business.

Oracle is an active supporter of Java, and is aggressively positioning itself as a provider of Internet technology and a major supplier of ASP software. Larry Ellison's latest edict to his development groups is that every product must be able to be hosted by an ASP. Oracle also has its own ASP operation.

During February 2000, Oracle launched into the WAP arena by announcing a new service, Oraclemobile.com, aimed at providing free personalised information to users through their mobile devices.

Infrastructure offerings

Figure G4.7 indicates the current coverage of Oracle's products in terms of our technology map.

Figure G4.7 **Oracle's offerings**

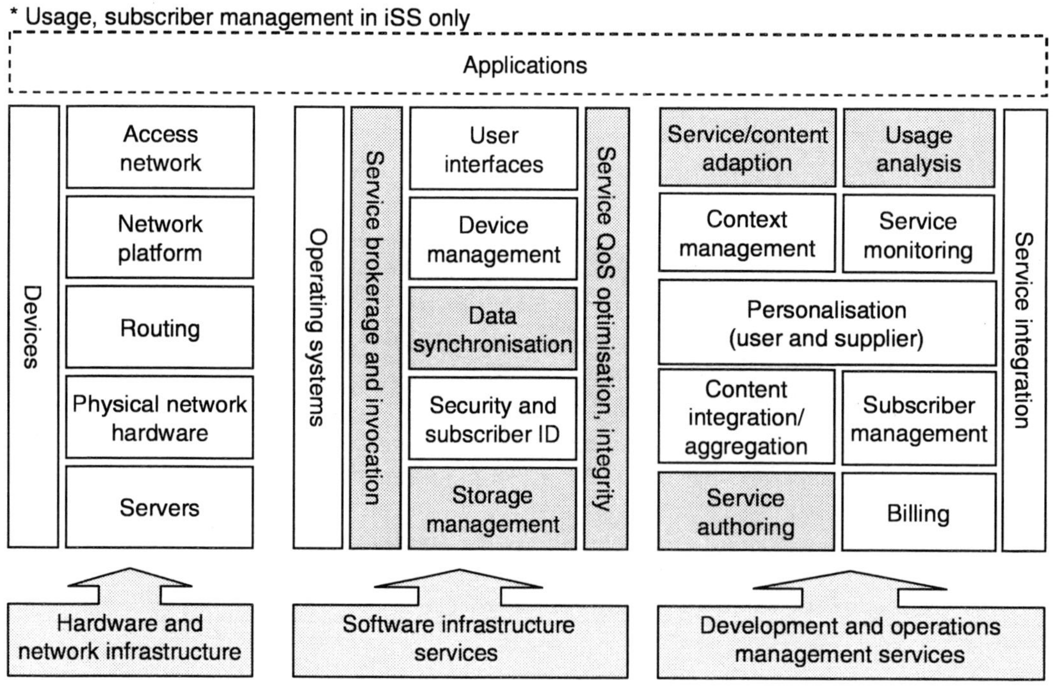

Source: Ovum (Pervasive Computing: Technologies and Markets/Chapter G)

Oracle positions its foundation infrastructure products – particularly the 8I and 8I Lite databases, the AQ and AQ Lite message queuing middleware and the Internet Application Server – as essential infrastructure components for every e-services provider and dot.com. None of these components is premium-priced, and all of them are designed to be implemented by customers with minimal consulting intervention – they are true 'shrink-wrapped' products for medium-sized and large enterprises.

Oracle is increasingly deploying its infrastructure technologies and products on a common base platform called the Internet Platform, which comprises a combination of the Oracle Internet Application Server and the Oracle 8I DBMS. The Internet Application Server provides an environment for the development and deployment of applications for the Web.

One of Oracle's major non-traditional areas of business is its Interactive Service Solution (iSS) solution, which it uses to construct server platforms for service providers wishing to deploy interactive TV services. iSS is a combination of code frameworks, middleware products and consulting services. Its foundation provides functionality for reliable and scalable content serving, subscriber management and usage tracking. In particular, the platform implements the return path infrastructure that enables service users to request and browse content, and perform transactions. iSS was used by BSkyB as the foundation for its interactive offerings, and Oracle claims iSS supports the leading digital interactive television middleware types (Microsoft, Liberate and OpenTV).

Oracle's Portal-to-Go offering is a set of portal infrastructure technologies for use by wireless service providers. Like iSS, Portal-to-Go is based on the core Oracle Internet Platform. (Oracle claims that because the core iSS software stack is designed in separation from particular middleware technologies, it works with Portal-to-Go to deliver content and interactive services to other platforms – for example, to mobile phones via WAP and WML.) Portal-to-Go implements content adaptation, service navigation management, and state and cookie management; as well as letting subscribers 'pull' content and services to them, Portal-to-Go can also 'push' content and services to subscribers.

Sphere of influence

Figure G4.8 shows where Oracle's influence is greatest in the major digital information delivery 'stovepipes'.

Figure G4.8 **Oracle's influence**

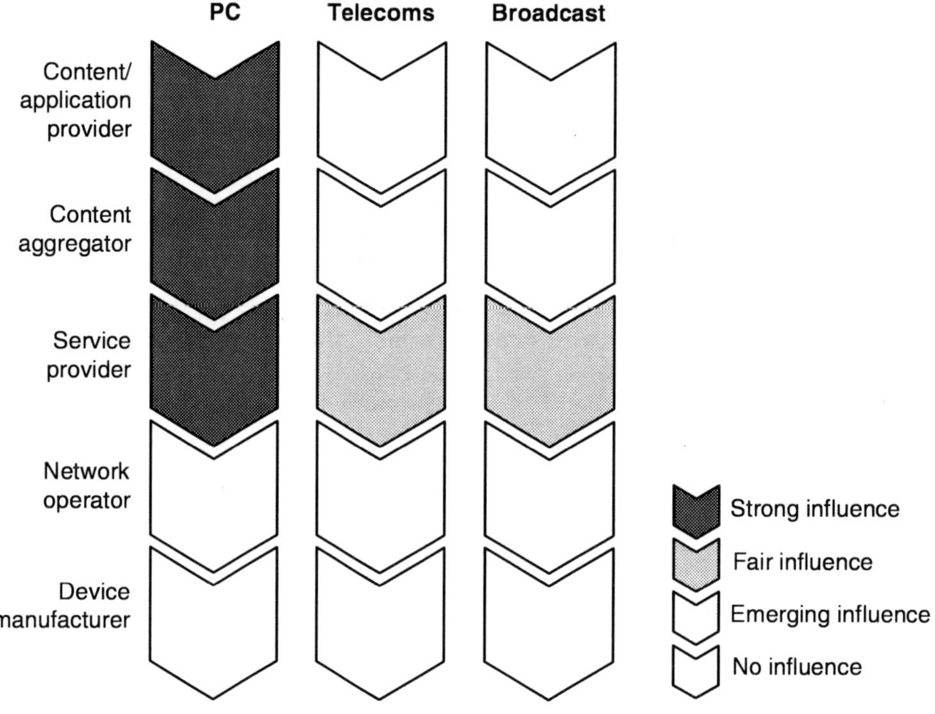

Source: Ovum (Pervasive Computing: Technologies and Markets/Chapter G)

Oracle has significant influence as a technology provider to content and application providers due to its DBMS server products, which it claims power a large proportion of the Internet-based applications (including e-commerce applications) deployed on the Internet.

Oracle is using its influence as a reliable, scalable back-end infrastructure provider to push into providing infrastructure and services for aggregators and service providers in mobile networking and broadcast media (interactive services).

Oracle targets iSS at the new wave of service providers working in broadcast media to deliver interactive services – primarily in digital TV. It provides infrastructure to support wireless Internet service providers through its Portal-to-Go offering.

G4.5 Sun Microsystems

Sun Microsystems was founded in 1982 as a hardware manufacturer, and became a public company in 1986. The company's founding premise was the proliferation of open systems technology, and it was a key player in the popularisation of Unix operating systems. Initially it found favour within the educational and scientific research markets, but with the rise in popularity of RDBMS technology, Unix – and Sun – gained popularity as a platform for hosting those systems, and this activity fuelled the first big growth phase of the company.

In 1995, when the Worldwide Web was becoming widely recognised as a powerful force in the IT industry, Sun announced that it had invented a platform-neutral programming language and operating environment ideally suited to network computing – Java.

Sun is engaged in three major spheres of activity with regard to pervasive computing:

- development and promotion of Java by the Consumer & Embedded Technologies unit, which is taking Java technologies to client and server devices beyond the realm of traditional workstations, including feature phones, smartphones and PDAs. The unit is currently working on at least 11 technology standardisation programmes, with third parties active in wireless Internet connectivity, telematics and in-car information systems, digital television and home networking – including DVB, ARIB, OSGi (Open Services Gateway initiative), the WAP Forum, 3GPP, ETSI and Symbian
- development of service provider and network operator hardware infrastructure (through its line of Netra carrier-grade servers) and management (through the Solstice Enterprise Manager)
- operation of the iPlanet joint venture with AOL/Netscape, which is developing e-commerce and wireless Internet infrastructure.

The company's corporate strapline is 'the network is the computer' – a message intended to convey the idea that Sun was enabling a new wave of network-based (rather than PC-based) computing architecture. Java technology, in its various forms and packages, is now the company's most well-known product. However, the company claims that 80% of the Internet backbone traffic passes through Sun systems.

Sun wants to play a leading role in the evolution of pervasive computing. It sees Java technologies as some of the major pillars of any pervasive computing architecture, and is spending a lot of time, money and effort to ensure that those technologies become widely used. However, Sun is not interested in making money directly from pervasive computing infrastructure products – rather, it wants to influence the direction of major consortia and individual vendors, to ensure that Java technologies end up in standards and products that are developed by third-party organisations.

Infrastructure offerings

Sun's Netra carrier-grade servers are high-end, fault-tolerant hardware systems that share their operating system (Solaris) and development environment (Java) with Sun's other platforms. Sun is confident of Netra products' fault-tolerance and availability capabilities, claiming, for example, that Netra ft 1800 can recover from any hardware failure within one second, with no data loss.

Sun is also using its hardware systems expertise in the client device market with its new range of thin-client, Java-based information appliances called SunRay.

Sun's iPlanet joint venture with AOL/Netscape is yielding software products that Sun can use to round out its infrastructure solutions. The new iPlanet Intelligent Communications Platform bundles together several of iPlanet's application server products, offering wireless messaging, calendaring, wireless connectivity and a messaging directory service, and exposing development interfaces that allow customers (whether service providers or corporates) to extend and build applications on the base platform. However, the platform is not built on iPlanet's own application server infrastructure product.

Sphere of influence

Figure G4.9 indicates the current coverage of Sun's products in terms of our technology map.

Figure G4.10 shows where Sun's influence is greatest in the major digital information delivery 'stovepipes'.

Figure G4.9 **Sun's offerings**

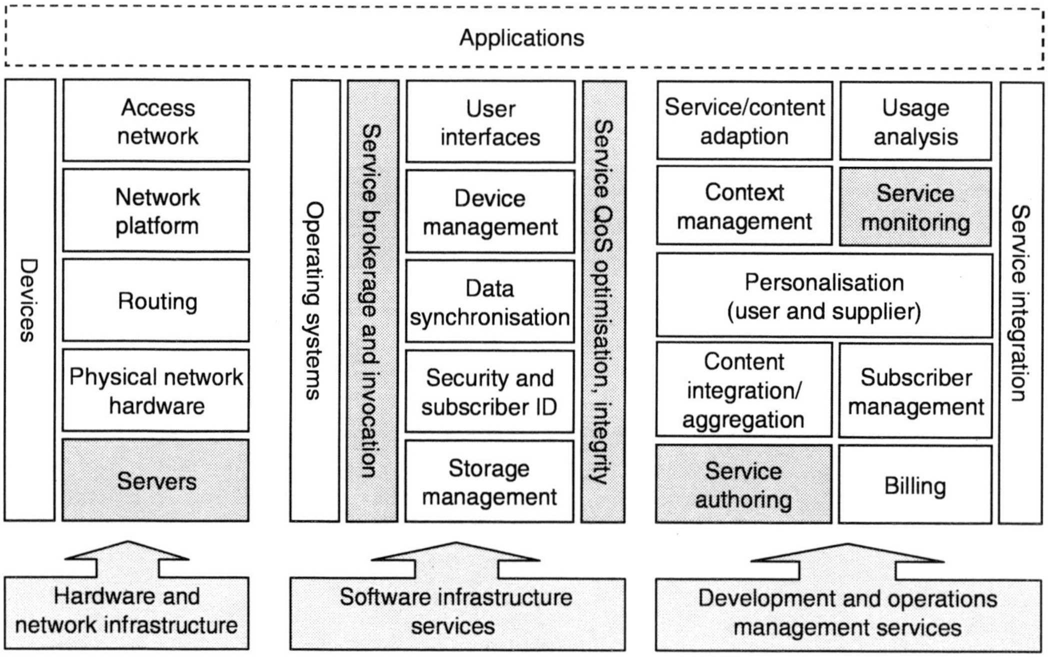

Source: Ovum (Pervasive Computing: Technologies and Markets/Chapter G)

Figure G4.10 **Sun's current influence**

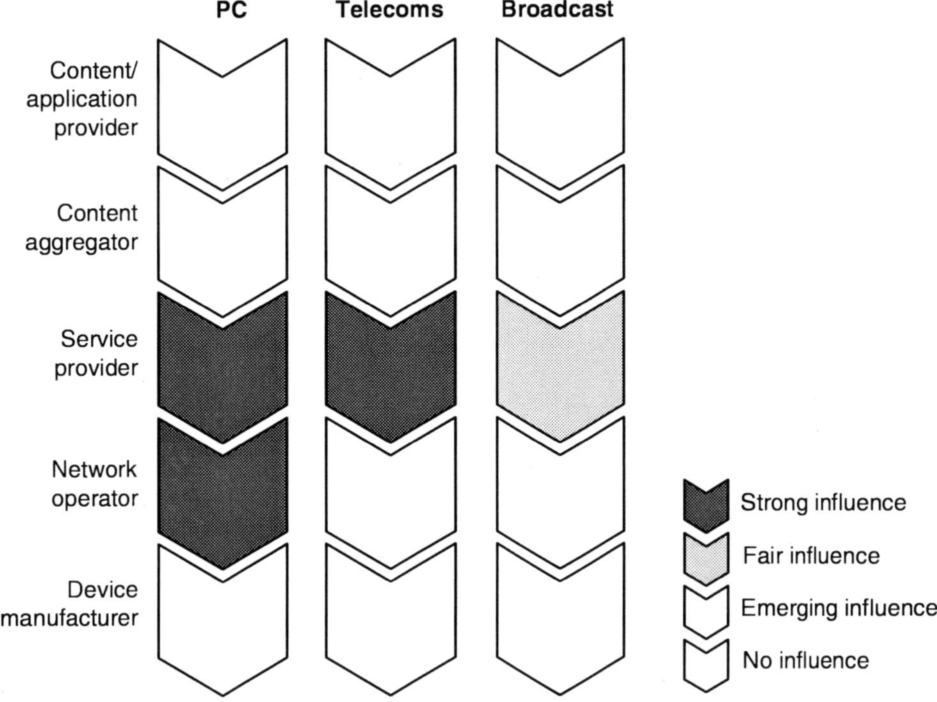

Source: Ovum (Pervasive Computing: Technologies and Markets/Chapter G)

Sun has a significant degree of influence in the service provider and network operator communities due to the popularity of its hardware platform and Solaris Unix variant operating system. The company's long association with the Internet, the Worldwide Web and e-commerce (together with its aggression towards Microsoft) have served to boost its penetration in these communities. The company is looking to capitalise on this position of strength through its new ServiceProvider.com industry initiative. This initiative is intended to offer service providers packages of Sun products and services, and business assistance, at competitive prices to both stimulate the growth of the service provider community, and also Sun's place as a supplier within that community.

Sun's high profile work with the Java standard means that it has an important, though indirect, influence on the development of pervasive computing devices. A diverse range of equipment manufacturers have already licensed Java technology (especially the J2ME and embedded Java variants) from Sun for use in their devices. Java can already be found as the runtime environment in phones, PDAs, home network gateways and set-top boxes. Nokia and Motorola are planning to use Java in their new smartphone ranges, and Java is already supported on Palm PDAs. It forms the basis of the OSGi's home network gateway initiative, and can be found in Motorola's set-top boxes. It is likely that the importance of Java in the mobile communications, digital TV and automotive channels will grow over time as the Java footprint continues to be optimised and the standard becomes more accepted.

In February 2000, the company increased its efforts to corner the home networking market, announcing a deal with the home appliance control firm Echelon Corporation. The deal allows Sun to embed Echelon's LonWorks network control software into its Java Embedded Server software for set-top boxes, residential gateways and other home appliances, to connect these devices over the Internet. Sun is likely to face stiff competition in this area from Microsoft and its own, well supported Universal Plug n' Play standard, which also has the support of Echelon.

G5 Device/network infrastructure providers

The companies are given in alphabetical order.

G5.1 Cisco Systems

Cisco Systems supplies IP networking solutions to enterprises and public carriers. It is the world's leading supplier of IP routers and LAN and WAN switches, IP firewalls and IP management tools. Cisco has headquarters in San José, California, and sales and support offices in 75 countries. Its target markets are enterprises, service providers and small to medium-sized enterprises; it has also introduced a consumer line of business to target Internet products and services for the home. Cisco has a highly acquisitive strategy and aims to capitalise on its market-leading enterprise position and move into the carrier infrastructure market to compete more evenly with Nortel and Lucent; it also aims to move into cellular infrastructure.

Cisco's leading role in IP network infrastructure provision makes its strategy crucial to the future of pervasive computing. The more pervasive IP networking is, the easier the pervasive computing vision will be to implement. The company's vision centres around the provision of 'New World networks', which are optimised around packet switching, through the central use of IP infrastructure as an integration layer. Cisco believes that IP's inherent scalability and reliability make it the most suitable technology for integrating different network technologies and applications, rather than ATM. For example, Cisco advocates direct implementation of IP on Sonet/SDH or even directly on DWDM, rather than via ATM.

The 'missing link' in the IP story is quality of service (QoS). This is where Cisco's strategy meets with its core technology strength – its IOS technology, which is embedded in its switches and routers. IOS is an embedded intelligent networking platform that allows Cisco and its customers to provide IP-based services directly in the network. Cisco has already used IOS as a foundation to deliver various types of QoS-enhancing service – directly in its routers and switches, and also in complementary server-based products. Functions include:

- data caching
- load balancing
- class-of-service implementation through RSVP
- multicasting
- VPN support
- address management
- voice-over-IP
- security.

The company sees migration towards unified networks based on IP as a way for service providers to reduce costs and enable easier creation and provision of value-added services. It is an enthusiastic supporter of IPv6 and is building support for IPv4-to-IPv6 mapping through the IOS platform.

Cisco's vision for IP and for its IP-centric infrastructure takes it beyond the enterprise in two directions: into carrier networks and into homes. The company is a key player in the Internet Home Alliance, which brings together a variety of standards initiatives (including the OSGi – Open Services Gateway initiative) and seeks to promote the use of home networking and broadband access services. Within the enterprise space, the company's focus is now broadening to encompass (largely through acquisitions) wireless LAN and voice-over-IP technology provision.

Cisco's strategy for the cellular market is one of partnership and independent development. The company has joined with Alcatel and Motorola to develop GPRS infrastructure solutions in Europe. Cisco sees 3G network upgrades in particular as a major market opportunity, as they require the deployment of new network infrastructure and also bring a much more IP-centric architecture to mobile networks.

Cisco also works with partners – notably Telcordia and Motorola – to provide systems integration services for carriers. The partners complement Cisco both technically and through their knowledge of current engineering practice within fixed and cellular carriers.

Figure G5.1 shows Cisco's current offerings.

Figure G5.1 **Cisco's offerings**

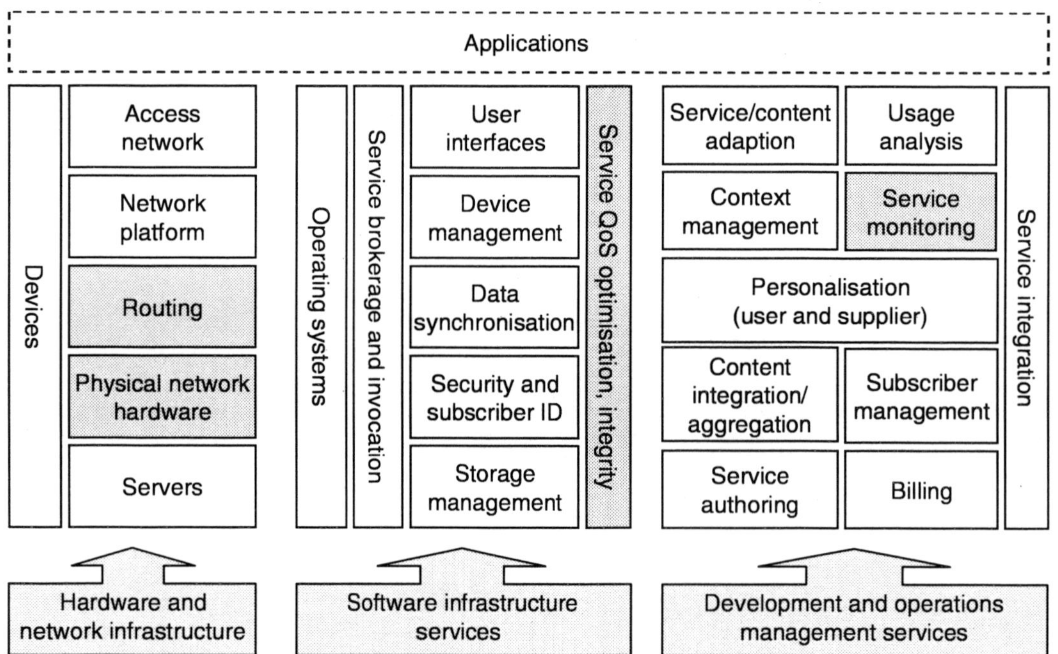

Source: Ovum (Pervasive Computing: Technologies and Markets/Chapter G)

G5.2 Ericsson

Ericsson is one of the world's leading suppliers of public circuit-switched network equipment. It is a major supplier of fixed and mobile networks. It is especially strong in Europe; its US presence is largely based on sales to mobile network operators and sales of international gateways. In the context of pervasive computing, the company is keen to become a major provider of both next-generation network equipment and mobile networking technologies – everything from handset hardware to application platforms. It is a major contributor to the WAP Forum and the Bluetooth SIG, and a major investor in Symbian. It has developed a close relationship with Microsoft, with which it is developing a set of mobile application platform components and other wireless application technologies.

Ericsson's next-generation network infrastructure portfolio is called Engine. The Engine products are designed to allow operators straightforward upgrade paths from circuit-switched to packet-switched networks. The company estimates that its market share of circuit-to-packet migration network orders is more than 80% in Europe and 40% worldwide.

Apart from its Engine next-generation fixed network infrastructure, Ericsson also builds and sells multi-service (basic telephony, ISDN and ADSL) access gateways, IP edge routers and IP core routers, optical transmission and switching systems. At the service layer Ericsson offers voice-over-IP and IP telephony servers.

The company is also a leading supplier of enhanced second-generation (2G+) mobile infrastructure and, via its acquisition of Qualcomm, is now building a network infrastructure platform that shares common elements across implementations of GPRS, cdma2000 (both 2G+) and W-CDMA (3G) networks, which will provide operators with predictable upgrade paths. The Qualcomm acquisition also brings Ericsson a considerable amount of mobile IP expertise.

For service providers, Ericsson is starting to build capability to provide a mobile application platform through its WAP gateway implementation. It has a significant software engineering and systems integration capability, which allows it to take new technologies to early adopters quickly. For example, it is partnering with Italian mobile network operator ViaSat to deliver content, applications and services to vehicles with installed GPRS terminals. The partnership envisages the network service will be able to offer infotainment services as well as vehicle management, safety and emergency services.

Ericsson is a leader in handset technology development. Its R380 EPOC-based smartphone was the first EPOC-based voice-centric handheld device to be released; its new Communicator EPOC-based platform is at the forefront of connected data-centric handheld technology. Communicator products will offer users mobile access to web browsing (WML or HTML), messaging, imaging, telephony and PIM applications in one integrated handset. Communicator products will also have built-in Bluetooth connectivity and an integrated GPS receiver. The company claims that its Bluetooth implementation is the first fully functional implementation to reach the market. It also delivers a development kit that it offers to third-party software developers, to help them build Bluetooth-enabled applications for its mobile handsets. Wind River (profiled in *Section G7.6*) is a Bluetooth licensee.

At the application level, Ericsson's stake in Symbian gives it some benefits. Sybase has already ported its UltraLite DBMS to EPOC and has licensed the technology to Ericsson; and the company has also gained a degree of influence over the J2ME specification through its involvement with the company. Ericsson is partnering with Motorola and Nokia in the Mobile Electronic Transactions (MeT) initiative, which aims to establish a common set of protocols and technologies for mobile e-commerce.

Figure G5.2 shows Ericsson's current offerings.

G5.3 Motorola

Motorola is one of the world's leading technology suppliers. It sells communications (mobile and fixed) terminals and networking hardware, embedded semiconductor solutions and embedded systems for transportation, networking, manufacturing and imaging companies, and digital and analogue systems and set-top boxes (Motorola merged with leading set-top box manufacturer General Instrument in January 2000) for broadband cable operators.

Figure G5.2 **Ericsson's offerings**

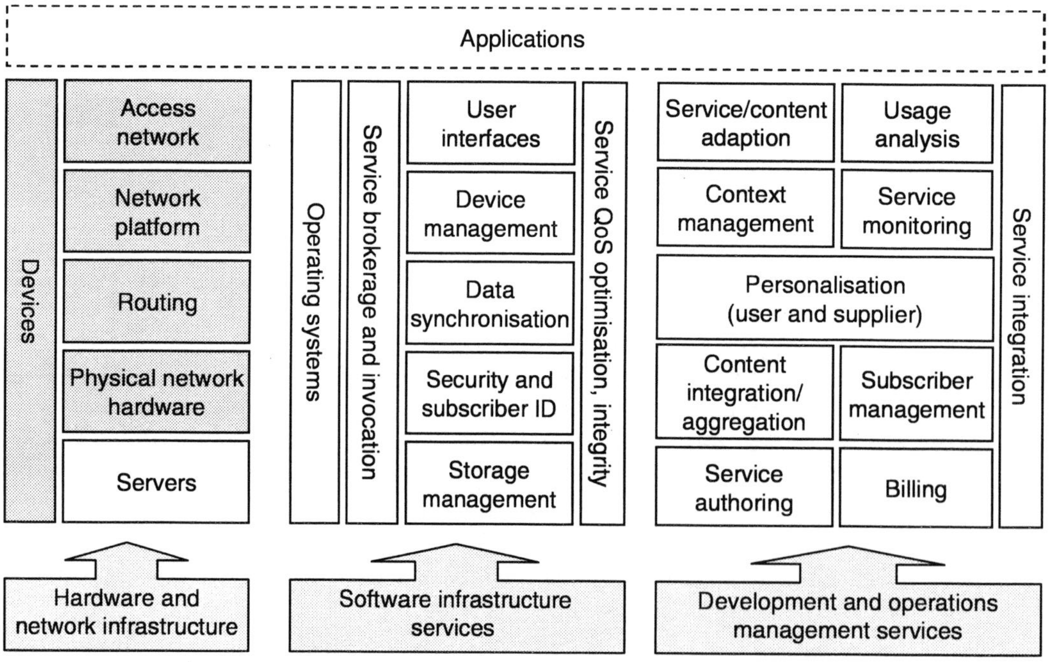

Source: Ovum (Pervasive Computing: Technologies and Markets/Chapter G)

Digital DNA is a new brand established by Motorola to encompass all its strategy-related initiatives. The strategy represents a shift for the company away from being a mere component supplier to being a solution provider, selling software infrastructure and services as well as hardware. It brings together current Motorola offerings across all its major business segments, and is organised around different solution usage scenarios:

- on the person – solutions for mobile personal communications

  Motorola feels that semiconductor developments have been key to the development of wireless, and that its expertise in this area positions it well to address the next generation of personal communications devices. With Digital DNA, Motorola (already a leading supplier of system components for wireless devices) now offers a complete software stack (based around Java) and can supply complete devices. As well as its traditional mobile phone terminal market, Motorola is now addressing the market for PDAs

- in the home – solutions for interactive broadband services

  Motorola sees the home as being at the centre of the consumer's universe of information access. It believes that consumers will wish to access a variety of services, such as banking, shopping, video conferencing and video-on-demand, delivered via multiple network technologies such as satellite, cable, xDSL, wireless and ISDN.

  By 2004, Motorola believes that a typical European home will have several digital devices, with 86% having at least one digital device, 76% with two or more devices, and most homes being online. It sees Digital DNA technology as the enabler for connectivity, entertainment and interactive solutions in the home, with its Streamaster architecture at the heart, acting as the network gateway

- on the move – solutions for driver information systems, telematics and vehicle control

  this area of the strategy focuses on the provision of semiconductor and software products to enable applications and services to be delivered to vehicles

- in the network – solutions for next-generation network infrastructure

  the Digital DNA strategy in this area centres on the Smart Networks Platform, which represents Motorola's efforts to speed the development of next-generation telecom networks. The platform includes a new PowerQUICC(TM) processor family, software and tools.

Figure G5.3 shows Motorola's current offerings.

Figure G5.3 **Motorola's offerings**

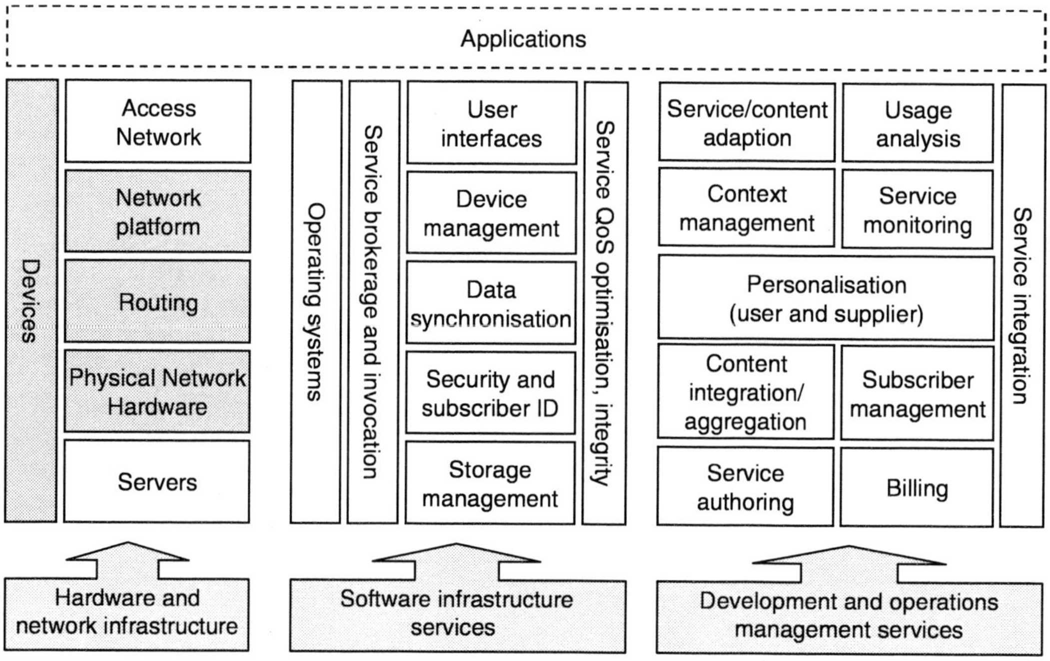

Source: Ovum (Pervasive Computing: Technologies and Markets/Chapter G)

G5.4 Nokia

Nokia started life in 1865 as a wood-pulp mill, manufacturing paper. Since the 1990s, it has focused on delivering telecommunications technology. The company now employs 60,000 people, approximately one-third of whom work in research and development. It achieved net sales of $19.9 billion in 1999; more than 65% of this figure came from Nokia's mobile phones division.

Nokia is a strong player in the mobile arena, as a supplier of handsets, mobile network infrastructure and application platforms. It claims to have sold its GSM technology to 87 operators in 39 countries, and its 2G+ (HSCSD and GPRS) technologies to more than 20 customers. It also has operations that provide infrastructure for delivering fixed broadband services to the consumer, SoHo and SME markets.

In order to achieve a position of strength in the wireless Internet market, the company wants to shift its focus from being a 'plumber' to being an end-to-end platform provider offering hardware, network infrastructure, software and systems integration expertise. The company wants to transform customers' views of its products so that they see them as personal communications devices; it also wants to transform people's views of access networks into personalised services portals. There are five interesting strands to its strategy:

- on the handset, Nokia aims to build a platform capable of serving sophisticated applications and content. The company is an active licensee of Symbian's EPOC and is also working with Palm to deliver an application delivery environment on its high-end voice handsets that can host EPOC applications natively, or Palm applications via emulation on EPOC. It has forged a partnership with RealNetworks to bring RealPlayer streaming media software to the EPOC platform. It has also worked with Macromedia to develop a version of Macromedia's Fireworks graphics authoring toolkit, which can generate images that can be shown on Nokia's WAP-capable feature phones
- the company is working with a number of software infrastructure suppliers, including BEA and TIBCO. BEA and Nokia have a technology and co-marketing partnership that sees BEA use Nokia's WAP gateway, and Nokia use BEA technology in its mPlatform – a wireless portal and application platform for wireless service providers, which implements OTA data encryption, customer care and billing functions. Together, the companies see their combined value proposition as providing reliable, scalable, secure platforms for wireless e-commerce (which is virtually identical to IBM's proposition). The company is also helping TIBCO to WAP-enable its ActivePortal solution, which is an integration framework for pulling together disparate data sources in a portal using high-performance messaging middleware
- to stimulate use of wireless Internet, the company is enhancing some of the standard services offered to mobile users. One example is its Multimedia Message Service (MMS), which has been specified with a view to standardisation in the WAP Forum and 3GPP (the group that is setting technology standards for third-generation wireless services). The specifications will include full interoperability between SMS and e-mail. The first stage of its development is the combination of hard-coded digital images with text messages. The company is also developing phone–camera interfaces and devices capable of displaying colour photographs; eventually, it sees MMS as being able to include user-created pictures, data, text, audio and video
- Nokia has created a 3G Service Creation and Execution Platform (SCEP). The company positions this as an environment that can be used either solely by a service provider, in partnership with Nokia itself, or via a third-party software provider. The platform is designed to allow a service provider's network to communicate with application servers run by third-party service and content providers. The company also claims that the platform can integrate multiple network elements and protocols, making it possible to deliver individual services that use UMTS, WAP and IP

- Nokia is starting to act as a systems developer and integrator for operators and corporate users. It can provide these customers with server solutions that include a range of integrated content and other applications. It is also creating web-based content- and application-developer communities that can add value to its server solutions.

In the broadband home access space, Nokia Home Communications (part of the Nokia Venture Capital business unit) builds and sells set-top boxes and broadband customer premises equipment to residential consumers and SMEs. Nokia's Media Terminal is a digital set-top box that can be connected to broadband IP services via ISDN, PSTN, xDSL or cable modem. The device's programming interfaces are built on a Linux system, and allow services and applications to be delivered using a variety of web-friendly and digital TV-friendly content formats. The application platform foundation is a PAL/NTSC-optimised version of the popular open-source Mozilla web browser (which also powers Netscape's offering). Nokia's Home Communications unit is also co-developing home networked appliances with 3Com and Whirlpool; it is also an active member of the OSGi.

Nokia's broadband customer premises equipment product line is centred around multi-terminal shared ADSL modems for residential access that allow multiple PCs and Media Terminals to share the same xDSL connection, and an SDSL/WLAN gateway for SoHo and SME users.

Nokia is committed to implementing IPv6 support in its wireless access network infrastructure products. It sees IPv6 as a critical enabler of interactive services on mobile access platforms, claiming that it 'promotes IPv6 and supports a gradual, controlled shift to IPv6 in mobile networks'. Effectively, this means that it is planning a migration strategy for 2G (which uses IPv4), and building new 3G infrastructure using IPv6, with IPv4 translation for backward-compatibility.

Figure G5.4 shows Nokia's current offerings.

Figure G5.4 **Nokia's offerings**

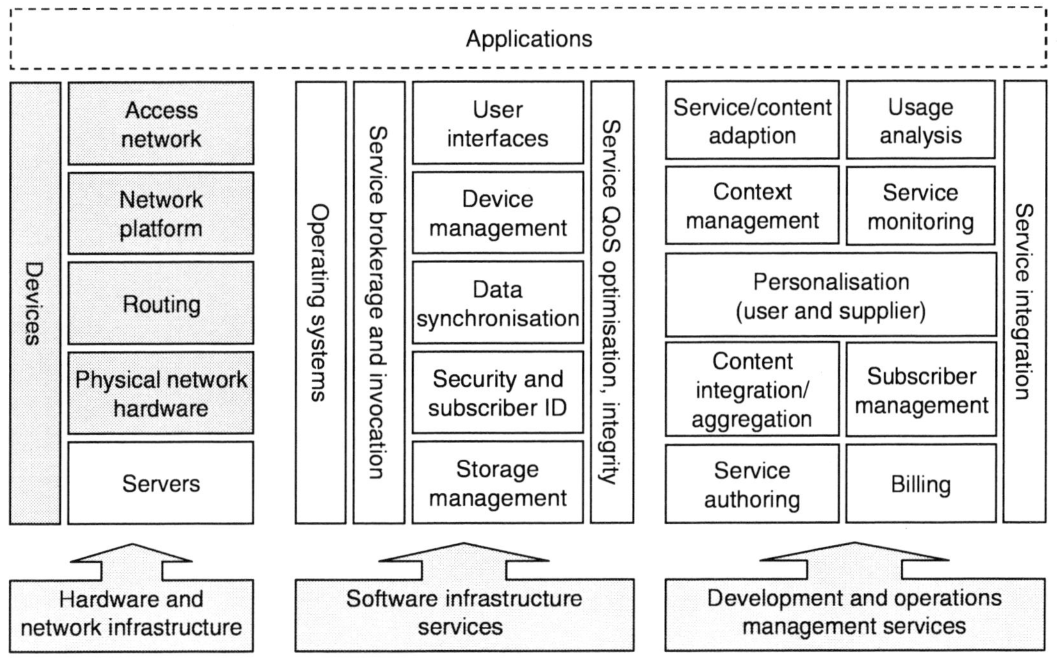

Source: Ovum (Pervasive Computing: Technologies and Markets/Chapter G)

G5.5 Palm Computing

Palm Computing is currently the leading supplier of PDAs worldwide, with its range of Palm Connected Organizers. The company started out as a division of 3Com, but was spun out of its parent company as a separate entity in March 2000.

Palm claims it has a market offering in all the delivery channels considered in this report. In addition to its PDA range, it has licensed the Palm operating system (PalmOS) to some mobile phone vendors, and has recently entered into a partnership with Delphi Automotive to deliver in-car information systems.

Palm sees itself primarily as a provider of portable computing devices for 'power users' – who use products in both corporate and consumer (personal) contexts. The company aims to make its products appealing to broad swathes of the mass consumer market, rather than selling its products as premium value items. However, within its product range it has carved out a space at the top end of the PDA market, and prices its products in that space accordingly. The company claims that its hardware products typically have a sales lifespan of between 12 and 18 months.

The company is increasingly putting strategic effort into its Palm.net network access and portal service, and into licensing the PalmOS platform to other device manufacturers.

PalmOS devices 'natively' operate personal information management (PIM) applications (calendar, notepad, address book and mail client) and some other general productivity services. The operating system also ships with HotSync synchronisation software. However, its partners develop and sell both horizontal (such as customer relationship management and intranet access) and vertical (such as healthcare, transportation and education) enterprise applications that run on PalmOS devices.

As Palm-based devices go wireless, the company points out that it believes people will still want to use their devices when not connected to a network. This is what makes its devices and its PalmOS platform fundamentally different to the technology approaches developed by some other wireless Internet infrastructure vendors (such as Phone.Com). From this base, Palm is keen to enhance the capabilities of the core platform, as well as develop compelling network services for connected users.

Figure G5.5 shows Palm's current offerings.

Figure G5.5 **Palm's current offerings**

Applications

Devices
Access network
Network platform
Routing
Physical network hardware
Servers
Hardware and network infrastructure

Operating systems
Service brokerage and invocation
User interfaces
Device management
Data synchronisation
Security and subscriber ID
Storage management
Service QoS optimisation, integrity
Software infrastructure services

Service/content adaption
Usage analysis
Context management
Service monitoring
Personalisation (user and supplier)
Content integration/ aggregation
Subscriber management
Service authoring
Billing
Service integration
Development and operations management services

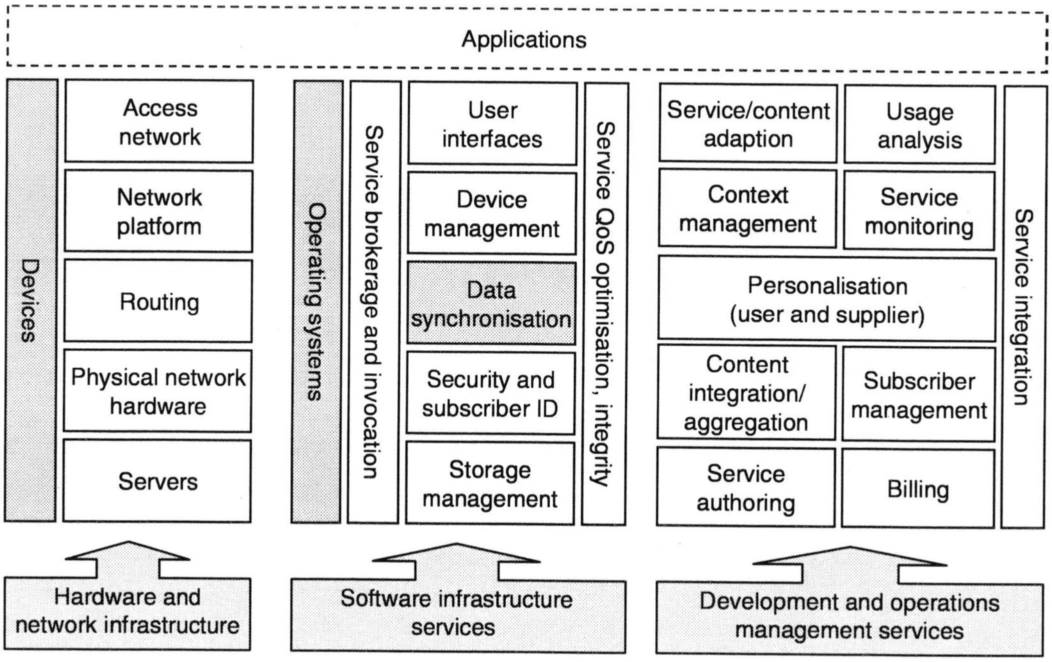

Source: Ovum (Pervasive Computing: Technologies and Markets/Chapter G)

G5.6 Psion

Psion produces connected PDA devices (Wireless Information Devices – WIDs) for the business and consumer markets. Psion believes that PIM and corporate application access will be the two 'killer' applications for WIDs and is focusing its efforts on these areas. It is positioning its devices at the upper end of the mobile terminal spectrum. All Psion's products are based around the EPOC operating system from Symbian (formerly the Psion Software Division, which was spun off to form the new company).

Psion's strategy centres on the production of WIDs as a means of providing enriched wireless Internet services. The WID includes significant local processing and storage facilities. Psion expects that WIDs will eventually act as terminals for both voice and data, but it is currently focusing only on the data side. The company is working on a joint venture with Motorola to bring voice and data WIDs to market.

Psion positions its products to address business and consumer markets. Its range of personal organiser products (Revo, Series 5mx and Series 7) are targeted at consumers, whilst the Netbook is Psion's first product to address the enterprise market.

The personal organiser products primarily focus on PIM, providing comprehensive calendar and scheduling functions, along with facilities for synchronising and accessing data whilst on the move. Other included applications focused on scaled-down personal productivity tools, such as a spreadsheet, word processor or database.

The Netbook is geared more towards mobile business applications. Psion ships a comprehensive set of application development facilities for the platform, including software development kits for Windows 95/98/NT, C++ and Java. The types of application that Psion is attempting to address with the Netbook include wireless field sales access to Internet and intranet data, rugged mobile use in a service or manufacturing organisation and home banking and shopping.

Figure G5.6 shows Psion's current offerings.

Figure G5.6 **Psion's current offerings**

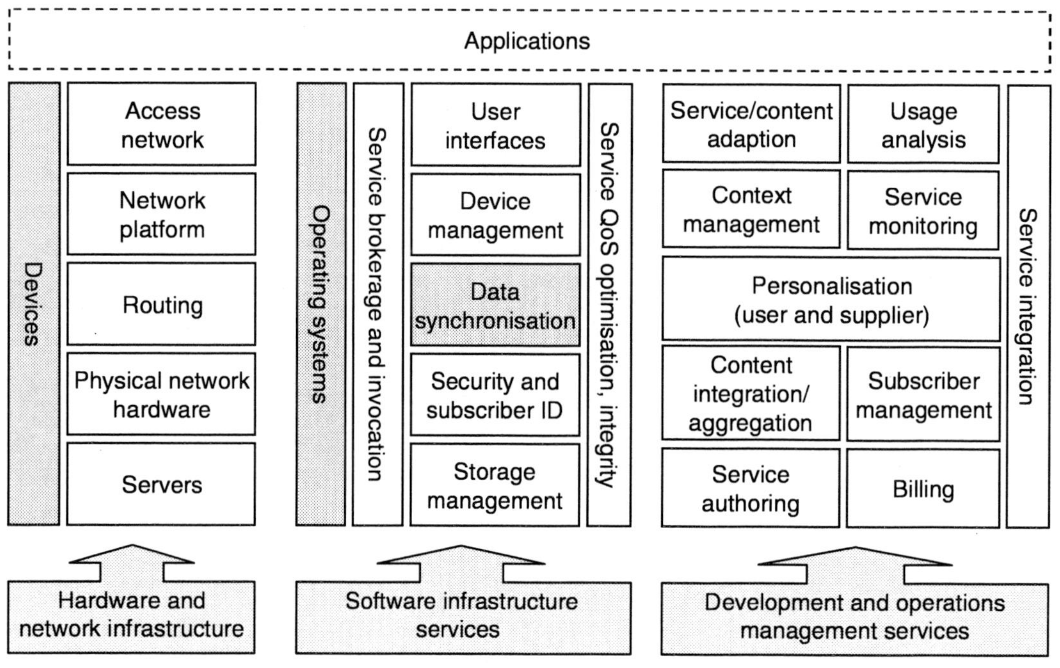

Source: Ovum (Pervasive Computing: Technologies and Markets/Chapter G)

G6 Software infrastructure providers

The companies are given in alphabetical order.

G6.1 BEA

BEA Systems was founded in 1995 to market, develop and sell an 'enterprise middleware platform based on enhanced distributed transaction processing technology and professional services'. The business plan was developed on the basis that the technology would have to be acquired from other companies. Since its incorporation, BEA has pursued an aggressive acquisition strategy – buying the rights to Tuxedo from Novell in 1996, followed by the purchase of DEC's middleware portfolio and NCR's TopEnd.

BEA is one of the leading suppliers of back-end corporate infrastructure for large-scale transactional systems – including e-commerce applications. Currently, it has no desire to step outside this role, but it is making full use of its position in its strategy and branding. BEA's core products are priced as serious enterprise or service provider infrastructure – this is no mass-market value proposition.

BEA believes that development of multichannel service delivery capabilities will vary widely across market segments, due to geographical, regulatory and social factors. It believes that, however market development occurs, service providers will want to treat all delivery channels as extensions of a single e-services infrastructure back-end – with the branch point between infrastructures for different channels being the 'presentation layer'. Essentially, BEA believes that it sells a common platform foundation for multichannel service delivery. The company expects Java technology to be pervasive in this environment.

BEA's product line centres on server-side infrastructure that supports the development and deployment of large-scale transactional applications. Of particular relevance to pervasive computing are BEA's WebLogic Commerce and Personalisation servers. Both these 'servers' are in fact bundlings of the WebLogic application server with additional software components. The Personalisation server includes a set of Java components that make it easier for developers to build portals that can be personalised and transactional applications. The Commerce server is a superset of the Personalisation server, and also ships with components for portal development, content management, business and rules processing, and a set of commerce processing pipeline components.

BEA's WebLogic Mobile Commerce solution is the fruit of a recent co-development and co-marketing partnership with Nokia. BEA claims that it supports the assembly of personalised WAP services and deployment of transactional WAP-based applications. The solution is an amalgamation of WebLogic Server 5.1, the Commerce server component bundle, the Nokia WAP server and a collection of BEA consulting services.

WebLogic is a line of application server products that provide development and runtime services to customers building transactional e-commerce applications. The WebLogic product line is highly focused on Java, but BEA also markets its distributed transaction-processing monitor, Tuxedo, as an 'e-commerce platform' in its own right, targeted at more traditional (non-Java) transactional e-commerce applications.

Figure G6.1 shows BEA's current offerings.

Figure G6.1 **BEA's offerings**

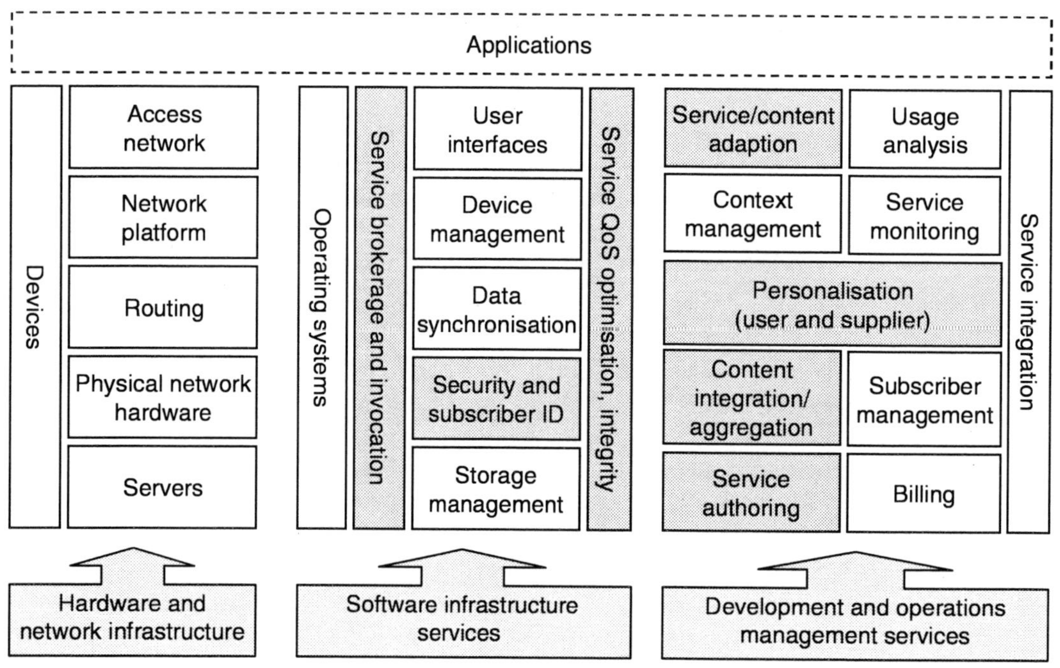

Source: Ovum (Pervasive Computing: Technologies and Markets/Chapter G)

G6.2 Centura

Centura Software Corporation supplies database and development products aimed at developers wishing to build and deploy component-based applications. These applications can be scaled from smart devices to the Web and operate in both the Windows client-server and Internet worlds.

Centura positions itself as an enabler of wireless connectivity solutions that enable applications running on a variety of devices to access back-end systems and business logic in realtime. It believes that its strong background in application development, coupled with its expertise in embedded realtime database systems as a result of the acquisition of embedded database specialists Raima, leave it well placed to realise this strategy.

The company is positioning itself to appeal to markets where there is need for zero latency whilst exchanging data between wireless devices and corporate intranets, and where realtime access is required to update business information.

Solutions are delivered through a combination of the eSnapp and db.Star products. eSnapp is a connectivity solution that allows enterprise data and business logic to be accessed in realtime from handheld devices, PDAs and other information appliances. eSnapp allows information to be gathered and transmitted to a central repository in realtime, via a wireless LAN or cellular connection, and uses event-driven messaging that allows specific processes to be automatically triggered when a specific data condition is met.

db.Star provides a small-footprint, embedded-database engine, which has a 15-year history of use in embedded applications. db.Star, which is open source software, requires 200kb of RAM, or 40kb if the access is read-only.

Figure G6.2 shows Centura's current offerings.

G6.3 Inprise/Borland

Inprise was originally founded as Borland in 1983 to market the Turbo Pascal compiler for PCs. The company suffered significantly throughout the 1990s as it fought to obtain, and retain, a place in the chaotic development tools market. It acquired a number of middleware technologies in order to add value to its tool offering. By 1998, the company had a strong portfolio of middleware technologies, including DCE-based middleware (Entera) from the company's acquisition of Open Environment in 1996, as well as COM-based middleware (MIDAS) and, more recently, a CORBA ORB from the purchase of Visigenic in February 1998.

By the time the company was renamed Inprise, it had already begun to refocus its strategy on the provision of strategic middleware, backed by a strong line in development tools. The company is extending this focus into the wireless Internet arena with its development tool support for wireless devices via JBuilder Handheld Express, and integrated middleware and application server infrastructure.

Inprise is organised in three divisions:

- Enterprise – which sells VisiBroker and the Internet Application Server
- JBuilder – which sells the eponymous Java development tool

Figure G6.2 **Centura's offerings**

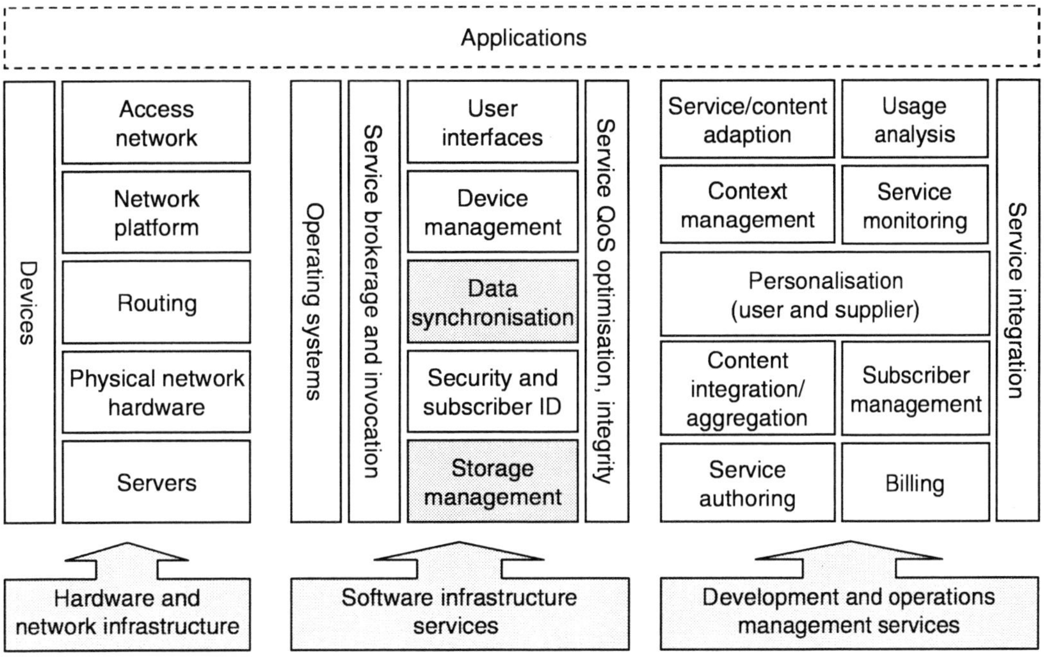

Source: Ovum (Pervasive Computing: Technologies and Markets/Chapter G)

- Borland – which sells the rest of its development tools (C++ Builder, Delphi and Kylix).

Two of Inprise's main offerings – its JBuilder tool and its Internet Application Server infrastructure – play a role in pervasive computing.

The newest release of JBuilder (version 3.5) is written from the 'ground up' in Java and is designed to be easily extended by third parties. Inprise has used the open tools interface (OTI) feature that enables this to create a special version of the tool called JBuilder Handheld Express. This can be freely downloaded from the Inprise website, and allows JBuilder developers to create and deploy Java applications that run on PalmOS devices. In a separate development, Gemplus used the OTI to build a version of JBuilder that developers can use to build Java applications for deployment on its smart cards.

The Inprise Application Server is based on the VisiBroker ORB, acquired when Inprise bought Visigenic. The latest version supports WAP client access as well as HTTP access.

Inprise's mission is to enable the development of enterprise class business applications using its broad range of tools and middleware. With its latest tool and middleware platform releases, the company is making it clear that it views the support of multiple access platforms to be a key requirement for enterprise applications going forward.

Figure G6.3 shows Inprise's current offerings.

Figure G6.3 **Inprise's offerings**

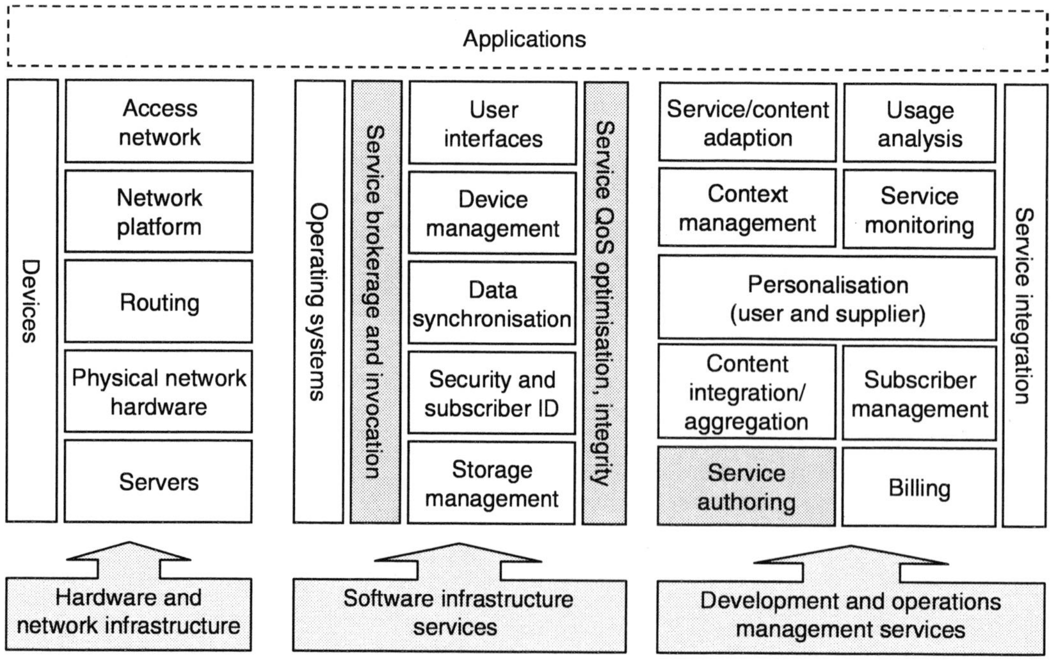

Source: Ovum (Pervasive Computing: Technologies and Markets/Chapter G)

G7 Ones to watch

G7.1 Aether Software

Aether Software is the software products division of Aether Systems, which focuses on providing software solutions for extending enterprise applications to wireless devices. Through its ScoutWare family of products, Aether Software provides the software infrastructure for delivering corporate information to any mobile device over any network. Aether Systems uses the software to offer hosted wireless applications.

All Aether Software's products fall under the ScoutWare brand. The product range comprises

- ScoutSync – synchronisation server software that enables connection between enterprise applications and remote devices
- ScoutIT – a management tool for the administration of handheld devices and applications
- ScoutWeb – a content management tool for handheld devices
- ScoutArchitect – a visual design tool for mobile applications
- Aether Intelligent Messaging (AIM) – a development environment and messaging software for integrating enterprise applications with wireless applications, which is the core technology behind all Aether's products.

Aether Software's partnerships and strategic alliances include 3Com, Palm, Research In Motion, AT&T Wireless services, Bell Atlantic Mobile, Reuters (Aether partnered with Reuters to form the European joint venture Sila Communications, which aimed to provide wireless access to corporate information, Reuters content, Internet information and applications, e-mail and secure transaction capabilities), Nextel, OmniSky (a joint Aether/Palm wireless ISP venture) and Visa.

Aether Software positions its products to address wireless connectivity within the enterprise and business-to-business arenas. It has no plans to address other markets in the short term.

G7.2 Echelon

Echelon is a network infrastructure company that concentrates on network-enabling everyday devices – from washing machines to valves – using its LonWorks technology, which has been adopted as a standard by a number of industry organisations. Many of the patents that the company holds are licensed without royalties or licence fees. Echelon's technology strength, combined with its open approach to doing business, has won it some high-profile infrastructure partners – including Cisco, Sun, Toshiba and Motorola. The company currently has around 175 employees, and in 1999 recorded a net loss of $3.9 million on revenues of $37.5 million.

LonWorks technology is embedded in devices, and used to build distributed 'control networks' – collections of devices that communicate with one another to perform a control application (such as security, lighting or power consumption management). Historically, the company concentrated on applying its technologies via OEMs and systems integrators to specialised vertical industry control applications, but the company's new focus – Internet and intranet connectivity – is bringing it much more strongly to the networked home appliance market. Cisco, Toshiba and Sun in particular are working with Echelon to improve their market positions in this area.

The outcome of Echelon's collaboration with Cisco and Toshiba was the i.LON 1000 Internet server, which was launched in October 1999. Since then, its partnership with Sun has led to a development programme that will see Sun's Java Embedded server (a product from its Consumer & Embedded unit) integrated with the i.LON 1000 server. The resulting product will conform to the OSGi's residential gateway specification.

Echelon believes that the market opportunity for home networks is considerable, and that there is likely to be room for more than one standard. Consequently, as well as being an active participant in the OSGi, Echelon is also a backer of Universal Plug n'Play (UPnP).

G7.3 NetMorf

Boston-based NetMorf is a new company that aims to provide a standard mechanism to deliver content to a wide variety of device types through its SiteMorfer product. SiteMorfer uses one common mark-up language at the back-end, enabling mobile applications to communicate with different devices in a scalable, reliable and secure manner. It provides a platform to enable the delivery of content and transactions in a format optimised for a wide variety of mobile devices, including WAP phones, pagers, PDAs, pocket PCs and custom devices.

SiteMorfer uses its own mark-up language (SML) but is designed so that it can quickly interface with databases, content and application servers, e-mail systems, and transactional back-ends. SiteMorfer supports XML, HTML, Oracle, SQLServer and ODBC, among others. Currently on its v2.0 release, it incorporates a GUI-based development environment designed for delivering mobile business applications that allow data sources to be linked to devices and new transactions to be added with minimum programming. SiteMorfer also provides a range of services including cookie proxy management, session management, security and automatic device formatting. SiteMorfer is also integrated with Allaire's ColdFusion and JRun web development and deployment platforms.

NetMorf targets a wide range of organisations, including business-to-consumer and business-to-business e-commerce sites, corporate intranets used for mission-critical operations (salesforce automation and dispatch) and online service providers (stock trading, banking and travel).

G7.4 Phone.Com

Phone.Com was founded as Libris by Alain Rossmann in December 1994. Rossmann is now the company's chairman and CEO. The company rose to fame as Unwired Planet in 1996, with the commercial release of its browser and server software, UP.Browser and UP.Server, which allowed mobile phone users to access information services using web-like formats and protocols. In 1997, Unwired Planet founded the WAP Forum with Motorola, Ericsson and Nokia. Since becoming Phone.com in April 1999, the company has acquired several small vendors of complementary technologies – including ApiON (a WAP software supplier), @Motion (a voice portal vendor), Paragon Software (a vendor of over-the-air data synchronisation technology), and Onebox.com (an ASP that focuses on delivering unified messaging services).

As Unwired Planet, Phone.Com entered the wireless Internet infrastructure market as a provider of client-server infrastructure for basic information access. However, it believes this type of infrastructure is becoming increasingly commoditised, and is keen to move up the value chain in providing turnkey solutions for mobile network operators, built upon its stack of wireless Internet applications and server infrastructure.

The company positions its infrastructure products and services as enabling the following types of application:

- carrier-centric – including location-based services, bill payment and realtime service provision
- Web companion – adjunct to fixed Internet usage
- consumer – including infotainment applications
- enterprise application access – e-mail and directory applications, and access to vertical (for example, field sales or customer service) applications.

Phone.Com's customers are mobile network operators, not consumers. The company licenses its server software on a per-subscriber basis, and its client browser software on a one-off basis. It either sells server software to mobile operators or hosts it itself – this is particularly useful for operators undertaking small-scale service trials. Phone.Com has more than 60 customers, who between them operate services for more than two million customers (although it is unclear how many of these are only using trial services).

G7.5 RealNetworks

RealNetworks specialises in the provision of streaming media tools and infrastructure for the business and consumer markets. It develops and markets software and services that enable audio, video and other multimedia services to be delivered to PCs and other electronic devices. The company claims an installed base of more than 130 million for its flagship RealPlayer client software.

RealNetworks positions itself firmly around its core expertise as a provider of streaming media infrastructure solutions. The company feels that it has played a key role in the creation and evolution of streaming media technology and also stresses the additional expertise it can offer to its customers in the form of additional services and consultancy as a result of this.

The company has more than 750 partnerships with organisations from a variety of industries, including terminal providers such as Nokia, and broadcasters and content providers such as the BBC and AOL.

The company operates mainly on a premium-value revenue model, based around the licensing of its server products to organisations wishing to make use of streaming media. It believes that, as a result of its entrenched position at the back-end (nearly all heavy-duty streaming media applications currently available are based around RealServer) and the size of the installed base for its RealPlayer client software, it is ideally placed to capitalise on any market opportunity for streaming media.

G7.6 Wind River

Wind River was formed in 1981 as a provider of embedded software for a wide range of devices. Wind River's software has been deployed in more than 100 million units – it has even seen its technology reach Mars as part of Nasa's path finder mission. The company claims more than 50,000 active developers worldwide, and has separate business units focused on consumer, networks, platform, services, and transportation, defence and industrial customers.

Wind River's technology used in network infrastructure (ATM switches, hubs and cellular base stations), automobiles, factory automation, set-top boxes (it co-develops systems for the AOLTV platform), digital cameras and many other types of appliance. The fact that its products are tried and tested in many different devices and applications puts Wind River in a strong position to capitalise on the growth in the market for new information appliances that pervasive computing is likely to bring.

Wind River's strategy centres on delivering a mechanism for the rapid development of software platforms that can be tailored to devices – that is, they supply a kit for building a platform, rather than the platform itself. Their Tornado embedded software development environment comprises three closely integrated components:

- Tornado Tools – a suite of development tools for embedded software, which includes a target hardware simulator for rapid product development
- VxWorks – Wind River's realtime operating system
- a full range of communications options to allow the device to connect with a host.

The company has a strong position in this market and is likely to find itself in competition with HP's Chai and Sun's Embedded Java products – Wind River was the first company to achieve full Java compatibility in a realtime operating system. With strong experience as an embedded systems supplier and many deployments in mission-critical applications already achieved, Wind River looks set to continue to be a major player in this market.

H Implications for suppliers

H1 Key messages for suppliers

H1.1 Three principles of pervasive computing supply

Multichannel electronic delivery of content, applications and services will represent more than 40% of total Internet service revenues by 2005 – nearly $1.3 trillion. The majority of today's players, together with a multitude of new entrants, will – indeed should – be very eager to play a part in this market.

However, successful development of pervasive computing requires all supplier communities to abide by the following three principles of product development, product marketing and market development:

- do not over-hype your products or services, no matter how tempting. Creating unrealistic user expectations will harm you in the long term
- implement open interfaces to your products and services using standard protocols and data formats as a matter of priority. This alone will not draw the best partners to you, but it will be a partnering prerequisite
- no single supplier, or even supplier community, has the ability to address all the issues that are critical to long-term success. No matter how painful it may seem, you will have to build bridges with others to bring compelling products and services to market.

H1.2 Building the hybrid software/network perspective

Supplier communities must realise that what they do not know is as important as what they do know:

- software-centric players understand issues surrounding the delivery of specialised products and services to highly segmented markets, and differentiating those products and services based on features and functions
- network-centric players understand issues surrounding the high-quality delivery of mass-market services that are differentiated based on price and performance.

Both network and software perspectives are vital, yet there are very few suppliers that recognise the importance of a hybrid perspective.

H1.3 Summary of key messages

Figure H1.1 summarises our key messages for the major supplier communities that will play a role in pervasive computing.

Figure H1.1 **Summary of messages to supplier communities**

2001–2002	2003–2004	2005–2006
Device manufacturers		
New devices by themselves are not enough – build complementary services in conjunction with established service providers Implement standards in the platform to maximise availability of content, applications and services	Your ability to provide or brand high-quality services, as well as your market position as a device manufacturer, will dictate success or failure Back-end software infrastructure is crucial in delivering compelling services – partner with large infrastructure players	Broaden device capabilities and provide an open platform – but balance these against potential security and reliability implications. Work with experienced platform vendors to avoid making 'tiny PCs'
Network operators		
Use network intelligence not just to enable quality of service, but also to track aggregate usage activity Concentrate on the value of compelling services, rather than the cost of your infrastructure and operating licences	Mine your user and usage knowledge base to provide value to other players beyond provision of a 'blind bit pipe' Form partnerships to bring new services to market – success requires an understanding of delivering specialised services to niche markets, differentiated through advanced functionality rather than price and performance	Use your operational coverage and experience of delivering high-quality services to underpin the operations of, and links between, complex chains of pervasive computing service providers – but involve software infrastructure providers in your efforts
Content/application providers		
Delivering your assets through multiple channels requires short-term investment in (re)designing them correctly Choose your infrastructure partners carefully – their ability to execute is critical to your long-term success	Do not shy away from delivering paid-for content – partner with operators and service providers that can implement micro-payment and EBPP schemes, and with infrastructure providers that can offer cross-platform security solutions	Make sure your pricing and business models are consistent across channels Partner globally to ensure your assets are tailored for particular geographic markets
Service providers		
Let the strength of your brand decide your path to market – whether wholesale or retail service provision (you can do both)	Do not focus exclusively on complete ownership of the customer as your point of market leverage. In the pervasive computing future, customers will have the freedom to 'own' themselves. You need to be prepared to share your ownership	Make sure your pricing and business models are consistent across channels Form global partnerships to ensure your services are tailored for particular geographic markets
Infrastructure suppliers		
Time-to-market is critical for your customers: form partnerships to build the right solutions quickly, but implement standards to maximise the breadth of their applicability	Smaller players must be prepared to work with the big players in order to get their technologies to market – or to work with service providers that can resell their technologies wholesale to other service providers. There will be a rapid increase in the number of infrastructure service opportunities for players wishing to take this route to market	Supporting content, application and service specialisation in a scalable fashion is the major challenge – network and software infrastructure vendors must partner or merge to build the critical mass required to become a multichannel platform player

Source: Ovum (Pervasive Computing: Technologies and Markets/Chapter H)

H2 Implications for device manufacturers

H2.1 Key messages

- For the vast majority of device suppliers, success in pervasive computing will require more than just delivering the 'sexiest' device
- You will have to complement your device offering with digital content, applications and services – but bring these to market by partnering with established service providers; do not attempt to build a service-provider business from scratch
- Keep services/portals relevant to your core device offering(s), ensure they add value and do not price them too highly, as this will stifle take-up
- Use standards to bring the widest universes of content, applications and services to your user base – but do not rely on them to solve all your problems. Form partnerships with experienced software infrastructure providers to ensure that your platform is good enough to deliver the right mix of services
- Be aware that implementing an open platform will decrease your hold over the supply chain – but that not having control over it is a precursor to your success. You must compete based on the quality of your partnerships, not through a market stranglehold.

H2.2 Market factors affecting device manufacturers

Market development

Pervasive computing will bring great opportunities for device manufacturers to access new markets and find new ways to compete with their rivals – but these opportunities will also bring new sources of competition to device markets, from consumer electronics and home appliance manufacturers as well as from 'traditional' computing device players. In the longer term, device disaggregation is likely to affect device markets – particularly in the area of mobile personal devices.

2001–2002

The pervasive computing device market in 2001–2002 will be characterised by:

- intense competition – between existing players, from players 'crossing over' from segment to segment (for example, PC manufacturers moving into PDAs and in-car systems) and from new entrants such as consumer electronics and home appliance manufacturers
- the continuation of 'hard' constraints on the capability of mobile devices – specifically, network capabilities and battery life
- the steady spread of Internet technology, content and applications into both mobile and broadcast supply chains – particularly in Asia on the mobile side.

2003–2004

By 2003–2004, the device market will be characterised by:

- the much greater influence of applications on the technology and quality-of-service capabilities of devices
- use of multiple devices by sophisticated users
- a steady erosion of the concept of distinct business and consumer users of computing devices, as employed people use the same devices in both home and work roles
- removal of battery life constraints, and improvements in network connectivity for mobile devices
- the 'Bluetooth effect' – where personal area network technology is pervasive to the degree that disaggregated devices start to be both practical and compelling for heavy users of computing devices.

2005–2006

The following market influences will occur in 2005–2006:

- broadening penetration of access networks and protocols that can carry voice, data and video to both consumers and businesses
- increasingly convergent personal communications, infotainment and e-commerce applications, with many devices becoming less like specialised platforms and more like general-purpose computing devices.

Strengths and weaknesses of device manufacturers

Pervasive computing offers highly attractive business development opportunities to existing device manufacturers. However, pervasive computing requires software and services components, as well as device innovation – and many players have limited experience of delivering software products or services.

Strengths

- Device capabilities and form factors control users' experiences and service capabilities
- Many products have 'personal relationships' with users
- Many vendors have highly recognised brands

Weaknesses

- Hardware-centric business models are increasingly tough to implement successfully – they require high levels of research and development investment, and only succeed when new products sell in huge volumes
- There is lots of potential for hardware commoditisation and price undercutting by competitors – competition is often a price/performance 'drag race'
- Many vendors have limited experience of software or services markets

H2.3 Opportunities, challenges and strategy options

Figure H2.1 shows the opportunities, challenges and strategy options for device manufacturers in pervasive computing.

Figure H2.1 **Options for device manufacturers**

Opportunities	Challenges	Strategy options
Create a new 'Internet appliance' device	Devices are only one part of the equation – success will be difficult without complementary content, applications and services Brand visibility is critical	If you do not have an established brand, take the OEM route to market If you have an established brand, make sure you form partnerships with content and application providers and/or well-branded service providers Concentrate on building open, but secure and reliable platforms – partner with infrastructure vendors
Create value-added portal or content aggregation services to complement new smart, connected devices	Experience of delivering software and e-services with incumbents in those markets is likely to be limited Competition from dedicated online aggregators Need to give users access to widest possible range of services	Build specialised portals that extend the value of the device and enhance its use Keep platform open to stimulate availability of content, applications and services – but balance this against security and reliability risks (do not build 'tiny PCs') Keep the cost to consumers down; differentiate from corporate offers Partner with experienced access service providers Partner with other aggregators where possible to offer the most compelling range of services to users
Create value-added services for enterprises	Experience of delivering software and e-services with incumbents in those markets is likely to be limited Competition from enterprise software players Security concerns will be paramount	Partner with experienced access service providers Partner with experienced infrastructure suppliers to build integration links with popular enterprise software products Partner with experienced infrastructure suppliers to solve security issues
Deliver certain device features or functions as e-services	Need to become a service provider Security concerns will be paramount	Resell white-label service provider offerings rather than build a service provider operation Focus on delivering the content and services Build 'bullet-proof' device security through partnerships

Source: Ovum (Pervasive Computing: Technologies and Markets/Chapter H)

H3 Implications for network operators

H3.1 Key messages

- You can play a powerful role in the pervasive computing revolution by offering network services – but only if you understand your target market and work with other established players to build the right offerings
- You have lots of specialised strengths – these go way beyond mere ownership of the 'bit pipes'. The user information that you have the potential to mine is valuable – use it
- You will not succeed if you try to do everything yourself. Success requires a hybrid IT/telecoms view and a shift in focus away from delivery of mass-market network services offered on the basis of price/performance, towards delivery of specialised services for highly segmented audiences, differentiated on features and functions
- Do not just see users asin terms of ARPUs – they will be turned off by information/advertising overload. Start by thinking about what content, applications and services *people* want; rather than by thinking about how much money you need to gain from each *subscriber* in order to recoup investments. Partner with others to explore this question.

H3.2 Market factors affecting network operators

Market development

Network operators will be pressured by high levels of competition and harsh market conditions in the short to medium term as they build out 'packet-friendly' networks and work to build business models that rely on more than voice carriage. Network operators that survive and thrive will face steadily increasing demands for bandwidth in all types of access network; first, from the growth in the number of devices that will occur and secondly, from the increasing richness of the content, applications and services delivered to devices by service providers.

2001–2002

During 2001–2002, network operators' role in the pervasive computing revolution will be affected by the following factors:

- there will be a great deal of diversity in the capabilities of different kinds of access network; many of those in use will not have been designed to be 'data-centric'
- strengthening demand for network bandwidth for data communication in developed, industrialised countries, due to increasing numbers of new smart, connected devices
- strong levels of competition between access network operators, with competition particularly fierce in deregulated markets
- declining revenues to operators from carrying voice traffic – particularly in fixed telecoms.

2003–2004

The period 2003–2004 will see the following factors introduced into the network operators' market environment:

- widespread rollout of point-to-point broadband networks to the home; broadband to the consumer PC
- gradual improvement of network bandwidth available to carry data to mobile devices
- 'packet-friendly' infrastructure beginning to be deployed throughout all types of access network
- high levels of competition in the application and content provider communities, which will bring increasing demands for data bandwidth in all types of access network.

2005–2006

The period 2005–2006 will bring increasing demands for data bandwidth across all types of access network, due to the increasingly converged nature of personal communications, e-commerce and infotainment applications.

Strengths and weaknesses

Network operators' ownership of the delivery channels for pervasive computing means that they have the potential to play powerful roles in the pervasive computing revolution. However, they will face increasing levels of competition; mobile operators in particular, in some countries, face the prospect of having to recoup significant licence and infrastructure investment costs. Without a fundamental shift in mindset, network operators will be relegated to 'blind bit carriers' and will cede any control they currently have to other types of player.

Strengths

- Network operators have ownership of the distribution channels for content, applications and services
- They have the potential to own important context and activity information (for example, subscriber location)
- Many operators have extensive cash reserves

Weaknesses

- Lack of data-centric infrastructure brings the risk of network operators being relegated to 'blind bit carriers'
- Growth in wholesale telecoms markets means barriers to entry are relatively low – there is great potential for competition from new entrants
- Some network operators (particularly mobile operators) may have to recoup high infrastructure and operating licence costs

H3.3 Opportunities, challenges and strategy options

Figure H3.1 shows the opportunities, challenges and strategy options for network operators in pervasive computing.

Figure H3.1 **Options for network operators**

Opportunities	Challenges	Strategy options
Content/application aggregation and portal provision	Experience of delivering software and e-services with incumbents in those markets is likely to be limited Competition from dedicated aggregators Need to give users access to widest possible range of services	Build portals around specialised applications/content that extend the value of the network and enhance its use – for example, location-sensitive applications Partner with experienced access service providers Unless you are very large and powerful, partner with other aggregators to take your offering to market If you feel you are sufficiently powerful, offer development services to other, smaller operators
Application/service hosting for new entrant service providers and corporate customers	Lack of experience of building, tailoring, integrating and delivering mainstream software applications Lack of experience of building and operating application infrastructure	Partner with infrastructure suppliers to build application server infrastructure Partner with dedicated systems integrators and ASPs to build, tailor and integrate applications

Source: Ovum (Pervasive Computing: Technologies and Markets/Chapter H)

H4 Implications for content and application providers

H4.1 Key messages

- In order to re-use your content or application assets across multiple delivery channels, you will have to do a lot of work in the short term – but it is vital that you do this, in order to reap rewards in the longer term
- Digital rights management infrastructure is critical to your ability to make money from your assets, but implementing it requires wide-ranging partnerships with software infrastructure, network and device suppliers
- Choose your software infrastructure partners carefully – their ability to help you deliver your assets across multiple channels with minimum effort is critical to your long-term success. Their level of commitment to standards is key. The more open the infrastructure through which your assets are deployed, the wider your potential audience
- Make sure your pricing and business models are consistent across multiple channels. Users will exploit weaknesses and/or inconsistencies to their advantage – and your disadvantage

H4.2 Market factors affecting content and application providers

Market development

Content and application providers' desire to re-use their assets across multiple channels, at potentially low incremental cost, is a chief driver of the pervasive computing revolution. Worries about the long-term viability of the 'fixed Web' channel as the sole distribution mechanism for digital content and applications is forcing suppliers to look to augment their revenues elsewhere – at the wild frontiers of wireless Internet and interactive TV services. However, suppliers that seriously attempt to become major pervasive computing players will have to make significant investments.

2001–2002

In 2001–2002, content and application providers' potential roles in the pervasive computing revolution will be influenced by:

- high levels of competition and over-supply of 'commodity' application functionality – particularly in the corporate space
- supplier worries about attainable levels of return on investment that are possible through the 'fixed Web' channel
- initial moves by major suppliers into wireless Internet and interactive services.

2003–2004

The period 2003–2004 will see further complications of the landscape for application and content providers, caused by:

- initial rollouts of multichannel applications and content by market-leading suppliers
- PCs joined by PDAs, TVs and voice handsets as the key delivery channels for content applications – with high degrees of variety in access platform capabilities requiring specialised approaches to delivery.

2005–2006

In 2005–2006, the increased levels of convergence between infotainment, e-commerce and personal communications applications will bring new opportunities for competition, and will force providers in these areas to significantly broaden their technology portfolios and partnership programmes.

Strengths and weaknesses

Content and application providers' major strength is that they have significant experience of creating the main source of value in pervasive computing – the content and applications themselves. However, this is balanced by their major weakness – that they tend to hold entrenched views of delivery 'stovepipes' that are realised in their product designs and implementations.

Strengths

- Expertise in creating a real source of value in pervasive computing – content and applications
- Many suppliers have strong business (and sometimes consumer) brands
- Large, committed customer bases
- Corporate application providers in particular have 'sticky' relationships with their customers

Weaknesses

- Most suppliers have 'uni-channel' device-coupled views of the world, in which applications are optimised for delivery over particular networks, to particular types of device
- Web-centric players in particular lack experience of tackling localisation and device-specialisation issues
- Suppliers have a general lack of understanding of real-world technical issues associated with electronic content or application delivery – in particular, network issues.

H4.3 Opportunities, challenges and strategy options

Figure H4.1 shows the opportunities, challenges and strategy options for content and application providers in pervasive computing.

Figure H4.1 **Options for content and application providers**

Opportunities	**Challenges**	**Strategy options**
Re-use web-based assets across mobile and broadcast delivery channels	Localisation of content and applications – telecoms and TV services are not 'English-only' Content regulation exists and differs by geography Different modes of user interaction	Work with local partners Check regulation laws. Partner with providers that understand the issues Build context management into application architectures, in partnership with specialist infrastructure providers Use partnerships with infrastructure providers to re-design applications in order to separate interfaces and navigation from 'core' logic
Re-use broadcast assets across mobile and web delivery channels	Highly restricted access platforms – require sophisticated adaptation Digital rights protection Different modes of user interaction in mobile and web channels	Work with content adaptation and streaming media market leaders to ensure the widest possible platform coverage Build context management into application architectures, in partnership with specialist infrastructure providers Mix implementation of content security (through partnerships) with business model innovation (offer something free of charge) to stimulate content or application usage

Source: Ovum (Pervasive Computing: Technologies and Markets/Chapter H)

H5 Implications for service providers

H5.1 Key messages

- You have the opportunity to play many key roles in the pervasive computing revolution, because your ability to deliver content and/or applications as services is a vital precondition of their delivery within a pervasive computing environment
- Success depends on more than just interposing yourself between one or more content and application providers, and users. Without an established brand behind you, it may be best to provide wholesale technology e-services rather than consumer-focused services
- Customer 'ownership' is a dangerous pursuit, as it may shut you out from lucrative collaborative partnerships with other providers. Exchange of information with other providers is likely to be vital to your success in the long term
- Partner with software infrastructure as well as network infrastructure players – you will not succeed without their expertise
- Your ability to store, manage and use usage context information does not just enable you to offer customers seamless multichannel experiences. It can help you add further value by allowing users to personalise their own online universes, and avoid information overload.

H5.2 Market factors affecting service providers

Market development

Service providers have opportunities to play many important roles in pervasive computing. Excluding the big brands, revenue opportunities for the majority of providers are more likely to come from serving corporate customers, or other service providers via brokering or management services, than directly from consumers.

2001–2002

The period 2001–2002 will see service providers' markets characterised by the following:

- frantic searching for sustainable revenue streams by the remaining web-based players
- rapidly increasing levels of interactive advertising to consumers in particular
- rapid proliferation of wireless Internet services, many re-purposed from existing web services
- steady spread of interactive TV services and portals, many of which are owned and operated by 'web and wireless' provider alliances.

2003–2004

In 2003–2004, service providers' markets will be shaped by:

- the crumbling of 'walled gardens' offered by service providers in wireless Internet and interactive services, and their replacement by open (or semi-open) access to third-party content, applications and services
- tighter, more wide-ranging but more short-lived partnerships between service providers, enabled through e-services technologies, in order to deliver subscribers more open access to content, applications and services
- increasingly pervasive use of interactive advertising, bringing with it the danger of information overload for subscribers and a subsequent backlash.

2005–2006

In 2005–2006, service providers will become as much aggregators of relationships as they are of content and applications. The chains of suppliers involved in delivering content, applications and services to users to multiple access platforms will be considerably longer and more complex, and activity will need to be increasingly tightly co-ordinated electronically.

Strengths and weaknesses

Many of today's service providers already have experience of delivering online services; even more hold positions of power due to their ownership of customers through billing relationships. However, many service providers have limited experience of delivering 'real' software applications, and still need to get to grips with the concept of platform openness as an enabler rather than a weakness.

Strengths

- Ownership of the customer through the billing relationship
- Large customer bases
- Emerging wholesale markets mean many can be small – and therefore (in theory) nimble and quick
- Some have existing content/application relationships with web-based suppliers

Weaknesses

- Service providers often have a strong network focus and often do not have experience of software or e-services issues
- They are still getting to grips with the implications of open platforms – how to compete as service providers without locking customers in.

H5.3 Opportunities, challenges and strategy options

Figure H5.1 shows the opportunities, challenges and strategy options for service providers in pervasive computing.

Figure H5.1 **Options for service providers**

Opportunities	Challenges	Strategy options
Create multichannel consumer portals	Competition from device manufacturers and network operators, among others Content and service localisation and device specialisation Context management Different applications require different quality of service environments	Focus on delivering offerings that add value to the billing relationship – for example, the involvement of micropayment and EBPP – but be prepared to compete with operators Build services in partnership with a large software infrastructure supplier, to solve the technology complexity issues Build 'franchise' relationships with local partners that can adapt content, applications and services
Multichannel enterprise application access services	Limited experience of delivering corporate business applications Delivery of applications as services means applying quality of service management principles to things you do not own Customers will dictate access devices and networks	Work with corporates, ASPs and integration specialists Implement collaborative service management frameworks to help you manage service chains – work with leading-edge management technology providers Build relationships with multiple network operators in different geographies
Provide e-infrastructure services (for example, device management e-services) to other service providers	Lack of software infrastructure expertise	Partner with software infrastructure vendors, and focus on providing customer care/billing/service management expertise

Source: Ovum (Pervasive Computing: Technologies and Markets/Chapter H)

H6 Implications for infrastructure vendors

H6.1 Key messages

- You are key to the development of pervasive computing – but unless you work with each other (particularly across the network/software divide) you will not reap the rewards
- Only the biggest providers will be able to build end-to-end solutions for customers. If you are not one of them, it makes sense for you to work with a major supplier, rather than try and usurp them. You will have to work with them anyway
- Do not try to make everything perfect. Time-to-market is critical – particularly in the short term
- In the medium to long term, most of the value-add you provide to your customers will be in helping them deal with the complexity inherent in the specialisation of content, applications and services, rather than their homogenisation
- Internet services or corporate application infrastructure specialists must work with partners – including specialist technology providers, service providers, network operators and device manufacturers – to provide the right offerings to customers of wireless Internet and interactive TV services

H6.2 Market factors affecting infrastructure vendors

Market development

Infrastructure is the 'glue' of pervasive computing – infrastructure providers are the most critical players in the pervasive computing revolution. The degree of market development depends on their ability and desire to deliver the technologies that other suppliers need in order to succeed. Most players are highly motivated by fierce competition and the threat of commoditisation.

2001–2002

The period 2001–2002 will see the following market factors affecting infrastructure suppliers' operating environments:

- the steady commoditisation of base-level software infrastructure and subsumption of some functions into network infrastructure
- a network infrastructure focus on serving basic build-out opportunities in mobile networks
- very high levels of competition across both software and network infrastructure markets
- continuing hype of a level more often associated with the fashion industry than technology industries
- some visionary infrastructure providers already providing e-services and wireless Internet infrastructure.

2003–2004

In 2003–2004, the following market factors will influence infrastructure vendors' markets:

- the largest infrastructure providers will begin to offer true multichannel application infrastructure solutions
- quality of service and security issues will increase in importance in software and in IP networks
- the requirement for service specialisation (localisation, personalisation and device-specific adaptation) will bring scalability and complexity challenges for application server suppliers
- the provision of infrastructure for interactive TV services will be more of a mainstream activity for providers
- the widespread adoption of the 'software as services' delivery model by software infrastructure providers – particularly where technology services can be delivered to other service providers.

2005–2006

In 2005–2006, increasing levels of convergence between different application types will bring renewed complexity to quality of service and security issues in the delivery of content, applications and services to multiple access platforms. There will be significant interworking between online service providers, and a correspondingly high level of demand for infrastructure that can help service providers share information securely.

Strengths and weaknesses

Infrastructure providers bring a focus on quality of service and an understanding of operational complexity issues to the pervasive computing movement – but, unfortunately, these strengths are shared between two communities that have historically not worked with each other to any great degree: software and network infrastructure vendors. Their combined strengths put them in very strong market positions; their weakness is their lack of understanding that partnering with the other is vital to their success.

Strengths

- Strong technology expertise, which is required by everyone else
- The largest and most experienced players are trusted brands
- Many (particularly network infrastructure suppliers) have a 'hygiene' focus

Weaknesses

- Software vendors do not understand carrier-grade requirements and network management issues
- Network vendors do not understand software stacks, the implications of open systems and application development issues
- Software vendors do not think in terms of appliances – they think in terms of PCs

H6.3 Opportunities, challenges and strategy options

Figure H6.1 shows the opportunities, challenges and strategy options for infrastructure vendors in pervasive computing.

Figure H6.1 **Options for infrastructure vendors**

Opportunities	Challenges	Strategy options
Build multichannel application server platforms	Network infrastructure providers have limited experience of commercial software architectures and integration issues Software infrastructure vendors lack expertise in delivering carrier-grade solutions	Network infrastructure vendors should partner with large software infrastructure vendors Software infrastructure vendors should partner with large network infrastructure vendors
Build specialised tools for wireless Internet and interactive services	Lack of skills in broadcast and mobile networks Competition from infrastructure vendors in other supply chains	Foster relationships with service providers and infrastructure providers in broadcast and mobile networks; focus on openness and extensibility to provide the competitive edge over specialists Build offerings quickly, but make sure you build extensible solutions – not closed 'sticking-plasters'
Build multichannel service authoring tools	There are lots of difficult technologies to include and address – including personalisation and context management Requires a new architectural approach Ability to localise content and applications is vital	Partner with vendors of multichannel application platforms. Foster communities of industry-specialised third parties (including network infrastructure vendors) that can deliver value-added components
Build quality of service optimisation, security and application integrity assurance technologies	Need to integrate server-hosted, device-hosted and network-hosted functions Need to integrate service provider management platforms with corporate infrastructure (in some cases) Specific to particular access platforms; scope for loss of focus Very complex technology and global reach required to build multichannel capabilities	Implement standard interfaces and protocols wherever possible Provide technologies for monitoring and management; publish interfaces to third-party management technology specialists Focus on enhancing security and reliability across a range of access platforms Use location- and device-independent technology base wherever possible to maximise return on investment Software infrastructure vendors should work with a wide range of device, network infrastructure and device- or network-specialised quality-of-service infrastructure suppliers
Build open service management platforms for multichannel infrastructure	Competition from established network/service management players	Focus on building an open architecture for service management to differentiate the platform; work with best-of-breed integration platforms to provide this Integrate platform offering with smart network infrastructure to leverage packet-friendly network capabilities

Figure H6.1 **Options for infrastructure vendors** (continued)

Opportunities	Challenges	Strategy options
Build integration solutions to enable service provider interworking	Privacy and security regulations differ by geography and industry Cultural resistance to information sharing	Work with local partners in each market Go for hosted solutions that broker information, rather than implementing direct transfer of information; work with trusted local third parties to facilitate this
Transform products into e-services to ease customer cost-of-ownership and maintenance issues	Few players understand the true operational implications of network-based service provision – they are not service providers themselves	Design products for e-services delivery, but resell through dedicated e-services providers

Source: Ovum (Pervasive Computing: Technologies and Markets/Chapter H)

J Market development scenario and forecasts

J1 Summary

Market push and user pull will drive an inexorable move towards the interconnection of devices, networks and applications. This is reflected in our core scenario, which focuses on the requirement for infrastructure development to deliver multiple applications over multiple channels.

What is more uncertain, however, is how these trends will develop over time and geography. The level of uncertainty about the scale and speed of change means that several alternative scenarios must be considered.

By 2005, Internet service revenues attributable to pervasive computing access – that is, revenues obtained by Internet service providers from multichannel access – will be nearly $1.3 trillion. This is more than 40% of total global Internet service revenues. It will come from:

- e-commerce transaction revenues
- access fees
- online advertising revenues.

Pervasive computing will have a dramatic effect on the software infrastructure spend of suppliers and users. In 2005, software infrastructure spend within pervasive computing projects will reach nearly $21.5 billion worldwide. Much of the spend will be driven initially by the adoption of platforms designed from the outset to be multichannel; the re-engineering of legacy applications will follow later.

J2 Market development

J2.1 It's about infrastructure

Pervasive computing is about making applications, content and services available to many devices and therefore enabling ubiquitous user access to things of value. Our definition of pervasive computing reflects this:

> *Pervasive computing is a vision of the future of digital information and computation, in which digital content, applications and services are made available in an integrated, personalised way to users, and accessed by users, via a diverse range of devices and access networks.*

This implies that it is not a focus on any one application, service, device or network that is important, but rather on the infrastructure 'glue' that binds applications together, and to their users – regardless of the access platform they use. Our market scenario therefore concentrates on issues that relate to the development of the software and network infrastructure to support pervasive computing, rather than on the services and applications themselves.

Pervasive computing infrastructure will affect, and be affected by, four market developments:

- the creation of multichannel applications, content and services that will enable users to access them via multiple platforms
- the enhancement of access platform capabilities in line with the applications that users want
- the opening of industry structures and increasing interworking between providers, to enable true user mobility between applications, content, services, devices and networks
- the strategies and spheres of influence of leading infrastructure suppliers, and the creation and proliferation of technology standards.

J2.2 Market drivers

There are three core trends in market development that are leading us towards a pervasive computing world:

- the convergence of information types and industries

  where the Internet has provided the foundation for convergent development
- diversification of information access methods

  in terms of devices types, networks, interfaces and applications
- the transformation of products into services

  as the software industry redefines its business models towards a managed ASP (application service provision) approach, and as computing hardware, automotive and home appliance manufacturers start to deliver features of their products as managed services.

Applications

A change in focus from products to services is central to the development of pervasive computing – represented by the ASP trend in the software industry, and similar changes in the telecoms arena.

This will lead to the death of the application as we know it by 2005, when applications will have become highly granular bundles of functionality, capable of being assembled in a variety of packaged forms.

Users

A move to pervasive computing is characterised by the increasing power of the end user, through the importance of personalisation and context management and the ease with which multichannel access can lead to supplier switching.

The control of information about user preferences will be crucial in a pervasive environment. Multichannel services require the management of context information to add value and to prevent user backlash – for example, allowing users to specify preferences and avoid being deluged with information 'pushed' to them.

Devices

The disaggregation of devices will become a feature of many device types, allowing experimentation with a much wider range of form factors and functionality packages than before. The end result of this experimentation will be greater device variety. Rich interfaces will develop through advances in core technologies, such as speech recognition.

There will be lots of opportunities for new players – especially those with a broad portfolio of products.

Infrastructure

In networks, the benefits of a widespread move to an all-IP world are evident and well documented.

Pervasive computing massively increases the base of computing devices, or at least, it has the potential to. Unsurprisingly, this is also seen as a great opportunity to increase the market for computing infrastructure at all levels.

Suppliers

Suppliers are generally driven towards pervasive computing by a combination of the negative aspects of their current positions, coupled with the desire to make the most of exciting opportunities to reach new communities and add value for their existing customers.

Amongst device manufacturers, intense competition for will lead to massive investment in functionality and innovation. Furthermore, device manufacturers see significant opportunities in the provision of complementary Internet-based services.

For network operators, the threat to long-term revenues posed by the inevitable commoditisation of basic voice services, and the lure of new value-added revenues from data services, provides the impetus to enter into pervasive computing.

Services

A combination of multichannel delivery, personalisation and context-based specialisation means that the provision of individualised services will become increasingly important to the software industry. This effect is particularly significant in key competitive areas such as e-commerce.

Re-using assets across multiple delivery channels will require a lot of work in the short term.

J2.3 Market challenges

Suppliers need to be aware of the critical importance of personalised, location and channel-aware service management – getting this right will be difficult and will require the co-operation of a number of players in any supply chain.

The major technology challenge is to deliver infrastructure that can deal with specialisation in general – personalisation, location sensitivity, device adaptation and localised content and services – while also delivering high performance, reliable services to thousands or possibly millions of connected users.

Users

Many users will not be technology-literate. Simplicity of user interface, balanced with richness of experience, will be a key technology challenge for device manufacturers and service designers.

Localisation issues are often forgotten by those with a Web heritage. The democratisation of information access means providing access to people that do not use computers or the Internet at work, as well as to those that do not speak English.

Consumer (perceived) need is a relative unknown across most access channels. Business models and tariffing packages are key components of the mix that will take time to get right. Context management makes this more difficult as users are increasingly segmented by a rich mix of activities and attributes rather than simple demographics. Context management can also be seen as the users' weapon in preventing information overload.

Applications

Applications tend not to exist in isolation, and as the environment moves towards multichannel access, the supply landscape will become more crowded as users are given the choice of many similar application portfolios from a variety of suppliers.

However, in many areas, successful applications may not translate well to other delivery channels – for example, rich media applications via mobile access.

The gradual convergence of infotainment, e-commerce and personal communications will affect the development of pervasive computing, positively in some ways, but also by potentially reducing the differentiation between offerings.

Devices

Pervasive computing brings applications and services to users that may be relatively inexperienced in using computers, and also to devices that have not previously been viewed as computing platforms. Many of these devices will be smart versions of existing devices – others will be completely new, but all will face key challenges:

- tension between familiarity and ease of use on one side, and functionality on the other
- managing expectations in terms of reliability, performance, cost and complexity
- the tension between platform openness requirements and the negative security and reliability implications that these can bring (for example, third-party software that harms your device, or viruses).

Infrastructure

Pervasive computing requires end-to-end solutions to issues such as context and QoS (quality of service) management. The level of co-operation required, both technically and commercially, is daunting.

The focus of technology will shift over time from dealing with physical heterogeneity (in access networks and devices) to dealing with complexities regarding specialisation and facilitating the 'death of the application'.

Standards in the different industries that will play a part in the development of pervasive computing are not always compatible. XML (extensible mark-up language) has been touted as an integration panacea, but the development of XML-based solutions brings a whole new set of infrastructure challenges.

Suppliers

Device manufacturers will be vulnerable to 'cherry picking' by niche suppliers of more simple devices, particularly as devices disaggregate.

Finer segmentation of user requirements means smaller user segments, where high sales volumes are unlikely.

Network operators run businesses that are largely predicated on voice services. Data service provision is a new and complex area. Operators may not have the skills required, and will have to acquire them either internally or through partnership.

Pervasive computing requires partnerships between organisations and industries that have historically been widely separated.

Pervasive computing means that users can potentially move more easily between service providers.

Services

The challenge of pervasive computing is its complexity – it requires the management of delivering different information types to different devices over different networks.

Service management will become more complex with the move to multichannel delivery, and as applications evolve to become a collection of co-operating software services that enable user activities over the network.

J2.4 Uncertainties and alternative scenarios

As with most market developments, particularly those that bring together a number of different technology areas, industry supplier groups and application areas, the future of pervasive computing is clouded by a considerable amount of uncertainty. Two key uncertainties are the level of consumer demand for the sort of interconnected applications delivered by pervasive computing infrastructures, and the level of integration that can be achieved in practice.

For most applications, the challenge is to scale up to the mass consumer market. Demand for integrated access to corporate data and applications, through a variety of access channels, is already established – it is a key feature of most user surveys. However, corporate customers may be early adopters, but they will also be more demanding, and solutions will typically require higher levels of systems integration.

The level of integration of infrastructure, services and business relationships is a rich mix. Guaranteeing end-to-end service for a wide range of applications across multiple delivery channels is a complex task.

Figure J2.1 shows four alternative scenarios for the development of the market, according to consumer demand and the level of integration between infrastructures, services and business relationships. Ovum's core scenario, which underpins our market forecasts, is built on the fourth scenario.

Figure J2.1 **Alternative market development scenarios**

	Low integration	**High integration**
Corporate demand plus high consumer demand	Scenario 3 Uni-channel delivery Scalability issues emerge, such as personalisation and location Frustrated demand because of service duplication and incompatibility	Scenario 4 Widespread consumer use Scalability issues are great Branding is more important 'Cherry picking' of service/access/ device combinations leads to the commoditisation of basic service packages
Corporate demand plus low consumer demand	Scenario 1 Predominantly uni-channel delivery Niche segments receive more attention Premium business services Premium device prices	Scenario 2 Widespread business use of generic applications Differentiation on quality of service

Source: Ovum (Pervasive Computing: Technologies and Markets/ Chapter J)

Scenario 1 – low consumer demand and low integration

- Corporate demand for access to data and applications is met in a largely access-specific fashion.
- Niche, high-spending segments receive the most service provider attention because of the high level of systems integration work required for most corporate clients.
- Most corporate usage is by large companies or very small organisations.

Scenario 2 – low consumer demand and high integration

- The integration of basic and generic business applications such as messaging across multiple access channels stimulates corporate uptake.
- QoS and security form the basis of most service differentiation.

Scenario 3 – high consumer demand and low integration

- A 'stovepipe' approach, where specific operator/content partnerships compete for user attention and loyalty. Bigger content owners strike multi-network deals.
- User frustration and dissatisfaction at perceived lock-in is high.
- Mass-market adoption brings scalability issues, particularly those concerning the provision of services based on location and personalisation.

Scenario 4 – high consumer demand and high integration

- Consumer usage is high, but this brings issues of scalability.
- Branding becomes more important than infrastructure ownership.
- 'Cherry picking' of service/access/device combinations leads to commoditisation of basic service packages.

Ovum's core scenario, which underpins our market forecasts, is built on this fourth scenario. *Figure J2.2* shows an expanded version of the core scenario. This shows the effect of pervasive computing on the following areas:

- applications
- user and service management
- digital information supply chains
- regulation
- software infrastructure
- network infrastructure
- devices.

Figure J2.2 **Market development scenario**

2000–2002	2003–2004	2005–2006
APPLICATIONS		
General observations		
Multichannel applications emerge, aimed at the business sector, through the development of 'add-ons' to existing web-based applications (the first wave of multichannel applications) Most applications are still uni-channel	Wider use of integrated applications in the top end of the consumer market Multichannel applications designed from the 'ground up' begin to be widely deployed (the second wave of multichannel applications) Businesses increasingly adopt multichannel intranet solutions	Differentiation on quality of service in key business markets New multichannel applications are highly personalised and granular (the third wave of multichannel applications) Some consumer packages are undercut by simple, low-functionality packages Many older applications are re-developed as 'proper' multichannel applications; many providers focus on better integration as popular applications begin to converge
Personal communications management		
Corporate unified messaging gathers pace Early consumer unified messaging Advanced personal communications services will be launched by some operators in the US Convergent billing and basic services launched by operators with a fixed–mobile portfolio	Call management functionality is increasingly bundled with unified messaging services to create advanced personal communications services	Services offered to everyone in developed markets as part of a flat-rate pricing plan Intelligent management of personal communications is commonplace Use of intelligent agents and avatars
Commerce		
Mobile e-commerce generally limited to simple applications that focus on existing commercial agreements between trusted parties TV shopping still largely phone-based	Generic security emerges on mobile channels. Mobile e-commerce usage becomes widespread for small purchases Business-to-business commerce is still the big money-maker in fixed environments T-commerce (television e-commerce) take-up begins Early rollout of targeted e-commerce applications to vehicles (for example, purchasing navigation information and e-tolling) and home appliances	Mobile devices widely used as a personal 'point of presence' for small transactions and authentication E-commerce applications becoming well integrated across PC/TV and mobile platforms Payment mechanisms well integrated with multichannel platforms

Figure J2.2 **Market development scenario** (continued)

2000–2002	**2003–2004**	**2005–2006**
Infotainment		
Content formats and application sets still limited by distribution channel and device type TV is the dominant platform, followed by the PC	Internet on TV, TV on Internet bring a more converged model to interactive infotainment services Mobility-aware infotainment is widely available	The delivery of television-quality programming on the Internet becomes common, but broadcast (wireless and cable) continues to dominate television delivery Targeted elements of rich media programming adapted for mobile networks
Corporate business applications		
PC is the dominant platform PDA-based access starting to become popular	The ASP effect: more applications are delivered as services Multichannel intranets gain acceptance Widespread PC/PDA application integration	PCs and PDAs remain the core devices for corporate applications, although modular communicators also widely used
Remote asset management		
The PC is the dominant platform – except for the use of handheld devices in some vertical markets	Mobile platforms become more widely used to access management services – particularly in the consumer sector, as home networks become more widespread	PC and personal mobile devices are still the main platforms for remote asset management
Users and service management		
Independent user populations split by access network and device type Most service management is based on simple identity and basic profiling Some very early integration of applications management and context – location services in mobile, for example	Context management across multiple channels becomes more widely recognised as a key differentiator	Consumer demand for mobile and integrated applications becomes more widespread Intelligent assistants for context management appear in multichannel environments, to help users cope with information overload
SUPPLIERS		
Wireless Internet is the focus of early collaboration between IT and Telecoms sectors. Consumer electronic and broadcast industries still largely independent Some large joint ventures between content providers and network operators	Joint ventures between the network, software infrastructure and content worlds increasingly common Branding companies start to take market share with convergent services. Service providers begin to move towards flat-rate pricing for all services	Brokerage models increasingly common as partnerships between players become easier to construct and deconstruct – due to the ASP effect and advanced use of integration technologies
REGULATION		
Regulation split largely by access network and geographic region Privacy is an issue	Moves to harmonise the regulation of infotainment and commerce across delivery channels, based on generic consumer protection and privacy legislation	Regulation of services is based on general consumer protection legislation

Figure J2.2 **Market development scenario** (continued)

2000–2002	**2003–2004**	**2005–2006**
SOFTWARE INFRASTRUCTURE		
Bulk of application hosting platforms and application development/service creation tools are uni-channel Focus on the construction of new interfaces to existing applications and content through content adaptation tools – enabling the first wave of multichannel applications	More infrastructure focus on platforms designed form the outset to be multichannel, in order to facilitate the second wave of multichannel applications Infrastructure provider shake-out as true research and development investment requirements start to emerge Research and development focuses on XML-based cross-supplier interworking technologies Some development of re-engineering legacy applications for integration with multichannel platforms	Focus on integrating multichannel platforms with legacy infrastructure, cross-supplier interworking (facilitating the third wave of multichannel deployment activity)
NETWORK INFRASTRUCTURE		
2G+ arrival in the developed world boosts the wider market by the end of 2001. WAP takes off in late 2001 Some early 3G rollout xDSL rollout maintains the disparity between the fixed and mobile worlds Move to IP-based infrastructures, but harmonisation across access network types is poor	3G rollout in developed countries begins but is slow and patchy Personal area networks start to become mainstream as the mobile and home electronics industries adopt interconnected devices xDSL rollout accelerates in 2001 and overtakes cable modems in 2002 IP core networks with edge variations Satellite starts to be relegated to niche distribution networks	Wider 3G rollout, largely for capacity reasons in most countries Many homes with broadband Internet connections have home networks that interconnect PCs, televisions and appliances
DEVICES		
Limited voice recognition and unified messaging Largely text-based interfaces on most mobile devices Battery constraints slow the growth of mobile platform capabilities Security and reliability are key customer issues Modular devices emerge	Modular devices, connected by some form of local networking, become more widespread The PC and handset remain the dominant communicating devices, (for e-mail and voice respectively), but the PDA and other hybrid communicators increase in importance In-car systems come to market, pre-installed in prestige vehicles	Large and diverse range of device types Hybrid interfaces commonplace, with basic control through natural language Modular devices commonplace Most portable computing devices have voice communications capability Networked home appliances start to replace standalone models in developed countries

Source: Ovum (Pervasive Computing: Technologies and Markets/ Chapter J)

J3 Global pervasive computing – service revenues

Figures J3.1 and *J3.2* show the regional development of pervasive computing applied to service revenues from Internet access, commerce and associated services.

By 2005, Internet service revenues attributable to pervasive computing access – that is, revenues obtained by service providers that offer multichannel access – will be nearly $1.3 trillion. This total will come from:

- e-commerce transaction revenues
- access fees
- online advertising revenues.

Over the forecast period, the pervasive computing phenomenon will largely be found in the developed world, where sufficiently high penetration of Internet access is spread across multiple delivery channels relatively evenly. In some regions, the levels of Internet access may be equally high, but not pervasive. Ovum's report *Ovum Forecasts the Internet and E-commerce*, on which our pervasive computing forecasts are based, indicates that the greatest degree of balance between access channels will occur in North America and Western Europe.

Figure J3.1 **Internet service revenues from pervasive computing, $ million**

	2001	2002	2003	2004	2005
World	**51,793**	**170,752**	**399,644**	**766,170**	**1,258,119**
North America	41,311	125,988	273,625	503,421	837,119
South & Central America and the Caribbean	80	258	1,526	3,654	6,180
Western Europe	6,840	32,783	94,926	198,762	311,959
Central and Eastern Europe	19	56	193	620	1,313
Central Asia	20	85	423	1,184	2,382
Asia-Pacific	3,513	11,515	28,686	57,939	97,998
Middle East and Africa	10	67	264	590	1,168

Source: Ovum (Pervasive Computing: Technologies and Markets/ Chapter J)

J3.1 Pervasive Internet service revenues will be almost half the total

Figure J3.3 shows the growth of multichannel service revenues as a proportion of overall Internet service revenues. The figure shows that by 2005, more than 40% of global Internet service revenues will be attributable to pervasive computing access.

Figure J3.2 **Internet service revenues from pervasive computing, $ billion**

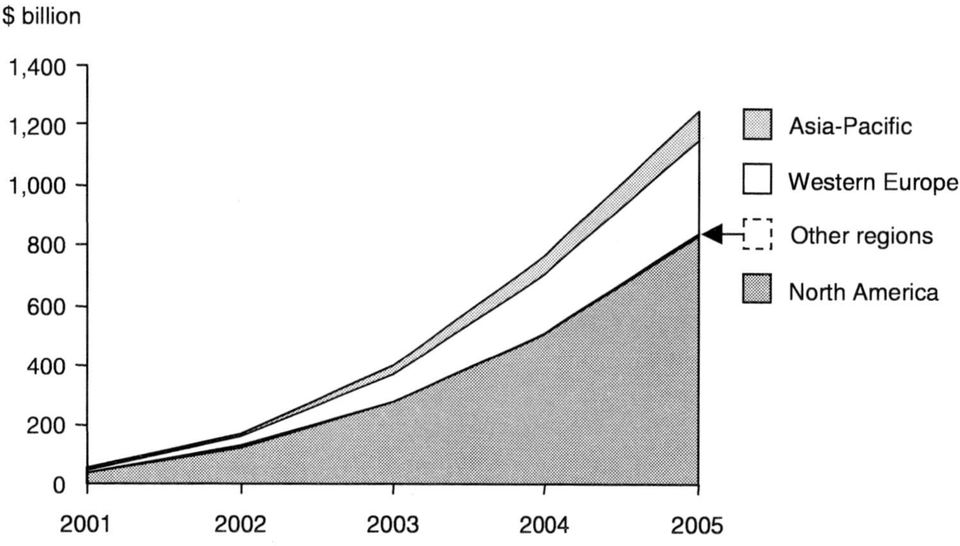

Source: Ovum (Pervasive Computing: Technologies and Markets/Chapter J)

Figure J3.3 **Global pervasive Internet revenues as % of total Internet revenues**

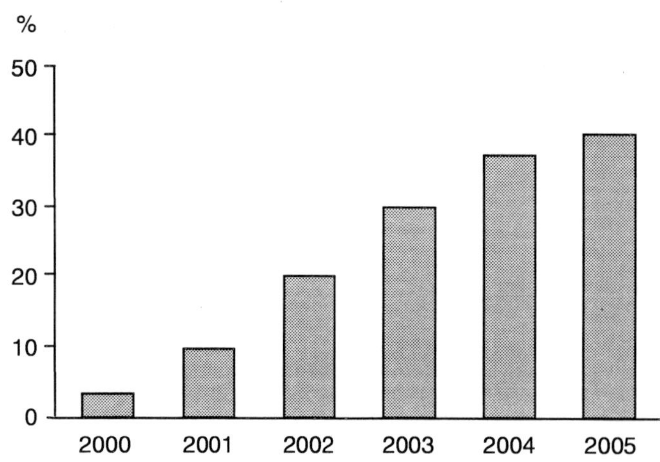

Source: Ovum (Pervasive Computing: Technologies and Markets/Chapter J)

J4 Global pervasive computing – software infrastructure spend

Pervasive computing will have a dramatic effect on the software infrastructure spend of suppliers and users. *Figures J4.1* and *J4.2* show software infrastructure spend by adoption wave. The three waves are:

- wave 1 – enabling multichannel access to existing applications and services using content adaptation tools
- wave 2 – generating entirely new applications and services on integrated multichannel platforms
- wave 3 – re-engineering legacy applications to multichannel platforms, and a focus on cross-supplier interworking.

In 2005, software infrastructure spend within pervasive computing projects will reach nearly $21.5 billion worldwide. Much of the spend will be driven initially by the adoption of platforms designed from the outset to be multichannel; the re-engineering of legacy applications will follow later.

Figures J4.3 and *J4.4* show the development of regional software infrastructure spend. The infrastructure opportunity is by far the greatest in North America and Western Europe. Surprisingly, the long-term opportunity in Asia-Pacific is significantly lower than that in North America – despite Asia-Pacific's current advanced state in the provision of mobile data services compared to the rest of the world.

The balanced provision of multichannel access creates an environment in which pervasive computing can flourish; the dominance of the mobile access channels in Asia-Pacific means that the opportunity for pervasive computing is limited compared to North America and much of Western Europe. This does not mean that the absolute level of Internet adoption will necessarily be lower – just less involved with pervasive, multichannel access.

Figure J4.1 **Global software infrastructure spend by adoption wave, $ million**

	2001	2002	2003	2004	2005
Total	**757**	**2,877**	**6,510**	**12,302**	**21,488**
Wave 1	603	1,688	2,510	3,134	2,807
Wave 2	154	901	2,547	5,445	11,878
Wave 3	0	288	1,453	3,722	6,803

Source: Ovum (Pervasive Computing: Technologies and Markets/ Chapter J)

Figure J4.2 **Global software infrastructure spend by adoption wave, $ billion**

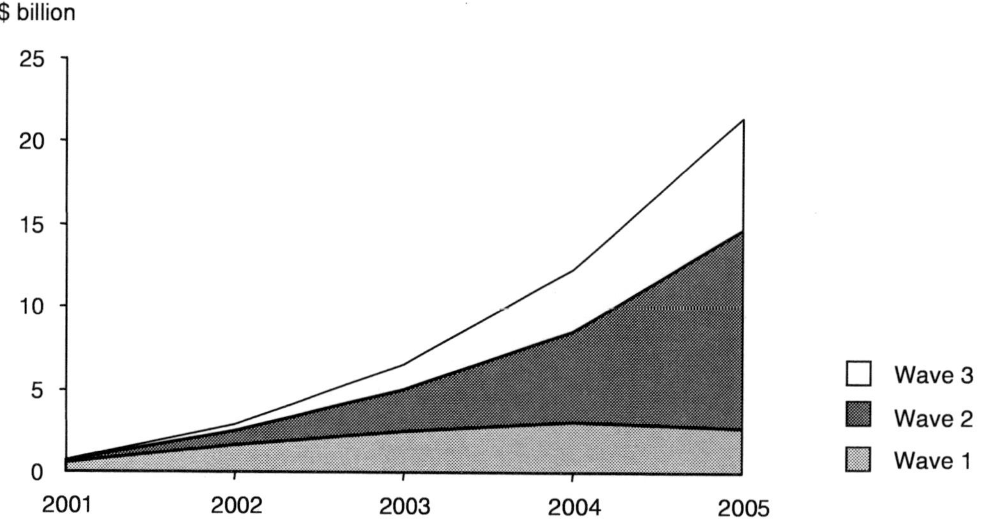

Source: (Pervasive Computing: Technologies and Markets/Chapter J)

Figure J4.3 **Regional software infrastructure spend, $ million**

	2001	2002	2003	2004	2005
World	**757**	**2,877**	**6,510**	**12,302**	**21,488**
North America	416	1,538	3363	6293	11,047
South & Central America and the Caribbean	17	74	186	350	587
Western Europe	158	610	1,408	2,695	4,739
Central and Eastern Europe	6	22	52	101	188
Central Asia	23	100	256	500	842
Asia-Pacific	128	497	1,157	2,187	3,777
Middle East and Africa	9	36	89	176	308

Source: Ovum (Pervasive Computing: Technologies and Markets/ Chapter J)

Figure J4.4 **Regional software infrastructure spend, $ billion**

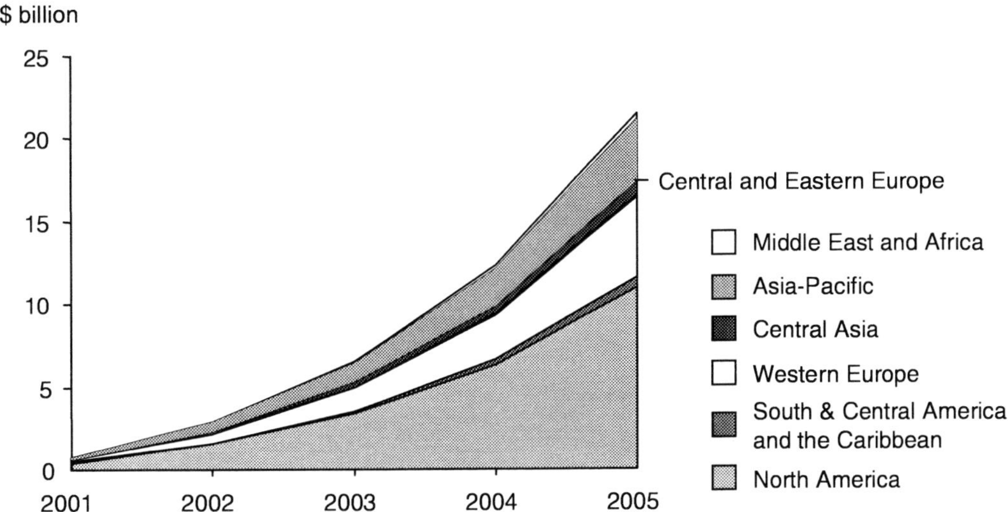

Source: Ovum (Pervasive Computing: Technologies and Markets/Chapter J)

J5 Forecast methodology

J5.1 Overview

Our forecast model is based on forecasts of Internet penetration and service revenues given in Ovum's recent report, *Ovum Forecasts the Internet and E-commerce*; it also utilises software product expenditure forecasts in Ovum's forthcoming report, *Ovum Forecasts Global Software Markets.*

We have layered a simple model on these forecasts that estimates the proportion of Internet activity that can be attributed to pervasive computing, in terms of service revenues derived and underlying spend on software infrastructure. Spend on network infrastructure and device hardware has been excluded from these forecasts.

Figure J5.1 shows the forecast process.

Forecast notes

The forecast figures are for 1 January of the year concerned, except in the case of revenue and spend figures, which refer to the whole year.

The forecasts are presented in US dollars.

North America includes the US and Canada but excludes Mexico, which is included in the South & Central America and the Caribbean region.

Figure J5.1 **Forecast process**

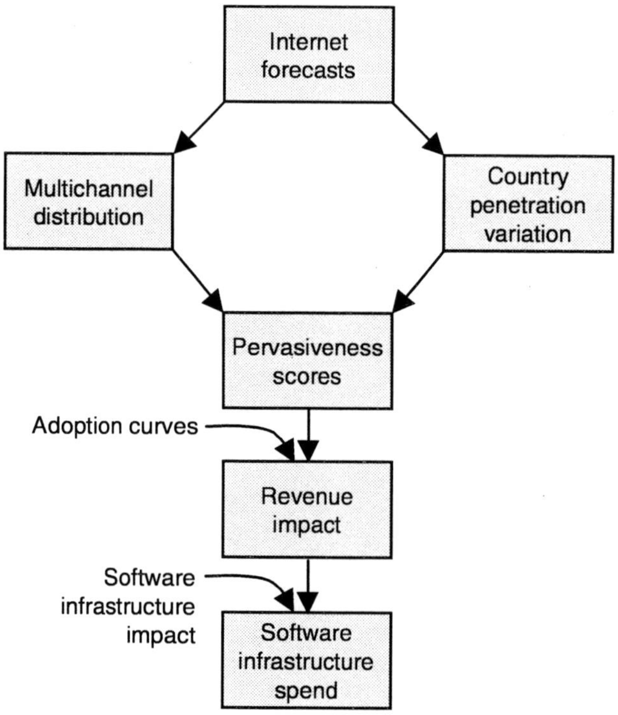

Source: Ovum (Pervasive Computing: Technologies and Markets/Chapter J)

J5.2 Base forecasts

Two recent reports from Ovum provide the base data for our pervasive computing forecasts:

- *Ovum Forecasts the Internet and E-commerce* supplies forecasts of the penetration of multiple access channels for Internet services by country, which we use to derive our 'pervasiveness scores' for each country; these drive our forecasts of service revenues attributable to pervasive service access
- *Ovum Forecasts Global Software Markets* supplies forecasts for the size of the global software infrastructure market, from which we derive our forecasts of software infrastructure spend related to the development and deployment of pervasive computing content, applications and services.

J5.3 Pervasiveness scores

Countries and regions will feel the impact of pervasive computing at different rates and in different ways. When the basic economic and demographic factors that affect the take-up of all telecommunications and computing infrastructure have been taken into account, then the development of pervasive infrastructures depends on two broad themes:

- the absolute level of Internet penetration of the population
- the degree to which this penetration is spread across multiple delivery channels.

Our model uses a simple scoring system to rate the pervasive-readiness of each country. The regional pervasiveness scores are shown in *Figure J5.2*.

Figure J5.2 **Regional pervasiveness scores**

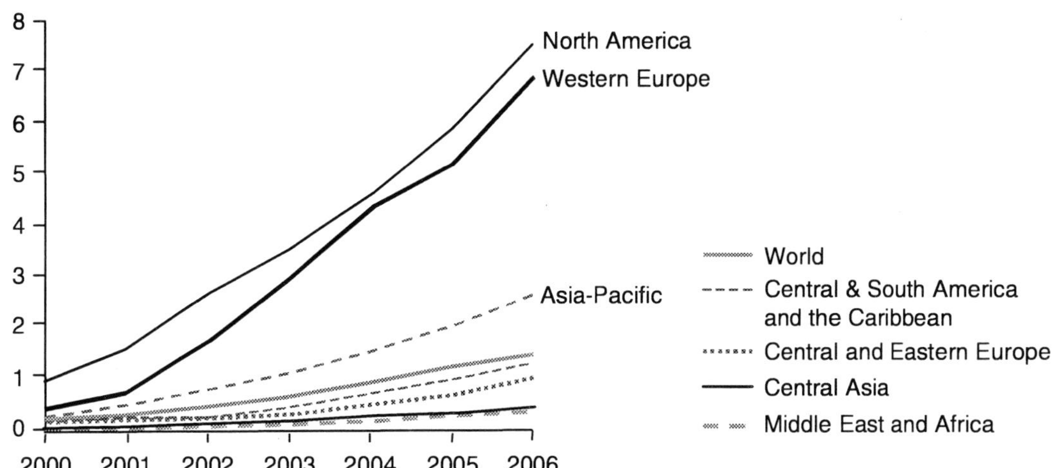

Source: Ovum (Pervasive Computing: Technologies and Markets/Chapter J)

The scores are useful only as a relative indicator of the scale and speed of development in a region. *Figure J5.3* shows this clearly – and in particular the dominance of North America in the early days of pervasive computing. Note the way in which Western Europe develops rapidly, partly as a result of mobile access, and partly as a result of the development of broadband access channels.

Figure J5.4 shows the pervasiveness scores for each region, relative to North America's regional score.

Figure J5.3 **Regional pervasiveness scores relative to North America**

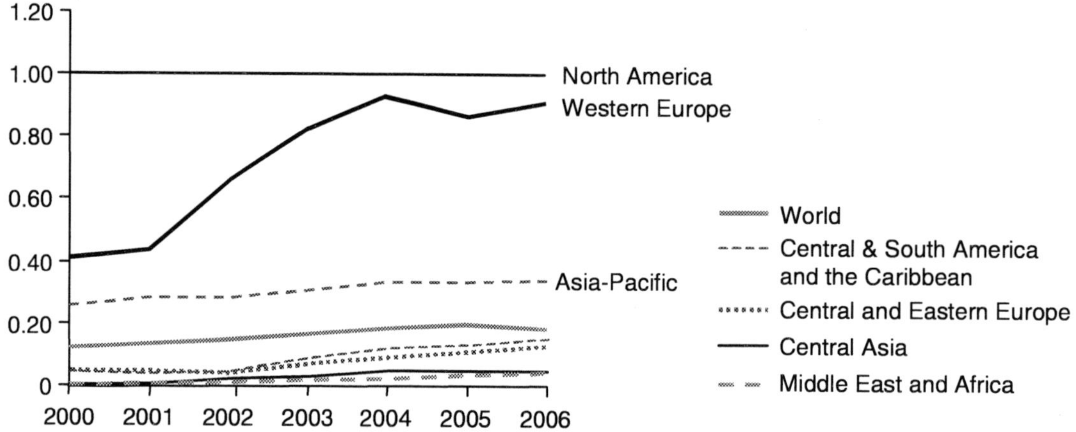

Source: Ovum (Pervasive Computing: Technologies and Markets/Chapter J)

Figure J5.4 **Regional pervasiveness scores relative to North America**

	2000	2001	2002	2003	2004	2005
World	**0.12**	**0.13**	**0.15**	**0.17**	**0.19**	**0.20**
North America	1.00	1.00	1.00	1.00	1.00	1.00
South & Central America and the Caribbean	0.05	0.05	0.04	0.10	0.13	0.14
Western Europe	0.41	0.44	0.66	0.83	0.92	0.87
Central and Eastern Europe	0.04	0.03	0.03	0.05	0.08	0.09
Central Asia	0.01	0.01	0.01	0.02	0.03	0.04
Asia-Pacific	0.26	0.28	0.28	0.30	0.33	0.34
Middle East and Africa	0.02	0.01	0.02	0.04	0.04	0.05

Source: Ovum (Pervasive Computing: Technologies and Markets/ Chapter J)

J5.4 Adoption curves

Our forecasts for the rise of pervasive computing usage and software infrastructure spending are based three waves of adoption, derived from the market development scenario outlined in *Figure J2.2*.

The three waves are:

- wave 1 – enabling multichannel access to existing applications and services, using content adaptation tools
- wave 2 – generating entirely new applications and services on integrated multichannel platforms
- wave 3 – re-engineering legacy applications to multichannel platforms, and focusing on cross-supplier interworking.

These waves represent three stages of application development and deployment activity, which we use to calculate our software infrastructure spend forecasts.

The implications of these adoption waves for pervasive service access are given in *Figure J5.5* and shown graphically in *Figure J5.6*. The method we used was to apply the adoption curves to the North American market – as depicted in the figures – and then use that as a baseline for other regions using the relative pervasiveness scores given in *Figure J5.4*.

Figure J5.5 **North America – percentage of service accesses that are pervasive**

	2000	2001	2002	2003	2004	2005
Total	**4**	**9.5**	**24**	**35**	**43**	**47**
Wave 1	4	7.5	15	17	17	13
Wave 2	0	2	7	12	16	22
Wave 3	0	0	2	6	10	12

Source: Ovum (Pervasive Computing: Technologies and Markets/ Chapter J)

Figure J5.6 **North America – percentage of service accesses that are pervasive**

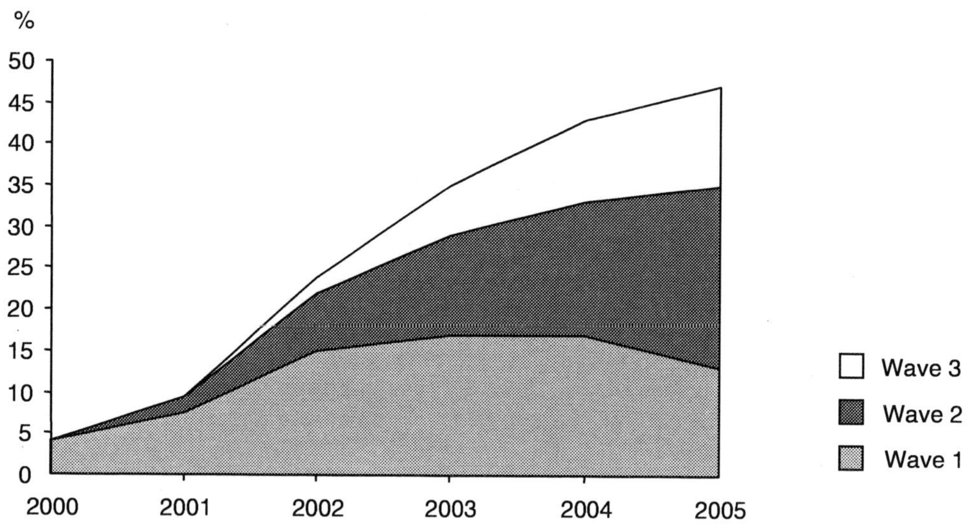

Source: Ovum (Pervasive Computing: Technologies and Markets/Chapter J)

J5.5 Impact on service revenues

The different waves of adoption will have different effects on service revenues:

- waves 1 and 2 will increase revenues per user by an estimated 20%, as the benefits of multichannel access are delivered to the end-user base for existing and new services
- wave 3 is about re-engineering and integration, leading to cost reductions in infrastructure and the potential commoditisation of basic services. Here we estimate pervasive revenues of 90% compared with earlier solutions.

Figures J5.7 and *J5.8* show the effects that the three waves of adoption will have on service revenues.

J5.6 Software infrastructure impact

In order to calculate the overall impact on software infrastructure spend, we have used forecast data from *Ovum Forecasts: Global Software Markets* to provide our base data. The report forecasts the growth of particular categories of software infrastructure over time.

In order to derive revenue curves for expenditure on software infrastructure products, we have estimated the total percentage of expenditure within each infrastructure category that will be spent on infrastructure for pervasive computing. These estimates are driven by our application development and deployment waves, and the ways in which different types of infrastructure product will be used within each wave of activity. *Figure J5.9* shows the percentage of software infrastructure spend on pervasive computing compared to total spend.

Figure J5.7 **Percentage of service revenues attributable to pervasive access**

	2000	2001	2002	2003	2004	2005
Total	**5**	**11**	**28**	**40**	**49**	**53**
Wave 1	5	9	18	20	20	16
Wave 2	0	3	8	14	19	26
Wave 3	0	0	2	5	9	11

Source: Ovum (Pervasive Computing: Technologies and Markets/ Chapter J)

Figure J5.8 **Percentage of service revenues attributable to pervasive access**

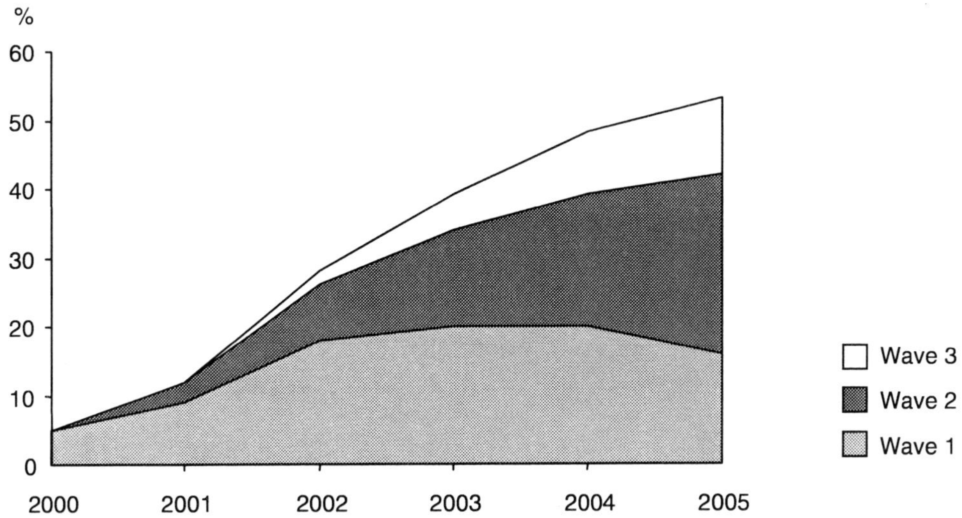

Source: Ovum (Pervasive Computing: Technologies and Markets/Chapter J)

Figure J5.9 **Percentage of software infrastructure spend on pervasive computing**

	Operating systems	Application servers	EAI*	Other middle-ware	DBMS	Tools	Testing and security	Systems management
Total global spend, 2001 ($ million)	19,639	4,066	3,050	9,393	13,662	8,051	3,903	11,954
% spend on pervasive computing, 2001	0.5%	3.0%	0.8%	0.7%	0.8%	3.6%	0.8%	0.2%
Total global spend, 2005 ($ million)	26,472	10,737	11,715	11,634	18,927	18,085	13,427	15,964
% spend on pervasive computing, 2005	9.0%	48.8%	16.3%	4.5%	9.0%	28.0%	31.5%	2.8%

Note: EAI = enterprise application integration

Source: Ovum (Pervasive Computing: Technologies and Markets/ Chapter J)

Appendix: Key technology standards

1 Standards are crucial – but are they working?

The role of open standards in enabling pervasive computing cannot be understated. The notion of delivering any application, to any device, over any network has a basic requirement for interoperability between different devices, networks and services. Infrastructure suppliers too will have to ensure that their products and services can work together with those of others in order to provide end-to-end solutions.

Suppliers understand the importance of standards and are committing large sums of money in order to implement them in their products. However, it is folly to assume that standards alone can bring the levels of interoperability that pervasive computing requires between applications, networks, devices and service providers. Standards provide good 'lowest common denominator' solutions to interoperability problems, but commercial partnerships bring more resilient remedies.

The evolution of IP into a globally accepted networking protocol, as a key enabler of the Internet and the Worldwide Web, has already played an important part in driving developments in pervasive computing. However, its transformation into a universally available piece of pervasive computing fabric is not a foregone conclusion. There remain three significant challenges to be overcome by suppliers in order to make IP suitable as a core piece of pervasive computing technology: device addressability, quality of service assurance and IP mobility.

Above the level of the network, application infrastructure for pervasive computing is currently creating the most interest in standardisation. It is software infrastructure that will directly enable pervasive computing applications, not physical devices and networks. The 'any application to any device over any network' ideal means that content, application, device and infrastructure providers' markets will be maximised if suppliers can agree on a common application infrastructure specification that can be implemented on multiple devices. Consequently, a great deal of work is being done by suppliers in order to create *de jure* and *de facto* standards. WAP, XML and Java all have their part to play in the armoury of the cross-platform application developer, but none of these can address the whole range of applications and devices:

- WAP is a set of protocols and formats optimised for delivering relatively non-interactive services to access platforms with limited processing and networking capabilities
- XML is a very flexible language for building languages that describe data – and consequently is a very useful tool where suppliers need to have their products exchange data. However, XML is highly abstract by itself and certainly does not offer a complete application infrastructure. It is merely a foundation for exchanging documents that contain structured data
- Java is a secure, cross-device application operating environment that comes in several flavours – optimised for mobile devices, desktop devices, smart cards, servers and even TV set-top boxes. However, for now, devices need certain levels of capability just to run the Java environment. Where Java is not the native operating environment used within the device, its use is therefore constrained – and 'Java-native' devices are few.

There is room today – and there will continue to be room tomorrow – for multiple application infrastructure specifications and implementations. Microsoft will be a key player, as will Symbian; Java implementations will also be popular. The wide variety in devices, networks and usage scenarios means that, in reality, there is no one homogeneous market for platforms.

XML has a wide role to play outside the provision of application infrastructure, however. It is already being used to enhance prospects for multichannel content delivery, and for the advertisement by mobile devices of their capabilities to remote application platforms. It is also a key component of most business-to-business application integration suites, which are likely to form the operational backbones of tomorrow's service provider information-sharing initiatives.

2 Bluetooth

2.1 Summary

Bluetooth is a widely backed standard for close-range wireless networking. Despite its relative youth, it is already influencing the product strategies of device manufacturers and software infrastructure suppliers across multiple supply chains. Whilst currently suffering from the high cost of its components and delays in product development as a result of the sheer size of the Bluetooth Special Interest Group, the technology has received sufficient investment to ensure its success and it is likely to become more influential (and useful) over time as more Bluetooth-enabled devices become available and the cost of components falls. Its main threat comes from other wireless networking standards such as IEEE 802.11; its main counter to the threat of competing technologies is its potential pervasiveness.

2.2 What is it?

Bluetooth is a short-range wireless networking specification that is being developed by the Bluetooth Special Interest Group (SIG). The idea originated in 1994, when Ericsson Mobile Communications initiated a study to investigate the feasibility of a low-power, low-cost radio interface between mobile phones and their accessories, with the aim being to eliminate cables between mobile phones and PC cards, headphones and desktop devices.

The Bluetooth SIG was not formed until February 1998, when Ericsson was joined by Nokia, Intel, IBM and Toshiba to transform the idea into a standard for short-range wireless connectivity. Since the formation of the SIG, its membership has grown to more than 2,000 companies, making it the fastest growing industry standard ever.

The Bluetooth specification, which is distributed freely to companies wishing to build Bluetooth-compatible devices, comprises two main technologies: the radio transmitter/receiver, which allows devices to communicate with each other, and the underlying network logic, which makes the communication meaningful.

Bluetooth operates over 79 different frequencies within the unlicensed 2.4GHz radio band (the band used by high-end cordless phones). It employs a technique known as ‘frequency hopping’, rapidly shifting between channels within the band range to find the free frequency with least interference and noise. ‘Spread spectrum’ technology is also used to allow devices to transmit on up to five frequencies simultaneously.

Bluetooth devices can transmit and receive over a distance of approximately ten metres, although this can be boosted to up to 100 metres by an amplifier. A group of devices communicating within a ten-metre range of each other is known as a ‘piconet’. Since Bluetooth devices can support three voice channels operating at 64kbit/s or one data channel, they can achieve data rates of up to 1Mbit/s. Bluetooth devices can be set to either transmit their own availability and capabilities (master), or just listen for other devices (slave). Typically, devices that have a permanent power connection (such as a Bluetooth-enabled Internet router or PC) will transmit their availability, as they do not have the power constraints of mobile devices such as phones and PDAs.

The master/slave relationship, voice-to-data conversion and error correction is handled by the link processor. This must be functionally identical on all

Bluetooth devices, because it handles the 'behind-the-scenes' negotiation through which devices identify their type, as well as their capabilities and which of those capabilities are available to be accessed by other devices. Also built into the link processor are the APIs (application programming interfaces), which allow software to operate over Bluetooth in the same way that it would over a conventional network connection.

Once a device detects the presence of another Bluetooth-enabled device in the vicinity, the devices exchange information on their capabilities and a piconet is established. Up to eight devices may exist on the same piconet, and frequency hopping allows multiple piconets to exist in the same area. It is even possible to bridge multiple piconets to merge them into a single entity.

2.3 Areas of influence

Figure 2.1 shows the influence of Bluetooth on players within the PC, telecoms and broadcast industries.

Of all the standards that are influencing the development of pervasive computing, Bluetooth is the one that has caused the most excitement. Bluetooth offers a mechanism for seamless connectivity between devices, which opens up possibilities across a variety of applications and services in a number of markets and industry sectors.

The technology has a great deal of support and, although the number of implementations is currently low, the levels of industry backing and financial investment in the technology are sufficient to ensure its future.

Figure 2.1 **The influence of Bluetooth**

PC
Telecoms
Broadcast
Content/ application provider
Content aggregator
Service provider
Network operator
Device manufacturer
Strong influence
Fair influence
Emerging influence
No influence

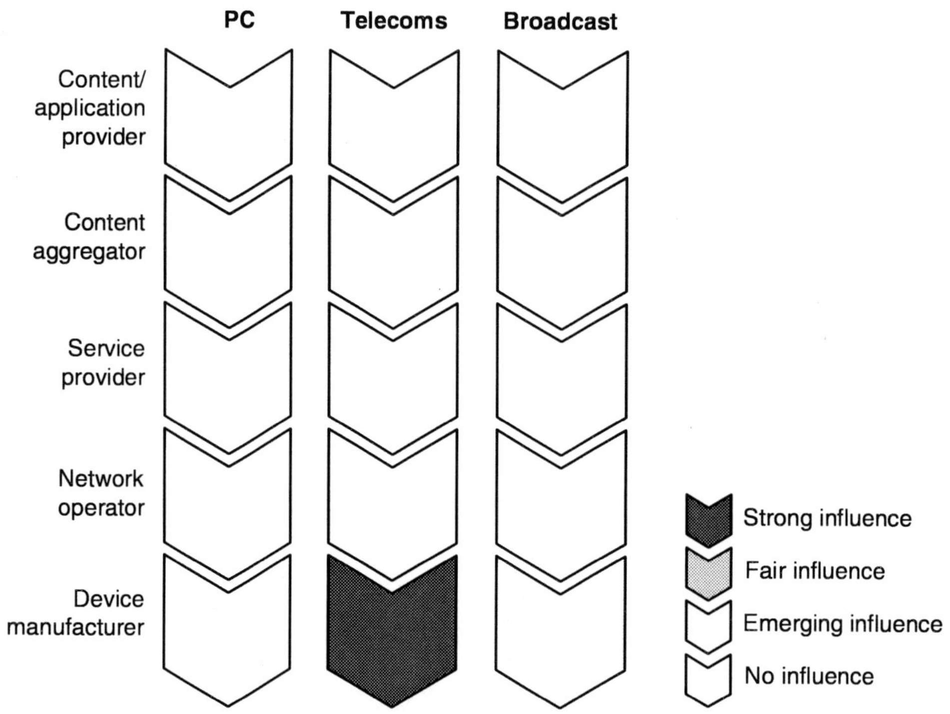

Source: Ovum (Pervasive Computing: Technologies and Markets/Appendix)

The major mobile phone and PDA manufacturers have announced their intention to incorporate Bluetooth into their devices and the first wave of such devices is likely to be available in 2001. There are some compelling applications for Bluetooth in the area of mobile computing. Examples include:

- the 'three-in-one' phone

  a Bluetooth-enabled handset that functions as a portable phone in the home (fixed line charge), a mobile phone whilst on the move (cellular charge), and a 'walkie-talkie' when within range of another Bluetooth-equipped phone

- the Internet bridge

  a Bluetooth-enabled PDA or laptop could be used to surf the Internet by using a Bluetooth phone to access a PSTN adapter or cellular device

- interactive meetings

  Bluetooth could be used to exchange meeting documents and business cards wirelessly

- wireless headsets

  a Bluetooth headset allows for a wireless connection to a phone or other Bluetooth-enabled device.

- synchronisation

  Bluetooth can be used to automatically synchronise a calendar or contact database between various devices – for example, when you enter your office, your phone and PDA automatically synchronise with your PC.

Bluetooth has also attracted wide-ranging support from manufacturers in the consumer electronics market. Again, although there are few implementations today, Bluetooth's influence in this market is likely to grow over time as the cost of components continues to fall and other Bluetooth devices proliferate.

Bluetooth is likely to find its way into the PC market by default as the technology first makes its way into devices that users will want to connect to PCs. There are compelling applications for introducing Bluetooth to PCs, not least to reduce the tangle of wires connecting the PC to peripherals that can be found underneath most desks today. Once again it is likely that Bluetooth's influence in this channel will increase over time.

There are also compelling applications for Bluetooth in the in-car systems market. Again, the standard is likely to become more influential in this channel over time, although this channel is likely to lag behind others, as vehicle manufacturers will wish to see evidence that the technology is reliable and widely supported before incorporating it into their new models.

Bluetooth is principally a network standard, but it is also influencing, to a lesser extent, the way new devices are developed. Device manufacturers are currently working to reduce the number of components required in Bluetooth modules to two – one for the radio and one for the microprocessor – so that everything can fit onto a single chip of less than half a square inch in size. Reducing the number of components will serve to reduce manufacturing and assembly costs, currently an inhibiting factor to the widespread adoption of Bluetooth, and improve reliability. At the moment it costs around $30 to enable a device with Bluetooth, and this is too high for the technology to become a commodity. In order for this to happen the price would have to fall to less than $5 per device.

The high level of industry support and backing for Bluetooth means that it is also influencing the development of software infrastructure. Software providers are keen to ensure that their products will be compatible with what they see as being an important future standard, despite the fact that at present there are very few Bluetooth devices on the market.

2.4 Bluetooth evolution

When Bluetooth products become available it is likely that they will be popular because of the flexibility and ease of use that the standard affords. It is, however, likely to be several years before we see a sufficient base of devices for the standard to really take off; the value of Bluetooth as a connectivity option only becomes compelling when all the things you might want to connect to are also Bluetooth-enabled. Progress is being slowed by the cost of the technology, which still needs to fall before manufacturers begin to include it in all of their base offerings as standard, and also due to the size of the membership of the Bluetooth SIG – developments are being slowed by the need to get products officially authorised by a review board before they can officially use Bluetooth branding.

Perhaps the most interesting thing about Bluetooth is the possibility it offers for the deconstruction of devices into individual components, allowing for new form factors and device types. A simple illustration of this idea is the wireless headset. By having a separate wireless headset, there is no longer any need to include one in (for example) a mobile phone, which allows the phone to become a small device that acts purely as a cellular receiver and can be attached to a belt, and purely as a transmitter for any Bluetooth devices wishing to use the cellular network (such as PDAs and laptops).

3 DVB-MHP

3.1 Summary

The DVB standards portfolio is the closest thing the broadcast media industry has to a standard platform for digital broadcast. The MHP standard, which extends the DVB platform to facilitate interactive services, is gaining important supporters. DVB-MHP has a key role to play in influencing the diffusion of interactive services that use broadband content, both within and outside the broadcast media supply chain. As broadband content providers and aggregators begin to look for ways to re-use their existing interactive services across multiple delivery channels, the DVB-MHP specification is likely to influence the direction that many players take and the partnerships that they form. MHP takes Java technology into interactive broadband services – the corollary of which is that it brings the requirements of broadband application players closer to what mainstream development tools can offer.

3.2 What is it?

The Digital Video Broadcasting standards body came into being in 1993 as an evolution of the European Launching Group (ELG), a group made up of television broadcasters, consumer equipment manufacturers, media interest groups, carriers and regulators with a common interest in overseeing the development of digital terrestrial broadcasting in Europe.

The group drafted a Memorandum of Understanding that set out basic principles, allowing commercial competitors to appreciate their common requirements and agendas in what was then a departure into unexplored territory. The memorandum was signed by all members in September 1993 and the ELG became the Digital Video Broadcasting Forum.

The DVB Forum provided the focus for gathering all the major European television interests into one group. It promised to develop a complete digital television system based on a unified approach. Initially, the forum focused its efforts on satellite and cable delivery of broadcast digital television services. Fewer technical problems and a simpler regulatory climate meant that they could develop more rapidly than terrestrial systems. By 1997 DVB's successes led it to move towards developing global digital TV standards.

The first generation of set-top boxes, however, employed a wide range of middleware, which prevented convergence to a single standard. In order to overcome this, the DVB Forum specified the Multimedia Home Platform (MHP) software. MHP is an API that incorporates existing Java specifications such as JavaTV and Java Media Player, alongside other standards such as HTML and HAVi. This makes it extremely interesting, as it provides a mechanism for enabling connectivity between a wide range of devices and standards. The first MHP implementation was made by Dutch electronics giant Philips, which recently announced that it had licensed the technology to US set-top infrastructure supplier Liberate. DVB-MHP has also been adopted by a number of other infrastructure suppliers and set-top box manufacturers in order to ensure that their products are compatible with the DVB standard.

The DVB standards are open and based on the MPEG-2 coding system, which means that they can be easily carried from one medium to another (for example, satellite to cable and cable to terrestrial). This is important because of the complexity of the modern distribution environment. All the manufacturers making compliant systems are able to guarantee that their DVB equipment will work with other manufacturers' DVB equipment.

3.3 Areas of influence

Figure 3.1 shows the influence of DVB on players within the PC, telecoms and broadcast industries.

Because the DVB standard is specific to digital video broadcasting, its influence is primarily in the broadcast media supply chain. Within this market it exerts influence over devices that must be built to conform with the standard, and the networks over which the data must be carried. However, recent developments in the PC supply chain – in particular a number of moves by Microsoft – mean that elements of the DVB standard portfolio are likely to have a degree of influence here as well. A new alliance, the PC DTV Promoters Group, backed by Microsoft, Intel and a number of other companies with a vested interest in digital TV on PCs, was recently formed in order to push further developments in this area. Microsoft has recently announced plans to incorporate digital TV APIs in future releases of its Windows 2000 operating system. All these developments will need to take into account the DVB MHP standard to ensure cross-platform compatibility.

Figure 3.1 **The influence of DVB**

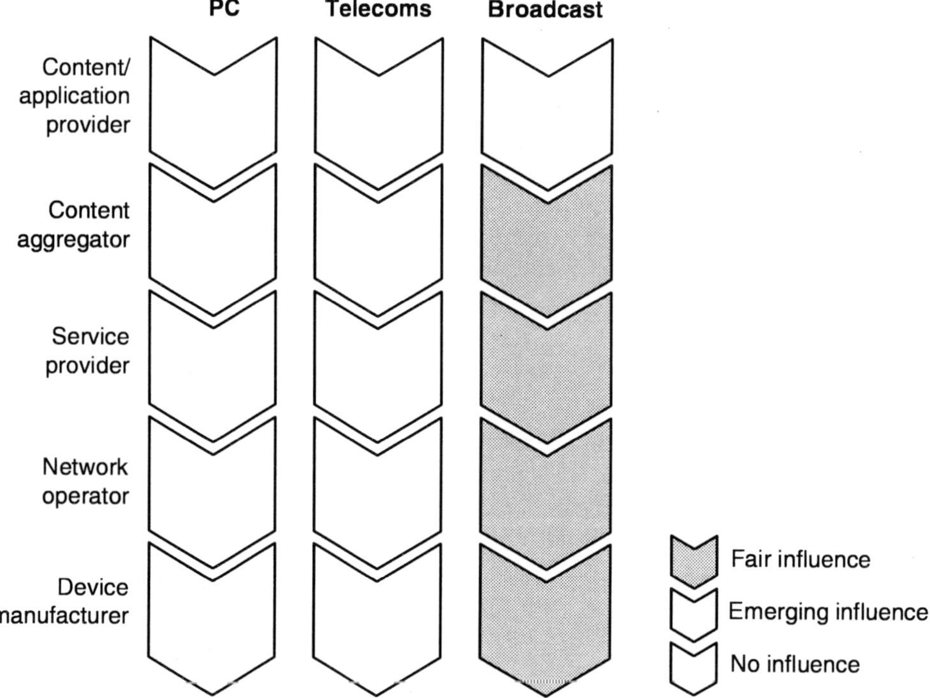

Source: Ovum (Pervasive Computing: Technologies and Markets/Appendix)

As the DVB standard originated in Europe, this is where it exerts the most influence; in other parts of the world there are different standards for digital video broadcasting. There is, however, some support for the standard in Asia-Pacific, where it has been embraced by several large consumer electronics manufacturers.

4 IP

4.1 Summary

IP (Internet Protocol) is a packet-switched networking protocol defined by the IETF (Internet Engineering Task Force) and used to underpin nearly all corporate data applications. It is increasingly becoming part of the fabric of telecommunications and broadcast networks. Pervasive computing is made much easier if IP is available as a common network protocol – however, 'IP everywhere' is a fiction today. A chief concern regarding the development of pervasive computing is the degree to which the IT community regards the availability of 'IP everywhere' as a foregone conclusion: the truth is that, as a contributor to pervasive computing, Internet infrastructure is similar to a leaking dam.

IP-related technologies will not collapse immediately, but neither are they a reliable foundation for the future. Many technical changes to Internet protocols, such as those aimed at address re-use, are filling the cracks without addressing fundamental structural weakness. While this continues, progress to improve the Internet will be slow, as each fix can reveal further weaknesses that require more fixes. Suppliers are working towards providing IP everywhere, but many of the issues are complex to resolve and require commercial and regulatory, as well as technological, changes.

4.2 Areas of influence

Figure 4.1 shows the influence of IP on players within the PC, telecoms and broadcast industries.

Figure 4.1 **The influence of IP**

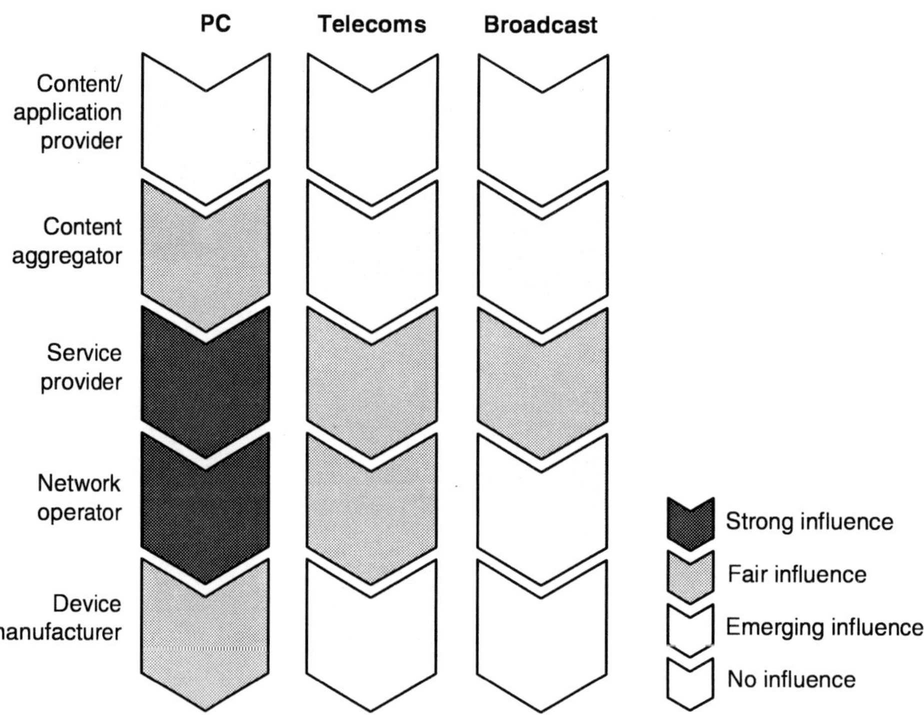

Source: Ovum (Pervasive Computing: Technologies and Markets/Appendix)

IP's influence is mainly felt in the IT supply chain. Infrastructure suppliers are pushing IP out into mobile and broadcast networks, as well as public access networks and core telecommunications networks, but the degree to which its influence spreads as an element of the pervasive computing fabric depends on suppliers and standards bodies resolving three key issues:

- addressability – the addressing scheme used in current implementations of IP (IPv4) uses four bytes. This means that, in an ideal world, there are approximately 4.3 billion possible unique addresses for devices and gateways. However, in practice the world is rapidly running out of IP addresses. Some applications can be built to allow network hosts to be dynamically assigned network addresses, but the technologies being used are only short-term solutions to the addressability problem
- quality of service – IP was designed specifically to ignore network performance issues – indeed, the protocol was designed to maximise communications resilience at the expense of performance. This was fine when the application of the protocol was to allow defence institutions to communicate in the event of a nuclear attack, but when the application involves transmission of voice or video the demands are significantly different
- mobility – today, telecommunications services are delivered through fixed telecommunications networks, mobile telecommunications networks and the Internet. In order to be part of the fabric for pervasive computing, IP infrastructure needs to be made available in the same way on all three types of network.

4.3 How is IP evolving?

Addressability

IPv6 is a set of extensions to the core IP protocol that aims to improve upon IPv4 in the areas of:

- scalability – it uses a six-byte, rather than four-byte addressing scheme, which in theory provides for more than 280 trillion individually - addressable network hosts
- security – through reference to the IPSec specifications
- ease of configuration
- network management.

Much of the original pressure for IPv6 focused on the shortage of addressing space caused by the four-byte limitation in IPv4. With the growth of Internet hosts on a sharp upward curve and every user requiring an address, it looked as though available addresses would soon run out.

In the short term, network address translation and re-use protocols such as DHCP (dynamic host configuration protocol) seemed to remove the problem. However, the problem of using address translation is that it breaks applications that expect a static mapping from source to destination addresses, or which include addressing information in the payload (as FTP does). It also causes problems with corporate firewalls, which can view legitimately applied address translation as a potential security breach. Address translation is a bad idea born of a need for a quick fix. It is still being adapted to try to fix some of the problems it has created.

IPv6's adoption has not been as rapid as the standards bodies hoped, however. Today, IPv6 is in use within the '6Bone' – a testing network set up in 1998 – but not in many other networks. This is chiefly because there is still no commercial case for IPv6. The need for a new protocol stack and conversion devices still outweighs the benefits of extensibility. However, the extension of IPv4 with network address translation (NAT) has been pushed to its limits and has proved to have many shortcomings. Bigger addresses are becoming a technical imperative that will drive IPv6.

The impetus for change will receive a major boost from third-generation (3G) cellular networks. With this technology, it will become essential to allocate an IP address to every user. Sheer weight of user numbers makes IPv6 essential and it will be the only option for 3G mobile carriers. As one of the major 3G mobile network infrastructure providers, Nokia is a strong proponent of IPv6.

Mobility

Over the past two years, major advances have been made under the banner of the 'next-generation network', which will provide for the convergence of the network services that are currently delivered through the networks of ISPs, fixed carriers and cellular carriers. A common service model will apply across all infrastructures, so that a carrier can define a service that spans all access technologies according to user needs. In the future, it will be possible to have a single mobile communications terminal that:

- works in multiple countries
- provides Internet access and voice communications
- is secure and affordable.

However, we are some way from this situation. And the solutions to today's 'mobility gaps' are not technological – they will have to come from commercial and regulatory spheres.

Although the grand vision of network integration is highly desirable, the reality is that the telecommunications industry will not deliver it overnight. Mobility of IP connections in the fixed network can benefit from a range of current IP initiatives, but the lack of a commercial case for IP roaming is limiting deployment. Convergence between the PSTN and IP is progressing well, but the inclusion of cellular networks is barely considered. More effort is needed to ensure that IP and its associated services can be delivered seamlessly through fixed and cellular access. Securing the goal of mobility is possible, but action must be taken now and with a broad enough consideration of the issues. Regulatory decisions are needed and these will influence the future of the market for a generation.

Those taking the decisions must consider a range of market factors, including:

- convergence between IP, the PSTN and 2G/3G cellular
- market positioning of incumbent and new entrant operators in the fixed, cellular and ISP sectors
- development of IP for roaming, quality of service and cellular applications
- evolution of CDMA and GSM carrier networks

- standardisation initiatives and vendor positioning
- regulatory issues associated with IP interconnect and 3G spectrum management.

There is little evidence that such a holistic view of the market is being taken by industry players. Issues must be addressed as IP continues to spread into networks, or the current 'stovepipe' development of fixed, cellular and IP networks will continue, and barriers for users will remain. Telecoms operators should be required to produce plans for network integration.

The mobility world seems to have an alarming number of standards bodies chipping away at it – from the heavyweights (such as the IETF and ITU-T), through to quasi-standards bodies (such as 3GPP), to fully industry-sponsored organisations (such as the Softswitch Consortium and the WAP Forum). Even a cursory examination of the work being carried out by these organisations reveals technical overlap and a different view of the role of IP. History proves that they are likely to select different technical options, and this will hamper the deployment of networks. There is a need for co-ordination of effort amongst the standards bodies, or else technical confusion will be added to the long list of hindrances to the establishment of mobility within networks.

Quality of service

Quality of service (QoS) is a concept that is completely absent from the IP technology deployed today. As IP becomes more of a proposition for implementation within the core of carrier networks, the QoS issue must be addressed.

MPLS, diffserv and RSVP

Carriers have faced a number of problems with managing their IP networks. Most stem from the limitations of classical IP routing, which does not support fast re-routing or traffic engineering. It relies on building routing tables – a slow process – that reflect the topology of the network rather than the loading and stability of network links. The process was designed with survivability of the network (rather than predictability or performance) in mind.

In today's Internet, survivability is still an issue – but at the level of service restoration within milliseconds rather than a gradual re-establishment of links. Traffic engineering has become essential to ensure consistency of service provision to end users.

Carriers will only offer services differentiated by QoS to end users when they have confidence in the internal operation of their network. Even then, the granularity of QoS specification offered is likely to be coarse. Carriers often give the impression that they are offering coarse-grained QoS – 'platinum', 'gold' and 'silver' – because they think their customers cannot understand anything else. However, there are leading-edge users that understand their demanding requirements very well. Carriers will need coarse-grained QoS because it is easy to sell and price, but their networks need to have a higher degree of capability for leading-edge users and for internal operation. Diffserv is well-suited to coarse-grained QoS specifications. RSVP is better suited to fine-grained QoS specifications. MPLS provides the traffic management that is essential to the delivery of any QoS.

IP multicast

Multicasting, which is traffic flowing from one to many users at the same time, can be provided either at the server layer or by multicast protocols (such as DVMRP and PIM). Server-layer solutions are most often deployed today and use servers to replicate content to users that require it. The replication and user subscription functions can also be carried out by routers through the use of a multicast protocol. This has benefits for carriers, as traffic can be managed more effectively – but thus far, relatively few carriers have enabled it in their production networks since it introduces an overhead that is hard to justify with relatively few users.

The alternative server-layer approaches of webcasts and streaming have proved satisfactory with today's limited user base and low bandwidth. As demand for content grows, so will interest in multicast protocols.

Implementation of multicasting breaks down into two issues:

- identification and maintenance of the group of recipients
- building a distribution tree and traffic distribution to multiple users without unnecessary duplication.

Since users can join and leave multicast groups on a regular basis, the topology of the network defined by the locations of the group members is constantly changing. In comparison with unicast routing, multicast routing generates many more route changes. Where MPLS is employed, this means that the process of setting up new label-switched paths must be faster than that required for unicast routing.

IP multicasting 'in the network' is championed by – amongst others – Cisco Systems.

5 Java

5.1 Summary

Java is a platform-independent operating system and programming language that is becoming widely adopted across the range of delivery channels we consider in this report. It is most established in the corporate IT realm on the server, but in telecommunications and broadcast media Java-based client operating environments are starting to be the focus of supplier interest. The 'Java promise' of a secure, network-aware, cross-platform operating environment is stimulating interest in the technology as an enabler of both wireless Internet and interactive TV services. Java also has a part to play in the evolution of networked home appliances – it forms the basis of the OSGi's (Open Services Gateway initiative's) home network gateway specification. 'Java everywhere' is not a prerequisite for the spread of pervasive computing, but its cross-platform nature means that it is a major potential source of pervasive computing infrastructure technology.

5.2 What is it?

Sun Microsystems launched Java, its platform-independent programming language and operating environment, in 1995, in response to the growing influence of the Web on IT. The stated aim of Java was to enable network computing, allowing a new wave of network-based (rather than PC-based) computing architecture. Java technology, in its various forms and packages, is now the company's most well-known product.

Whilst Sun continues with its own pervasive computing efforts through the Consumer and Embedded Systems unit of its JavaSoft division, many other companies are basing their own pervasive computing initiatives around Java technologies.

The Java operating environment specifications are produced by Sun's JavaSoft division in 'families' that are intended to be hosted on different-sized platforms. J2EE-compliant products are intended to be hosted on servers, J2SE-compliant products are intended to be hosted on PCs, J2ME on smartphones and PDAs, and Java Card on smart cards.

It is important to note that Sun's Java Soft division has turned over responsibility for the development of many Java specifications to the Java Community Process (JCP) – an open consortium of companies with interests in Java. In particular, many of the specifications that make up the J2ME environment have been produced through the JCP.

All JavaSoft's new technology releases ship with open specifications. In addition, most new technology releases are accompanied by reference implementations of those specifications, along with their source code, and also, in some cases, by test suites that third parties can use to test the compliance of their products with the specifications.

The Java technologies that are most significant in the pervasive computing market are J2ME, Jini and Java Embedded Server.

Java 2 Micro Edition (J2ME)

J2ME is a family of Java environment specifications, designed to be suitable for consumer appliances and embedded systems. Within this specification family, Sun and the JCP have created a variant called the Connected Limited Device Configuration (CLDC). The J2ME CLDC is designed for mobile devices that must operate with limited power, limited network connectivity and constrained memory and processing capacities.

At the heart of the CLDC are:

- the K Virtual Machine (KVM), which is a Java Virtual Machine designed from the ground up to operate in severely restricted environments. The KVM can run in 160kb of memory
- the Mobile Information Device Profile (MIDP) API specifications, which allow devices running the CLDC to tell network-based services what their capabilities are – in terms of user interfaces, storage, networking and so on. MIDP thus allows network-based services to deploy content and applications tailored to the capabilities of particular devices.

Motorola is one of the specifiers (and adopters) of the J2ME CLDC. Symbian has ported J2ME to the EPOC operating environment. Nokia, Ericsson, NTT DoCoMo, Research In Motion, Samsung and Palm Computing have all licensed the J2ME specification from the Java Community Process.

Jini

Jini is a set of lightweight Java middleware services that enable distributed Java programs to collaborate over an IP network connection to achieve particular tasks. Jini was designed primarily to enable smart devices to communicate with each other and with remote servers – consequently, its likely influence will be strongest in networked home appliances and mobile computing. The technology enables programs to publish requests for services, for other programs to advertise their capabilities and for requesters and providers to be 'matched up' and connected transparently to software developers and device users. Jini has not yet been widely adopted by the Java application developer community, however – this is probably because the technology suppliers in the markets that it is most likely to influence are still getting to grips with implementing the basic Java platform.

Java Embedded Server (JES)

JES is a binary Java executable software product that complies with the OSGi's specification for a residential network service gateway. Sun believes that this product has a potential role to play not only in the home networks market, but also as a service gateway to sophisticated in-car networks. Sun has collaborated with Echelon to combine JES and Echelon's LonWorks lightweight networking technology, thus producing a Java-based home network gateway product.

5.3 Areas of influence

Figure 5.1 shows the influence of Java on players within the PC, telecoms and broadcast industries.

Figure 5.1 **The influence of Java**

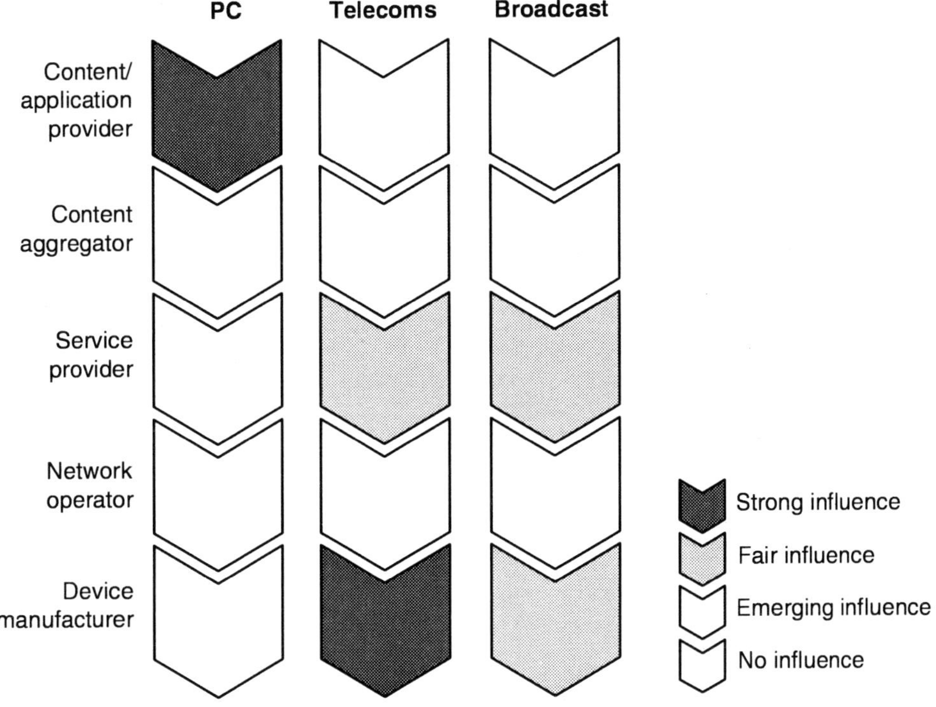

Source: Ovum (Pervasive Computing: Technologies and Markets/Appendix)

Java technologies have already been embraced by a range of device manufacturers within the pervasive computing space. This has been brought about mainly through the development of J2ME, which has been designed specifically to work within the constraints of devices with limited resources in terms of processor power, memory and storage requirements. Java is most established in the PC channel as a platform for development of server-based web applications, where the technology is implemented by the vast majority of application server vendors (with the exception of Microsoft).

Java is already starting to move into the telecommunications stovepipe – particularly the mobile voice handset market. Java is also established in the PDA market and is supported by Palm, which currently holds the greatest share of this market. The Palm VII includes a WAP microbrowser from 4thpass, which is built around Java.

Java also has a potentially strong role to play in the emerging market for networked home appliances, as it forms the basis of the OSGi's home network gateway specification.

6 WAP

6.1 Summary

WAP is a standard set of network protocols, optimised for delivering simple information services, infotainment and e-commerce applications to mobile access platforms with limited capabilities. The WAP environment is modelled on the same principles as the web browser, but severely cut down. To date, WAP microbrowsers have only been deployed in limited ranges of 'feature phones'. WAP has experienced technology and marketing problems since its launch (a significant problem being that most implementations are incompatible with each other) but, despite this, it still has an important part to play in stimulating demand for wireless Internet applications. The window of opportunity for the technology is limited, however, as over time the design criteria for WAP and its mark-up language, WML (wireless mark-up language), will be rendered obsolete. There are also moves to transform WML into a dialect of XML that is much easier to reconcile with other mark-up languages – principally HTML.

6.2 What is it?

The WAP Forum was formed in September 1997 by Motorola, Ericsson, Nokia and Phone.com in order to define a standard for enabling access to Internet content from mobile terminals. It has now expanded to include more than 200 members, including operators, infrastructure suppliers, software developers and content providers.

WAP has been designed to enable access to web-based information, coded in WML within the constraints of the small screen of a mobile terminal and the characteristics of the mobile network (which is limited in terms of speed, bandwidth and latency). Ovum's view of WAP is that:

> *WAP is a widely backed standard supporting Internet content access and call management functionality for small screen wireless devices.*

WAP is actually a stack of protocols, rather than a single network protocol. The stack comprises:

- WTP, the connection protocol (a role similar to that of IP)
- WSP, the session protocol (a role similar to that of TCP)
- UDP (User Datagram Protocol), the low-level transmission protocol that also underpins SNMP
- WTLS, a transaction-level security layer that mirrors SSL in terms of functionality.

The WAP specification relies on the presence of a host machine running a WAP gateway to translate between the WAP protocols and the native protocols of the Web.

There is much confusion within the industry regarding what WAP is capable of delivering now, and will be capable of delivering in the future. At present, only simple information services are available over WAP and there are still some unresolved technical issues such as end-to-end security, interoperability between gateways and handsets, and limitations of second-generation networks, which are preventing the delivery of value-added services such as call management and 'push' information delivery. These services are instead being delivered through implementations of proprietary extensions to the standard.

6.3 Areas of influence

Figure 6.1 shows the influence of WAP on players within the PC, telecoms and broadcast industries.

WAP services are targeted specifically at mobile devices, particularly those with small screens such as voice-centric handsets. While it is possible that WAP services may be delivered to other types of terminal such as PDAs, and terminal devices fitted in cars, it is unlikely because the larger screens and enhanced processing capabilities of these devices make other delivery mechanisms more appropriate. The WAP specifications are influencing the direction not only of device manufacturers, but also network operators and service providers that need to optimise their infrastructure for delivering WAP applications.

Figure 6.1 **The influence of WAP**

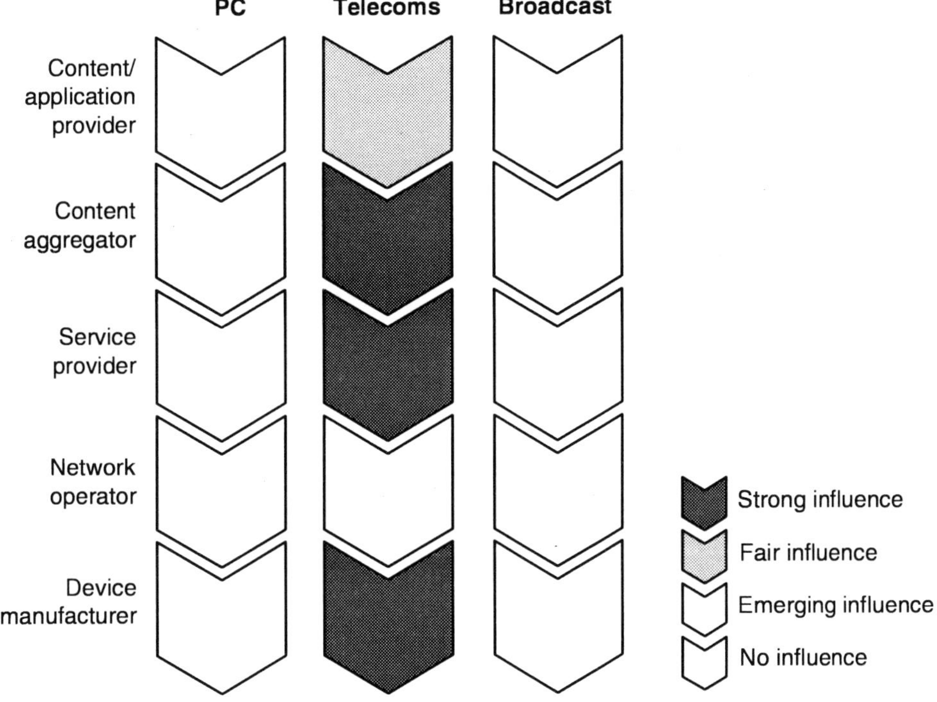

Source: Ovum (Pervasive Computing: Technologies and Markets/Appendix)

At present WAP is limited primarily to delivery of simple 'infotainment' services, such as news, weather, stock quotes and horoscopes. Whether it will become a popular technology for delivering services over more capable third-generation networks is highly uncertain. The removal of today's severe constraints will bring opportunities to deliver richer, more interactive applications, and with it the requirement for more sophisticated infrastructure platforms.

7 XML

7.1 Summary

XML (extensible mark-up language) describes the structure and meaning of documents containing data. Its openness and simplicity is generating great interest within supplier communities, because it provides a relatively low-cost, low-risk mechanism for the sharing of data between different applications, service providers and device types. There are many potential applications for XML technology within pervasive computing infrastructure – and the ease of information exchange that it allows will be a key factor in the development of pervasive computing.

However, XML is not a 'silver bullet'. The language by itself does not solve any problems – parties that want to exchange information must also agree on a common XML vocabulary, described in document type definitions (DTDs), or agree to implement a translation layer. Either way, the parties have to collaborate in order to create an environment in which exchange can take place. Dynamic exchange of data between two software products that have not 'met' before is only possible if the two products have been designed and built with a common vocabulary (hence the standardisation of the MIDP specification within the J2ME CLDC, for example).

7.2 What is it?

XML, like HTML, is a sub-set, or dialect of SGML (standard generalised mark-up language – ISO 8879), which is an international standard for the structural and content mark-up of electronic documents.

Like HTML, XML documents are made up of a number of text strings held within angle-bracketed tags (for example, <TITLE>Consultant</TITLE>). However, this is where the similarity ends.

HTML is made up of a set of predefined tags. These tags specify only how a web browser should interpret the document for display on screen. If publishers use a tag that is not part of the HTML specification (and which is therefore not supported by the web browser), the tag will be ignored.

XML tags do not describe how data should be displayed on a screen – XML is a specification for self-describing documents. XML documents provide, along with the document data itself, document type definitions that are descriptions of how the data is structured and, to a certain extent, what it means.

7.3 Areas of influence

Figure 7.1 shows the influence of XML on players within the PC, telecoms and broadcast industries.

Figure 7.1 **The influence of XML**

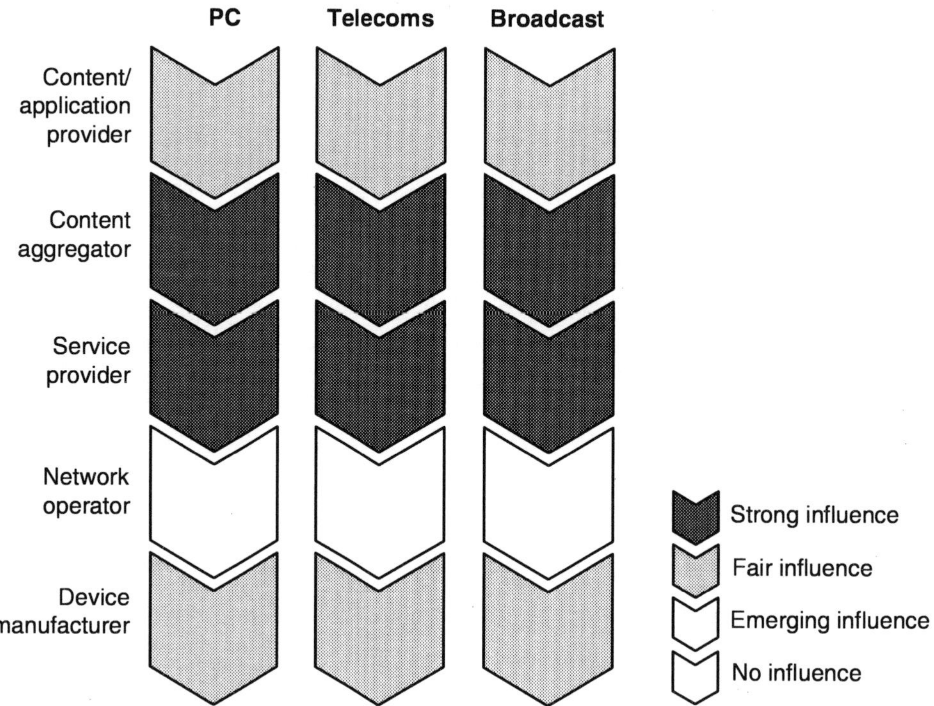

Source: Ovum (Pervasive Computing: Technologies and Markets/Appendix)

- As an open specification of a self-describing document format, XML has applications wherever the open exchange of metadata – data that describes data – is required. XML therefore has great potential strengths as a solution component for many integration or translation problems – and the evolution of pervasive computing brings opportunities for plenty of those. For example:
- access platforms must be able to register their capabilities with service providers' application platforms
- application platforms must be able to adapt content and application interfaces for delivery to multiple access platforms, with varying capabilities
- service providers must be able to exchange operational information with other providers, in order to facilitate unfettered service navigation, interactive advertising, accurate billing and good customer service.

XML documents can be transported across the Web using existing transportation protocols, so a communications and security structure is already in place for anyone with web access. The majority of software infrastructure vendors are now using XML as a platform to make their products and technologies more open. Microsoft and IBM have used XML as the basis for their Simple Object Access Protocol (SOAP) and it is the basis for other Internet-based brokerage and invocation services such as UDDI and XAML.

XML is not a complete solution for exchanging data between different applications and devices, however – it does have limitations. XML only provides a syntax for describing data; neither vocabulary nor semantics are inherent in it. It is purely a vehicle for the exchange of information, not a mechanism in itself.

This a common misconception about XML that vendors have done little to dispel. In order for applications to exchange data using XML, it is necessary to have a further, higher level of abstraction to describe the XML documents themselves. Document type definitions provide this extra level, and therefore serve as a means to validate XML documents, but it remains necessary for software applications or companies that wish to exchange data using XML to agree on the document type definitions that they will use.

XML cannot, therefore, be regarded as a universal data exchange solution. It requires significant supporting software to process documents, which rules it out as a complete solution. It does, however, provide a common coding format that can be used by services.

8 Other standards

8.1 HAVi

HAVi is a standard that supports communication between digital home appliances and electronic goods, with a focus on home entertainment products. The standard was launched by a group of eight leading manufacturers (Grundig, Hitachi, Matsushita Electric Industrial Co, Royal Philips Electronics, Sharp, Sony, Thomson Multimedia and Toshiba).

The HAVi specification is audio and video device-centric. It has been designed to meet the particular demands of digital audio and video, with a focus on the control and content of digital audio and video streams. It defines an operating system-neutral middleware that manages multi-directional audio and video streams, event schedules and registries, and provides APIs for the creation of software applications.

HAVi uses IEEE 1394 (also known as i.LINK or FireWire) as the connection medium between devices. This is an appropriate protocol because it has sufficient capacity to carry multiple audio and video streams simultaneously, and it also supports digital copy protection.

As leading manufacturers of consumer electronics are already committed to producing HAVi-compliant products, it is likely that the standard will be influential in home networking. Due to its strong focus on audio and video devices, it is unlikely to compete directly with other home networking initiatives, such as those of the OSGi and the UPnP (Universal Plug and Play) Forum. Indeed, there is evidence of HAVi integrating with other standards – for example, its use within DVB MHP.

8.2 IEEE 802.11

IEEE 802.11 is a standard for wireless local area networking. Commonly available, it operates in the same area of radio spectrum as Bluetooth. This presents a problem, as IEEE 802.11 signals are significantly more powerful than those of Bluetooth, resulting in the scrambling of Bluetooth signals when the two are used together. Engineers are currently tackling the problem from both ends, but until a solution becomes available the problem could constrain the adoption of IEEE 802.11 or Bluetooth, or both.

A group of computers that communicate over an IEEE 802.11 LAN can communicate at speeds of up to 11 million bits per second and, whilst companies with wired networks that offer better connection speeds are unlikely to wish to switch to IEEE 802.11, it does provide a simple, cheap, wireless networking alternative in new offices or for smaller companies. The technology is also being pitched as an attractive option for home networking for those that do not wish to install a hard-wired network such as Ethernet. Apple Computers has already targeted this market with its 802.11-based AirPort wireless LAN system, which enables wireless connectivity between Mac computers at distances of up to 30 metres. A number of companies are manufacturing 802.11 adapters for use with PCs.

8.3 Universal Plug and Play

Universal Plug and Play (UPnP) is a networking and service invocation framework that is designed to enable peer-to-peer network connectivity of PCs of all form factors, intelligent appliances and wireless devices. It is a distributed, open networking architecture based around TCP/IP and the Web, which seeks to enable networking and data transfer between networked devices. It is particularly targeted at the markets for home networking, and networking within small businesses and commercial premises.

Whilst the idea for UPnP originated at Microsoft (the 'plug and play' concept was first implemented in Microsoft's Windows 95 operating systems as a means of simplifying the addition of new hardware and peripherals to PCs), the standard is being developed by the Universal Plug and Play Forum. This association is made up of more than 120 companies and individuals from a variety of companies representing the consumer electronics, computing, home automation and security, home appliance and computer networking industries.

UPnP is based around HTTP, XML and browser technologies. It uses common protocols and requires no device drivers, and is programming language and operating system 'agnostic'. However, since it is XML-based, vendors must agree on document type definitions on a per-device basis.

UPnP devices are designed to operate without needing to be configured. New devices have the ability to connect straight to the network, announce their presence, obtain an IP address and convey their capabilities upon request, as well as learn about the presence and capabilities of other devices on the network. UPnP is based around open Internet standards, as the UPnP Forum (following Microsoft's lead) expects that mixed-media, multi-vendor networks will be a common scenario in the future.

The principal competition for the technology comes from Sun's Jini and the OSGi's home network gateway initiative, but the UPnP Forum feel that, because their architecture is based around the open standards of XML and HTTP and does not require a specific execution environment, it represents a more attractive proposition.

Whilst the UPnP Forum is well supported in terms of its membership, we are yet to see any implementations of the technology outside Microsoft's own products. However, as Microsoft is such a well established manufacturer and is well supported by partners and developers, it is likely that UPnP will become more influential over time.

8.4 OSGi

The Open Services Gateway initiative (OSGi) is an independent non-profit organisation based in the US, supported by more than 60 companies worldwide. It seeks to define and promote open specifications for linking networked consumer and business devices to the Internet in residential or small/remote office environments.

The OSGi is engaged in defining a set of APIs and providing a sample implementation of a services gateway architecture. This services gateway is inserted between the external network and internal network and devices. The OSGi believes that this services gateway will facilitate the development and deployment of a wide range of advanced network-based services. Service providers will deliver 'just-in-time' value-added services to the services gateway, with the gateway providing a service distribution, integration and management point.

The gateway specification is based on Sun's Java technology, which the OSGi believes to be appropriate, as Java is an open standard itself. (Responsibility for defining the home gateway specification has now been transferred to the OSGi from the Java Community Process.) It uses a 'thin server' architecture, which it claims helps to standardise the delivery of services to gateways. As it is based on a three-tier computing model (device, gateway and back-end) and on open standards throughout, the OSGi claims that it is compatible with existing computing infrastructures (including Windows-based ones).

The OSGi is designed to complement most other residential gateway and home networking standards initiatives currently underway. It focuses on the application layer and is designed to be able to work with a variety of network protocol, transport and device technologies. Where there is an existing Java standard in play, such as Jini, the OSGi can use it. Where there is a standard that is not Java-based, such as HAVi or Universal Plug and Play, the OSGi is working to accommodate these standards.

The OSGi focuses entirely on the home network market and, in particular, on defining a standard implementation for a home network gateway. It is in this area, therefore, that it has most influence. To a lesser extent, it also has an influence over devices in the consumer electronics area, as these must be designed to be compatible with the home network gateway specification. Like Universal Plug and Play, there are few implementations of the technology today, but the standard is well supported and its influence in home networks is likely to increase in the future.

Notes for readers

- Whilst every care is taken to ensure the accuracy of this report, the facts, estimates and opinions stated are based on information and sources which, while we believe them to be reliable, are not guaranteed. In particular, it should not be relied upon as the sole source of reference in relation to the subject matter. No liability can be accepted by Ovum Limited, its directors or employees, or by the authors of the report for any loss occasioned to any person or entity acting or failing to act as a result of anything contained in or omitted from this report, or our conclusions as stated.
- The organisations studied illustrate the activities of participants in the sectors in which they operate. The inclusion or exclusion of a company does not imply a judgement of the value of its activities.
- Trademarks are implicitly acknowledged.

About Ovum

Ovum is an independent research and consulting company, offering expert advice on IT, telecoms and e-commerce. Our mission is to help you make successful decisions. The authority, quality and clarity we apply means our analysis of key developments is highly respected worldwide.

With expected sales in 2000 of more than $30 million and growth of more than 50% per annum, Ovum now has offices in London, Boston, Melbourne and Buenos Aires. Our 300 staff are dedicated to delivering authoritative analysis, tailored consulting and customer support to over 10,000 senior executives around the world.

Ovum publications

Director Products and Services
Martin Garner

Reports Manager
Philip Carnelley

Managing Editor
Daniella Domlija

Editors
Suzanne Mucci
Lee Hope

Proofreader
Debbie Thornton

Designers
Katy Peek
Kate Hunter
Nicola Rickard

Publications Manager
Hugh O'Neill

Electronic publishers
Natasha Cox
Claire-Laure Thomas
Anthony Blears

Fulfilment Manager
Joanna Clayton

Ovum's research methodology

Ovum's reports are based on primary research. The authors, who are all experienced consultants, interview suppliers, users, policymakers and standards bodies to gain a thorough understanding of the market.

This research is used to produce a picture of market development and forecasts of the market's value to suppliers. The authors explain and defend their conclusions in a presentation to Ovum's senior managers and consultants.

The draft text is reviewed by senior Ovum staff and external experts to ensure that the conclusions and supporting information are presented clearly, consistently and credibly. Each company profiled has the opportunity to comment on the text of the profile before publication.

Ovum consulting

Ovum's consultancy business benefits from £3 million worth of worldwide research for our reports and continuous information services.

Consultancy projects include:

- research and analysis of European markets
- evaluation of the commercial potential for emerging technologies and products
- advice on business strategy and policymaking in these markets.

Our consultancy clients include most of the world's leading computer and communications companies and a number of government agencies.

To learn more about how Ovum's consultancy services can help you, please contact Duncan Brown at dwb@ovum.com or on +44 (0) 20 7551 9000.

How Ovum can help you

Ovum publishes a wide range of reports and continuous services on IT, telecoms and e-commerce. Our ongoing research programme analyses key developments worldwide. We ensure that you benefit from accurate and independent information and advice, through:

- IT strategy reports
- software evaluations
- e-commerce reports and services
- telecommunications market reports
- telecommunications advisory services.

A list of current reports and services is printed opposite. All information is available in both paper and electronic formats (Ovum Online delivery, HTML, Adobe Acrobat and Lotus Notes).

If you would like to find out more about any Ovum report or service, please contact us in one of the following ways:

Fax

Fill in the information request form opposite and fax to:

- Europe & the rest of the world: +44 (0) 20 7551 9090/1
- North America: +1 781 246 7772
- Asia-Pacific: +61 (0) 3 9606 0799

Post

Send your completed information request to us at any of the addresses below:

- Ovum Ltd, Cardinal Tower, 12 Farringdon Road, London EC1M 3HS, UK
- Ovum Inc, 301 Edgewater Drive, Suite 220, Wakefield MA 01880, USA
- Ovum Pty Ltd, Level 6, 388 Lonsdale Street, Melbourne VIC 3000, Australia
- Ovum, San Martín Street 674, Floor 5 (A), 1004 Capital Federal, Buenos Aires, Argentina

Telephone

For more information on reports you are interested in, call us on:

- Europe & the rest of the world: +44 (0) 20 7551 9000
- North America: +1 781 246 3773
- Asia-Pacific: +61 (0) 3 9606 0499
- South America: +54 11 4893 2902.

E-mail

Let us know which Ovum report you saw on this form by e-mailing us on info@ovum.com.

Faxback information request form

Fill in and fax back today • Please include a fax cover sheet

London **+44 (0) 20 7551 9090/1** **Melbourne** **+61 (0) 3 9606 0799**
Boston **+1 781 246 7772**

Name ______________________
Position ______________________
Organisation ______________________
Telephone ______________________
Fax ______________________
E-mail ______________________

Address ______________________
____
____
____
Country ______________________
Type of business ______________________

All reports are available in electronic or paper formats

Please send me details of Ovum's Consultancy services ○
Please send me details of Ovum's Telecoms products and services ○

Please send me more information about (tick where necessary):

Software evaluations and IT strategy reports

Application development

Ovum Evaluates: Client-server Development Tools ○
Ovum Evaluates: Configuration Management ○
Ovum Evaluates: Software Testing Tools ○
Ovum Evaluates: Web Development Tools ○

Business applications

Application Service Providers: Opportunities and Risks ○
Ovum Evaluates: Corporate Financial Systems ○

Customer relationship management

Ovum Evaluates: Call Centre Software for CRM ○
Ovum Evaluates: CRM in the Front Office ○
CRM Strategies: Technology Choices for the Customer-focused Business ○
Next Generation Call Centres: CTI, Voice and the Web ○

Knowledge management

Ovum Evaluates: Data Warehousing Tools and Strategies ○
Ovum Evaluates: Integrated Document Management ○
Knowledge Management: Building the Collaborative Enterprise ○
Ovum Evaluates: OLAP ○
Repositories and XML: Technology Choices for Metadata Management ○

IT infrastructure

Application Servers: Creating the Web-enabled Enterprise ○
Enterprise Application Integration: Making the Right Connections ○
Ovum Evaluates: Enterprise Middleware ○
Ovum Evaluates: Service Management for E-business Applications ○

E-commerce market reports and advisory services

E-business Security: Solutions and Opportunities ○
E-commerce Services for Electronic Merchants: Market Strategies ○
E-services@Ovum ○
Smart Card Systems: Multi-application Technologies and Strategies ○